SOYINKA'S LANGUAGE

Obioma Ofoego

 KWARA STATE UNIVERSITY PRESS

© Obioma Ofoego 2016

All rights reserved. No part of this book may be reproduced or transmitted in any form or by any means without prior written permission from Kwara State University Press.

Front cover picture: Ogun, Yoruba god of Iron

First published 2016

Published by

Kwara State University Press
Kwara State University, Malete
PMB 1530
Ilorin, Kwara State

ISBN 978-978-53920-4-3

Designed and typeset by Agbo Areo Book Publishing Consultancy Services, Ibadan

Acknowledgements

My debt to Professor Christiane Fioupou cannot be repaid. I salute her herein. Professor Biodun Jeyifo's great generosity of spirit is here warmly acknowledged. To Professor Olabiyi Yai, my deep and abiding gratitude, beyond what I hope plain in this work. I am also pleased to acknowledge Professor Abiola Irele, Agbo Areo, and Kwara State University Press, without whom this book project would never have materialised. I benefited from an AMID research grant from the Université Toulouse II-Le Mirail in 2011, which enabled a two-month research-visit to Ife and Ibadan. From my time in Ife, I must thank the Anyadike family, munificent hosts; Arthur Anyaduba and Mrs Ogunleye, phlegmatic teachers; and, from Ibadan, Professor Niyi Osundare, for the whistle-stop tour and *ad hoc* interpretations from *Kongi's Harvest*. To M.D.S. Lazarus, Alex Gil, and Sasha Rubel; to Diana Ardissone; and to my siblings Lydia, Chidozie and Nicola: my thanks. Especial recognition is reserved for my wife, Laura Petrecca. All the book's flaws and obscurities are irrevocably mine. It is dedicated to my parents, Richard and Pearl Ofoego.

List of Abbreviations

ADF	*A Dance of the Forests*
BE	*The Bacchae of Euripides*
DKH	*Death and the King's Horseman*
JM	*Jero's Metamorphosis*
MLAW	*Myth, Literature and the African World*
MS	*Madmen and Specialists*
SB	*The Strong Breed*
TBJ	*The Trials of Brother Jero*
TBM	*The Burden of Memory, The Muse of Forgiveness*
TI	*The Interpreters*
TLJ	*The Lion and the Jewel*
TMD	*The Man Died*
TR	*The Road*

Contents

Acknowledgements.. vi

List of Abbreviations.. vii

Introduction... 1

I: The Issue of Language, or Words' Consequence:
Lessons in Seduction and Conversion........................ 16
The Lion and the Jewel: Learning on the Job................ 19
The Jero plays, or How Words Change Under
Historical Pressure... 39

II: The Passing of Worlds, and the Language of Teaching... 70
The Road: Prof. Made New..................................... 73
Madmen and Specialists: Murdering to Dissect............ 107

III: The Blind Spot of Justice, or What Does The
Onlooker Say?... 140
The Strong Breed: Tranquil Recollection and
Present Circumstance.. 143
A Dance of the Forests: Foreknowledge, or the
Language of Emptiness I.. 155
The Bacchae of Euripides: Foreknowledge, or the
Language of Emptiness II....................................... 180
Coda: *The Burden of Memory*: Of Senghor, and
the Language of Forgiveness................................... 197

IV: The Language of Being and Non-Being.................. 210

The Man Died: Solitude... 213
Myth, Literature and the African World: Using and
    Abusing the *Cogito*.. 236
V: *Death and the King's Horseman*: Rhetoric and
    Insinuating Possibility.. 259
    The Couple Pilkings.. 259
    Give and Pull.. 294
    Death, and the King's Horseman................................. 315
    Conclusion... 330
Bibliography.. 337
Index... 358

Introduction

> They were now on the portion of the new road that had been built. It made one feel lost like a grain of maize in an empty goatskin bag. Obika changed his machete from the left hand to the right and his hoe from right to left. The feeling of openness and exposure made him alert.
>
> — Chinua Achebe, *Arrow of God*[1]

As part of a lecture given on the occasion of Wole Soyinka's seventieth birthday, Biodun Jeyifo proposed a discussion at once funny and complex of *'igilango Geesi'*, or 'big English'. It was a term applied, in his greener youth, he says, both 'to a person whose mastery of the English language was superlative, so superlative indeed that such mastery of the language went beyond the competence of the "owners" of the language, the English themselves', *and* to instances of exhibitionist display or (inadvertent) misuse.[2] This phenomenon, and its exploitation in literature, is linked to a few historical elements.

The first element concerns the enlarged imaginative perspectives that come with any new language, through and beyond what might have been the grievous historical experience of its adoption or enforcement. To offer a simple example from the Nigerian literary context in English, the geographical broadening of perspectives to issue from the colonial experience

---

[1] Chinua Achebe, *Arrow of God* (London: Heinemann, 1986 [1964]), 80.
[2] See Biodun Jeyifo, "'Oguntoyinbo': Wole Soyinka and 'Igilango Geesi'", Lagos, Nigeria, 5th July 2004. The lecture was later published as *'Oguntoyinbo:* Wole Soyinka and "Igilango Geesi,"' *Philosophia Africana,* Vol.11, No.1 (March 2008).

was intelligently met in a specific dramatic type, the teacher-turned-by-reading. On the tongue of this dramatic type, it was as if geographical enlargements or the falling away of horizons reduced words' mass, traded in their gravitational bind to common earth for the sheer upward elation of newness and creativity and exploration. The second element, though no less important, is that the English language, in Nigeria as in other colonial contexts, presented a rhetorical *and* moral challenge to the serious thinker or writer, with which to counter colonial and imperial racist tropes from within that very language. The usage of the English language, that is, was inextricably bound up with moral imperatives, issuing from historical circumstance.

The third element is implicit in the previous two, yet speaks more directly to our literary purposes. The challenge of English was the challenge of learning a *craft*, the craft of writing in forms not yet seen; the challenge of expanding the sensibility and moral imagination of a Yoruba and Nigerian and African public, in a new language; the challenge of remaining attentive to the danger of being cut off from one's own community in a new language, a danger which has the writer, like Obika in the passage quoted in the epigraph to this introduction, alert to a feeling of openness and exposure. The terrain of this feeling, in Soyinka, is language. This is how I understand Dan Izevbaye's point that Soyinka's (and others') ideological choice to write in English, as well as their respective African languages, represented an attempt 'to control the dominant language of the new reality' in a style 'mimetic of the cultural synthesis' that created it.[3]

---

[3] Dan Izevbaye, 'West African Literature in English,' in *The Cambridge History of African and Caribbean Literature*, eds. Abiola Irele and Simon Gikandi (Cambridge: Cambridge University Press, 2004), 480. For a seminal discussion on Soyinka's relationship to two important Yoruba predecessors, D.O. Fagunwa, whose *Ogboju Ode ninu Igbo Irunmale* (1938) Soyinka translated from Yoruba into English, and Amos Tutuola, see Abiola Irele, 'Tradition and the Yoruba Writer,' in *Critical Perspectives on Wole Soyinka*, ed. James Gibbs (London: Heinemann, 1980), 45-68.

The title of this thesis should be taken as an allusion to Frank Kermode's *Shakespeare's Language*. In that study, Kermode reserved his critical attention for Shakespeare's *poetry*, the unlikely achievements of his dramatic verse. This had a few methodological consequences: a sensitivity towards hearing as a *technical* difficulty, Shakespeare's poetry making quite considerable demands on the audience's ear; a qualification of the notion that the stage-production is what matters most, for '[f]ollowing the story', writes Kermode, 'and understanding the tensions between characters, is not quite the same thing as following all or even most of the meanings.'[4] In other words, poetry plays a substantive role in the very interpretations directors and actors choose to give to the stories they stage and act; to the impression and trace the audience carries in its gut at the end of a performance. The deeper assumption is that Shakespeare both moves us through the language of the possible reality he presents, *and* that this poetic representation spills back over into our experiential knowledge of the real world. Arduous interpretation, therefore, comes to serve a cognitive end, opens up and smoothes the passage for art's flowing back into life.

There is good precedent for bringing together Shakespeare and Soyinka in Soyinka scholarship, precedent which stands beyond the fortuitousness of shared initials, or local bragging rights.[5] In his 1983 essay on Aeschylus, Euripides, Shakespeare

---

[4] Frank Kermode, *Shakespeare's Language* (New York: Farrar, Straus, Giroux, 2000), 5.

[5] This precedent was perhaps first established with Eldred Durosimi Jones' dedication to his seminal early study of Soyinka, *The Writing of Wole Soyinka* (London: James Currey, 1988 [1973]): 'For W.S., our W.S.' His rapprochement between Shakespeare and Soyinka comes in a spirit of collegiality, not antagonism. Before his study on Soyinka, Jones had published the critical works *Othello's Countrymen. The African in English Renaissance Drama* (London: Oxford University Press, 1965), and *The Elizabethan Image of Africa* (Charlottesville: University Press of Virginia, 1971).

and Soyinka, for example, Philip Brockbank made the point that centuries, millennia even, are relatively brief periods when considered in an anthropological perspective, which is to say that the poetic imagination is, ultimately, not limited to place and historical moment, but is rather informed by enduring human responses.[6] The imaginative distance between Shakespeare and Soyinka, he continues, belies the historical distance separating the two, to the extent to which *Soyinka* can retrospectively illuminate certain moments in Shakespeare:

> It is not merely that Shakespeare and the Greeks have had an influence upon Soyinka; it is rather that influences – current and flowing-in from the remote past – are by his work made more accessible to us in plays that have gone before.[7]

In this thesis, I shall be specifically concerned, in the manner of Kermode, with Soyinka's language, with the words and poetry of his writing, predominantly for theatre. *Soyinka's Language* sounds like a vast title, but it will be taken in an extremely narrow sense. It does not refer to Yoruba, which I do not speak, and therefore has little to say of the (no doubt) extremely rich interplay which exists between Yoruba and English, across Soyinka's oeuvre; nor, for instance, does it embrace Pidgin English, of which I have only limited knowledge. No doubt, the emphasis on words leads me into what some will consider an undue veneration of the arrangement of words on a page, at the expense of what Femi Osofisan used to like to call theatrical 'mechanics', or the inherent flexibility of theatre as it

---

[6] Philip Brockbank, 'Blood and Wine: Tragic Ritual from Aeschylus to Soyinka,' in *Perspectives on Wole Soyinka: Freedom and Complexity*, ed. Biodun Jeyifo (Jackson: University Press of Mississippi, 2001), 77. First published in *Shakespeare Survey*, Vol.36, No.1 (1983), 11-20.

[7] Brockbank, "Blood and Wine," 78.

responds to expediency.[8] There is probably some truth in such a charge. I would simply hope, however, that where my readings are judged excessive or irrelevant or foolish, they will, as Stanley Cavell, another fine reader of Shakespeare, once wrote, simply drop away as worthless.[9]

This emphasis on poetry, on words, is proper to my intellectual training and background. It is also, however, given the enormous and quite overwhelming critical corpus concerning Soyinka's oeuvre, a means of resisting what T.S. Eliot might have called the idea's violations of the mind, by which he meant the danger of receiving an idea so quickly that we ignore its means of expression. In the same perspective, I have found useful the distinction Kermode (drawing on Spinoza) elsewhere makes, between 'meaning' and 'truth': 'meaning', that is, as what is written (and, we would add, spoken), and 'truth', as what is written (and spoken) about.[10] The trick is not to conflate the two, but to hold them apart, the better to see the human sense caught between.

An essential thread in *Shakespeare's Language* is the idea that Shakespeare is *thinking* through language, that the poetry of his plays is the expression of a specifically literary intelligence at work; and that this is an intelligence which is being honed with every play, a *developing* intelligence. In other words, Shakespeare, for Kermode, is interested in the language of thought, both as a writer who is trying to express something,

---

[8] See, for example, Femi Osofisan, "Drama and the New Exotic: The Paradox of Form in Modern African Theatre" [1978] and "Beyond Translation: A Comparative Look at Tragic Paradigms and the Dramaturgy of Wole Soyinka and Ola Rotimi," [1980] in *The Nostalgic Drum* (Trenton, New Jersey: Africa World Press, 2001), 44, 61.

[9] Stanley Cavell, *Disowning Knowledge in Seven Plays of Shakespeare* (Cambridge: Cambridge University Press, 2003), 5.

[10] Frank Kermode, *The Genesis of Secrecy: On the Interpretation of Narrative* (Cambridge, Massachusetts: Harvard University Press, 1979), 119.

and as a writer who is representing characters trying to express something. The idea of writers, in general, as thinking, as *intelligent*, as engaged in a cognitively creative process, is an important one, and I have tried hard not to reduce Soyinka to an effect or a symptom of his own work. If there is any benefit of being a literary academic, it comes precisely in the leisure which we are able to bestow upon texts to disentangle their meanings, to paraphrase Dr Johnson, often, indeed, where the author him- or herself was content to abandon the attempt.

There is an obvious danger in any critical enterprise, of seeing only what one wants to see, of using the writer as a screen for the airing of one's own views. Whether we think of this as a hermeneutic circle, or, as I prefer, as seeing one's own eye in the microscope, like James Thurber,[11] in the last instance interpretation must live and die by its capacity of persuasion, evinced in the *mutual* endowments of artistic and critical creativity. In the context of Yoruba artistry, Olabiyi Yai has provided extremely rich insights which I have found useful in trying to guide my own attempts here.[12] In glossing the Yoruba '*iba*' or homage, "*Gbenagbena se tire tan/O ku ti gbenugbenu*" ['Here ends the work of the sculptor/Let the critic start his own'], Yai observes that a '*gbenugbenu*' (or 'one who carves with his or her mouth [voice]') is not a critic in the standard English sense, if by that we consider the critic's activity to be radically distinct from the artist, but rather one whose task is 'to continue the work of the sculptors by other means. The public expect them to orally perform a text that at once reflects the sculpture and departs from it.'[13] He goes on, movingly, to place this bind of reflection and departure,

---

[11] James Thurber, *My Life and Hard Times* (Paris: Hachette, 1955), 61-4. I first came across the reference in Kermode, *The Genesis of Secrecy*, 27.
[12] Olabiyi Babalola Yai, 'Tradition and the Yoruba Artist,' *African Arts*, Vol.32, No.1, Part 2 (Spring 1999), 32-5+93.
[13] *Ibid.*, 32.

of acknowledgement and leave-taking, whose apparently paradoxical sense is tightened in phonic likeness and difference, into a discussion of the Yoruba concept of àṣà, or 'tradition'. Àṣà, that is, deriving from the verb ṣà, meaning selection, discernment, discrimination, as 'a tradition that is permanently open to innovation informed by preceding phases in the process.'[14] Where new elements are added which evince an ignorance of the earlier elements of the process, the word used, continues Yai, is aṣa, whose tonal shift conveys the uncanny effect engendered by attempts to break completely from precedent. Tradition, then – the verb used with àṣà is da, meaning to break, to split, to create, to depart – is by definition *informed* departure from what has come before. The point is not so much whether etymological conjecture should be tested against current usage, whether it can withstand the charge of 'semantics as frozen history', in Darko Suvin's phrase.[15] Yai's deeper point, if I have read him correctly, is that *intelligent* selection among any number of possibilities is the condition of both the work of art's significance, *and* the significance of the critical work, for its human community. The measure of the artist, and critic, is the extent to which his or her usage of the tools and imaginative resource available to him or her, successfully flows into and away from precedent. The measure of this study, in turn, will be the extent to which it can be judged to have reflected and departed from Soyinka's language, and the creative intelligence which animates it.

Although the principal emphasis is on words, there is, nonetheless, a quiet underlying narrative. In *Shakespeare's Language*, Kermode argues in the direction of Shakespeare opening up a new language of interiority, of silence. In Soyinka's major plays, however, the enduring intention,

---

[14] *Ibid.*, 34.
[15] Darko Suvin, *To Brecht and Beyond: Soundings in Modern Dramaturgy* (Sussex: The Harvester Press, 1984), 51.

which reaches a form of climax in *Death and the King's Horseman*, seems to me quite different. Soliloquies, monologues, self-address, are not the space for a new poetic language of subjectivity to develop, but rather symptomatic of a wider danger to which Soyinka is constantly attentive: the danger, that is, of falling into an existentialist conception of being, and, as corollary, to words' being cut off from the common human constituency and experience which gives them life. An important undercurrent in the poetry of Soyinka's theatre, that is, is the search for a poetic language which both moves us towards, *and* leads us away from, the self-sufficiency of thought and language.

It was, in truth, Chinua Achebe who first spelled out to me this continuous search for balance, *for the artist*, between common language, and flight from common language, in his poem 'Beware Soul Brother'.[16] If, because of the epigraph to *Things Fall Apart*,[17] the bind between Achebe and the Irish poet W.B. Yeats has often been thought of in terms of the vulnerabilities issuing from broadening perspectives – the widening gyre, the spiralling falcon[18] – an equally profound principle of literary construction is moving, it seems to me, in both. Yeats, in Frank Kermode's gloss,

> said that the System enabled him to hold together reality and justice in a single thought. Reality is, in this expression, the sense we have of a world irreducible to human plot and human desire for order; justice is the

---

[16] Chinua Achebe, "Beware, Soul Brother," in *Beware, Soul Brother* (London: Heinemann, 1972), 29-30.
[17] Chinua Achebe, *Things Fall Apart* (London: Penguin, 1958).
[18] W.B. Yeats, 'The Second Coming,' in *The Collected Poems of W.B. Yeats*, ed. Richard J. Finneran (New York: Simon and Schuster, 1996), 187: 'Turning and turning in the widening gyre / The falcon cannot hear the falconer; / Things fall apart; the centre cannot hold; / Mere anarchy is loosed upon the world.'

human order we find or impose upon it. The System is in fact all Justice; in combination with a sense of reality which has nothing whatever to do with it, it became a constituent of poems. [...] For a moment, in that expression, Yeats saw himself as an emperor dispensing equity, transcending both the fact and the pattern; it is what poets do. Only rarely did he forget that whatever devotes itself to justice at the expense of reality, is finally self-destructive.[19]

Kermode goes on to speak, quite beautifully, of the tension 'between a paradigmatic order where the price of a formal eternity is inhumanity, and the world of the dying generations',[20] and of the tension between pattern and fact, which is transcended in the poem or artwork, of which consolation is the paradoxical prize: for what we accept as consolation must not be all formal beauty, all justice, in Yeats' special sense, but must instead draw into the stylistic arrangements of its eternal artifice the roughness and hard-headedness of reality. Achebe's poem 'Beware, Soul Brother' could be seen as an arresting instance of just such a transcendence of fact and pattern:

> Our ancestors, soul brother, were wiser
> than is often made out. Remember
> they gave Ala, great goddess
> of their earth, sovereignty too over
> their arts for they understood
> too well those hard-headed
> men of departed dance where a man's
> foot must return whatever beauties
> it may weave in air, where
> it must return for safety
> and renewal of strength.[21]

---

[19] Frank Kermode, *The Sense of an Ending* (Oxford: Oxford University Press, 2000), 105.
[20] *Ibid.*, 106.
[21] Achebe, 'Beware, Soul Brother,' 29–30.

These lines provide a memorable lesson in the orchestration and feel of long sentences. They begin with a compact reminder, and we, the young, dutifully prepare to hear the lessons we imagine familiar on that sermonly 'Remember'. And yet – wisdom's ruse – the ensuing run and release has us groping for rhythmed footholds along the slackened rope. The governing poetic intelligence is moving here in syntax, quietly swelling and gathering toward that pivotal word – 'where' ('where a man's foot') – which, in turn, and quite wonderfully, can cast meaning forwards and backwards like a roving searchlight only if we push it through a little more slowly and firmly in the throat; if, that is, we take our time over saying it, as if, indeed, it were worthy of chewing and rumination. If this is an *ars poetica* – the dancer performing a synecdoche for the artist – it is one in which the same motion discloses the better to occlude, for the perfect tense of the indirect statement ('they understood') holds the *content* of that 'where' at a distance, in a place which lies forever beyond. The lesson of these lines, therefore, does not move us towards imitation – it cannot – but simply towards vigilance and awareness in whichever search for concord we may be embarked upon, whichever search for harmony is proper to our time and circumstance.

The techniques Achebe uses are suitably discreet (warnings require elegance to disarm the inevitable resistance). The poet's slight impatience before the mere stylistic arrangements of the dancer's foot is brought out by the omission of the definite article – 'whatever beauties it may weave in air' – which subtly suggests an indifferentiation of place, and, in turn, that beauty abstracted from place is no beauty at all. The stakes of the dance gain dimension through Achebe's conscription of Igbo metaphysics in the lure of *Igwe* or Sky,[22] the seductive heresy

---

[22] Michael Echeruo spoke most eloquently of this in his inaugural Ahiajoku Lecture "Aha m efula [May my name not be lost]: A Matter of Identity"

of which is here intimated in the foot's climb, against the supremacy and moral safeguard of *Ala* (or *Ani)* or Earth.

The moment which best expresses the artist's complex bind to community, however, comes with the word 'return'. Firstly, there is the transitive sense – to return beauty – beauty's very being as conditional upon its acknowledging its obligations to earth, to community; and secondly, as complement, there is the *intransitive* sense of return – return as homecoming – the sense that the acknowledgement of debt to community is not merely a curb on individual freedom, but rather a renewal of the individual's protection. That is to say that *Ala* or the moral order of community is, in this poem, a demanding presence; it is both a form of coercion, *and* a form of protection; it is, writes the poet, both beauty's condition of existence, and the limit of its dance.

What happens if this balance is ignored? What happens if 'justice', in Yeats' sense, prevails over 'reality'? The poem continues, shifting the theme and energies of artistic balance into one-leggedness, and ruffling the settled equanimity of the old proverb ('If a fowl comes to a land it does not know, it stands on one leg') into full warning:

> Take care, then
> mother's son, lest you become
> a dancer disinherited in mid-dance
> hanging a lame foot in air like the hen
> in a strange unfamiliar compound.[23]

(1979), observing: *'Igwe ka ala* was quite simply not only a devilish sect but a heretical one. Its very name was a daring – a consciously daring – challenge to the supreme deity of the Igbo people. This cult placed *Igwe* above *Ala*, and claimed him as supreme. To propose that was in itself an abomination, that is to say, a defilement of the Earth, *imerụ ala.* In short, Umunneora and *Igwe ka ala* must be seen in the history of our institutions as phenomena which came closest to setting up a god cult above that of *Ala* herself, the ultimate sanction to morals.' http://ahiajoku.igbonet.com/1979/ Accessed 12th September 2011.

[23] Achebe, *Beware, Soul Brother*, 30.

The distance separating the fowl's prepared alertness ('standing on one leg') and the dancer's lame, hanging foot – note the new dissonant note of plangency of that 'in air' where before it held the tension of impatience, as if warning still had grip – is as small as it is irreversible. The artist's devotion to 'justice' or perfect forms at the expense of reality, as Kermode tells us, comes with death.

These terms, it seems to me, can usefully be used of Wole Soyinka too, to demonstrate how the *literary* argument of his plays, the argument of poetic language, which is irreducible to any overarching idea, enacts the pursuit for balance between 'justice' and 'reality', in Yeats' specific sense, between self-assertion, or indeed self-sufficiency, and common meaning; to suggest how words are constantly pulling towards drift or inertia or autonomy, and how they must be brought back to earth, to reality, to life. (And this is a corrective, perhaps, to the peculiar agonism which opposes the two great Nigerian writers, Soyinka and Achebe, instead of showing us capable of receiving both, and the richer for it.)

This study of Wole Soyinka's language casts this *linguistic* undercurrent into relief against certain themes. (The corpus I have chosen to study has been dictated, through and beyond personal preference, by the extent to which this movement between self-sufficiency and commonality can be analysed in words. There is, in any case, no desire to be exhaustive.) Each chapter is organized chronologically, from *The Lion and the Jewel* (1959–60) to *Death and the King's Horseman* (1975), although this organization is not hidebound (I speak of *The Burden of Memory* [published in 1999], for example, and do not hesitate to draw on Soyinka's autobiographies of the 1980s, where necessary). I have deliberately avoided a chronological progression from chapter to chapter, however – the organization of the study is more trellis than cone. Hopefully, the reader will progressively test the interest of a particular chapter's thematic or conceptual investigations against the study's parallel investigations. This organization responds, in general, to my conception of artistic and critical creativity: how both are constantly nourished and stimulated by what appears to be the least predictable of sources, how their intelligence is diamond-faceted. And it seems to me perfectly apposite, in particular, when approaching the oeuvre of Wole Soyinka, this most eclectic, and 'eclectric',[24] of minds.

The first chapter, then, which is concerned with *The Lion and the Jewel* and the *Jero* plays, analyses the ways in which words have a way of penetrating us, of undermining our attempts to stand apart; and how those words might have consequences, spill over into life. That is to say, how language, and skilled language-use, is not merely for display, but matters only to the extent to which it comes to impinge upon the real world, the way we live and move. In the second chapter's discussion of *The Road* and *Madmen and Specialists*, the emphasis is placed on the linguistic or poetic implications of passing between two historical moments, on how quickly language becomes strange to us, where yesterday it was coherent to our perception. I use 'teaching', which depends for its communication on shared conventions, as a point of ingress. The starting point for the third chapter is the ambivalence of the notion of onlooking, how it might provide 'objective' distance (theory) and how, at the same time, distance might

---

[24] Wole Soyinka, "Between Self and System: The Artist in Search of Liberation" [1974] *Art, Dialogue and Outrage: Essays on Literature and Culture* (London: Methuen, 1993 [1988]), 43: 'One of the tribulations of an eclectric approach to creativity – which I consider the only reliable antidote to the ever-changing monomania of the artistic world – is that genuine eclesticism *[sic]* manifests itself more in awareness than in application.' The typo 'eclectric' can happily pass as a neologism expressing the illuminating energy of a creative mind.

also weaken our human understanding, our empathy. I shall be focussing on the language of a few onlookers in Soyinka's sceptical interrogations concerning procedures of justice, in *The Strong Breed, A Dance of the Forests* and *The Bacchae of Euripides*. The coda on *The Burden of Memory, The Muse of Forgiveness* concludes the chapter with an appraisal of Soyinka's reception of Senghor's language of forgiveness. The fourth chapter represents something of a departure, in that I concentrate my readings on prose. What is implicit in the previous chapters – the staging of self-sufficiency, and the warding off of the dangers self-sufficiency presents, for characters and writer alike – is situated in the literary context of tragedy, the genre which subjects our most fundamental conceptions of being to severe interrogation, breaking them down, even. Proceeding from a discussion of a specific chapter in *The Man Died*, I will analyse a few West-African conceptions of being, and the literary responses which such conceptions might demand. The chapter concludes with a reflection on Soyinka's (Yoruba) conception of being as articulated in *Myth, Literature and the African World,* and the rhetorical tools he deems proper to tragedy, as available, notably, in Yoruba oral poetry. The fifth and final chapter constitutes the culmination of my reflection. For it seems to me that *Death and the King's Horseman* most insinuatingly and richly enacts the search for balance between commonality and flight, between return and departure, between being and non-being, in and through poetic language.

A final observation on the word 'formalism', which shall be put to a few different usages throughout the course of this study. The only conscious usage I have made of Russian formalism, in any of its diverse manifestations, comes with an unsystematic borrowing of a few of Viktor Shklovsky's insights. Shklovsky's energy of mind is a joy to share in, and his undoubted achievements came in insisting on formal schemata, on the discontinuities of word, character, genre, chronology and structure of which the total work becomes an expression. In this study, I have not hesitated to speculate, in the manner of Shklovsky, as to what I think may plausibly be schemata which Soyinka might have used or reworked, at times trying to imagine with him, upstream, so to speak, why a certain choice might have been taken, how a certain text might have been 'made'.[25]

Shklovsky, however, had an almost perversely ludic indifference to history (though this aversion was itself a deeply felt and acutely intelligent response to the dimming of perception of his automatized age). His failure lay in thinking that the identification of literary schemata was sufficient of itself. There is a sadly apocryphal anecdote involving Shklovsky and Trotsky, reported by Darko Suvin —

> SHKLOVSKY: As a literary critic, I'm not interested in war.
>
> TROTSKY: But war is interested in you.[26] –

in which we understand the real sense in which stopping with the identification of schemata is to forget the point of art in general, which must be the world in which we live and move. To that world, we now come.

---

[25] See, for example, Viktor Shklovsky, "The Making of *Don Quixote*," in *Theory of Prose* [1925], trans. Benjamin Sher (Illinois: Dalkey Archive Press, 1990).

[26] Relayed in Darko Suvin, *In Leviathan's Belly: Essays for a Counter-Revolutionary Time* (Rockville, Maryland: Wildside Press LLC, 2012), 166.

I

The Issue of Language, or Words' Consequence: Lessons in Seduction and Conversion

Among the many remarkable passages in Seamus Heaney's prose collection, *Finders Keepers*, there comes the following reflection on the use of language in a political situation whose violence and various divestments might recall any number of post-colonial contexts:

> In Ireland for decades we were exercised by a problematic *ceist na teangan* or language question that concerned itself with the contesting claims of Irish and English to be the right language of the country. Through the collaboration of these two poets [Paul Muldoon and Nuala Ni Dhomhnaill], what was problematic has become productive, even arguably reproductive: when Muldoon translated *ceist na teangan* as 'the language issue' – issue having associations not only of new life springing from an old source but of a handout of provisions or equipment that you make the best of – when he translated the title in this way, new thinking was being bred out of the original words and it seemed as if the two languages were wanting to indulge in the old clandestine pleasures of 'touching tongues'.[27]

Muldoon's translation brooks no elision or attenuation of those problems or even irreversible difficulties which inhered and inhere yet in the political situation of Northern Ireland,

---

[27] Seamus Heaney, *Finders Keepers: Selected Prose 1971–2001* (London: Faber and Faber, 2002), 380.

writes Heaney, just as it pays full heed to the survival and modulation of creativity in and through the embrace of two tongues, to the *issue* which is both renewal and *ad hoc* survival kit. Passage through Ireland should not seem entirely arbitrary in this context. When the Welsh poet, Stewart Brown, and the Yoruba poet, Niyi Osundare, in what I assume to be one of those occasional parallel epiphanies, arrived at the same metaphor of illicit and pleasurable exchange in thinking of Yoruba poetics held and reduced and enlarged in and through English – 'When two languages meet, they kiss and quarrel'[28] – it is because they are alive, as poets, to just these complex senses of issue, the re-creative pleasures to be had in and despite situations of historical expediency. Indeed, as Abiola Irele and Simon Gikandi have reminded us, Irish writers came to assume a certain importance within Molly Mahood's teaching project at the newly independent University of Ibadan, and, by extension, among those to form the nascent national lettered elite: the example, that is, of new life springing from an old source (the colonial language), evinced in a coherent body of letters; the robust example of expediency.[29]

In a different essay, Seamus Heaney, because from W.H. Auden, writes of the artistic manifestation 'which has less to do with argument or edification than with the fact and effort of articulation itself' as evinced in Christopher Marlowe's

---

[28] Niyi Osundare, 'Yorùbá Thought, English Words: a Poet's Journey Through the Tunnel of Two Tongues,' in *Kiss and Quarrel: Yorùbá/English, Strategies of Mediation*, ed. Stewart Brown (Birmingham: Birmingham University African Studies Series, No.5, 2000), 15.

[29] Abiola Irele and Simon Gikandi, Introduction to *The Cambridge History of African and Caribbean Literature*, xi. Mahood, the editors continue, envisioned the university as 'the enabling environment for the formation of a new literary culture, in what Stanley Fish was later to call 'an interpretative community,' for which the colonial language stood to function as the determining cohesive element.' (xi)

poem, 'Hero and Leander.'[30] That poem, writes Heaney, is

> a work happily in love with its own inventions, written at the height of the young master's powers, a work which exercises itself entirely within the playhouse of erotic narrative in the tradition of the Latin poet Ovid, but which remains responsive to and transformative of the real pains of love.

I shall be considering a few Soyinka plays – *The Lion and the Jewel* and the *Jero* plays – in just this perspective, as a celebration 'of the fact of articulation itself'. My sense is that Soyinka, in these three plays, is a writer indulging in exercises in language, in happy invention – at first inconsequential perhaps, though nonetheless innovative and creative and exploratory; and that, with the second *Jero* play, he moves to test the limits of what indulgent exercise can offer, pushing playful language into a realm of consequence, and comedy to breaking point.

---

[30] Heaney, *Finders Keepers*, 269.

1
The Lion and the Jewel: Learning On The Job

While the odd reader might see in *The Lion and the Jewel* (1960;[31] first published in 1963) an 'argument' on the relationship between tradition and modernity,[32] I think we are better served by considering it part youthful showing-off or leg-stretching, and part cheerful celebration of language, a prelude to greater things; what I have called, in the chapter title, 'learning on the job', or apprenticeship. And though the playhouse tradition is different from Marlowe, we remain with the entwinements of sex and language. Sex, like language, 'is subject to the shaping force of social convention, rules of proceeding, and accumulated precedent',[33] notes George Steiner, and, he

---

[31] A short version of *The Lion and the Jewel* was produced in 1959. See James Gibbs, "The Masks Hatched Out," in *Theatre Research International*, Vol. 7, No. 3 (Autumn 1982), 180–206. As a general rule, throughout this study I provide the date of completion and first publication for each play. Where the two coincide, I have simply provided the year.

[32] See, for example, Mpalive-Hangson Msiska, *Postcolonial Identity in Wole Soyinka* (Amsterdam: Rodopi, 2007), 57: '[...] in *The Lion and the Jewel* Soyinka examines the relationship between tradition and modernity and finds that a modernity that fetishises surface things rather than its essential spirit ends up being inimical not only to the progressive elements within the discourse of modernity itself but also to those of tradition, creating conditions for more exploitative interpretations of tradition to assume a validity that a more critical view of modernity would easily have undermined.' This is a bizarre sentence, and is surely out of step with the play's spirit.

[33] George Steiner, *After Babel: Aspects of Language and Translation* (London; New York; Toronto: Oxford University Press, 1975), 38; ch.4.

speculates reasonably, the two most likely developed in close-knit reciprocity. Steiner's general argument is directed against semantic formalism, against its underlying assumption as to the possibility (and desirability) of formal systems which would theoretically account for all the creative possibilities of language. For Steiner – and this is one of the lessons of literature – creativity comes rather in non-logical sequence, in indirection; it comes in nonsense, in lying, in reciprocal incomprehension, and in wrong-footing; in such is the condition of our renewal. These rhetorical instances are creative not from nothing, but precisely through and against accumulated precedent. To step beyond the rules of precedent, goes the implication, is to step into sterility, or loneliness, the peacock preening and strutting in the dark.

No doubt it behoves us as teachers to attend first to ourselves, to hear ourselves as we speak and write, for it might seem condescending at best, and hypocritical at worst, to castigate a teacher for his shortcomings, thinking that in our own students, upon our own disquisitions, our teachings do not die. But Lakunle, bookish school-teacher and young pretender to the affections of Sidi, the belle of the village Ilujinle, really is foolish; his lesson, which works through the commonplace, is negative – *ex nihilo* creation is no creation at all. In their double acceptation as both the source of arguments and as observations, commonplaces, part of Lakunle's staple, carry the pall of rhetorical exercise, of rote or formal rearrangements, which, of course, was one of their principal functions in ancient Greek and Roman rhetoric; that is, their formal usefulness in constructing an argument around any subject, through the assistance of formulas, tropes, and memory. The importance of Lakunle's tropes of modernity comes not in their argument – we do not learn anything new – but quite precisely in their 'conspicuosity', as he might have said: that is, they are important insofar as they show a speaker 'happily in love with his own inventions', the technical term 'invention' meaning the development and refinement of ideas. We lose part of the humour of the play if we do not first hear Lakunle's pleasure in speaking for speaking's sake, there being pleasure to be had simply in the organization and construction and arrangement of sentences, in the eternal (and inhuman) forms we can construct when freed from reality. The comma in the sentence 'No wife of mine, no lawful wedded wife',[34] well expresses the moment of reflection, projected imagination and *jouissance* which formal fictions can briefly bring. Steiner speculates again, a little grandly: 'If coition can be schematized as dialogue, masturbation seems to be correlative with the pulse of monologue or of internalized address.'[35] If the official reason for Lakunle's delay comes in the bride price, that pulse of monologue, no doubt, carries its own form of solace.

'One little thing and you must chirrup like a cockatoo' (*TLJ*, 9), opines Sidi, and there is the persistent sense that Lakunle is waiting, simply waiting for something he recognizes in the storehouse of his readings to be able to disburse words; waiting for that trigger, however oblique or light the touch, to take up his old stylistic arrangements. We rightly laugh at Lakunle's instant soulfulness (7; 10), his lissome glide into pulpit declamatory (9), his besotted genuflecting (19), sensing beyond them books' emasculation of his sexual purpose – academics might be familiar with the charge – their divestment of his voice, which comes to us through a crowded gutter of literary sources (the symptom of a limited availability, perhaps). A quick stock-taking of this effluence might include fairy tales ('I know he has dungeons. Secret holes where a helpless girl will lie and rot for ever. But not for nothing was I born a man.

---

[34] Wole Soyinka, *The Lion and the Jewel* in *Wole Soyinka: Collected Plays 2* (Oxford: Oxford University Press, 1974), 9.
[35] Steiner, *After Babel*, 39.

I'll find my way to rescue her. She little deserves it, but I shall risk my life for her.' [50]), the happy ending proving elusive; those perfectly balanced Victorian expressions of self-help, self-interest and moralising ('Idlers all of them, good-for-nothing shameless men casting their lustful eyes where they have no business' [4]); (Victorian?) misogyny ('as a woman, you have a smaller brain than mine' [5], or again: 'This is divine justice that a mere woman should outstrip him in the end.' [12]); the Bible, itself short of female exemplars, though Lakunle has managed to rustle up a few ('My Ruth, my Rachael, Esther, Bathsheba' [19]); the benighted grandeur of Gibbon's *Decline and Fall* (the Englishman's infamous judgement on Ethiopia, or 'Ethiopia',[36] reapplied to Ilujinle: 'We must be modern with the rest or live forgotten by the world' [34]); the triteness of magazine-talk ('I seek a life-companion' or 'Sidi, I seek a friend in need. An equal partner in my race of life.' [9]); and, finally, two re-workings from *Macbeth* – the lofty though feeble 'No, no, I won't. This foolery bores me. It is a game of idiots. I have work of more importance' (14) or the amusing and vulnerable 'Do not unman me, Sidi. Speak before I burst in tears.' (53).

These two threads bind together in the prelude to Lakunle's moment of recognition, as he begins to think that he will be forced into marrying Sidi, or words with actions:

> LAKUNLE: But I must prepare myself.
> I cannot be
> A single man one day and a married one the next.
> It must come gradually.
> I will not wed in haste.

---

[36] See Edward Gibbon, *The History of the Decline and Fall of the Roman Empire*, Vol. 4, ch.XLVII, 1996 Project Gutenberg Edition ebook: 'Encompassed on all sides by the enemies of their religion, the Aethiopians slept near a thousand years, forgetful of the world by whom they were forgotten.'

> A man must have time to prepare,
> To learn to like the thought. [...]
> [*The singing group is now audible even to him.*]
> What is that? The musicians?
> Could they have learnt so soon?
> SADIKU: The news of a festivity travels fast. You ought to know that.
> LAKUNLE: The goddess of malicious gossip
> Herself must have a hand in my undoing.
> The very spirits of the partial air
> Have all conspired to blow me, willy-nilly
> Down the slippery slope of grim matrimony.
> What evil have I done...? Ah, here they come!
> [*Enter crowd and musicians*]
> Go back. You are not needed yet. Nor ever.
> Hence parasites, you've made a big mistake.
> There is no one getting wedded; get you home. (55-6)

The first lines dispense with the polysyllables, replaced by sturdier one- and two-syllable words, and this well conveys Lakunle's thinking he has all the time in the world, time to plot and consider and learn to like the thought. (We should think of this speech – and here there is ample precedent – as progressively falling away from contact with its nominal addressee, Sadiku; as becoming a monologue, whence his surprise on hearing the singing group.) Notice the pun on 'undoing', which means both 'downfall' and 'not-doing' – Lakunle's foible. I imagine the rhythm here to pick up, an acknowledgement of outside pressures – though there is still one rhetorical foot in quotation, so to speak – as he is forced by outside circumstance back into direct address.

We have spoken of ancient Greek and Roman rhetoric only because Lakunle's tongue flaps to a foreign rhythm. Niyi Osundare once observed in a gloss of a Yoruba dictum – '*Omi tootoo/Omi o/Omi la te/Ka to te yanrin*' ['Water is supreme/ Oh water/For water is what we tread/Before we step on sand']

– that eloquence, which is to say speaking well as opposed to merely speaking, is anchored in the memory of proverbs, aphorisms, idioms and gnomic sayings, 'the scriptless library of an oral culture'; and by implication, that eloquence is the constant return to and renewal of common rhetorical precedent.[37] One of the sources of much of the fun and traction Soyinka gains in this play, as indeed in his later oeuvre, comes in the distinction between voluntary and involuntary memory: whether in the undercutting of the one by the other, or in the oscillations between the two. In the uses to which conversion is put, come a host of examples.

What A.D. Nuttall has observed of Protestant spiritual autobiographies in general seems to me true, *mutatis mutandis*, of Lakunle in particular: that 'conversion, once a single event on, say, the road to Damascus, becomes in Puritan spiritual autobiographies such as John Bunyan's *Grace Abounding to the Chief of Sinners* a sort of oscillatory constant', that 'Protestants talk endlessly of "assurance", not because they have it, but because they don't.'[38] This theme of ill-assured conversion, this drawing attention to the fact that no *tabula* is ever fully *rasa*, that we are born into the words of our ancestors and that we live and die, in a sense, always through and against them; this sense that no form of absolute break can (or should) be voluntarily achieved, Soyinka has understood perfectly.

The point which most seems to stoke his dramatic and critical intelligence seems to be that lack of assurance which

---

[37] Niyi Osundare, "Stubborn Thread in the Loom of Being: The Writer as Memory of the World," slightly modified version of the S.A. Yoder Memorial Lecture presented to the Convocation of Goshen College, Indiana, October 21, 1998, in *Thread in the Loom: Essays on African Literature and Culture* (Trenton, New Jersey: Africa World Press, Inc., 2002), 17.

[38] A.D. Nuttall, *The Alternative Trinity: Gnostic Heresy in Marlowe, Milton, and Blake* (Oxford: Clarendon Press, 1998), 36.

wilful rupture must of necessity bring about, and the subsequent search for order – artificial, extrusive, never quite enough – with which we attempt to assuage our unease. There is a moment in the prose of *Ìsarà* (1989), for instance, in which 'Josiah contented himself with a silent prayer of thanksgiving, which he divided evenly between the presiding spirits of *osugbo* and Christ the Son of God, ensuring in his now-practised way that he gave precedence to neither.'[39] That phrase, 'Christ the Son of God', delicately expresses the intrusions of voice through the third-person narration, the sound of the performance of assurance through quotation. Or elsewhere, the false exchange between Simon Pilkings and Joseph in *Death and the King's Horseman* (1975):

PILKINGS: Does seeing me in this outfit bother you?

JOSEPH: No sir, it has no power.[40]

Here we should (literally) hear the dissonance of studied or rote-learning in Joseph's voice, the dissonance of earnest correctness, of the self-regulating prudence which can never fully compensate for not being at one with oneself. And later in that same play, Amusa ('Amuser'?) snapping to attention before the girl's summons, starched joke-butt to the women's play, easy prey to the confusion and vulnerabilities to which constant pretence gives rise. And, as Soyinka's suggestive reading of Mongo Béti's *Le Pauvre Christ de Bomba* in *Myth, Literature and the African World* (1973–4) shows, it might also perform a more telling structural purpose: to undercut colonial literature's tropes of self-sacrifice.[41]

---

[39] Wole Soyinka, *Ìsarà: A Voyage Around Essay* (London: Methuen, 1989), 23.
[40] Wole Soyinka, *Death and the King's Horseman* (London: Methuen, 1975), 27.
[41] Wole Soyinka, *Myth, Literature and the African World* (Cambridge: Cambridge University Press, 1976), 98: 'The only reprisal from the victims of his spiritual assault is to witness the reversion of his prize

This one enduring idea – the oscillatory constant born of ill-assurance – assumes different tonalities according to genre and context and artistic purpose. Back in the comic world of *The Lion and the Jewel* and Ilujinle, the lower frequency of that oscillation is expressed through physicality. Against Lakunle's tendency to self-absorption – recall, for instance, that odd intransitive deployment of the verb love ('I want to wed because I love' [*TLJ*, 9]) – other characters pull and slap him outwards, into reality, into the world. His attempts to stand apart, to 'rise above taunts and remain unruffled' (5), to remain loftily aloof, to refuse 'drawing in' (5), or his performances of indifference ('I wouldn't demean myself to bandy words with a woman of the bush' [33]), tend to be counterbalanced by fearful retreat, as if he is not enough convinced of his own loftiness to feel assured of protection. (And he is right.) He retreats in panic from the threats of Sadiku (there is something of the *vade retro* about his 'Keep away from me, old hag.' [21; 23]); he scarpers before the revelation of Sidi's conquest (53); and he is, finally, given two shoves that sit him down hard against a nearby tree (52; 57), a repeated opportunity to test whether the smell of wet soil is indeed too much for his delicate nostrils, in the words of Sadiku's taunt (33). This form of physicality is enriched by a more subtle because less resistible element: the sense of ease

---

convert to the joys of polygamy. The poor Christ of Bomba is an equally stubborn prelate. He is even more manic in his encounters with 'heathen' practices but by contrast, is revealed as a man tortured by increasing doubts. His inner reflections promise a conversion, some hope for the salvation of the man is awakened in the breast of the reader. But Mongo Beti is not about to redeem his gull. The ramifications of a venereal denouement cover the Father Superior with the stench of failure. Beti's thesis reads: the Church is, by its very nature (doctrine and practice), a contagion; Mongo Beti's expositions are masterly erosions of the Christian myth.'

and belonging to be had in a common vocabulary, most obviously in the mime; and the 'drawing in' which flirting induces, enjoyable to the extent it is inconsequential, as with the author's parting indulgence to his creation which well expresses the quickness of recovery proper to the young: '*A young girl flaunts her dancing buttocks at Lakunle and he rises to the bait.* [...] *Lakunle last seen, having freed himself of Sadiku, clearing a space in the crowd for the young girl.*' (58)

In *The Lion and the Jewel*, Ilujinle is both a coherent community and one whose young are, we imagine, increasingly turned to horizons beyond, another way of saying that 'coherence' is loosening. This spatial broadening enables Soyinka to play around with the weight of words on the young characters' tongues. It is no coincidence that the dictionary proved a common trope in plays of malapropism along the Gold Coast in the first half of the twentieth century, from which Soyinka's early creation takes and gives back richly – from Sekyi's *The Blinkards* (think Mrs Brofusem looking up the 'pronounciation' of the word 'petal', or Mr Tsiba looking up 'transparent', to understand the phenomenon of blushing[42]) to James Ene Henshaw's contemporary *This is Our Chance*.[43] In Soyinka's play, however, the interest comes less in malapropism, a trick as easy as its effect is short-lived, and more as he moves in the gaping hole between *langue* and *parole*, between language as

---

[42] Kobina Sekyi, *The Blinkards* (Ibadan; Nairobi; Lusaka: Heinemann Educational Books, 1974 [1915]), 20, 33. Sekyi took his epigraph from Robert Burns – 'O, wad some pow'r the giftie gi'e us/Tae seen oursel as ithers see us.' We might add hearing to seeing.

[43] For a general presentation of a few characteristic features of the Anglicized élite of this society in the first half of the twentieth century, see P.F. de Moraes and Karin Barber, eds., *Self-Assertion and Brokerage: Early Cultural Nationalism in West Africa* (Birmingham: Centre of West African Studies, 1990).

an aggregate of formal definitions and language as a living thing. Learn a language with a dictionary, Adorno remarked, look up all a word's meanings ten or twenty or thirty times, and you will still have no clear grasp of what they might come to mean in changing contexts, their proper weight on the tongue; rather their meanings will always and necessarily be too light or too heavy, too broad or too narrow.[44] He could have been thinking of Lakunle's description of the bride price he refuses to pay:

> LAKUNLE: A savage custom, barbaric, out-dated,
> Rejected, denounced, accursed,
> Excommunicated, archaic, degrading,
> Humiliating, unspeakable, redundant.
> Retrogressive, remarkable, unpalatable.
> SIDI: Is the bag empty? Why did you stop?
>
> LAKUNLE: I own only the Shorter Companion
> Dictionary, but I have ordered
> The Longer One – you wait!
> SIDI: Just pay the price.
>
> LAKUNLE [*with a sudden shout*]: An ignoble custom, infamous, ignominious. Shaming our heritage before the world. (8)

Lakunle's listed words are funny because they enact perfectly the imprecision of words, of learning, when deprived of context. The pause for breath following the word 'redundant' suggests that Lakunle's final intention is not one of precision, but rather of proliferation, profusion, display. As such, it will take something more than Sidi's unswerving insistence on payment of the bride price to interrupt the young teacher's rhetorical stride – indeed the phoneme /aɪ/ of 'price'

---

[44] Theodor W. Adorno, 'The Essay as Form,' trans. Bob Hullot-Kentor and Frederic Will, *New German Critique*, No. 32 (Spring–Summer, 1984), 161.

actually triggers the remaining words Lakunle knows beginning with the letter 'i', which turns out to be the dying splutter and jerk of a surrogate memory. Nevertheless, the simple thrust of Sidi's point cannot be wished away. Lakunle, and by implication, any rhetoric which is not re-creative but draws on a limited stock, is on borrowed time (this looks forward to the bishop's 'running out of grammar' in *The Road*[45]*;* eloquence which does not bend tongue and ear to common precedent, the better to invent, which is not also shaped by response, is no eloquence at all. Sidi's casual command 'Just pay the price' means both 'pay the bridal price', and deliberately preserves the idiomatic 'suffer the consequences of your actions'. In other words, just accept that you cannot marry me, the village belle, and drop the whole charade.

Words have a way of penetrating us, despite our defences or protested indifference or mockery. Of *The Lion and the Jewel*, Biodun Jeyifo has observed, usefully, that 'the play of conflict and opposition is constantly shifting and moves from Lakunle and Sidi to Lakunle and Baroka and finally to Baroka and Sidi' and that 'it is these rhetorical improvisations that give the language of the play its very rich, suggestive texture'.[46] This creative enmeshment is assured by a basic idea. Each character has a weakness, momentary or characteristic, readily identifiable by others and occluded from him- or herself: in Lakunle, the wagging tongue of a 'sprig of foreign wisdom' (51); for Sidi, youthful callowness; in Baroka, the wincing insecurity of old age

---

[45] The observation belongs to Samson: 'We wanted to see which of them would win, whether Professor would get cramp for in the neck or the bishop would run out of grammar.' See Wole Soyinka, *The Road*, in *Wole Soyinka: Collected Plays 1* (Oxford: Oxford University Press, 1973), 164.

[46] Biodun Jeyifo, *Wole Soyinka: Politics, Poetics, and Postcolonialism* (Cambridge: Cambridge University Press, 2004), 108.

amid the encroaching shadow of change; and for Sadiku, the momentary dropping of her guard, or the vulnerability which wish-fulfilment can induce.

The bond between Sidi and Lakunle, then, is not all rebuff and impermeability. Of course, Sidi rightly dismisses Lakunle's nonsense as the symptom of foolishness, though reader and audience should not stop there. Against her commonsensical mockery of his chat – 'I had enough of that nonsense yesterday' – his pirouetting response is an inadvertently funny blend of register and reference: 'Nonsense? Nonsense? Do you hear? Does anybody listen? Can the stones bear to listen to this? Do you call it nonsense that I poured the waters of my soul to wash your feet?' (7) This well captures Lakunle's adoption of a sort of platonic idealisation of sex; love as intransitive, the woman as the object of man's humility, in the gesture of Jesus before his disciples. And yet Sidi does acknowledge a certain dependence on Lakunle, firstly with regret ('we really cannot do without your head' [4]), and later, in a moment of unguarded celebration ('The school-man here has taught me certain things and my images have taught me all the rest.' [21]).

In truth, both have had their heads turned – a word which, significantly, binds looking elsewhere, a change in state, and going mad – by print: Lakunle in the words of books, Sidi in her magazine-image. For just as Lakunle's usurped tongue ably assists in his 'undoing', so Sidi's voice and mind are interrupted by quotation: 'The book? Did you see the book that would bestow upon me beauty beyond the dreams of a goddess? For so he said. The book which would announce this beauty to the world – have you seen it?' (11) Experience here is something conferred from without, not lived, and as a result the first person swells: 'Known as I am to the whole wide world, I would demean my worth to wed a mere village school teacher.' (12) The normal construction would have 'it' in the place of 'I', but Sidi's new-found confidence struts loudly.[47] Even Sidi's coming to 'know' things – 'He's old. I never knew till now. He was that old...' (21) – comes from these extrusive sources, and in this sense, can only rejoin the flightiness of Lakunle's words. She pronounces her own worst condemnation, ambivalence stalking the proud assertion, flipping the claim of self-creation into a boast of her own ignorance or not knowing: 'I have learnt nothing of anyone.' (43) In both, distant horizons – Lagos, beyond the seas, the mad outer world, the stranger – become the arbiter of taste and good judgement, the great distances gradually or suddenly weaken and undo the bonds which once obtained between words and their usage.

In the dancing scene between Sidi and Sadiku, between village belle and the senior wife of old chief Baroka, we first hear the subtlety of counterpoint between Lakunle's trite 'romantic' outpourings[48] and old-school marriage obligations.

---

[47] We should probably add that, in a different key, these glossy magazines, as with Lakunle's misogyny or Baroka's leadership, might take on a darker note. In Soyinka's 1981 childhood biography *Aké*, 'glossy' images are again coupled with the notion of 'fulfilment of promise', though in the depressing context of skin-bleaching: 'A girl decides at last on one of several competing brands of "skin-tone" creams, already picturing her skin bleached lighter, if the glossy poster on the wall fulfilled its promises.' See Wole Soyinka, *Aké: The Years of Childhood* (London: Methuen, 2001 [1981]),157.

[48] See Emmanuel Obiechina, *An African Popular Literature: A Study of Onitsha Market Pamphlets* (London: Cambridge University Press, 1973), 40: 'What has happened in Africa has been that the combined onslaught by St Paul, St Augustine and St Ambrose, Shakespeare and Jane Austen, Marie Corelli and Bertha Clay, and those indefatigable spinners of tales about love-lorn maidens and dashing young men who dominate the "true" romance magazines, has proved too strong for the fragile defences of the customary code of sexual morality and marriage. The result has been the emergence of romantic love as a vital factor in modern West Africa.'

Previously, Sadiku has tried to recall Sidi to herself: 'But Sidi, are you well?' asks Sadiku, before observing, 'Such nonsense never passed your lips before. Did you not sound strange, even in your own hearing?' (21) To no avail, alas: 'Sadiku,' remarks the young girl, 'I am young and brimming; he is spent. I am the twinkle of a jewel but he is the hind quarters of a lion!' (22) Sidi is not hearing herself as she speaks: a twinkle is ephemeral, and must fade and die, whereas at least hind quarters are grounded – the wrestling with words and in body gives later resonance to this. Yet Sadiku herself will be subject to the same alarmed questioning not too long after, by the very one she has just accused of madness: 'Sadiku, are you well?' and again 'Stop your loose ranting. You will not move from here until you make some sense.' (31) That word 'loose' is charming, quietly conveying the unseaming or outrunning of thought by word.

At the risk of my being prosaic, Sadiku is dancing at night, and the sense of communion between her and Sidi as they celebrate Baroka's supposed impotence, the elision of physical difference before female solidarity, is assisted by darkness. Perhaps this facilitates or even accounts for her yielding to the temptation, against her better judgement ('Baroka is no child you know, he will know I have betrayed him' [32]), which sets the final events of the play in motion. The run of words in Sadiku's solo song and dance had shown someone controlled enough in thought and imagination to develop and hone and sheen a metaphor – always a satisfying thing. From 'Race of mighty lions, we always consume you, at our pleasure we spin you, at our whim we make you dance; like the foolish top you think the world revolves around you', we move to 'it is you who run giddy while we stand still and watch, and draw your frail thread from you, slowly, till nothing is left but a runty old stick.' (30) The imagery of spinning is used to intimate man's and her man's finite condition, a yarn, with its finite amount of thread, speaking to the body's irreversible decline in time. And even though she is here dancing to a misconception, I must add that I always have the impression that the force of her celebration might outlast Baroka's success, that the strength of her feeling, patiently curated, is not prey to collapse at the first disappointment; that her victorious sense of Baroka's ending is strong enough to last her disabusal. Her experienced 'Too late for prayers. Cheer up. It happens to the best of us' (53) bespeaks, perhaps, a victory *deferred*, rather than lost.

If Lakunle fails, it is because he fails at charm, ignores the forms of address necessary to seduction. If Sidi fails, it is because she is not attentive to the palpable hits she scores – the most resounding instance being her ruthlessly pinning Baroka's old age in the phrase 'Once upon a time' (42), which suggests not only the eclipse of his powers but that they are of the realm of fairy tale, the imagined – because she plunges too deep into the enjoyment of Baroka's misery, as once she did to Lakunle (12), and is burnt therein. What of Baroka? It is poetically right that a satire on mishearing and sex plays with double-entendre, and the play's best gag belongs (inadvertently) to Lakunle. 'I seek redress!' (53), he intones, taking Baroka's seduction of Sidi for abusive, little hearing in that upright declaration the muted association with straightening or erecting. (This sense came to English through French, and still comes quicker to the French- or Italian-receiving ear – *'redresser'*, *'raddrizzare'*.) For, at that same moment, by the litmus test of manhood, Baroka is being proved the most diligent of pupils.

To the audience, Baroka's will and intention had already been felicitously announced in the word 'purpose', deployed expertly in his faux-lachrymose confession to a generally suspicious but in this instance, sadly unsuspecting, Sadiku: 'The scorn, the laughter and the jeers would have been bitter had she consented and my purpose failed, I would have sunk with shame.' (27) The 'purpose' of this permanently rutting old man – 'He loves this life too well to bear to part from it' (24) opines Lakunle, in one of his rare concessions to the solidity of monosyllables – is, of course, to bed nubile women. To the extent to which Baroka 'confesses' his shame instead of having others point it out, to the extent to which he seeks to control its issue, his is an investment in a fiction of shame, not without its attendant risks – we can never fully control what others will say – the better to carry off the prize.

Baroka's triumph is perhaps ultimately attributable to his grasp of nonsense. 'One hardly thinks the Baale would have the time for such childish nonsense' remarks Lakunle, to which Baroka responds: 'A-ah Mister Lakunle. Without these things you call nonsense, a Baale's life would be pretty dull.' (16) We earlier noted that words' unmooring seemed to be linked to a broadening of perspective, as if these seductive vistas and the imaginative projections they elicit involve both a gain and a considerable loss. The summons of huge distances which is set here for comic purposes (where in tragedy the governing of space requires greater control if effect is to preserve its bite), for triviality, in no way diminishes the elegance of the ruse with which Baroka seduces Sidi. The ruse works through the enlistment of the postal service. Chinua Achebe once recalled the mixture of fear and admiration instilled in him and his friends, during his childhood, by the letter-van of the postal service – His Majesty's Royal Postal Service as it was then, today just another privatised company – which they captured in the nickname *Ogbu-akwu-ugwo*, Killer-that-doesn't-pay-back.[49] Baroka has astutely latched onto Sidi's similar youthful blend of fear and wonder (at what we might take to be a more or less contemporary moment), though here it works, crucially, through Sidi's own image flying throughout the land

---

[49] Chinua Achebe, *Home and Exile* (Oxford; New York: Oxford University Press, 2000), 76–8.

on stamps; that is, it gains traction and purchase through Sidi's own conscription into the idea, it gains grip on her imagination through an indirect and disarming appeal to her vanity.

The ancient Greeks, who had a wonderful moral vocabulary, might have seen in Baroka's seduction a classical expression of 'nikhedonia', the enjoyment and savouring of a victory one knows to be imminent. Once Baroka thinks he has triumphed, once he suspects that his triumph is complete and assured, he allows his tongue to trip and stroll freely in mocking ambivalence, experience's strut and luxuriation before the callowness of youth – undoubtedly more pleasurable precisely because youth has proved surprisingly spirited. Sidi's drowning self-contemplation, her ingenuous 'perching' on the bed, is, then, an invitation to rhetorical brazenness too good to turn down: 'I hope you will not think it too great a burden, to carry the country's mail all on your comeliness' (47), he purrs, a game of homophony in which 'mail' refers to the stamped letter, but 'the country's male' to the Baale himself. The delicious or outrageous sense, depending on the sensibility, in which, victory assured, he verbally paws his prey, is developed in his slightly perverse use of ambiguity, the undertow of easy-flowing sententiae:

> BAROKA: we must leave
> Virgin plots of lives, rich decay
> And the tang of vapour rising from
> Forgotten heaps of compost, lying
> Undisturbed... (47)

The surface meaning is well-trodden ground, a conservative idyll of untouched community coterminous with Nature, as against industrial encroachment. Yet 'leave' means not only 'leave untouched', so to speak (where it goes with 'lying undisturbed'), but also something which approaches the opposite sense, 'leave behind' or 'quit', which in turn makes of that 'Virgin plots of lives' – notice the accent on the 'Virgin'

– a not-so-oblique reference to young Sidi, the once bold interlocutor now charmed into silence. Furthermore, it intimates what is to come, the renewal that Baroka is seeking, the intention to stay that intruding whiff of his own decay, his decline into irrelevance, forgotten by the community, alive only in his elegies for himself, the log-tossing, leopard-and-boa-hunting, silk-cotton-tree-climbing, first-pod-breaking-man – of yesterday. Wonderfully, that 'lying undisturbed' ceases to be an orthodox conservative yearning, but becomes suggestive of what he wishes to do, of the 'cooling aftermath' he now imagines imminent: lying *down* undisturbed, the plot cultivated. Conservatives and reactionaries, alas, are perfectly capable of playing with the tropes of their own discourse, a principle further refined in what is shortly to come, seduction's tipping-point, the proverbial point of no return:

> BAROKA: Our thoughts fly crisply through the air
> And meet, purified, as one.
> And our first union
> Is the making of this stamp.
> The one redeeming grace on any paper tax
> Shall be your face. And mine,
> The soul behind it all, worshipful
> Of Nature for her gift of youth
> And beauty to our earth. (48)

We earlier mentioned Lakunle's tendency to the intransitive ('I want to wed because I love' [9]), to which we might have added his abstract usage of certain nouns of foreign provenance – faith (7), 'the love of spirit not of flesh' (54) – in Sidi's riposte, 'words which always sound the same and make no meaning.' (8) It is clever that Baroka's reclaiming of these words – 'The school teacher and I, must learn one from the other. Is this not right?' (49) – grounded in the postal stamp, is quite exactly a rejection of platonic abstraction or 'undoing', and that it comes with a new deeper or heavier tonality to the words *in*

Sidi's hearing, for well must the same words of Lakunle continue to ring in her head. The trick for Baroka is to 'sound like the school teacher' (48) but to retain address; to reflect just as he departs. 'I can no longer see the meaning, Baroka. Now that you speak almost like the school teacher, except your words fly on a different path, I find...' (48) That word 'almost', which expresses the difference between identity and likeness, tells us, if we are to take seriously what Sidi says she is hearing, that there are two different orders of speech here, and that we, the audience, should be alive to the fact that Sidi now hears two, where before she could only hear one.

It little matters what the specific word is that breaks her alert tension or wariness into vulnerability or passivity or confusion: the point is more the cumulative effect of familiarity and strangeness, carefully constructed through the words 'Nature' and 'grace' and 'soul' and 'beauty' and 'earth'; and, as corollary, her enlargement which has nothing to do with the additions or elaborations of conceptual knowledge, nothing to do with the acquisition of information, the capital of England, say, but rather with the deepening of experiential knowledge, the sense that empty words, which is to say words which we use without thinking, might be reinvested again, take on a new weight and tonality, which holds them both to past usage and an uncertain present, which has us looking forward and backward at once, unsure and excited.

As he nears the moment of 'doing', the old fox allows himself one last flourish:

> BAROKA: The old must flow into the new, Sidi,
>   Not blind itself or stand foolishly
>   Apart. A girl like you must inherit
>   Miracles which age alone reveals. (49)

What might, in a context of innocence, have been merely preachy, is here a smutty gag which works with 'flow', 'the inheriting of miracles', we are to assume, thereby becoming a technical point of sexual pedagogy. (And observe how it is all conceived as the opposite of 'standing foolishly apart', the emasculations of the contemplative attitude of the would-be scholar.) Here he is again, with a little more subtlety this time, though no less cheek: 'the rugged wine acquires a full and rounded body... is this not so – my child?' (49) All is irreproachable innocence if we take this as a disembodied reflection on experience and becoming; all is impudence and guile if we hear in that word 'acquires', as we should, the physical acquisition of imminent sexual conquest, and in that 'full and rounded body' the issue thereof. Sidi nods, overcome, and as the old man takes a bow, we move on to consider another sleek tongue, operating in the same rhetorical realm of persuasion, only in the realm of soul-seduction: Brother Jero.

2

The *Jero* plays, or How Words Change Under Historical Pressure

In approaching Soyinka's two Jero plays – *The Trials of Brother Jero* (completed in 1960; first published in 1964) and *Jero's Metamorphosis* (1973)[50] – I wish to begin with a simple observation: that in and between these two plays, Soyinka puts the 'trial' to quite different ends. In the earlier play, it seems to me, the trial should suggest most immediately the sense of 'trials and tribulations', whose levity has the twin-advantage of appealing to popular Yoruba – and more widely West African – literary and dramatic forms involving the trickster figure,[51] as well as the plangent though ultimately comic Christian tradition of suffering here on earth. In *Jero's Metamorphosis* – we must simplify for now – history enters the picture, and with it, a new rhythm. The all-too-human trials and their attendant sentences, which constitute both the organizational principle and end of the action, are trials under the new military state, not of individual doubt or testing – yet theatrical, and the implied link should not be missed – but culminating in public execution. Where in *The Trials of Brother*

---

[50] Wole Soyinka, *The Trials of Brother Jero; Jero's Metamorphosis*, in *Wole Soyinka: Collected Plays* 2.
[51] See, for instance, Ulli Beier, '*Esu-Elegbara:* Ambivalence in Yoruba Philosophy,' [1991] in *The Hunter Thinks The Monkey Is Not Wise... The Monkey Is Wise, But He Has His Own Logic*, ed. Wole Ogundele (Bayreuth: Bayreuth African Studies Series 59, 2001), 29–35.

Jero we are dealing with a principle of concatenation, a series which we might imagine endless, day upon day differing only in detail but not in substance or form; in *Jero's Metamorphosis*, time and space take on flesh.

As *The Trials of Brother Jero* concludes, Brother Jeroboam, the beach prophet and protagonist, has successfully eluded his creditor, Amope, had her husband and his disabused 'disciple', Chume, interned in a mental institution, and successfully manipulated a Member of Parliament, with promises of greatness sanctioned by God's favour, into becoming a potentially lucrative client. Although the final word of the printed version of the play is 'Master', uttered by the spellbound MP, the words which come just before have a deeper structural significance:

> JEROBOAM: And so the day is saved. The police will call on me here as soon as they catch Chume. And it looks as if it is not quite time for the fulfilment of that spiteful man's prophecy. (*TBJ*, 171)

This passage provides both formal closure (the definitive evasion of the problems of this day) just as it recognizes that tomorrow will hold its own problems (danger, as is proper to the genre, is only ever deferred, never fully resolved; rest is really only respite, salvation really only rescue). This constant oscillation between safety and danger is perhaps one meaning of the threat of the aged prophet whom Jero, a former protégé, has outwitted and ousted from his patch of land on the beach: 'May the Wheel come right round and find you just as helpless as you make me now...' (146) This is a good metaphor, for it speaks to chance, and therefore preserves in its threat a residuum of instability, a constant remainder beyond mere planning.

And yet although we understand the basic connection between land competition among beach prophets and the exponential rise in land price on the beach, Soyinka's artistic intention in *The Trials of Brother Jero* is not directed thereto. Space and the beach remain abstract, for the governing principle of this reworking of 'trials and tribulations' is chance and reversibility. A simple way of clarifying this is in the idea of 'professionalism'. Professionalism, unlike in *The Road* (1965),[52] is a subject of private, sweet and sighing melancholy. Brother Jero has the time and leisure to talk to the audience in direct address, and, one suspects, is not truly pressed by the fear of starvation or death (the genre does not allow for permanence, either in contentment or in disinheritance). The structural purpose that Jero's desire for professionalism enjoys works in this sense. His desire to stand out is the first motion of plot: for in order to acquire the accoutrements of professionalism – professionalism in this context is enhanced by ornament of both word and cloth – he acquires an ecclesiastical cape from Amope (another word for this slightly fantastical word is 'stole', an ecclesiastical vestment, and perhaps a more appropriate rendering of his means of acquisition):

> JERO [*Stands upright, divine rod in hand, while the other caresses the velvet cape.*]: And it is not what I would call a luxury, this velvet cape which I bought from

---

[52] In *The Road*, the meanings of 'professionalism' have more profound implications. Samson, the recently jobless passenger-tout who used to work with the coast-to-coast driver Kotonu, tries to stand out and apart before the indifferentiation of capitalist demands, before his own replaceability or anonymity in a trade in which mortal substitutions are daily; he tries to insist upon his skill, that said skill should properly confer upon him an individual identity, and yet this insistence is aired and expressed in bored unemployment: as a cinema-show or conjured dream to a man – Salubi, the assistant driver, himself seeking a licence – whom he holds in contempt ('They have no pride in their job. Part-time tout, part-time burglar. In any case they are the pestilence of the trade. No professional dignity.' [*TR*, 153]), or in morning's sullen soliloquies, or in drunken bravado ('Na me be dat. As you see me like this, I am a quiet, peace-loving man, but when we get to motor park, I don't know my brother again.' [225]), the hollowed

her. It would not have been necessary if one were not forced to distinguish himself more and more from these scum who degrade the calling of the Prophet. (*TBJ*, 153)

The proliferation of prophets, or false prophets, suggests the passing between two moments, between ease and leisure and the wistfulness for ease and leisure ('Charlatans! If only I had this beach to myself.' [153]), yet goes no further.

There is a sense in which *The Trials of Brother Jero* might be seen as a series of 'How-to' manuals or user-guides. Soyinka is quite attracted to the simple rhetorical possibilities which come from a logical understanding of a specific métier. We have already witnessed something of a classic 'How-to' moment in *The Lion and the Jewel*, in the scene between Baroka and his newest wife (the favourite), which we might subtitle 'How-to-pluck-hairs-from-an-armpit':

> BAROKA: You are still somewhat over-gentle with the pull
> As if you feared to hurt the panther of the trees.
> Be sharp and sweet
> Like the swift sting of a vicious wasp
> For there the pleasure lies – the cooling aftermath.
> [...] But – A-ah – Now that was sharp.
> It had in it the scorpion's sudden sting

---

and fleeting consolations of wish-fulfilment. Perhaps, so the implication goes, professionalism in *The Road* has not so much to do with dignity, if by dignity we mean respect for humans in life as in death, for it is a surfeit of dignity, or respect, or feeling, that has led to Kotonu's skirting spiritual destitution; perhaps professionalism means grabbing whatever chance one gets – 'I think they say beggar no get choice' (153), as Salubi remarks generously, and damningly – and Kotonu's peering into loss, his slow step into the shoes of Sergeant Burma, the war veteran who lived off the wreckages of accidents on the road, dramatises the problem effectively. For if Kotonu falls into one type of professionalism, coherent with a new order, he loses human dignity – and Samson loses his hopes of exercising his job as he conceives it, and with it, his own claims to professionalism.

> Without its poison.
> It was an angry pull; you tried to hurt
> For I had made you wrathful with my boast.
> But now your anger flows in my blood stream.
> How sweet it is! A-ah! That was sweeter still.
> I think perhaps that I shall let you stay,
> The sole out-puller of my sweat-bathed hairs.
> Ach! [*Sits up suddenly and rubs the sore point angrily*]
> Now that had far more pain than pleasure
> Vengeful creature, you did not caress
> The area of extraction long enough! (*TLJ*, 25, 26)

This well captures the unequal balance of a certain type of (exclusively old-school?) marriage, in which an unpleasant job, deemed a favour or honour, nonetheless holds the light solace of being capable of inflicting a sting. So what we have is Soyinka imagining how best to pluck an armpit – or rather, how best a man might wish to have his armpit plucked by a woman – and, in the fiction, a convincing enactment of that ideal by its tumbling away, as jealousy and spite and petty vengeance replace the bartered tenderness which comes with being the Favourite. Notice how unruffled general truths held in the opening imperative 'Be sharp and sweet' give way to live commentary; we reach an ideal sort of balance in the middle of the speech, as plucking and suddenness of sting decant, we must imagine, into the most soothing of cooling aftermaths; only Baroka no longer has control of the rhythm, or rather the rhythm of his Favourite's thoughts, for here we are dealing with practice not with theory, and the cooling aftermath is interrupted prematurely, the suddenness of the sting now slow to resolution.

In *The Trials of Brother Jero*, Amope, to whom Jero owes money, provides another straightforwardly amusing exercise for Soyinka, this time in a rhetorical genre with which we are all too familiar, both in others and in ourselves, though we tend to be more indulgent with ourselves: complaint. And Soyinka has perceived two things which I take to be universal in this most quotidion of genres. The first is the egocentricity of it all, in that all experience can be gathered and made to cohere around and within one's own person: 'I suppose we all do our best' (*TBJ*, 147); 'it's a tough life for a woman' (148); 'I can look after myself. I've always done, and looked after you too' (148); 'if I wasn't the kind of person who would never think evil of anyone – even you – I would have said that you did it on purpose' (149); 'There are women who sleep in beds of course, but I'm not complaining. They are just lucky with their husbands, and we can't all be lucky I suppose', 'Thank God I am not the kind of woman who...' (149). This convincingly plays on those effortless slides between material desire, which further diminishes the little she actually has, and the moral hypocrisy of claiming defencelessness, which lends to the whole a sort of sanctimonious, calculated impermeability.

As genres of complaint are calculated, they are, however, vulnerable, which is to say conditional or dependent. If Amope keeps up her patient monologue, '*spoken almost with indifference*' (148), it is that 'almost' which carries the pepper, and when Chume eventually '*gets on his bike and flees*' (149), Amope, as she must, '*relapses and sighs heavily*' (149). For such forms of deadened creativity or word-churning, coming from boredom perhaps, need an audience, and the rhetorical challenge for Amope comes in an address: to control the give and pull of the rope which binds her husband to her words, to balance self-address with audience address, so to speak, allowing the rope to run variously along her tongue from complaint to accusation to self-pity to instruction to questioning to elicit in him sufficient guilt to feel indebted, though not enough for him to feel resentment at her claims – another reason as to why it is so important for those malnourished on complaint constantly to switch perspective, to trade in argument or reasoned follow-through for a kaleidoscope of trailing recriminations.

At the centre of the play stands Jero's *ars praedicandi*, and his lessons in how to be a prophet – *not* a false prophet, for a prophet, here, is only a prophet by the success with which he meets, not by any relation to the Most High – descry two different forms of teaching. The first is of the order of (mere) description:

> JERO: It becomes important to stand out, to be distinctive. I have set my heart after a particular name. They will look at my velvet cape and they will think of my goodness. Inevitably they must begin to call me... the Velvet-hearted Jeroboam. (153)

Jero's aspiration later receives a purely imagined fulfilment, robust enough momentarily to do away with his diagnostic standing apart, to enfold him – though only, it turns out, the better to accentuate the melancholy of an illusion ending, the coming apart of wish and reality:

> JERO: The Son of God appeared to me again this morning, robed just as he was when he named you my successor. And he placed his burning sword on my shoulder and called me his knight. He gave me a new title... but you must tell it to no one – yet.
>
> CHUME: I swear, Brother Jero.
>
> JERO [*staring into space*]: He named me the Immaculate Jero, Articulate Hero of Christ's Crusade. [*Pauses, then, with a regal dismissal*] You may go, Brother Chume.
>
> CHUME: God keep you, Brother Jero – the Immaculate.
>
> JERO: God keep you, brother. [*He sadly fingers the velvet cape.*] (163)

In terms of genre, this miniature vision points beyond the (deliberate) limits of *The Trials*, and suggests a dramatic line which Soyinka might pursue elsewhere: the coming together of articulacy and immaculateness, perfect because memory-less artifice, the flight from the stain of too much reality, from assimilation into the group as if one's own talents and gifts did not deserve a special place. The end to the indignity of a woman-creditor's morning window-ambush.

Nonetheless, in *The Trials,* the earlier play, standing apart is the more common posture, and it is perhaps therein that Soyinka most approaches his protagonist. The link between the ways in which a writer orders through the plot, and the ways in which a specific character might manipulate his fellow men and women, comes firstly in the staging of worshipful enthusiasm, and next with the venal motivations of a 'public servant', the MP earlier mentioned. Charlatanry, as Soyinka has well understood, requires control, perhaps indeed a greater honing of control and awareness, at least in the ways in which we use words, than other trades; that apparent paradox which sees verbal richness as requiring the greater precision. The linchpin of this charlatanry's axle turns on its deferral of the fulfilment of its dependents. This is expressed, true to Christian form, as a test which, like sustaining belief following the aftermath of conversion, is lived, as we have already remarked of the early Protestant tradition, in a sort of permanent tension, between the remorseless threat of collapse, and the straining towards constant renewal. This is channelled into the word 'trial', which is used in two opposing senses. It is, first of all, Jero's means for preserving Chume as client, Chume's apparently helpless exposure to the daily exactions of Amope's caw being quite easily conscripted into a spiritual narrative:

> JERO: Brother Chume, this woman whom you so desire to beat is your cross – bear it well. She is your heaven-sent trial – lay not your hands on her. I command you to speak no harsh word to her. Pray, Brother Chume, for strength in this hour of your trial. Pray for strength and fortitude. (157)
>
> The Lord says that you may not beat the good woman whom he has chosen to be your wife, to be your cross in your period of trial, and will you disobey him? (158)

Certainly, in such an environment, the reward Chume seeks is not otherworldly, but, as the previous prayers have spelled out for us, very much of this earth. Difficulties, or 'trials', are rationalised not as being the price to pay for salvation, but rather as the means to achieve what we want in the here and now. As soon as this slow-burning contract becomes subservient to a more pressing need – in other words, once Jero realizes that Amope, his creditor, is Chume's wife – the trial becomes something else. Or rather the opposite sense always felt as implicit in 'trial' – that of having passed the test, of having suffered sufficiently into truth, of arrival – becomes operative, reminding us that continuity of words is not continuity of meaning. The specific colour which this takes gains strength from a previous, casually misogynous, genealogy:

> JERO: I was only thinking how little women have changed since Eve, since Delilah, since Jezebel. But we must be strong of heart. I have my own cross too, Brother Chume. This morning alone I have been thrice in conflict with the Daughters of Discord. (162)

Women are Jezebel, the wicked wife of Ahab eaten by dogs; women are Delilah, the treacherous Philistine responsible for men's emasculation or swerving from purpose; women are Eve, the founder of strife in the world. More conveniently, women can be gathered up into the *fourre-tout* of 'the daughters of Discord'. Jero indeed skilfully weaves Amope into this group, to give it flesh from within, as he enjoins Chume to beat her in private as a means of removing her from his doorstep: 'Remember, it must be done in your own house. Never show the discord within your family to the world. Take her home and beat her.' (162) That word 'discord' is now both the abstract personification, and (Amope's) flesh and blood.

It might well be that any sales job requires such verbal skills, just as much as does attending to customers and worshippers on the beach. Here, however, Soyinka is able to stage and explore, through the generic context of prayer, the curious terrain of possession and awareness, of self-abandonment and self-control, evinced in leader and chorus alike. Anyone who has been to a 'lively' Christian service will know that there are degrees of involvement in worship, and here, Jero and Chume are the bookends of a sliding scale. Involvement in worship, however, is not all immersion and surrender. Chume performs quite well that recitative genre of conversational enthusiasm in prayer, against Jero's counterthrusts: 'My life is a hell... This woman will kill me... Only this morning I... All the way on my bicycle... And not a word of thanks... All she gave me was abuse, abuse, abuse... Nothing but abuse... If I could only beat her once, only once' (156). Jero is playing for time, waiting to see which way he needs to spin Chume in order to defuse his yearning for the quick release that a flurry of fists might provide. It is just as Chume goes to articulate his specific wish that Jero intervenes, not by argument but rather by that far more effective principle of authority, shouting down: 'Forgive this sinner, Father. Forgive him by day, forgive him by night, forgive him in the morning, forgive him at noon...' (156). (And notice those rhetorical commonplaces used for padding out the time, handy general nouns such as 'day' which can readily be declined into their constituent parts, according to the need.) This shouting down in turn brings in a wider chorus of worshippers, well-versed in the rhetorical game, though Chume's continued calls for mercy retain one foot in the beating camp, so to speak.

A moment later, Chume is forced into deputizing for Jero, and constructs his prayer from the rhetorical resources he has available to him – relatively poor, of course, in relation to those of Jero. Again, however, he preserves that strong sense of individuality within collective prayer that one might expect attenuated or diminished by ecstasy. We follow him as he builds his prayer, the *accelerando* both coercive and exhilarating. 'Forgive her' becomes 'Forgive am' not just because he is more comfortable in Pidgin English, but also because he is picking up on the congregation's 'Amen' (were I to direct this play I would bring together the pronunciation of the two);[53] as he moves into his narrative of worldly ascent for all, an extended expression of his own personal frustrations, after a short period of finding his voice, he comes across the balanced syntactical construction that most suits him:

> CHUME: Those who be clerk today, make them Chief Clerk tomorrow. Those who are Messenger today, make them Senior Service tomorrow. Yes Father, those who are Messenger today, make them Senior Service tomorrow. [*The Amens grow more and more ecstatic.*] Those who are petty trader today, make them big contractor tomorrow. Those who dey sweep street today, give them their own big office tomorrow. If we dey waka today, give us our own bicycle tomorrow. I say those who dey waka today, give them their own bicycle tomorrow. Those who have bicycle today, they will ride their own car tomorrow. [*The enthusiasm of the response, becomes, at this point, quite overpowering.*] I say those who dey push bicycle, give them big car tomorrow. Give them big car tomorrow. Give them big car tomorrow, give them big car tomorrow. (160)

The repetitions provide Chume with that crucial stillness amid the swell to regroup or think of what to say next, and provide the congregation a point of silence to fully apprehend and grasp the arc of worldly ascent that Chume is depicting. The two short stage directions – the gradual ecstasy, the overpowering nature of the response – are quite important, and must be well attended to by the director: Soyinka is staging

---

[53] For a relatively early discussion of Soyinka's literary exploitation of Pidgin English in the *Jero* plays, see Tony Obilade, 'The Stylistic Function of Pidgin English in African Literature: Achebe and Soyinka,' in *Research on Wole Soyinka*, eds. James Gibbs and Bernth Lindfors (Trenton, New Jersey: Africa World Press, 1993), 13-24.

prayer as a derivative of farce, as possessing the autonomous rhythms of a collaborative illusion, just as he is pointing to its power *despite* this, to the fact that knowledge is, despite our better judgement, wholly susceptible to weakening. The word 'overpowering', which applies not to the congregation, who are obviously quite caught up in things, but rather to the audience of onlookers, well conveys the blend of emotive coercion and aggression involved in these moments. And it is important that it is a prelude to the final repetitions ('Give them big car tomorrow' [160]), in which we begin to hear the note of desperation, the tipping point in prayer at which one has expressed everything one wants, and can but give an expiring final gasp, loud and voluble, before tapering off.

In between these two prayers, we glimpse through a crack in the prevailing humour, the darkness implicit in exploiting people's desperation. There is an important sense, which we must not miss, in which the brief expression of Jero's passionless cruelty is indissociable from the attempt to stand apart; in which passionlessness is a logical expression of the distance necessary for manipulation. As Jero surveys his beach congregation, moving from a man seeking local political office ('a very safe prophecy' [157]), to someone seeking national political office (a riskier prophecy, born from a need for more worshippers), he comes to his 'most faithful penitent' (157) – and 'faithful' here means something like 'desperately vulnerable' – a woman desperate to have children:

> JERO: She wants children, so she is quite a sad case. Or you would think so. But even in the midst of her most self-abasing convulsions, she manages to notice everything that goes on around her. In fact, I had better get back to the service. She is always the one to tell me that my mind is not on the service... (157)

Jero, it would seem, does not permit himself the luxury of feeling sorry for her – a lofty and condescending stance, certainly, but which, at the very least, recognizes the truth of her suffering – for risk of losing control of his orchestration. This is, I think, the meaning of the *non-sequitur* 'Or you would think so', for in no way does her noticing everything around her render the fact of her not being able to have children any less sad – indeed it possibly renders it *more* sad. The point Soyinka is making here, through his heartless prophet, regards the ways in which awareness of and participation in illusion can coexist, the ways in which stillness and control can survive with movement.

The deeper rhetorical point concerns the rhetorical conventions which govern the words chosen in prayer, and the responses one might legitimately expect to elicit (if one infringes upon these, one is shouted down, and left invoking mercy); but also, the rhetorical conventions which govern physical movements in prayer, as if self-abasements carry both the metaphorical weight Jero intends of a loss of dignity ('self-abasing convulsions'), and the literal sense of lowering oneself to the floor, of rolling and the like. As prayerful *convention*, this self-abasement implies anything but the loss of awareness or repairs, anything but the negligence of disattention, and, in turn, becomes perfectly compatible with lucidity. As such, Jero's lucidity is made to respond to the childless woman's lucidity (based, of course, on the disastrous premise that Jero can do anything about it), in a pact whose daily enactment on the beach is the subject of the play. When Church Missionary Society (C.M.S.) missionaries first attempted to establish missions in Yorubaland, they faced a number of difficulties in communicating (and justifying) what they meant by 'charity'. Yoruba worship practice had historically assumed that no gift is gratuitous, but rather involves reciprocity, mutual attention, an I-give-that-you-might-give rule of thumb. J.D.Y. Peel quotes a certain James White, writing of his wife's 'charitable' activities:

> She was often regarded by the heathens as generous to a fault, for, say they, kindness ought to be shown only to those from whom we expect a return, either personally from themselves or from their relatives nor ought they

to be shown to strangers with whom we are not acquainted, and the question is generally put, and who is to thank you?[54]

A little over a century later, it would seem, the networks of giving and receiving have been turned and channelled through an imported Christian vocabulary, and protection has become purely formal, predatory.

Femi Osofisan once remarked in a penetrating essay that Soyinka's progress from *The Trials of Brother Jero* to *Jero's Metamorphosis* 'illuminates, even more than Jero's, Soyinka's own artistic metamorphosis.'[55] Osofisan is here identifying with the writer who wrote the play, not with the characters, and I mean to pursue his line of thought as I come to consider the latter play. There is a slight methodological or generic risk in eliding the two plays, or more specifically, of reading back into the first what we know of the second. Take the following line, for instance, of *The Trials*, spoken by Jero as his tribulations reach temporary resolution: 'I have already sent for the police. It is a pity about Chume. [...] With the influence of that nincompoop I should succeed in getting him certified with ease.' (171) Within the generic frame of the play, what might we impute to this? Any 'darkness' or profundity as to, for instance, Jero's willingness to send somebody to a lunatic asylum in order to escape a creditor, must be counterbalanced

---

[54] Quoted in J.D.Y. Peel, *Religious Encounter and the Making of the Yoruba* (Bloomington and Indianapolis: Indiana University Press, 2000), 87. For a detailed discussion of the importance of the principle of reciprocity or *do ut des* in historical Yoruba social and religious practice, see Karin Barber, "How Man Makes God in West Africa: Yoruba Attitudes Towards the Orisa," in *Africa*, Vol. 51, No. 3 (1981), 724-44.

[55] Femi Osofisan, "Tiger on Stage: Wole Soyinka and Nigerian Theatre," in *Theatre in Africa*, eds. Oyin Ogunba and Abiola Irele (Ibadan: Ibadan University Press, 1978), 158. The essay's intelligence is the more admirable for being contemporary with Soyinka's artistic production.

by the sense of inconsequentiality of actions proper to the genre, the sense that one can always escape the constraints of an action, the constraints of history. Oyin Ogunba inadvertently expresses the slight methodological risk quite well, in my sense, when he writes of the first *Jero* play's link to the Yoruba tradition of storytelling 'in which the narrator, especially in describing lovely rogues, for example in Tortoise stories, changes to the first-person narration for effect and brazenly declares how depraved he is.'[56] The word 'brazen' is perfect, holding as it does the transgressions which we admire because of their daring, but 'depraved' places us into a separate ethical field, one of moral corruption standing beyond the attenuations administered by style. This is not mere wordplay on my part: the satirical effect of *Jero's Metamorphosis* depends on the extent to which Jero is able to retain our admiration, despite the new and altogether more serious ethical context.

One symptomatic change in *Jero's Metamorphosis*, simple though suggestive, comes in the pedagogical skit between Chume and Major Silva, a Salvation Army officer charged with teaching Chume the trumpet. Unlike the perfect negative pedagogy of the final scene of *The Trials*, in this scene, theory is not coherent with practice. Chume's recent experience in the lunatic asylum, and, one imagines, Major Silva's foreign accent (that odd '*perfect RP plus a blend of Oxford*'[187], which perhaps intimates an awkward and oscillating accent, one which is undercut by its conformist zeal), account for the student's suspicion and hostility. It is not merely that Chume becomes 'Chummy' in Major Silva's mouth, but that a term of endearment ('chum', 'friend') is used as an alibi for condescension, and the upholding of hierarchies. I imagine we have all been in situations in which condescension, racism even, expresses itself through a bizarre sort of confident

---

[56] Oyin Ogunba, *The Movement of Transition: A Study of the Plays of Wole Soyinka* (Ibadan: Ibadan University Press, 1975), 65.

ignorance, as if the important thing were not your name, as such, as much as the generosity shown in the mere recognition of your presence. Certainly Soyinka shows us here he is attuned to these methods of ingratiation, which will be more urgently expressed later in prose.[57]

True to bad theory, Major Silva's terms are not only abstract (nothing wrong with that) but also obfuscatory. Chume legitimately asks how Silva can teach the trumpet when he does not play it. The major's weak response deftly sucks the life from the trumpet by transforming it into something altogether less effable, which is to say 'Music' with a capital 'm':

CHUME: You don't yourself blow trumpet.
SILVA: That indeed is true, but I do understand music and that really is what I intend to teach.(*JM*, 188)

Silva is a fool of a teacher, and we should not be too quick to take him beyond that category, but his crudeness at least makes clear one element which *could* speak to us as teachers, for otherwise it is too easy, we are too safe. He is incapable of describing what he means by 'flourish' ('Well, flourish is er... extra, you know, frills, decoration.' [190]), eventually falling back on that old platonic notion of purity, 'What we want is pure notes, pure crystal clear notes.' (190) Chume looks blank, and we side with him, rather than Silva. The most effective moment in the scene comes shortly afterwards, and revolves around the sense of 'pepper':

SILVA: Pepper?
CHUME: Enh, pepper. When you cook soup you go put small pepper. Otherwise the thing no go taste. I mean to say, 'e go taste like something. After all, even sand-sand get in own taste. But who dey satisfy with sand-sand. If they give you sand-sand to chop you go chop?
SILVA [*beginning to doubt his senses*]: Mr Chume, if I

---

[57] See, for instance, the opening interrogation scenes with Mallam D., in Wole Soyinka, *The Man Died: Prison Notes of Wole Soyinka* (Middlesex: Penguin Books, 1975 [1972]),44, 65.

tell you I understand one word of what you're saying I commit the sin of mendacity.
CHUME: What! You no know wetin pepper be? Captain Winston, as soon as I say pepper 'e knows wetin I mean one time.
SILVA: I do not know, to use your own quaint expression, wetin musical pepper be, Mr Chume. (191)

As the scene has evolved, differences of class have been progressively expressed through each character's retrenchment in a specific register: for Major Silva, a staid and pedantic standard English; for Chume, Pidgin English. In the above quotation, Silva's mystification before Chume's language triggers a reversion to an English which he takes for eloquence, and which he attempts to use as a means of reminding Chume of his own superior credentials. His slight disgust before Chume's terminology, which all but he readily understand, is heard in his reversion to Mr Chume over Chummy, a re-establishment of distance or order, and that funny incapacity to use the same metaphor which Chume uses, pepper, without adding in the qualifier 'musical', as if the 'quaintness' was too much for him to bear.

In an essay on Aristophanes' *Lysistrata*, Soyinka neatly describes one possible thread worthy of the satirist's intelligence:

> The sinister aspect of satire is easily overlooked – in exaggerating to a ludicrous degree it also poses a threat – suppose it really happens? Laughter, after all, is a two-sided affair: it expresses a superior attitude but it also covers up fear. The more effective satire teeters successfully on this knife-edge of laughter-superiority and self-centred fear; the posed thesis can be dismissed but its exposition has succeeded in arousing thoughts of possibilities.[58]

This speaks both to audience and writer, both to reception and construction, and well expresses that double perspective

---

[58] Wole Soyinka, "The *Lysistrata* of Aristophanes" [1964], *Essays*, 21.

which the writer must retain when writing satire. By the end of *Jero's Metamorphosis*, as we hope to show, dismissal can no longer come to us easily, both because of the nature of events, and because events now carry a sense of irreversibility, a sense that we must fall in with events if we are not to fall (or be pushed) by the wayside. This is signalled from the opening scene, which indicates the arrival of the military, and the institution of a 'pre-emptive' judicial apparatus, in which the verdict precedes the charge. The sort of state in which infraction is reducible to an official's sense of personal affront: 'You dare slander a senior government official of my department in my presence? I shall order an investigation and have you charged with...' (*JM*, 183). Mikhail Bakhtin, in writing of the chronotope ('the intrinsic connectedness of temporal and spatial relationships that are artistically expressed in literature'[59]), argued that:

> spatial and temporal indicators [in the literary chronotope] are fused into one carefully thought-out, concrete whole. Time, as it were, thickens, takes on flesh, becomes artistically visible; likewise, space becomes charged and responsive to the movements of time, plot and history. This intersection of axes and fusion of indicators characterizes the artistic chronotope.[60]

By way of example, Bakhtin discussed the chronotope of adventures of Greek romance, noting that there, 'the nature of a given place does not figure as a component in the event; the place figures in solely as a naked, abstract expanse of space.'[61] Time and space in the Greek romance, for Bakhtin, were therefore characterized by the reversibility of moments in time, and their interchangeability in space. Against this naked abstraction, however,

---

[59] Bakhtin, *The Dialogic Imagination*, 84.
[60] *Ibid.*, 84.
[61] *Ibid.*, 100.

any concretization – geographic, economic, sociopolitical, quotidian – [...] even of the most simple and everyday variety, would introduce its own *rule-generating force*, its own *order*, its *inevitable tie* to human life and to the time specific to that life.[62]

Following Bakhtin, it might be useful to think of the difference between *The Trials of Brother Jero* and *Jero's Metamorphosis* as a difference between an abstract order of time and space (reversibility, interchangeability), and a more concrete one (a rule-generating order, a tighter intersection between the axes of time and space). In other words, instead of the early play's undifferentiated sandy expanse (the beach) and its rhythm of 'trials and tribulations' (yesterday, today, forever as reversible), in *Jero's Metamorphosis,* the beach becomes more concrete; it becomes 'charged and responsive to the movements of time, plot and history'. To the movements of history, because the new military government has instituted a repressive judicial order, part of which entails the execution of people on the beach; to the movements of time and plot, because competition for land (and the spiritual monopoly that land ownership brings) among the beach-prophets is, as a result, greatly stimulated. It is the quest for a spiritual monopoly which organizes Jero's activities in the play, and to which we must now turn in more depth.

Sand is no longer mere décor, but is enmeshed in a wider thematic. For sand has become the scene of the Bar Beach Spectacular, the spectacle of execution – the Latin part of our ear should hear, in 'sand', associations with the 'arena' – and it is this fact, in turn, that has transformed sand into a commodity, land, to be fought over by the prophets. When Jero speaks of the 'sandy though arable beach' (176), the imagery of ploughing to receive the earth's dividends makes

---

[62] *Ibid.,* 100 (italics in original).

vivid the bond between 'propheteering' and death, for the growth of one is inseparable from the blood which will be po(u)red by the firing-squad. (The link between blood and ploughing has already appeared with Professor in *The Road*, and there too, the dramatic tension comes from a sinister motion of renewal, sustenance of sorts depending on blood spilt.[63]) Indeed Jero's successful attempt to reingratiate himself into Chume's good books works through the contrast of pointless self-sacrifice ('martyrdom') with (others') meaningful death, in the alliance between 'God's judgement and the law' (194), the executions which stand on the play's horizon. Jero's instruction to Chume, which might seem surprisingly vivid – 'Picture my blood sinking into the sand and mingling with the foam, your feet sinking into the gruesome mixture and growing heavy with the knowledge of eternal damnation' (194) – serves not to repulse Chume through the violence of its imagery, but to elicit in him revulsion for the idea of violence *without the lucrative supportive alibi of official justice,* an altogether different proposition. 'Spirituality, to take root, must have land to take root in' (210).

There is a striking moment in which Jero creatively conflates two verses from the same chapter of Matthew's gospel, to make a point to the yet suspicious Chume. J.D.Y. Peel has shown us the truth of the old saying that it is religion that creates Scriptures (not Scriptures religion) in a Yoruba context, observing on the basis of C.M.S. archives that a certain number of verses recurred among the early missionaries[64] with great frequency – notably Acts 17:16ff, in which St Paul at Athens sees a 'city wholly given to idolatry', and the altar 'to

---

[63] Soyinka, *The Road*, 159: PROFESSOR: 'I found this word growing where their blood had spread and sunk along plough scouring of the wheel.'
[64] The first C.M.S. mission in Yorubaland was established in the mid-1840s, in Abeokuta. For a useful discussion, see Peel, *Religious Encounter*, ch.5.

the unknown God'. The missionaries gained from this, in Peel's reading, 'a sense of how to proceed and what to say' and a 'boosting identification with the Apostles'.[65] In Jero's conflation, well over a century after the first Anglican missionaries set up in Yorubaland, religion is not merely choosing which Scriptures to pass off as important (the sense of Peel's 'religion creates Scriptures'), but is instead literally creating new scripture. The Bible, that is, has become a mere prop before expediency. The verses 'Blessed are the meek: for they shall inherit the earth' (*King James Version*, Matthew 5:5) and 'Blessed are the peacemakers: for they shall be called the children of God' (Matthew 5:9) become, in Jero's mouth, 'Blessed are the peacemakers for they shall inherit the kingdom.' (195) It is astute of Jero, who is trying to placate Chume for having had him interned in a mental hospital, to avoid eulogizing meekness; it is calculatingly intelligent to swap 'earth' for 'kingdom', assuming that Chume will understand that the kingdom, here, is very much of this world,[66] and that kingdom is therefore a promise of worldly riches; and it is crafty that this new scripture precedes and prepares Jero's offer of a promotion to Chume, which reminds us that 'peacemaker' is not a term that tends to inertia or surrender, but belongs rather to the active life, that it is a quality of those who *institute* peace, which is to say, those who institute a new order.

Peacemaking clarifies this play's construction, its departure from *The Trials of Brother Jero*. The formally unchanging mould of *The Trials*, in which Jero's stand-aside commentaries on

---

[65] *Ibid.*, 155.
[66] Cf. Christ's remark to Pontius Pilate, John 18:36: 'My kingdom is not of this world.' The separation between an earthly (political) realm and an otherworldly (spiritual) realm has of course been one of the central animating tensions of the history of Christianity, irrespective of denomination or Church. In *Jero's Metamorphosis*, we remain firmly on the side of this world.

more or less self-regulating mechanisms were the order of the day, is replaced by a mould, in which Jero is building from the inside towards a specific objective; *Jero's Metamorphosis*, that is, tends towards an ending which acknowledges irreversible change, change from which we cannot go back. This historical pressure is intimated *in language* from the opening scene. The difference between the opening scenes of the two plays is striking: on the one hand, soliloquy, melancholic opining, commentary, recollection; on the other, dictation, purposeful organization, enactment, *doing*. This is Jero speaking to his new secretary, Rebecca:[67] 'Distribute those invitations at once. Go to my tailor and ask him to deliver my order tonight. Prepare everything for the spiritual assembly. When the moment comes, all shall be made plain.' (177)

Jero's Metamorphosis enacts a reordering of church hierarchy – the 'rationalisation', as it were, which Peel, in *Aladura: A Religious Movement Among the Yoruba* (1968), had found in Max Weber's mature sociology of religion: 'To rationalize is to reorder one's religious belief in a new and more coherent way to be more in line with what one knows and experiences.'[68] In his discussion, Peel goes on to discuss the nature of reorderings within a specific branch of the Aladura movement (one of the more important renewal movements in Yoruba Christianity), the Seraphim Society, observing

---

[67] From *The Trials of Brother Jero* to *Jero's Metamorphosis*, Jero seems to have solved the problem of the temptations which the Daughters of Discord once presented. Rebecca is a *'demure young woman, quite attractive'* (*JM*, 175), and so constitutes something of the golden mean, the cake being there without provoking the temptation to eat, like the can of beer in the bag of the proverbial alcoholic, which keeps him from relapsing. As such, she makes the perfect aid to the prophet.

[68] J.D.Y. Peel, *Aladura: A Religious Movement Among the Yoruba* (London: Oxford University Press, 1968), 294.

that the eclecticism of its hierarchical codes of dress and adornment, most in evidence in anniversary processions, was expressive of the flexibility (and potential weaknesses) of the church's organization.[69] In his oft-cited response to Igbo historian and writer Chinweizu's essay, 'Prodigals Come Home',[70] in 'Neo-Tarzanism: The Poetics of Pseudo-Tradition', Soyinka cites Peel's study to counter Chinweizu's claim that indigenous religious systems have been able fully to domesticate Christianity, and goes on to make a clear link between 'fundamentalist Christian church[es] anywhere along the coast of West Africa', and his initial inspiration for the *Jero plays*: 'I wrote *Brother Jero* from personal contact with these churches; in youth I often attended the services or watched their ecstatic dancing through the windows.'[71]

---

[69] *Ibid.*, 75.
[70] Chinweizu, *Okike: An African Journal of New Writing*, No.4, 1973. The proscriptive thrust of Chinweizu's argument as to African poetics evolves over his collaborations with Onwuchekwa Jemie and Ihechukwu Madubuike, most obviously in *Toward the Decolonization of African Literature: African Fiction and Poetry and Their Critics* (London; Boston; Melbourne; Henley: KPI, 1985 [1980]). The polemic between Chinweizu and Soyinka reached surreal heights when Chinweizu read Soyinka's poem 'To My First White Hairs' as pandering to the blancophilia and Negrophobia of Western racism. I must quote Chinweizu, in the introduction to his *Voices From Twentieth-Century Africa* (London; Boston: Faber and Faber, 1988), xxvi: 'Does a welcoming of one's white hairs call for a derogation of one's black hairs? If not, why this voluntary exhibition of contempt for things black? This all suggests that the author of this confessional poem, though a Black, is so thoroughly Euro-assimilated that he responds to black and white with the impulses of a white racist! Vorster, Botha, Hitler and other white racists would be flattered to read the poem, and would gladly hail the poet as an auxiliary Bantu spokesman for white supremacy.' This is unworthy of the author of the poetry collection *Energy Crisis and Other Poems* (New York; London; Lagos: Nok Publishers, 1978).

The 'rationalization', true to historical form,[72] operates in part through the dress. 'By the cut of his tailor shall a man be known. Uniform maketh man' (206), notes the beach-prophet Caleb; and Chume's final consecration as Brigadier Joshua in Jero's 'army' is confirmed in his dress – in Jero's words, 'the very ornament of his rank' (212). Beyond this historical connection between costume or disguise and symbolic hierarchies within the religious reorderings of the Aladura church, however, Soyinka plays on the *rhetorical* sense of language's adornment or disguise. From the first scene, he puts to good use the connection between verbal and sartorial adornment common in English, 'appearance' speaking both to eloquence (clothing a legitimate thought), *and* to disguise, which is to say deceit, concealment, trickery. The play begins

---

[71] Wole Soyinka, "Neo-Tarzanism: The Poetics of Pseudo-Tradition" [1975], *Essays*, 301. It is worth recalling that the *Jero* plays enjoyed popularity along the West-African coast not simply because of their accessibility to amateur theatre troupes, but also because of the public's familiarity with the fundamentalist expressions of Christianity which form their starting point. See Peel, *Aladura*, xi: 'The Aladura movement (the word means 'praying') has been prominent in Yoruba religious life for nearly fifty years [i.e. since the first decade of the 20th century], and has spread from its source in Western Nigeria all along the West African coast from Calabar to Freetown.'

[72] See Peel, *Aladura*, 75: 'What brought the Seraphim to people's notice more than anything else were the huge anniversary processions, involving thousands of people arrayed in white robes with special uniforms and adornments for different ranks and sections. A contemporary report describes how Moses Orimolade and "his energetic assistant Captain Abiodun" sat together in a go-cart under a canopy very similar to that used at Corpus Christi and inscribed with a motto celebrating the power of the Trinity. Twenty-four elders with stars as ornaments on their clothes and long staffs accompanied them, followed by 3,000 members.' Peel goes on to note that, historically, the various titles did not correspond to any clearly marked functions, which caused great confusion in Seraphim organization.

with Jero dictating to Rebecca the speech he will later give to his brother-prophets, to convince them of the importance of forming a 'syndicate':

> JERO: ... in time of trouble it behoves us to come together, to forget old enmities and bury the hatchet in the head of a common enemy... no, better take that out. It sounds a little unchristian wouldn't you say? [...] we have to be careful about our brother prophets. Some of them might just take it literally. The mere appearance of the majority of them, not to mention their secret past and even secret present... (175)

'Appearance' here might mean 'turning up', as if the meeting itself would in fact be compromised by their (criminal) presence, but also chimes with 'secret', and of course, the disguise of uniform, or the hypocrisy of the cloth. These ambiguities are complemented in the risk of confusion between the literal and the metaphorical, the sense that we can no longer take for granted the simple distinctions of the old order ('bury the hatchet'). And what we might speak of as a 'constituency' is given life in language through the play which the words 'brother' and 'brotherhood' are made to undergo. Peel, again, has made the key point for our purposes. He has observed that the fraternal idiom of European Christianity, 'the brotherhood of man', proved difficult to translate into Yoruba, due to the Yorubas' age-related and gender neutral terms of siblinghood ('egbon', for example, can be used of men and women); and that the lack of a term which was 'both warm and ungendered to express religious fellowship was not easily shaken off.'[73] Here in *Jero's Metamorphosis*,

---

[73] Peel, *Religious Encounter*, 59. Peel is writing of the Yoruba reception of Christian missionaries in the second half of the nineteenth century, but Chinua Achebe memorably felt that, despite the clear and often considerable historical differences between the success of Christian

brotherhood is not seen to be an expression of fellowship, if by that we mean a community built on trust, but rather a network in which each man seeks to withhold things from his brother. (The name given to the cut-throat prophet Ananaias is probably a discreet reference to the biblical Ananias of Acts 5:1–10, who sells his land, only to withhold part of the profit from Peter and the Church. As punishment, he drops down dead. Ananias' wife, Sapphira, ignorant of what has happened, commits the same lie shortly afterwards, and meets the same fate.[74]) A pact between 'brothers' must therefore be sought for the safety of all. In other words, at a moment in which competition is taking off, in which ethical considerations are subordinated to considerations of profit and loss, the foreign expression of kinship ('brotherhood') is most apposite to express the fragile and predatory contract

---

missions in Yorubaland and Igboland, a similar strangeness must have attended upon Igbo communities with the arrival of the missions in Igboland. One possible point of ingress into *Things Fall Apart* lies in the rendering of brotherhood, and the extent to which one might reasonably credit a metaphor stemming from grace, over historical social ties. You will recall that extraordinary moment in which the author writes of the response of Nwoye, Okonkwo's son, to a Christian hymn, to the poetry of the new religion; of how that hymn of brothers seated in darkness and fear provoked in Nwoye a form of recognition which he is yet unable to understand, and which leads him into confusion. Perhaps recognition is too clear a word; but certainly a movement of the mind which reaches out towards resolution or understanding, the yearning which Ikemefuna's death has left in the kernel of his gut. And so the 'callow' youth reaches out into a new sense of appurtenance which seeks to straddle and contain the best of both, to ignore or at least attenuate the aggressive rendering sought by the Christian church, that perverse re-working of Matthew 19:29: 'Blessed is he who forsakes his father and his mother for my sake'. See Achebe, *Things Fall Apart*, 50.

[74] Not to be confused with Ananias of Damascus, under whose divine hand the scales fell from the eyes of Saul of Tarsus (later St Paul). See Acts 9.

binding them.

To stand apart is to be overrun – the professionalism of the world of Samson in *The Road*, not of the first Jero; and this is the lesson of Shadrach, a rival beach-prophet. In the past, indeed only yesterday, his congregation would have been sufficient to assure his authority and independence – 'We protest most strenuously at this barefaced conspiracy. We shall pursue it to the highest level. The leader of a flock twenty-thousand strong is not to be taken lightly we promise you:...' (211) – but the new congregation embraces both this earth and the kingdom, which is to say, to paraphrase Jero, those seeking morals to be drawn from the miserable end of felons, as organized by the state. And so when Jero remarks to Rebecca that 'The voice of the people is the voice of God' (177), he means this in the worst sense, the sense in which the voice of madness is taken for the voice of reason, because the voice of the crowd is the only voice we hear.

Jero's Metamorphosis is, formally, the opportunistic realization of a plan – whence Jero's final *'amiable charlatan grin'*, whence the sign-off ('After all, it is the fashion these days to be a desk General.' [213]) announced from the first scene. We began by speaking of the genre of the trickster tale, how it must avoid overly serious moral issues if it is to elicit in us an enjoyable hesitation between admiration of the trickster's verbal and imaginative dexterity, and admiration of his brazenness. However, when the moral issues raised or suggested *en sourdine* become 'difficult to dismiss', as Soyinka wrote of the trial in Aristophanes' *Lysistrata*, we must talk of something else.

The ancient Greeks had a word, 'apotrope', which literally means 'the warding off of evil', and which entailed the attempt to divert the violence of mythology into comedy. In other words, to perform an apotrope is successfully to defuse the potential violence held in myth, into a happy ending.[75] Such is the case in *The Trials of Brother Jero*, as (Christian) myth is quite easily contained within the harmlessness of humour. In *Jero's Metamorphosis*, however, the apotrope is never fully assured; Jero's final joke ('After all, it is the fashion these days to be a desk General' [213]) is never fully able to defuse the violence of the executions from which he seeks to profit. The personal gain of the prophet comes too close to connivance with the terrible spectacle of public execution, a contemporary event in the lives of Lagosians. Soyinka's critique endures not only through direct attack, then, but also, and perhaps more importantly, by bringing brazenness into contact with perversion, in language.

As the final scene builds to its climax, Jero gives the following instructions to Ananaias, who is now a most zealous conscript in his new army:

> JERO: Just lean on the rotting walls Ananaias and the Lord will do the rest. By dawn the entire beach must be cleansed of all pestilential separatist shacks which infest the holy atmosphere of the united apostolate of the Lord. Beginning naturally with Apostate Shadrach's unholy den. The fire and the sword, Ananaias, the fire and the sword. Light up the night of evil with the flames of holiness! Consecrate the grounds for the Bar Beach Spectacular! (212)

Soyinka would later write of the widespread destruction that 'prophetist cults' waged on sacred objects and art works across Nigeria, their sudden descent on the provinces of established churches, their 'hot-gospelling' in the heat of the bonfires for which they were responsible.[76] J.D.Y. Peel has

---

[75] I am here borrowing from Nuttall's insights in a quite different context. See A.D. Nuttall, *Shakespeare the Thinker* (New Haven; London: Yale University Press, 2007), 132.

provided the particular historical example of Efon, formerly a major centre of wood carving, which was almost entirely denuded of its carvings. The rationalization? 'Babalola told the Alaye that in the six days after the burning of the idols there would be more peace than in the six previous years.'[77] Such, historically, were the peacemakers. In *Jero's Metamorphosis*, although we have moved beyond that initial period of fury – to a point, indeed, where such fury has turned inwards, against brothers in Christ, fellow beach-prophets – the method of destruction has survived, in the suddenness of descent (surprise being a timeless warring advantage), in the use of fire (shacks being as vulnerable as wood sculpture – perhaps even housing wooden crucifixes, symbols to 'ward off evil' become catalysts of their own end).

What is strikingly new in Jero's speech, however, is the cogency with which it enmeshes spiritual and political registers. The 'cog' in cogency is oiled by metaphor. We earlier spoke of the play's opening scene, in which Jero expressed wariness at the 'unchristian' weight of his expression, 'bury the hatchet in the head of the common enemy' (175), how his brother prophets might take the expression literally. By the play's end, his language has attained a perfect 'christian' weight of expression. Metaphor does not undermine the literal sense; nor is it mere adornment of an underlying notion. Rather, it both enlarges *and* authorises the basic notion. Which is to say that the two are indissociable.

The phrase 'Lean on the rotting walls', for example, connects

---

[76] Wole Soyinka, "Theatre in African Traditional Cultures: Survival Patterns" [1982], *Essays*, 142. He continues thus: 'This period may also be justly said to constitute the lowest ebb in the fortunes of traditional theatre, participation in the cultural life even of the villages being subjected to lightning descents from the fanatical hordes of the prophetic sects.'

[77] Peel, *Aladura*, 95.

the methods of violence (tearing down the rickety walls of the temporary beach shacks; 'lean' also carries a hint of intimidation, of pressure physically applied) to a sense of moral duty (to rid the land of disease or 'rot'). The separatists – that is to say, those prophets, with Shadrach first in line, who are not prepared to join Jero's syndicated army – are to be removed in 'the cleansing of pestilential shacks'; and the word 'cleanse' communicates political and spiritual renewal (respectively, violence directed against a specific group of people, and 'cleansing the land', a phrase derived from Ezekiel 39:14, and common in evangelical parlance). 'The fire and the sword' are possible tools for the cleansing, and not just a poetic borrowing from the flaming sword of Genesis 3:24. The imperative 'consecrate' ('Consecrate the grounds') formally announces the dedication of the beach to a divine purpose (as a church might be 'consecrated'); and it links sacredness and destruction, reminds us of the Christian ceremony in which bread or wine are made into the body or blood of Christ, as if actions involving bodies are taking place, without the sacred mysteries of transubstantiation. If these possibilities held in language are not disturbing enough, the new army's coming together is sealed by Brigadier Joshua, formerly Chume, who plays 'Joshua Fit the Battle of Jericho', the city whose walls fell after the Israelites marched around them playing trumpets. The biblical episode carries the following descriptions:

> And they [i.e. the Israelites] utterly destroyed all that was in the city, both man and woman, young and old, and ox, and sheep, and ass, with the edge of the sword. (Joshua 6:20)

> And they burnt the city with fire, and all that was therein: only the silver, and the gold, and the vessels of brass and iron, they put into the treasury of the house of the Lord. (Joshua 6:24)

We now see the uses to which (Brigadier) Joshua might put 'pepper', as the strict tempo yields to an indigenous rhythm *'to which the Army march-dance out into the night.'* (213)

I am arguing that the thickening of time, its taking on flesh, and space's charged response to these movements of plot and history, are channelled and focussed into language; and more specifically, into a language whose violence and moral implications step beyond the rhetorical parameters of inconsequential fun and wordplay, as well as the generic boundaries of comedy. In other words, towards the end of *Jero's Metamorphosis*, there is a subtle passing, or suggestion of passing, from one world of convention (rhetorical, ethical) to another. It is just such a sense of passing – and Soyinka's alertness to the literary fact that there is no better way to express such passing than in language, in the weight and inflection of words – that forms the starting point for two of Soyinka's most formidable plays, *The Road* (1965) and *Madmen and Specialists* (1970). It is to these plays that we now turn.

II

The Passing of Worlds, and the Language of Teaching

> y, como yo soy aficionado a leer, aunque sean los papeles rotos de la calle... [and, as I am keen on reading, even broken scraps of paper on the street...]
> — Miguel de Cervantes, *Don Quijote*[78]

> What I seem to sense is that age being linked with wisdom and knowledge implies a humane and moral world, whereas in the industrial, technical, technological society one tends to get the impression of development without morality, without the ethical basis of living – those things seem to become irrelevant.
> — Femi Osofisan, "The Word in Disguise."[79]

The French poet and translator Yves Bonnefoy once wrote quite beautifully of the passing worlds of *Hamlet*, and the awakening

> to a condition that was undreamed of and unimaginable only the day before: a world without structure, truths which henceforth are only partial, contradictory, in competition with one another – as many signs as one could wish, and soon far too many, but nothing that will resemble a sacred order or meaning.[80]

---

[78] Miguel de Cervantes, *El Ingenioso Hidalgo Don Quijote de la Mancha*, http://quijote.bne.es/libro.html(consulted August 2011).
[79] Femi Osofisan, "Ninth Dialogue: The Word in Disguise," in *The Power of the Word*/*La Puissance du Verbe*, ed. T. J. Cribb (Amsterdam; New York: Rodopi, 2006), 178.
[80] Yves Bonnefoy, *Shakespeare and the French poet*, trans. John Naughton (Chicago; London: University of Chicago Press, 2004), 17.

Bonnefoy's terms are coherent with the Western sceptical narrative according to which the domineering heritage of Christian Truth fragmented following the Renaissance, leaving little but doubt and scepticism in its place. We know that historical expressions of Yoruba metaphysics were perfectly able to host competing claims to truth; were, indeed, conditional thereon.[81] Despite these significant differences, however, I think that the basic *artistic* challenge remains constant: how, that is, imaginatively to represent two historical moments felt at once to be continuous and discontinuous,

---

[81] For a canonical discussion, see William Bascom, *Ifa Divination: Communication Between Gods and Men in West Africa* (Bloomington and London: Indiana University Press, 1965). Soyinka, of course, has been tireless in insisting on the accommodativeness of truth in Ifá practice, as against in 'revealed' religions, in Nigeria and beyond. See, for instance, his (relatively recent) 'The Tolerant Gods,' in *Orisa Devotion as World Religion: The Globalization of Yorùbá Religious Culture*, eds. Jacob Olupona and Terry Rey (Wisconsin: The University of Wisconsin Press, 2008), 41: 'Ifá emphasizes for us the perpetual elasticity of knowledge. Ifá's tenets are governed by a frank acknowledgement of the fact that the definition of Truth is a goal that is constantly being sought by humanity, that existence itself is a goal that is constantly being sought by humanity, that existence itself is a passage to Ultimate Truth, and that claimants to possession of the distinctiveness of knowledge are, in fact, the greatest obstacles to the attainment of Truth. Acceptance of the elastic nature of knowledge remains Ifá's abiding virtue, a lesson that is implanted in the Yoruba mind by the infinitely expansible nature of the gods themselves.' The distinction between 'elasticity' and dogma is a distinction which Chinua Achebe, too, considered pertinent enough to make repeatedly. In his (relatively recent) essay, "The Education of a British-Protected Child," for example, he contrasts the 'middle ground', considered lucky in Igbo culture, with 'Fanaticism. The One Way, One Truth, One Life menace.' He continues: 'The preference of the Igbo is thus not singularity but duality. Wherever Something Stands, Something Else Will Stand Beside It.' See Chinua Achebe, "The Education of a British-Protected Child," in *The Education of a British-Protected Child* (London: Penguin, 2009), 5-6.

how to render existence as it is steadily stretched over the yawning hole between two worlds.

One lens through which Bonnefoy attempts to apprehend the passing of worlds in *Hamlet* is in teaching, and the language deemed proper to specific orders of knowledge – Horatio's scepticism, the references to Wittenberg, a medieval ethic of revenge. I would like us to keep this in mind as I turn to Olabiyi Yai's suggestive reflection, in a discussion of the formidable difficulties and problems which teaching faces in today's Nigeria – and Africa – following the experience and sequelae of colonialism. The logic of Yai's reflection runs thus: in a post- or neo-colonial cultural context, teachers who possess and guard a traditional structure of knowledge are relegated to the bottom of the hierarchy; as such, student-numbers decrease, and with this, transmission of knowledge is endangered; and, as a result, the *language* of these teachers' knowledge, and their rhetoric of transmission, fall beyond esotericism (implicit in any form of powerful knowledge), into exoticism, and disuse.[82]

My interest in *The Road* (1965) and in *Madmen and Specialists* (1970; first published in 1971) hovers above these two insights: firstly, the artistic challenge of representing an order passed or passing into present profusion – in *The Road*, we are plunged *in medias res*; in *Madmen and Specialists*, we are witness to the passage – and finding or recreating a generic house and language proper to both; secondly, though more pressingly in the case of the later play, the *rhythms* proper to teaching, how teaching and knowledge which depend on patience and initiation and time, from one day to the next, might see their historical experience and truth reduced, under unimaginable historical pressure, to billowing smoke.

---

[82] Olabiyi Yai, "The Word in Disguise," in *The Power of the Word*, ed. Cribb, 175-6: 'Il faut dire qu'il y a beaucoup de choses qui sont devenues ésotériques parce que précisément ceux qui possèdent ce savoir ont des doutes sur la valeur de leurs étudiants.'

1

The Road: Prof. Made New

As we move from *The Lion and the Jewel* (1959–60) to *The Road* (1965), the Nigerian dramatic type of the teacher-turned-by-reading is greatly stretched and strained beyond its stock expression. It is as if the inconsequentiality of the type, the resolutions easily administered by comedy, and the simple technical exercise of listening and speaking well, have been submerged by historical circumstances altogether more exacting, not liable to proleptic interception or staying, à la Baroka. Dan Izevbaye, many of whose reflections on *The Road* I have found useful here, once discussed with great acuity what 'realism' might mean in the play, which I here quote at length:

> At the immediate, theatrical level Professor is the 'professor' or 'conjurer' who communes with spirits, as well as the stereotype, so strong in Nigerian popular imagination, of the learned man who like Paul had gone mad with too much learning. Both types are socially identifiable. At this level Professor's image is mainly a device for theatrical appeal, and his 'meaningless' but impressive rhetoric would make sense. But social realism is not the intention behind Professor's image. It is rather that other side of him, the 'madness' of the intellectual so obsessed with learning that he remains blind to flesh and blood, or the inevitable 'madness' of the figure of satire, which points [to] the realism behind the portrait.[83]

---

[83] Dan Izevbaye, "Language and Meaning in Soyinka's *The Road*," in *Critical Perspectives on Wole Soyinka*, ed. Gibbs, 102.

The 'immediate, theatrical' level, it would seem, consists of two types, both derivative of society; and is, if I have understood Izevbaye correctly, characterized by two expressions of 'social realism'. Firstly, social realism as a device for theatrical appeal – the representation of a well-known social type – which is to say, a response which conforms to audience expectation. In this sense, Professor's words are but signs for something else, his madness an invitation to allegorizing; the assumption of his madness determines his reception, our not listening or receiving the words he speaks. Yet Izevbaye immediately proceeds to nuance or indeed correct this sense of 'social realism'. For the greater expression of realism, he seems to suggest, is rather found in Professor's blinding to 'flesh and blood', an idiom which is striking here precisely because it renders almost casually, that grave and material presence of death which informs the entire play.

Professor or the reader, that is, is no longer content with signs confined to books, but is now interpreting signs which have spilled out into the world around; which is to say, books (and the Book) are no longer able to provide the answers within their covers, to assure and secure an understanding of the world. And so the reader – Professor – now lives and moves in the world as if it and its human constituency were just another text to be deciphered, as if everything around him must ever reveal to him a hidden meaning, just as it moves to conceal it. For a play in which the understanding and experience of 'essence' beyond appearance is a recurrent motif, it is intelligent that the motions of interpretation should be enlisted to the purpose, for such motions belong to the interstitial place inhabited by the reader and interpreter, destined to see the illuminated, not the light.

What, then, of the relationship between or joining of Izevbaye's two senses of 'realism'? The title of this chapter is taken from William Empson's essay on *Hamlet* – "'Hamlet'

When Made New".[84] There, Empson connects the shape and motivation and genesis of Shakespeare's masterpiece to the expectations of his first audiences. Shakespeare had to tackle the problem of delay, writes Empson, for the audience, fresh from Thomas Kyd's earlier *Hamlet* (c.1587), could quite easily puncture the later play by simply shouting out, 'Get on with it!' ('whereas ten years earlier they would only have wanted to say "Shush."'[85]) And so – and herein lies the technical inspiration – Shakespeare makes the problem of delay large, a formidable subject in itself, beyond the deflating pretensions of the bored or smart-alecky audience. He turns, that is, a 'calculated collapse of a dramatic illusion into an illustration of the central theme.'[86] This is his conclusion:

> Those members of the audience who simply wanted to see a Revenge Play again, without any hooting at it from smarter persons, deserved to be satisfied; and anyhow, for all parties, the suspicion that Hamlet was a coward or merely fatuous had to be avoided. The ambiguity was an essential part of the intention, because the more you tried to translate the balance of impulses in the old drama into a realistic story the more peculiar this story had to be made. The old structure was still kept firm, but its foundations had to be strengthened to carry so much extra weight. At the same time, a simpler view could be taken; whatever the stage characters may say, the real situation in the theatre is still that the audience knows the revenge won't come till the end.[87]

I am interested in two points of continuity here with Soyinka's own outstanding imaginative inventions in *The Road*. Firstly, it seems to me that a crucial part of Soyinka's artistic

---

[84] William Empson, '"Hamlet" When New,' *The Sewanee Review*, Vol.61, No.1 (Winter 1953).
[85] *Ibid.*, 19.
[86] *Ibid.*, 24.
[87] *Ibid.*, 31.

intention is expressed precisely in the structure of Professor's delay, in our hesitations between shouting out 'But he is just a madman!' (the suspicion to be avoided) and our willingness, readiness even, tentatively to enter into his way of thinking and understanding. To return to the terms of the introduction, the confusion between exhibitionist display and genuine mastery, Soyinka has created a character who is explicitly *both*, who holds both extremes quite clearly, *and* who moves, as along a sliding scale, between those extremes, his words and phrases enmeshed and caught up in and, indeed, in a way, apposite to, the surrounding context. In the reading that follows, I conjecture as to one way in which this operates; if it focuses on Christian terminology, it readily acknowledges its partiality, just as it seeks to suggest that that terminology, ultimately, is itself reintegrated into the governing principle of the work, that of recycling and re-use and breaking down.

Dorrit Cohn once noted of the English present tense that it can be used to denote three temporal ranges: the punctual or one-off, expressing momentary action; the habitual, expressing repeated action; and the timeless, in generalizations or eternal truths.[88] In her brilliant discussion of Kafka's short story, "The Burrow", she goes on to show the uses to which the author puts an illogical usage of this tense. In that story, an animal's daily routine in his sovereign burrow, rendered in the habitual present, is disturbed by a hissing sound, and with it the durative present becomes the punctual present of a consciousness adopting and rejecting different hypotheses as to the origin of the hissing, the bewildering experience of simultaneous events. Kafka's intention in that fiction, she writes, is to dramatize his own paradoxical conception of human time, 'based on a denial

---

[88] Dorrit Cohn, *Transparent Minds: Narrative Modes for Presenting Consciousness in Fiction* (Princeton, New Jersey: Princeton University Press, 1978), 190.

of the distinction between repetitious and singular events.'[89] If this distinction is effaced, she continues, 'the durative silence always already contains the hissing sound, and the destruction it brings lies not in a single future moment, but in a constantly repeated present.'[90] I would like to pursue this idea with Professor.

These are Professor's first words, as he enters *'in a high state of excitement, muttering to himself'*, clutching *'a road-sign bearing a squiggle and the one-word, "BEND"'* (157):

> PROFESSOR: Almost a miracle... dawn provides the greatest miracles but this... in this dawn has exceeded its promise. In the strangest of places... God God God but there is a mystery in everything. A new discovery every hour – I am used to that, but that I should be led to where this was hidden, sprouted in secret for heaven knows how long... (157)

This is not the first mention of 'miracles' in the play ('Now that is a miracle' says Salubi, bemused at the reliability of his body-clock alarm, inviting Samson's counter 'There is a miracle somewhere but not what you say. Maybe the sight of you using a chewing stick.' [152]), but with Professor the notion is carefully wrapped in insinuating paradox: for how are we to understand the apparent conflict between that 'Almost a miracle' and dawn's exceeding her promise, her providing a miracle greater than the rule – between, that is, something which seems both to fall short *and* step beyond the rule? If we think that this is accidental, we are weakened in our assumption when the same form of contradiction recurs shortly afterwards, in different garb: if we are to understand 'a new discovery every hour' in apposition to there being 'a mystery in everything', as I think we are; if we are to

---

[89] *Ibid.*, 193.
[90] *Ibid.*, 197.

understand everything as being able to yield a level of meaning beyond appearances, or even as standing for something other than itself; then the phrase 'I am used to that' must take us by surprise, for it suggests that constant discovery or permanent mystery *and* familiarity are part of the same gesture of interpretation.

I want to argue that, in Professor's usage of language, and more specifically in his usage of the present tense, there is a discreet ambiguity as to the distinction between repetitious and singular events; between the everlasting truth of something and the punctual. And within the ambit of this logical contradiction, perhaps expressive of confusion in Professor's mind, perhaps expressive of the constitutive motions of interpretation, in vain do we listen ourselves for stable distinctions in his language; in vain do we seek to separate the newness of the wonder from the habitual, the one-off terrible loss from the terrible loss that is repeated daily. We think of Shklovsky's pithy remark that familiarity, or automatization, swallows things, clothes, furniture, one's wife or fear of war.[91] No such clear distinctions are provided here, in Soyinka's reader in whom familiarity and wonder can co-exist.

Professor offers Kotonu a tour of 'the new wonder' (158), a 'madness where a motor-car throws itself against a tree – *gbram!* And showers of crystal flying on broken souls.' (159) This is Professor's refusal of the contingency of the accident – for where there is only contingency, no reading or meaningful interpretation beyond mere appearance can be had – and it flows into the following grand statement:

> PROFESSOR: My bed is among the dead, and when the road raises a victory cry to break my sleep I hurry to a disgruntled swarm of souls full of spite

---

[91] Viktor Shklovsky, *Theory of Prose*, trans. Benjamin Sher (Illinois: Dalkey Archive Press, 1990), 5.

> for their rejected bodies. It is a market of stale meat,
> noisy with flies and quarrelsome with old women.
> The place I speak of is not far from here, if you
> wish to come... you shall be shown this truth of
> my endeavours – (159)

And so Professor's description of his sleeping place, his loud alarm, melts into what could be a general description of a site or a specific description of today's site ('a market of stale meat'), and 'the truth of his endeavours' receives both validation and qualification in the renewal of the quest with every crash. At the risk of seeing my own eye in the microscope, like James Thurber,[92] it does seem to me that recognizing the staging of the reader clarifies a certain aspect of *The Road*, the dangers of interpretation, of becoming blind through interpretation, through a private rhetoric, to the world around us; how Soyinka's at times terrifying extension of dramatic type, in an important sense, stages the madness and quelled humanity which comes in talking of truth while moving around corpses as if, to borrow from Kotonu, they didn't exist.

Let me pursue this effect a little. Christiane Fioupou once reproduced Soyinka's cheerful relish of his ambiguous characterization of Professor, from the programme notes of the Chicago Goodman Theatre 1984 production: 'Charlatan, outcast yet communal, teacher and quester, innocent and cunning, a stray among strays, priest and profaner, moulder and iconoclast'.[93] The language-effect I have been discussing, one specific expression of this ambiguity, is perhaps quite hard to hear, but Professor's hesitations, his hanging or suspension

---

[92] See above, 12.
[93] Wole Soyinka, "From the Director," *Stagebill, The Road* (Goodman Theatre of the Art Institute of Chicago, April 1984), 15; quoted in Christiane Fioupou, *La route: réalité et représentation dans l'oeuvre de Wole Soyinka* (Amsterdam: Rodopi, 1994), 275.

between exhaustive readings and lack or failure or incompletion, beyond appearances and forever on this side of plenitude, are channelled into a narrative conceit, from which, in turn, they receive enlargement. (We have seen, with Baroka's exploitation of the post office, how such conceits lend words purchase that otherwise they would not have.[94])

Imagine the following situation: you are speaking with a non-native speaker of English, say, who through excessive confidence or understandable confusion or melancholy, has a poor grasp of verbal usage. Each time the native speaker hears 'I am going to hang this,' or 'Put it!' or 'It was snuffed,' he or she feels within a strong sense of the need for resolution, and the corollary impulse to complete the sentence ('up', 'away!' and 'out', for instance). This principle of generating the desire for completion in interlocutor is available to writers as an active or operative technique before reader or audience, be it in word or syntax or generic structure – or, as is the case here, all three. It is exploited cleverly by Soyinka in *The Road*, through the conscription of John's gospel.

Dan Izevbaye observes that a Christian background is the 'point of departure for the evolution of Professor's philosophy, and the point of reference at every stage in his Quest', and that this Christian 'religious background becomes the language through which we understand the dramatic unfolding of Professor's experience.'[95] Soyinka's exploitation of his audience's basic Christian competence – more rigorously, their basic familiarity with John's prologue[96] – works by evoking the terms of revelation and providence the

---

[94] See above, 39-40.
[95] Dan Izevbaye, "Language and Meaning in Soyinka's *The Road*," 93.
[96] Perhaps what Okot p'Bitek (irresistibly) cites as the opening verses of John's Gospel in Acoli – translated back into English, we are told that the verses read 'From long long ago there was News, News was with the Hunchback Spirit, News was the Hunchback Spirit.' – is symptomatic

better to indicate their present hollowness. We do not need to know that John's gospel, more than the synoptic gospels, plays constantly on the initiated and the uninitiated, on high and low or deeper and superficial meanings – think Nicodemus struggling to imagine (or to avoid imagining) re-entering his mother's womb (John 3:4) – though all of this no doubt adds a nice touch. We do, I think, need to know that the various symbols of the gospel all, ultimately, relate to Revelation; and that the gospel's apocalyptic shape, as John Ashton has reminded us, does not end with Revelation, the imaginative horizon, but instead traces a hymn about revelation, guaranteed by God's providence, which culminates in *incarnation*; that incarnation is, in this narrative arc, 'the triumphant moment in which [God's] design [...] comes to fruition by descending to earth in human form and finding a home in the small community which was all there was to welcome him.'[97] In *The Road*, and nowhere clearer than in Professor's interchangeable talk of kernels and words and keys and hidden wisdoms –

> PROFESSOR: ... eventually the revelation will stand naked, unashamed... the subterfuge will be over, my cause vindicated... (160)
>
> Somewhere in that granary is that elusive kernel, the Word, the Key, the moment of my rehabilitation. From what cesspit was this object dragged that you set it against the select harvest of a faithful gleaner? (202)

---

of the currency which the prologue had, its importance in both Catholic creed and Anglican offices across Africa, and therefore its succulence as morsel for regurgitation among thinkers and writers. Quoted in Samuel O. Imbo, "Okot p'Bitek's Critique of Western Scholarship on African Religion," in *A Companion to African Philosophy*, ed. Kwasi Wiredu (Oxford: Blackwell Publishing, 2004), 371.

[97] John Ashton, *Understanding the Fourth Gospel* (Oxford: Oxford University Press, 2007), 504.

> Oh God Oh God, the enormity of unknown burdens, of hidden wisdoms... say the Word in our time O Lord, utter the hidden Word. (203) –

we are made to understand, through an incremental operation working in word and sentence and tense and idea, that we are now cut off from purposiveness or salvation, from the assurance of providence.

Of course, the author needs to be sure that the audience grasps this emptying, and he does this through Professor's private conversion and spiritual biography (or 'backsliding', as they say), which we have come to know by heart: how he was once a youth fired by evangelism to wage a war on worldly sinners; how, as lay-reader, his voice attracted many to the church; how he used to bow at every mention by the preaching bishop of the name of Jesus Christ; how said bishop, jealous of the Professor's voice, delivers a preach saturated in Christ, so to speak, which forces Professor to remain bowed, a bent yet sturdy bulwark against the bishop's rhetoric, limited in time and resource; how the excitement of the 'audience' or congregation, crowded on the nearby wall to view, was such that the wall collapsed under their weight, never to be rebuilt; how later, the aggrieved bishop would sneak up on Professor during the latter's Sunday school teaching, a figure of judgement motivated by revenge, to hear Professor's blasphemous aetiology of rainbow ('a promise that the world shall not perish from floods.') and palm ('a covenant that the world shall not perish from thirst.' [222]); and how, later yet, Professor, who had already 'heard the laughter of children' when the wall fell down in flesh and dust, leaves the Word hanging. For the conversion is deliberately placed under the sign of John. Here is Professor:

> PROFESSOR: If you could see through that sealed church window you will see the lectern bearing the Word on bronze. I stood often behind the

bronze wings of the eagle; on the broad span of the eagle's outstretched wings rested the Word – oh what a blasphemy it all was but I did not know it. (205)

The eagle is the symbol of John and his gospel (one recalls the fourth beast like a flying eagle, of Revelation 4:7), and the bronze eagle lectern, brought to Nigeria on the back of its popularity in Victorian England where it had supported the open Word in Anglican offices, testified to the continued privileged status of John as apart from the synoptic gospels in the formalized cycle of Bible readings at services.[98] (It is no doubt also worth recalling, with Peel, that St Peter's Church in Ake, Abeokuta, the earliest established church in Yorubaland and hometown of Soyinka, held an open Bible in its stained glass windows.[99]) Here, the eagle, left hanging in the coloured light of the tainted windows, a bird no longer soaring but awaiting definition, a sign in ellipsis, has become a symbol of how the Word is left hanging and shorn of resolution, a means of drawing our attention to the emptying of the Word of its former Christian significance.

This sounds abstract, but it does serve a purpose. We know that John's prologue is a midrash on Genesis 1, that his usage of 'logos' borrows from and transforms Jewish traditions of Wisdom seeking a home in the world, in its claim as to the

---

[98] See Michael Wheeler, *St. John and the Victorians* (Cambridge: Cambridge University Press, 2012), 42.

[99] Peel, *Aladura*, 48. See also Soyinka, *Aké*, 152: 'But the seasonal anthems rehearsed by the choir also exerted my voice. The tunes came out clearly enough, but not the words. These emerged as some strange language, a mixture of English, Yoruba and some celestial language that could only be what was spoken by those cherubs in the stained-glass windows, whose mouths sprouted leaves and branches as they circled the beatific faces of saints and archangels.'

incarnation of the Word of God.¹⁰⁰ Here we realize that all of this simply moves to draw our attention to the *materiality* of flesh unredeemed; the operation works through the recycling, re-use, re-incorporation, or the breaking down and reconstitution of the 'Word' into a wider and more complex linguistic economy.¹⁰¹ It is here that we must recall the second part of that important verse which now takes on a terrible resonance: 'The Word became flesh *and made his dwelling among us.*' (John 1:14; my italics.)

Christiane Fioupou has called our attention to the play's 'mobility' of 'language', both verbal (orders of meaning, register, translation) and theatrical (musical variations, dance, mime, the play within the play, flashbacks); a mobility which is, in turn, given historical anchoring and metaphorical resonance in the road – the road as point of convergence, of exchange and of transit, and, in this destructive and gruesome urban context, as the site in which the passing of things, the disruptions and sudden ruptures within the plenitude of a former order, is most acutely felt.¹⁰² Another useful word might be 'circulation', come to English through Latin because through French, which holds a semantic sense (what Dr Johnson used to call the 'reciprocal interchange of meaning'),

---

[100] See Richard B. Hays, "The canonical matrix of the gospels," in *The Cambridge Companion to the Gospels*, ed. Stephen C. Barton (Cambridge: Cambridge University Press, 2006), 70.

[101] Northrop Frye, when speaking of the metaphor of 'logos' as employed in John's gospel, once remarked, within the Vichian cycle that was his, that 'we' who inhabit the democratic age, with its descriptive framework of language in which 'the word has no power to be anything but a word', are no longer able to understand such a metaphor. Certainly *The Road* is a compelling riposte. See Northrop Frye, *The Great Code: The Bible and Literature* (London; Melbourne; Henley: Ark Paperbacks, 1982), 18-19.

[102] Christiane Fioupou, Avant-propos to *La Route* by Wole Soyinka, trans. Christiane Fioupou and Samuel Millogo (Paris: Hatier, 1988), 6.

an economic sense (currency and goods), and most importantly perhaps, the idea of a closed system or circuit in which vehicles move (in modern French, the word 'circulation', nicely, denotes both the movement of vehicles *and* traffic.) Fioupou's acute distinction in talking of the characters in *The Road,* that they all live, to varying degrees of danger, *on* and *of* the road,[103] expresses the human entanglement well – their moving according to that general principle of repair or re-use, a sinister circle of life in which the 'old flows into the new', to use Baroka's chat-up line in the most harrowing of keys,[104] in this play without women; and how this happens through language.

A simple example of this notion of flow and passage comes with Say Tokyo Kid, the gang leader and timber-lorry driver, when, after flexing his muscles and 'luxuriating in the feel of his strength' (170), he engages in the following exchange:

> SAY TOKYO KID: I don't carry no timber that ain't one hundred per cent fit. I'm a guy of principles. Carrying timber ain't the same as carrying passengers I tell you. You carry any kind of guy. You take any kind of load. [...]
>
> SAMSON: I don't know. I like to deal with people. Just think, carrying a dead load like that from one end of the world to another...
>
> SAY TOKYO KID: Dead! You think a guy of timber is dead load. What you talking kid? You reckon you can handle a timber lorry like you drive your passenger truck. You wanna sit down and feel that dead load trying to take the steering from your hand. You kidding?
>
> There is a hundred spirits in every guy of timber trying to do you down cause you've trapped them

---

[103] Fioupou, *La Route,* 36.
[104] See above, 42-3.

in, see? There is a spirit in hell for every guy of timber. *Feels around his neck and brings out a talisman on a string.* You reckon a guy just goes and cuts down a guy of timber. You gorra do it proper man or you won't live to cut another log. Dead men tell no tales kid. Until that guy is sawn up and turned to a bench or table, the spirit guy is still struggling inside it, and I don't fool around with him see, cause if your home was cut down you sure gonna be real crazy with the guy who's done it. (171-2)

Say Tokyo Kid's strength, not the contemplative self-absorption of today's gym community, is directly related to, even derivative of, his daily struggle. 'Guy' is a homonym which, here, means both 'man' and 'woodbeam', and this assures the open (or 'animist') passage between driver and load, between man and wood. (This wordplay is a skilled instance, I should add, of the more subtle colours which run under the cinema-bequeathed American or faux-American drawl; a timely reminder, that is, that we should not stop with the identification of formal registers, but instead be prepared to see how formal registers are exploited, kept fresh.) Say Tokyo Kid understands this perpetual tension between balance and imbalance in anthropomorphised terms, terms sufficiently grand, we should suppose, to communicate to him a sense of danger, and ensure his constant awareness on the road (and to that extent, it makes sense): the simultaneous sense of mechanical control and exponential force which we have when driving vehicles of large mass ('So when I carry a guy of timber, it's gorra be the biggest.' [172]), the affirmation of strength as a simultaneous recognition of its limits. The wider observation, of course, is that the dance of death and life is held and expressed, for Say Tokyo Kid, in language, in couplings and passage which we feel to be necessary.

The formal artistic aspiration is probably similar to that

which Soyinka had already observed of Tutuola's most accomplished fictions: the 'juxtaposition of analogous experience from the familiar', the sense of reality as a tight web enmeshing levels of perception, the importance for the reader, as for the audience here, to live that enmeshment as an experience in language, to emerge, as with the protagonists, wise from the stress of experience.[105] And here we see a kinship between Professor and the gang leader, despite everything. For the mythic vocabulary of Professor, too, becomes coherent in this urban context precisely because mythic logic works through breaking down and re-assemblage, through disintegration and reformation, through circulation; and so there arises a cogency and kinship in principle between his language and the circulatory principle of existence, or rather survival. The point I am making, in this rather roundabout way, is that the language in *The Road* is, in an important sense, associative – not expository – because that is proper to such a context of existence; and as such, that talk of the 'Word' or the 'word' is important for what it suggests and opens up and insinuates (or closes down and breaks down and re-articulates or joins), for its not being reducible to a symbolic or purposive order.

The first mention of Professor in *The Road*, coming in the mouth of Salubi, the trainee-driver – 'All I need now is a licence. It is only a matter of getting Professor to forge one for me.' (*TR*, 153) – has Professor as a forger, a word which means the illicit reproduction of documents, but which can also connote the reworking of old material. The second mention – 'You can't frighten me you hear. Who do you think is afraid of that madman?' (154) – has a double purpose: it suggests a lack of assurance before Professor's powers, an ill-assurance which is most dramatically evinced in Say Tokyo Kid; and it draws

---

[105] Wole Soyinka, "From a Common Backcloth: A Reassessment of the African Literary Image" [1963], *Essays*, 10, 11.

out an unobtrusive meaning buried in forgery, the skilled calculated temper coexistent with something more elemental and, indeed, dark. In fact, the entire first exchange between Salubi and Samson – the 'cinema show' – is itself a play with illusion and re-enactment, only this time in a major key, or at least consistent with the harmlessness and inconsequentiality of 'bored games', as it were, the improvised play within the play. Yet even here, Soyinka is at work. Consider the projections of Samson into richness:

> SAMSON: Sometimes I think, what will I do with all that money if I am a millionaire?
>
> SALUBI: First I will marry ten wives.
>
> SAMSON: [...] Me, I will buy all the transport lorries in the country, then make Kotonu the head driver. [...] You I will make my private driver – and if you come near me with a dirty uniform like that, I will have you thrashed like a horse. (154)

Soyinka is exploiting a possible syntactical construction of informal Nigerian English – the dropping of the conditional 'would' in favour of 'will', and the subjunctive 'were' for 'am' – to convey the freeing from conditionality which any reverie or projection aspires to – from frustrations, from insalubrious Salubis, as it were, from reality. This is true, it seems to me, to life: the forgetting of the conditionality of our wishes, the forgetting of our bound existences, in slippages as quick and easy and momentary as tense or mood or syntax can offer. As the projections fade, Samson's last words in Pidgin – 'God I go chop life make I tell true. I go chop the life so tey God go jealous me.' (155) – have lost the balanced serenity of the projection's midpoint, and are, we know, darkened by something more desperate, or wistful, or timebound, the return to reality.

Structurally, Professor's skill in forgery ensures that people are dependent upon him for their sustenance, tied to him irrespective of flight of fancy or caprice. Yet the protection which comes of dependence is a double-edged sword in this context, for one man's protection is another's divestment. If forgery, as we have remarked, depends on copying, on illusionism, the full social meaning of this, the human consequence, only coalesces when Samson realizes that Professor intends to transform Kotonu's driving licence into one for Salubi, that one person's sustenance is another's condemnation:

> PROFESSOR: Not so long ago I would have spurned such clumsy craftsmanship, built a new document from old electric bills and those government circulars in which food-sellers wrap their food. [...] Nearly a year since I celebrated my hundredth forgery. It is difficult always to forge from scratch, and I am getting old. Once I could do three licences in a week and not feel the strain. Now if I manage one, I feel the life has gone from me. This needs only a little adjustment. A neat transfer, not a basic forgery.
>
> SAMSON: But Professor, what about us? Our livelihood! I asked you to convince him to return to the road but you want to cut him out altogether. What will we live on? (188)

Here, wordplay acquires force as we realize that people are 'cut out of life' as they are 'cut out' of a photo, and, conversely, are restored to life as they are restored, through forgery. In turn, Samson's desperate question – 'What will we live on?' – sharpens our ears to that sense, which is never distant, that physical sustenance might come from death; that, should Kotonu fall into complete emptiness, Samson, too, will be forced to live, so to speak, on death.

I earlier spoke of 'reworking' because it preserves the sense that there is no creation for Professor *ex nihilo*, that his creativity is, in this peculiar context, a form of sinister renewal, that it is strange outgrowth from something else, be it a driving licence or a police report. The sense that words are somehow organic, or part of a turned organic process, has been prepared in Professor's opening scene, where he speaks of the word 'hidden, sprouted in secret', the word that 'was growing from earth' (157) until plucked; and, stemming from that word 'plucked', the word as fruit, albeit strange. He continues:

> PROFESSOR: Three souls you know, fled up that tree. You would think, to see it that the motor-car had tried to clamber after them. Oh there was such an angry buzz but the matter was beyond repair. They died, all three of them crucified on rigid branches. I found this word growing where their blood had spread and sunk along plough scouring of the wheel. (159)

The road is earth 'ploughed' by the wheels of the lorry, and 'cultivated' by blood, into yielding its strange fruit, the signpost. This association between blood and words is suggested, too, in the word 'matter'. 'Matter' is, of course, a general noun meaning 'business' or 'affair', but here it also holds the sense of *bodies* being beyond repair, of life being reduced to mere matter – and the logical continuation of the sentence clarifies this, confirming the passengers' death. Later in the play, the word is given a further suggestive inflection, as Kotonu describes Professor as 'Wandering over empty streets picking up his dirty pieces of printed matter' (166). Ostensibly, this is a reference to newspapers, as we later learn, but there is an irresistible association with Don Quixote, that classical expression of European literary modernity, wandering over the streets picking up 'broken scraps of paper' (and quoted in the epigraph to this chapter). Whether deliberate or no, this sews together different levels of meaning: the passing from one order to another, in which our mad readings are applied to anything upon which our eyes come to rest, a gesture towards certainty in a world of profusion.

And yet here, on the road of *The Road*, that word 'matter' carries an additional macabre note absent from '*papeles rotos*', a chiming reminder of our own materiality.

There are other fleeting and insinuating moments. There is an obvious bind between human parts and spare parts, terrifyingly expressive of the *quid pro quo* logic of the play's world. 'Hear them snoring as if their exhaust has dropped off' (153), remarks Samson quite scornfully, though this is cleverer than it seems: the basic idea is clear, that the sleeping thugs make a loud noise, just as a car would without its exhaust-pipe. Yet there is a sort of over-insistence on expressions of tiredness – 'drop off' means to fall to the ground, where now they lie, but it also means 'to fall asleep' – which, I like to think, hints at an underlying and more fundamental fatigue. Shortly afterwards, returning clients impatient for the 'Aksident Store' (151) selling spare parts, once run by Sergeant Burma, to re-open, engage in a macabre song:

> 1st MAN: [...] Spare plugs, fuses, petrol cover.
>
> 2nd MAN: Windscreen wiper twin carburettor.
>
> 3rd MAN: Tyre chassis hub or tie-rod.
>
> 1st MAN: Propeller pistons rings or battery
>
> 2nd MAN: Rugs car radio brakes silencer
>
> ALL: Where there is crish-crash call Sergeant Burma
>
> 1st MAN: Every seam of second-hand clothing
>
> 2nd MAN: Trousers sandals ties assorted
>
> 3rd MAN: Handbags lipstick cigarette holder (175).

The pivotal neologism is 'crish-crash': it enmeshes a type of stitch (cross-stitch) – itself a medical and sartorial word – with the vocabulary of the accident (crash), as if the two are indissociable and joined (not merely juxtaposed or neighbouring or contiguous) in language as in mind as in reality. The articulations between clothing and car parts are greased by the falling away of punctuation. (This song looks forward to the macabre Mendicants' song of *Madmen and Specialists,* as they rehearse the preparation of Si Bero's herbs:

GOYI: First the roots.
CRIPPLE: Then peel the barks.
AAFAA: Slice the stalks.
CRIPPLE: Squeeze out the pulps.
GOYI: Pick the seeds.
AAFAA: Break the pods. Crack the plaster.
CRIPPLE: Probe the wound or it will never heal.
BLIND MAN: Cut off one root to save the other.
AAFAA: Cauterize. [*MS*, 228]

The associative language works, through parody, the medical idea of breaking to mend, reducing to rebuild. 'Pulp' is the pivotal word, in that it can denote both plant and human 'flesh', and so opens up the passage to the medical and bodily resonance of 'plaster' and 'wound', sealed in 'cauterize'.)

In *The Road,* the elision between car- and body parts, we were saying, further prepares us for Professor's intriguing contrast, as he asks: 'What's the Ministry's needle after all except for sewing the Word together or the broken flesh. But mostly the tattered Word.' *(TR,* 196) I take this, in a sudden reversal, to mean that the Ministry of Health is more concerned with spinning its own tales or self-protective rumour than looking after the injured; that the 'tattered word' – another ricochet from the dirty bits of printed matter, 'tattered' being a word frequently used of newspapers – is more important than the battered and broken flesh.

In an important sense, the legacy of the departed Sergeant Burma, who returned from war in Burma no longer able, it would seem, to distinguish between war and civil society, or – an altogether more dangerous thought – simply judging such a distinction no longer pertinent, is a master-trope, emblematic and historical. Consider the following exchange:

> PARTICULARS JOE: Oh Sergeant Burma was a rich man. He searched the pockets before the police or the ambulance came. Looting was after all the custom in the front. You killed your enemy and you robbed him. He couldn't break the habit.
>
> SAMSON: But this is not war.
>
> PROFESSOR: Liar. Even these rags [*waving a newspaper*] understand its nature. Like a battlefield they always say. Like a battlefield. (218-9)

No longer able to break the habit, no longer willing to break the habit; war or not war; victims of misfortune or injustice, those dead bodies strewn across the battlefield or across the roads of Nigeria? And, finally, human or inhuman? For it is the meaning of humanity that is on the line, as Kotonu's attentiveness to the ambivalence at the heart of 'inhumanity', which Sergeant Burma so dramatically renders, shows: 'He wasn't human.' – 'But he was. He was. A man must protect himself against the indifference of comrades who desert him. Not to mention the hundred travellers whom you never really see until their faces are wiped clean by silence.' (167)

With one or two exceptions, these examples are all taken from the first half of the play, but it seems to me that from the first to the second part, there is a sort of rupture as a new rhythm enters. (Shklovsky once pointed out that, common to the history of the novel is the replacement, within the covers of the same book, of an 'old novel' by a 'new novel' based on new devices.[106]) If waiting is not itself the sole principle of construction, and the main expressive force of symbolism; if waiting is not, so to speak, the only focus of the play's

---

[106] Shklovsky, *Theory of Prose*, 77–8.

energies; what then? How do we anticipate the audience's boredom, their sense that we are not going anywhere despite all the talk, that the ambiguity of rhythm is not mere provocation? Is the foreclosure of Revelation and the breaking down of the 'Word' into associative polysemy and enmeshment in concrete context enough for the audience? Is the rhythm of association and circulation itself enough to ensure a tale of *suspense*, or purposiveness, rather than simply belonging to a descriptive order?

In *The Lion and the Jewel*, the conventions of comedy, albeit inversed, are sufficient to give direction and impulse to the play, to channel its linguistic play towards an end, to preserve the distinctions between ornament and melodic line. In *The Road*, however, the rhythm which characterizes the first half is a sort of peristalsis, an awkward hesitation between urgency and release, between intensity and familiarity, that apparent erosion or indeed collapse of the distinction between the one-off and the ever-repeated event. And I should add that it is not limited to Professor. Think of the first human motions on stage, with Samson. They unfurl against the ticking of the clock, whose hands strike the half-hour and the hour far more quickly than we would reasonably expect. Beyond theatrical expediency, the silent exposition of Samson's solitude in frustration, and the respectful acknowledgement of the audience's need to become accustomed to mood and ambience, Samson, shorn of work, condemned to aimlessness *and* caught in time's jaw, is lost to boredom *and* surprised by the passing of time.

In the second part of the play, the dependence on death for sustenance that has been intimated hitherto is clarified quite directly in the opening scene, when Professor remarks, following Samson and Kotonu's attendance of the funeral:

> PROFESSOR: And you brought no revelation for me? You found no broken words where the bridge swallowed them? [...] You neglect my needs and

you neglect the Quest. [...] Understand, that shop sustains our souls and feeds our bodies. We lose customers every day. [...] you bring back nothing at all. Nothing. How do you expect me to make out your statement for the police? (195)

Several of the earlier senses briefly emerge or coalesce here: broken words resonating with the earlier signpost; 'new spare parts' to re-enter circulation, culled from the debris of the crash; and, ultimately, one symbolic swallowing to feed others, for where the bridge 'swallows', from its digested fare do they glean to survive. More importantly, however, we have the sudden introduction of a 'police investigation'.

The first mention of the police in *The Road*, it is true, comes in the opening exchanges between Samson and Salubi. Samson is imagining himself as a millionaire, the founder of a driving racket across the country, with Professor as the expert forger of driving licences. 'The day the police catch you...' warns Salubi, only to be corrected: 'Which kind police? They will form line in front of my house every morning to receive their tip. No one will touch my lorry on the road.' (154) This is all orthodox enough, and no one will be surprised – though plenty outraged – at the idea of police collusion in criminality. There is, however, a clever gag which comes shortly afterwards which announces the tighter ambivalence to come. Flinging out coins by way of bribes, this is Samson, the animator of what Salubi will call a 'cinema show' (165) :

> SAMSON: [*dips in an imaginary purse, he is about to fling to them a fistful of coins when he checks his hand.*]: Now remember, officers first. Superintendents! [*Flings the coins. Salubi scrambles and picks up the money.*] Inspectors! [*Action is repeated.*] Sergeants! [*Again Salubi grabs the coins.*] Now that is what I call a well-disciplined force. Next, those with one or two stripes. [*Flings out more money. Salubi retreating to a new position,*

picks up the largesse.] Excellent! Excellent! And now, those who are new to the game. [*Same action.*] You may go now. And good hunting friends. (155)

Corruption is no unregulated free-for-all, and Samson's show respectfully preserves the sense of hierarchy which obtains in the shadows (or not). The gag I spoke of comes with 'stripes', which is a term used for medals of honour, usually awarded for military or police service, and, of course, slang for prison-wear; and happily, if we strain hard enough, it holds even the weals which prisoners come to bear after passage, weals administered by the same striped police officials. This would be satisfactory but inconsequential wordplay if Soyinka did not take the care to insinuate its direct link to Particulars Joe. 'Who are you chasing today?'(210) asks Samson of the policeman, when he enters the stage in the second part. 'Chase' is a standard synonym for hunt, the word Samson earlier used for the slackened activity of corrupt police officers, and we again chuckle as Particulars Joe sees a coin on the floor and goes to pocket it, the coin being a stray left-over from Samson's earlier show, for it is the striped officer collecting his dues in life as in the show.

In our discussion of the passage from *The Trials of Brother Jero* to *Jero's Metamorphosis*, we suggested, leaning on Bakhtin, that the difference is between one of abstract time and space, and an historical rule-generating order. The difference between Samson's illusion and Particulars Joe's appearance in the second part has the same function *within the same play:* that is, to contrast illusion with the real thing.

Izevbaye perceived one strand of generic tension, held in the term 'realism'. Another strand comes in what Biodun Jeyifo, cleverly, has drawn our attention to: a crime mystery or thriller placed within or on top of the metaphysical quest. I must quote him in full:

underlying the 'plotlessness' of the play is a structural mythos which combines elements of a 'crime mystery' with that of a 'crime thriller': on the day of the drivers' festival which happened before the play proper begins, the funerary 'egungun' masquerade was 'killed' but the body 'disappeared' and all the characters sense something fishy and untoward in this 'disappearance'. Particulars Joe, the corrupt policeman, is in fact on the trail of Professor, the real 'culprit'; at the end of the play, the body reappears in the 'resurrection' planned by Professor; consequently, this 'resurrection' and the terrified panic that it causes, lead to Professor's slaying at the hands of Say Tokyo-kid, the most terrified and at the same time the least intimidated by Professor's reputed occult powers. Of course, there is no 'crime' and the 'disappearance' of the body is more apparent than real and it is precisely the totally imaginary nature of these motifs that enable Soyinka's treatment of this mythos of 'crime mystery' and 'thriller' to give death, the disappearance ('flesh dissolution') of bodies and the mystery of life, part romantic, part tragicomic expressions through powerfully realized characters in the grip of processes of historical change they barely understand.[107]

The first quoted word 'underlying' recognizes that there is a difference in rhythm between circulation and waiting ('plotlessness'?); the purposiveness of crime fiction, in which the content of the crime is ultimately resolved; and intimates that we, the audience, feel its presence without that presence having to shout about itself. At the same time, Jeyifo's reading qualifies everything it says, all the standard tropes of the genre as deployed in Soyinka's play, with those inverted commas. Jeyifo, that is, shows himself extremely attentive to the ambiguities attending the staple tropes of crime fiction as evident here in *The Road* – what is the crime? who is the criminal? who, the detective?

---

[107] Jeyifo, *Wole Soyinka*, 143.

I would like to pursue the significance of the 'totally imaginary nature of these motifs', evoked in the above quotation. In an article published at least twenty years earlier, though in circulation years before, Jeyifo had offered an influential Marxist reading of *The Road,* which notably gave short shrift to exclusively metaphysical interpretations of the play.[108] *The Road,* argued Jeyifo in that essay, expresses in tangible and concrete ways the varied expressions of psychological instability and crises evinced in a human community subjected to daily violence. The socio-historical factor, he continues, comes in too rapid an urbanization, a spiritually denuding thrust into a sort of shadow capitalism which preserves the destructive features of that system *without* the technological and industrial advances. However, instead of seeking the grip for a Marxist reading at the level of *source* of violence, which seems to me too paradigmatic a reading (what can one say, ultimately, beyond the symptomatic diagnosis? – that the characters are a result of what they have lived, that their traumas reflect an underlying violence, and the like), perhaps we could turn, rather, to genre and the sociology of literary forms; which is perhaps another (provocative) way of saying that, in one restricted sense, Jeyifo's reading was, in fact, not Marxist enough (an orthodox enough Marxist complaint).

Franco Moretti has argued quite wonderfully of what he takes to be the classical period of detective fiction in the English novel (1890-1935), that its solutions only provide the *sensation* of scientific resolution, while all the while deliberately (and somewhat ironically) avoiding empirical testing. Detective

---

[108] See Biodun Jeyifo, "The Hidden Class War in *The Road* (first presented at the first annual Ibadan Conference on African Literature, University of Ibadan, July 1977," in *The Truthful Lie: Essays in a Sociology of African Drama* (London: New Beacon Books Ltd., 1985), 11-22.

fiction of this classical period, writes Moretti,

> perfectly satisfies the aspiration to certainty, because it rigorously avoids the test of external reality. It is science become myth; and hence self-sufficient. Detective fiction empties the proto-bourgeois ideal of experimental culture by subordinating it to a literary structure that is anything but experimental. The cultural model it promulgates must not be coherent with external reality, but only with itself. This perfect self-referentiality ultimately defines detective fiction as a hyper-literary phenomenon. [109]

One specific structural expression of this, which is quite to our purposes, comes in Moretti's discussion of the fictions of Conan Doyle, the mollifying tonic which such fictions offered to a paranoid and expanding society afraid of the sudden snapping of social control. And what the city or metropolis distils in frightening intensity (the fear that 'anonymity – that is, impunity – potentially reigns'[110]) is ultimately defeated in the form of the arrest, which is dependent on 'the new and perfect mechanisms of transportation and communication', on carriages and trains and letters and telegrams. 'They are the tacit and indispensable support of the arrest. Society expands and becomes more complicated: but it creates a framework of control, a network of relationships, that holds it more firmly together than ever before.'[111]

In *The Road*, the master-trope of the road has the clear purpose of expressing the destructive and necessary contingency at the heart of the city and, as corollary, the complete collapse of the fiction of a formal and coherent supportive network of control functioning to preserve the

---

[109] Franco Moretti, *Signs Taken for Wonders: On the Sociology of Literary Forms* (London; New York: Verso, 2005 [1983]), 149.
[110] *Ibid.*, 143.
[111] *Ibid.*, 143.

order of society. It offers an exploitation of the generic assumptions of classical detective fiction, as characterized by Moretti, a counter to its dilution of fears and anxieties in self-sufficient representations of scientific rigour, by confronting us with the terrible truth that at the heart of such order, contingency lies coiled. Soyinka, that is, is referencing the tropes, the better to hollow them out from within, just as society provides a shell without the substance, the urban shadow without its technological twin.

Before we come to Particulars Joe, the corrupt policeman, a word on chronology. We mentioned the 'police investigation' at the start of the second part, but it is not the police investigation which comes to occupy the stage, loosely, as we approach the end. That is, it announces the new rhythm, and prepares our confusion before the various declensions which police investigations, in the second part, will undergo. The central event in *The Road*, the accident involving Kotonu and the mask in possession, holds the various characters' trajectories turning and revolving in its gravitational pull. It gives coherence to what has come before, and opens up direction for the resolution of the various characters' quests. When it is revealed to us, it suddenly clarifies that language of waiting, of what we have felt to be a successive and endless rhythm of urgency and release, and gives it a meaning, an understandable impulse. For instance, no longer is Professor's quest eternally reproducible, no longer do we have that sense of what seems like an incommunicable reason for waiting, his 'watching, watching and waiting, waiting for the careless moment' (206) before the open window which he thinks closed, or reads closed; but rather we understand the 'miracle' of Murano, the importance of the abduction of the god, deliciously teased out in the eventual confession:

> PROFESSOR: And waiting, waiting till his tongue be released, [*desperately*] in patience and in confidence,

for he is not like you others whose faces are equally blank but share no purpose with the Word. So, surely Murano, crawling out of the darkness, from the last suck of the throat of death, and Murano with the spirit of a god in him, for it came to the same thing, that I held a god captive, that his hands held out the day's communion! And should I not hope, with him, to cheat, to anticipate the final confrontation, learning its nature baring its skulking face, why may I not understand... [*He stops, looks around him.*] (223-4)

This confession works when we hear it as self-address, the expression of a wish, aired here for the first time perhaps, tantalizing precisely because of the awareness of the unbridgeable gap between the thought and the experience or better, in that the thought itself posits itself as surrogate (or 'anticipation') of the experience, a theorist's wet-dream. The first two sentences are interrupted, so to speak, and the main verb we feel to be imminent is withheld and deviated by the word 'for', more justification of the intellectual project than anything else. The final elliptical question he hears in the silence around him, and this, of course, leads to his 'forgetting the mute one' in his own ritual.

And yet, in another sense, this central event does just the opposite, by creating more questions than answers. It might be useful to consider Kotonu, the former coast-to-coast driver. Before the action of the play begins, Kotonu has been forced to don a mask, to rescue himself and Samson from the angry followers of Ogun, whose ritual they have inadvertently interrupted by running over the masquerade, Murano. Yet the attempt at mere disguise and concealment is harried into something more serious, as Kotonu finds himself caught up as a surrogate in the ritual:

> KOTONU [*tearing at the clothes, demented.*]: It's all wet inside, I've got his blood all over me. [*They*

> *dance and whip one another around the masquerade, leaving a clear space for his frenzy.*] It's getting dark Samson I can't see. His blood has got in my eyes. I can't see Samson. [...] Samson where are you? My eyes are all clammed up I tell you. [... *His struggles become truly frantic, full of violent contortions. Gradually he grows weaker and weaker, collapsing slowly on the ground until he is completely inert. The dancers flog one another off the scene. A slow black-out, and a half-minute pause.*] (209)

The ritual itself, however, is itself carefully attended to by ambiguities: can Kotonu not see for the blood (Murano's blood in the mask)? Is that the darkness that encroaches over his sight? What is Ogunnian possession without the effort of will? Was he not already dumbly nodding and 'hopeless' *before* the ritual?[112] Salubi's quite nonchalant question to Samson as he quits the stage – 'Why you no surrender self?' (161) – is a call to acceptance of his present circumstance, but is given deeper hues in the play in what it anticipates or rather suggests of his former colleague: Kotonu imploring Professor – 'How much longer must I wait?' only to hear Professor's curt response – 'Like you all I also wait but you do not hear me complain.' (199); Kotonu, caught in immobility, his coast-to-coast days a canvas against which we retain but the memory of his actions, his current suspension, that 'No Danger No Delay Here Today Gone Tomorrow' (212) turned from being part of a praise-epithet to a slightly sinister commentary on

---

[112] Cf. Ketu H. Katrak, *Wole Soyinka and Modern Tragedy: A Study of Dramatic Theory and Practice* (New York; Westport, Connecticut; London: Greenwood Press, 1986), 71-2: 'Kotonu undergoes an experience of disintegration of self and then through the exercise of superhuman will, a restoration. The tragic actor, Kotonu, resists this initial plunge into disintegration, for it is a fearful and lonely journey through the metaphysical abyss.'

his present condition, the danger of delay, the contingency of life in such a context; Kotonu's very name, as Fioupou has told us, as held enigmatically in its Fon rendering, 'on the edge of the river of death';[113] Kotonu's *language*, undoubtedly the least poetic of all the characters, expressive of this flattened or dumb or dulled humanity. These are not problems that reach resolution in an ending, in an ideal of self-sufficiency, but rather seem endowed with a centripetal force.

Let us step back to Particulars Joe, for, as the policeman, he is the protagonist of the investigation, or should be. Jeyifo was, to my knowledge, the first formally to speak of his surface venality and mediocrity masking a deeper sharpness and astuteness,[114] to which we would only add that the latter seems to shape the former. Particulars Joe enters following the long black-out and silence after the flashback, which seems perfectly suited to the resolution of past event in present investigation. Only this is immediately qualified, as we learn that his timing is less than miraculous, as we hear his skilled precision of imprecision, his stringing together of descriptions expressly tailored to be impermeable to disproof:

> PARTICULARS JOE: Rather light in complexion, mind you it's bit dark in here, so you could easily think him a somewhat darkish fellow. He was wearing a huge agbada but then, he could have shed it while I was chasing him. (210)

Soyinka's artistic intention, therefore, is directed towards homology, towards superimposing the illusory motions of justice, the empty shell of a police investigation, on top of what we imagine to be the real thing. In other words, the confusion we referred to in the introduction between two orders of language, is here reinforced in *generic* ambiguity, to

---

[113] Fioupou, Avant-propos to *La Route* by Wole Soyinka, 11.
[114] Jeyifo, "The Hidden Class War," 13.

the ends just discussed. And so the tale of hit-and-run on the goat, is suddenly turned into the question directed towards Kotonu: 'You wouldn't know anything about that sort of thing would you?' (210) From there, he proceeds to an investigation of the 'Unreported accident suspicion of foul play and accessories before and after the fact.' (214) This is what journalists say when reporting, not what the police say of their own investigations, and translates the sense, starkly expressed with his sudden adoption of a *'dramatic-interrrogator pose'* (214), that Particulars Joe is representing justice in both senses of the verb, as representative and as dramatic enactment, as action and acting. And we might look to the following lines, too: 'And I hereby warn you that anything you say or do will be taken and used in evidence et cetera et cetera.' (214) This is a rather ominous reworking of the standard formula – anything you say or do *may* be taken and used in evidence. What was announced as a purposive police investigation, is quickly caught up and enmeshed in elision, indifference, forgetfulness, cowardice, incompetence, venality...

I have said that there is an irresistible sense in which the detective genre simply drops away. The passage to Professor's ritual experiment is opened up as Particulars Joe is forced by the thugs – a revealing role-reversal – to question Professor, though 'question' is no doubt too accusatorial a verb:

> PARTICULARS JOE: thinking sir, that as a man who wanders on the roads quite a bit and picks up significant events which would escape the ordinary eye, we were wondering sir, if you may chance to have er... discovered something which... er... might be able to assist the police in their investigations. (219)

Here, the principle of the police investigation, the search for clues which the 'ordinary eye' cannot see, which is to say read, doubles the language of Professor's extraordinary metaphysical quest, the picking up of significant 'events', which of course reminds us of those dirty bits of printed matter. But if two types of quest have here come together – the metaphysical and the more prosaic police investigation – it is the metaphysical which seems to edge the other from the stage. Particulars Joe's final words, a jittery entreaty as Professor's ritual continues apace ('I swear sir, I would sooner you forged a hundred insurance policies.' [226]), lead not to the resolution of a resolved crime, but rather to his simple dropping away (or watching on), as another crime is committed at the play's denouement, Professor slain by Say Tokyo Kid.

I would like to offer a conclusion by way of Christiane Fioupou's seductive conjecture on the *mise en scène* of *The Road* at the Chicago Goodman Theatre, as reported by Ketu Katrak.[115] According to Katrak, then, the production's final image was that of the mask which continued to spin beyond the death of Professor, providing the play a frame in Murano: from the coiled sleeper of the opening scene who is the first to awaken, to his final illusive parting. For Fioupou – though she retains the conditional, in French a mood often reserved for prudence, the holding open of possibility – this frame or closing of the loop, as represented in the Chicago production, could be seen to make of the whole play a movement of transition, the simple phase, the passing between day and night, life and death, the human and the divine, the representation of the suspension of death as materialized in the characters and the events of the play itself. She concludes, as far as insinuation or seductive conjecture allows for conclusion, writing that '*The Road* would be, then, a dramatization of the ritual space of *agemo*, time and death having yielded to spatialization throughout the play, a concrete representation of the road of transition, the juncture between

---

[115] See Fioupou, *La Route*, 173.

the worlds of the visible and invisible, between ritual and theatre.'[116] The notion of a yielding of time and death in spatial representation, a temporary thwarting of successiveness, is extremely suggestive.

We might seek confirmation in Murano, for his early role is not, in this perspective, what Izevbaye once called a discreet way of associating the opening scene with death[117] – the 'empty cups used at the last carousing' (152) speak rather to a lively (if not good) time the night before. The first to rise, he leaves the stage before the striking of the clock, before the reminder, for the rest of us, of our time-boundedness or obligations or, in this case, terrible lack of obligations, before the beginning of that rhythm of give and pull which we have suggested. And in that sense, I rather like to think that this opening prepares the contrast between an ideal or formally perfect sense of beginning and ending, in Murano, a perfect expression of transition which leaves just as it had come, on the one hand; and, on the other, the force of disruption which seems to characterize everything which comes within and between; our finite selves, life. The lissome illusion which is offered as conclusion – the terrific whirl and collapse of the *agemo*, the running of the chameleon's colours until nothing remains, the expert perfection of this danced language of passage and transition – paradoxically renders what comes in between more difficult to assimilate, carves it into relief, for it is not subject to illusory resolution. Using the frame of illusion, that is, the symbolic expression binding infinite to infinite, Soyinka is better able to express the terror and force of what comes in between, that is, life, this world, stale meat and the buzzing flies.

---

[116] *Ibid.*, 173-4.
[117] Izevbaye, "Language and Meaning in Soyinka's *The Road*," 91: 'However much we are consciously unwilling or unable to link the opening scene with death, the sprawling, motionless figures lying close by the Aksident Store must appeal to our subconscious by their likeness to death before the comedy takes over.'

2

Madmen and Specialists: Murdering to Dissect

In *Madmen and Specialists* (1970; first published 1971), we are witness not so much to 'what comes in between', as to the passage from what once was to what no longer is, or ever can be. I would like to begin with a few of the scenes involving Iya Agba and Iya Mate, two old women and protectors of traditional knowledge, through and against the activities of the Mendicants, variously crippled returnees from a recent war, and what we come to know of Dr Bero and the Old Man his father, who themselves have just returned from the war, damaged in mind. A good starting point comes with Biodun Jeyifo's conclusion in his reading of the play:

> the undergirding mythos here rests on the conflict between great, all-encompassing evil and forces and agents who act on behalf of a providential grace and munificence [...] and who have a keen, unromantic knowledge of evil and are thus not themselves averse to using evil to fight evil.[118]

I mean to explore the specific dimensions of this conflict, with regards to the old women and teaching. The notion of providence ('providential grace') seems to me an interesting and problematic word to use of the old women as, if anything, the play seems to gesture towards their apparent *absence* of foresight (the Latin basis is '*providere*', or seeing ahead), in the

---

[118] Jeyifo, *Wole Soyinka*, 143-4.

paradoxical measures that they are ultimately forced into taking to protect their knowledge.

It is, then, never possible to state with anything approaching assurance – audience hesitation, as in *The Road*, might even be the effect sought – that either of the two women possesses acute foresight with regard to imminent events. In the first scene in which they appear, Iya Mate observes to Si Bero, their young student, and Dr Bero's sister: 'Your menfolk are lucky. There will be leaves in their living-room – but not the kind that places the handprint of death on a man's heart.' (*MS*, 225) Shortly after, Iya Agba spots the presence of poison among the herbs which Si Bero has gathered, and the two women offer their young charge an important lesson:

> IYA AGBA: Poison has its uses too. You can cure with poison if you use it right. Or kill.
>
> SI BERO: I'll throw it in the fire.
>
> IYA MATE: Do nothing of the sort. You don't learn good things unless you learn evil. (225)

Both points are true, descriptively, but rather beg the question. Have the old women, at this stage, sensed any connection between the workings of evil and Si Bero's 'lucky menfolk'? Furthermore, if we are presented here with the theoretical *affirmation* of the women's knowledge and preparedness to cure evil with evil (based no doubt on precedent), how might such a theory, if pressed, move beyond words? how might it be recruited, in practice, should a new form of evil come into their lives?

The scene continues and so, seemingly, does the author's concern to cultivate this insinuation:

> IYA MATE: He'll come back. He and his father. There is too much binds them down here. They will take root with their spirit, not with their bodies on some

unblessed soil. [*She scrutinizes the hands carefully, bursts suddenly into a peal of laughter.*] These hands are not yet ready to wind shrouds. We shall drink palm wine soon, very soon when someone returns. (226)

This passage announces a dissonance between the protection and care of knowledge, amid the perversion of the wider condition of that knowledge's worth and meaning. 'Careful scrutiny', what the audience will come to know but already senses as being a dangerous misreading by Iya Mate, is, momentarily, diverted into reassuring laughter before Si Bero, a sister and daughter, into the celebration of the binding of root and spirit adjudged imminent. Despite our welling apprehension, however, our detection of authorial insinuation, there is always something shocking about the encounter between the earth mothers and the Mendicants which follows immediately on Iya Mate's prediction, and the women's song in Yoruba (*Ofegbe wa de'le o-Ofe*[Wind spirit, bear us home, wind-spirit] [226]) – something which pitilessly penetrates our studied defences.

The encounter, the only direct encounter between the old women and the Mendicants, clarifies through parody what will become the play's implicit moral challenge – whether you can cure poison with poison. In his fiction 'Pierre Menard', Jorge Luis Borges once spelled out to us the fact that the identity of a text is not reducible to its words. The pages of Pierre Menard's *Don Quixote* coincide, word for word and line for line, with Cervantes' earlier version. The differences between the two versions, however – and this is what renders Menard's version almost infinitely richer than the earlier one, writes the narrator – are related to time, for Menard's version must be considered as a stylistic decision taken against the intervening historical period, against the contemporary ideas of such figures as William James and Bertrand Russell and

Julien Benda.[119] In *Madmen and Specialists*, in the direct encounter between the old women and the Mendicants, Soyinka, albeit to different purposes, is drawing on a similar idea. He is using the passage of time to clarify and dramatize the ways in which identical words can be put to radically different meanings, held unto different worlds; and it is precisely the fact that the song is voiced at the same time, word for word and line for line, that allows us to see and hear both.

In an important sense, the battle for the play's heart will be determined by the extent to which we feel that the Mendicants' parody pushes the women's language into allegory, into exoticism, makes us *hear* the women's language as belonging to a past and stained order. Put provocatively: is it possible that the slightly antiquated English which Soyinka takes care to give his earth mothers serves *both* to lend grandeur and strength to their knowledge, *and* to suggest, terribly, the retreat of the holders of precious knowledge, and their language, under the pressure of parody, into the pallor of allegory?

The stage directions seem to be working in this sense:

> *The Mendicants look at one another, begin to beat time with them, then join the singing in a raucous, cynical tone. The women stop, amazed and offended. The Old Women fold their arms, retire deeper into the hut while Si Bero dashes out, furious.* (226)

The old women's deeper retirement or wilful enfoldment into shadow carries an almost mythical resonance – the solemn sense of departing or leaving – and a new note of passivity seems to inhabit their sense of 'being borne home'. Following Oyin Ogunba,[120] we might be tempted to interpret the play through spatial symbolism, expressed in the three levels of

---

[119] Jorge Luis Borges, "Autor del Quijote," *Ficciones* (Buenos Aires: Debolsillo, 2012 [1941]), 50.
[120] See Ogunba, *The Movement of Transition*, 213-219.

the scenography: Dr Bero's *'surgery down in a cellar'*, the *'level ground in the fore'* before Dr Bero's home, and the *'higher structure to one side in the form of a semi-open hut'*, where the old women sit (MS, 217). Ogunba argues for a schematic symbolism which remains stable throughout the play, according to which the cellar 'is the level below normal human dignity', the ground level the stage on which 'we see the people and their actions essentially from outside', and the higher structure proper to 'the skyey abode of the witches'.[121] It rather seems to me, however, that a crucial element of the play's intention, dramatically expressed in the encounter between the old women and Mendicants, comes through the mutual effects that one spatial level can bring to bear on another, the sense that the activities of one alter the others – which is, in a profound sense, the truth of community. In such a perspective, the women's being cut off from the ground feeds into the insidious sense which steals upon us, that they are, just perhaps, powerless before reality on the ground, before the Mendicants who, in turn, no longer understand or want to understand them, and mock in indifference.

I have spoken hitherto quite casually of 'earth-mothers', as if the meaning within this play were itself assured, but the metaphor of 'earth' – in Yoruba a ready metaphor for the moral values of the community (as, for instance, in Igbo) – is subject to some qualification as we progress. There is an important exchange between Iya Agba and Bero: 'We move as the Earth moves, nothing more. We age as Earth ages.' (259) And again, shortly afterwards, as Iya Agba mocks Bero's aspirations towards a sort of unbridled positivism:

> BERO: You are proscribed, whatever you are, you are banned.
> IYA AGBA: What can that mean? You'll proscribe the Earth itself? How does one do that? (260)

---

[121] *Ibid.*, 216; 217; 219.

Iya Agba is speaking of a consubstantiality of knowledge and nature, secured in the earth, the total framework in which all live and move. By the end of the play, what has become of this Earth and, by extension, this consubstantial bind? In the general introduction we spoke of Achebe's usage of the word 'return' in his poem 'Beware Soul Brother': return, that is, as both restitution and protection. Here, that bind of continuity cannot take root as it should. The 'debt' to be collected from Si Bero at the end of the play, the condition of protection, can only express itself in destruction rather than, as theoretically conjectured earlier, in righting poison with poison. We only fully understand this in the women's final exchange with their pupil, or former pupil:

> IYA MATE: Nothing we can do daughter. Evil hands soon find a use for the best of things.
> SI BERO: And the good that is there? Does that count for nothing?
> IYA AGBA: We'll put that into the test. Let us see how it takes to fire.
> SI BERO: Fire?
> IYA AGBA: It is only the dying embers of an old woman's life. The dying embers of earth as we knew it. Is that anything to fear? (274)

It is important to hear Iya Mate's expression of impotence, and the weakness of Iya Agba's response to Si Bero's legitimate question: must we destroy even the good, must nothing remain? What follows, indeed, must be heard and held against that earlier question, which now seems prematurely confident: how does one proscribe the Earth itself? The 'Earth itself' has dwindled into 'earth as we knew it', and the typographical clue reduces earth from being the total foundation of values, to being just one erstwhile frame of reference, weakened by and diminished into history, in the retreating and ashen knowledge of her, an old woman. And so it is that we come to understand how one can proscribe Earth or, more prudently, how 'Earth' can fall into proscription: by its moral foundation falling into irrelevance, by its being harried and compelled by historical pressure into destroying its own patrimony. The meaning of 'protection' turns from within, comes to denote an irreversible reduction of their precious knowledge to grey ash, a paradoxical destruction upon which survival now depends, and by which it stands threatened. The effect comes from what we might call 'cross-rhythm': that is, the counterpoint between the women's language, strong and slow, sustained by history, against the exponential motion of the plot; how quickly we have to come up with contingency plans before unforeseen historical expediency, how quickly all that knowledge can fall into disuse, how that lasting destruction, a day's work, can undo an age of accumulation.

* * *

The second and longer part of this chapter could be taken as a response to Eldred Jones' slightly elliptical conclusion, in his early reading of the play: 'The Old Man seems suddenly to have become possessed with the need to "practise" on the questioning cripple.'[122] A 'sudden possession'? Or is there a sense that this sudden possession has been carefully prepared? I will be arguing that the terrifying turned ritual which constitutes the play's climax is prepared in language, as wordplay eventually disregards the necessary moral distinction between play and life, between the hypothesis and the real, with fatal consequences.

In *Madmen and Specialists,* completed shortly after the end of the bloodshed of Biafra,[123] war provides the historical

---

[122] Jones, *The Writing of Wole Soyinka*, 123.
[123] Four major works would come directly from Soyinka's experiences during the war (and its prelude): *Madmen and Specialists* (1970), *The Man Died* (1972), *A Shuttle in the Crypt* (1972), and *Season of Anomy* (1973).

catalyst for the passing into the absurd: that decline into apparent anachronism of the certainties which but yesterday were hard-headed and sure and operative; the sudden or surreptitious strangeness in the language with which we had fashioned that world – we who stand now, with Si Bero, looking back on that world become little, within a new order or disorder which, perhaps, we feel to be stronger or at least more present.

In terms of technique, what better than a fool to bring to the audience an awareness of the difference between these two moments, to bring to us, by way of negative example, the understanding that we can never go back to things as they were before, that everything from the words to issue from our mouths to our assumptions about order and structure and hierarchy has been altered from the marrow? In *Madmen and Specialists*, Soyinka uses the character of the Priest to introduce the notion of rupture. The scene involving the Priest comes immediately after Si Bero's recognition that, to borrow Nuttall's paraphrase of Hegel, ethical fields are now disunified;[124] and as consequence, that she will not be able to choose to protect what she has learnt, that she must rather break her promise, which is to say her debt, leaving her with neither the possibility of staying in her 'own little world', on Bero's instruction, for recognition closes the door on return. This prepares the Priest's blindness. Most directly, he condescendingly insists to Si Bero that the medicine he has been taking during Dr Bero's absence is different, whereas it is the same (continuity taken for discontinuity); and all the while, he continues as if no major event has taken place, as if war is free of its own grim issue, as if it is of the order of inconsequence (discontinuity taken for continuity).

More importantly, I think, it is dramatically intelligent that

---

[124] Nuttall, *The Alternative Trinity*, 23.

the Priest should be a man without dimension, a caricature. That is to say, he is a caricature not simply because Soyinka wishes to get in a few cheap shots at the priesthood – the ministries from the tongue of the former chaplain Aafaa are, in any case, more trenchant – but because the rhythm of his speech and thought picks up exactly where it had been interrupted before the war, pursues false fictions of continuity or perfect cadences with the son who is no longer the image of the father, the brother who is no longer bound to the sister; a tongue which lives in comfort in cliché and idiomatic phrases – platitudes being the symptom of not receiving experience – rather than in dissatisfaction or frustration or anger or disappointment or melancholy, symptoms of that pressing for escape from ordinary language which should variously afflict us. This is best captured in his recollections of his erstwhile verbal jousting with Old Man:

> PRIEST: I couldn't believe my ears when he got up and said he was going to join you. At your age, I said, you doddering old thing? I used to call him that, you know, and he would call me the mitred hypocrite. All in play, of course, only in play. So he... where was I? (239)

It is important to hear the imbalance between the inconsequential phrase 'doddering old thing' and the far more incisive riposte 'mitred hypocrite', a direct insult rather than the teasing of foibles proper to peers; in overhearing himself – and in performance he might imitate the Old Man's voice – the Priest overhears that imbalance, the greater weight of Old Man's words, and so seeks to defuse it by invoking the lightness of jest. It is all to no avail, however, as the ellipsis preserves a tinge of sadness before his failure of self-persuasion, before the reminder he has given himself of the contempt in which Old Man held him. Even despite having been sufficiently shaken to accept the possible truth of what Bero is saying, the possibility of the young doctor having eaten human flesh on the warfront, he yet asks: 'I... er... couldn't simply come for drinks afterwards?' (240) – a desperate attempt not to yield fully to acknowledgement, preserving the smooth capsule in which priestly gourmandise can continue to express itself unhindered, despite it all. Such avuncular foolishness is marked by the Priest's inapposite vocatives (Si Bero remains his 'little lady', Bero his 'boy', his 'lad' or 'son' [238]), and can but swell our foreboding.

Albert Camus once defined the absurd as the divorce between man and his life, the actor and his stage; as depriving man of memories of a lost homeland, as well as the hope of a promised land to come.[125] Perhaps no Western writer better placed his fictions in an absurd present than Samuel Beckett. There is a convenient example in Winnie's opening 'prayer' in *Happy Days*:

> WINNIE [*gazing at zenith*]: Another heavenly day. [*Pause. Head back level, eyes front, pause. She clasps hands to breast, closes eyes. Lips move in inaudible prayer, say ten seconds. Lips still. Hands remain clasped. Low.*] For Jesus Christ sake Amen [...] World without end Amen [...] Begin, Winnie. [*Pause*] Begin your day, Winnie.'[126]

Winnie's language is a reworking of Thomas Cranmer's

---

[125] For a fuller definition see Albert Camus, *Le Mythe de Sisyphe: essai sur l'absurde* (Paris: Gallimard, 1942), 18: 'Quel est donc cet incalculable sentiment qui prive l'esprit du sommeil nécessaire à sa vie? Un monde qu'on peut expliquer même avec de mauvaises raisons est un monde familier. Mais au contraire, dans un univers soudain privé d'illusions et de lumières, l'homme se sent un étranger. Cet exil est sans recours puisqu'il est privé des souvenirs d'une patrie perdue ou de l'espoir d'une terre promise. Ce divorce entre l'homme et sa vie, l'acteur et son décor, c'est proprement le sentiment de l'absurdité.'
[126] Samuel Beckett, *Happy Days* (London: Faber and Faber, 1961), 9-10.

English translation of the *Gloria patri*, instituted in the Book of Common Prayer (1549; revised 1552; amended 1662) as part of the early Protestant Reformation in England.[127] It works by invoking the signs and phrases and plenitude of a (Christian) world's lost order, the better to inhabit its present emptiness, the liturgy of providence dwindled into circular psychological entrapment. Darko Suvin has cleverly remarked that the closed cosmos of Beckett's fictions achieves an intensity of claustrophobic effect through 'its constantly renewed comparison with more open alternatives,'[128] that the loss of order works dramatically to deepen our yearnings for arrival or transcendental stepping out and beyond, just as such credible escape-routes are foreclosed. This technical heritage – the creation of an effect of pressing down or narrowing or claustrophobia by the invocation of escape, Winnie gazing at zenith as her language turns in on itself – is put to good use in *Madmen and Specialists*, most obviously in plot. The Mendicants' circus tour, for instance, is constantly invoked, but is never more convincing than a horizon which has now

---

[127] For an interesting discussion of the permanence and importance of Cranmer's translations of Latin liturgy into English, which approaches Shakespeare and the King James Bible, see James Wood, "God Talk: The Book of Common Prayer at Three Hundred and Fifty," *The New Yorker*, October 22, 2012.
http://www.newyorker.com/arts/critics/atlarge/2012/10/22/121 022crat atlarge wood?current Page=all (consulted January 2013). In a discussion *of Madmen and Specialists* which I find quite esoteric, Ato Quayson states that Soyinka is reworking 'the mystery and numinousness inherent in the originating *biblical statement.*' (my italics) This is an error. There is a long and important literary tradition of English language writers reworking *Cranmer's translation of Latin liturgy*, not 'biblical statement', to which Soyinka, in *Madmen and Specialists*, belongs. See Ato Quayson, *Aesthetic nervousness: Disability and the Crisis of Representation* (New York: Columbia University Press, 2007), 134.
[128] Suvin, *To Brecht and Beyond*, 210.

receded beyond the reach of realistic desire, as is well expressed in the following early exchange:

> CRIPPLE: You're just a rubber ball, Goyi. You need a hand to throw with, anyway.
>
> GOYI: I can use my mouth.
>
> AAFAA: To throw dice? You'll eat sand my friend.
>
> BLINDMAN: Sooner or later we all eat sand.
>
> CRIPPLE: Hey, you're beginning to sound like the Old Man.
>
> AAFAA [*voice change*]: Did you eat sand, my friend? We'll make you the Ostrich in our touring circus.
>
> BLINDMAN: The limbless acrobat will now perform his wonderful act – how to bite the dust from three classic positions.
>
> GOYI: Upright, take off, and prone.
>
> CRIPPLE: We'll never go on that tour.
>
> AAFAA: Roll up – roll up. Presenting the Creatures of As in the timeless parade.
>
> BLINDMAN: Think we'll make that tour?
>
> AAFAA: We will. But until the millions start rolling in, we better not neglect the pennies. (218)

The context is one of begging, a deserted lane, where nobody comes and nobody goes any more. Through the word 'sand' (Latin: *arena*), as we saw in *Jero's Metamorphosis*,[129] we are gently elided into the spectacle and illusion proper to the arena, and are further assisted in this by Aafaa's ventriloquism, as he mimics Old Man's parodic circus instructions ('Did you eat sand, my friend? We'll make you the Ostrich in our touring circus.' [218]). The arena, however, as befits illusion, is itself associated with a wilful negation of knowledge (the ostrich with its head in the sand), and the illusion cannot survive the

---

[129] See above, 62.

stark contrast between acrobatics and Goyi's earth-bound wriggle (Goyi, note the stage directions, *'is held stiffly in a stooping posture by a contraption which is just visible above his collar.'* [217]). Aafaa seals the end of the illusion, the distance between present circumstance and future promise as large as that between begging on a deserted lane and gathering in the millions.

For my purposes, however, more important than this simple idea of confinement are the ways in which the 'constantly renewed comparison with more open alternatives' used to intensify claustrophobia, strike up a counterpoint with a semantic undercurrent involving bottoms and lowness, as well as a structural conceit involving (a)basements and depth. These come together to express complexly one of the play's central points of interest: our linguistic grounding; whether, that is, we use language, or whether language uses us.

This is cogently announced in the miniature scene which we might entitle *'Rem Acu Tetigisti'*, a Latin phrase meaning 'You have touched the matter with a needle'. Idiomatic renderings of this phrase – hitting the nail on the head, or putting one's finger on the nub, for instance – tidily express the motive of the Mendicants' discussion: to uncover Dr Bero's reasons for the inter(n)ment of his father, the Old Man; to 'get to the bottom of it'. Idioms, however, have a way of fading through usage, of being self-effacing, so that we no longer discern the early poetry they once held. Soyinka counters this by preserving the Latin and, in 'translations' or iridescence or fragmentation, extending the idiom beyond pithiness:

> BLINDMAN [*shrugs*]: When things go wrong it's the lowest who get it first.
>
> AAFAA: There is money at the bottom of it.
>
> CRIPPLE [*places Blindman's hand on his shoulder and starts off in the direction of the house*]: And we are at the bottom. So, let's go and make sure the woman doesn't stumble on any official secrets.

AAFAA [*checks*]: Rem Acu Tetigisti.
CRIPPLE: What? I don't get you.
AAFAA: R.A.T.! R.A.T.! I smell a rat.
GOYI: Is he having an attack?
CRIPPLE: What's up, Aafaa?
AAFAA: You said it yourself – Official Secrets. Official rat is what I smell. Yessir! We'll get paid something decent. Secret Service funds and all that. Let's celebrate. [...] I tell you the Cripple has Rem Acu Tetigistied it. Official Secrets that's what's at the bottom of it. Bottomless account. We'll get overtime and risk allowance. (222)

Aafaa's basic line of thought is the following: that by helping Bero with the important business of guarding the Old Man, he and his companions are in line for handsome remuneration; and this he posits against Blindman's resignation ('lowest' is a word used of hierarchy and, as we have seen, provides a literal echo for Goyi's limbless acrobatics), which is picked up by Cripple ('And we are at the bottom'). The phrase 'bottomless account', however, undercuts Aafaa's rounded speculation. An account is also a version of events, and so a bottomless account implies endless spinning of the same event – and it seems to me that this quieter sense provides the logical connection to the mock-trial which immediately follows. There, through various associations of the word 'needle', this specific sense of bottomlessness runs into the notion of centrelessness, provides a new angle on truth's malleability, on being lost and bewildered before truth's many different faces. Neither notion allows for stability, a grounding or fixed point of reference around which to organize meaning; both, rather, multiply possibility and association, overwhelm us in profusion. The needle, then, is a crotch, vulnerable and capable only of crooked renewal; the needle is a gun or torture instrument; and the gun and pain lead into the moment of truth, which, itself, is reversible, reworkable. And this, ultimately, leads to Goyi's being lost in words ('Where am I?' – 'Within the moment of truth, dear friend.' [223]), his failure to understand or follow his companions' endless declensions of words. As if he does not have the compass needed for safe navigation.

Perhaps it is only with the later reappearance of the word 'rat', where the connection between holes and the Mendicants as a group is rendered more explicitly ('I noticed rats. That means holes. You should see the rats. – They'll desert. – [*gazing round at the Mendicants*] I suppose so.' [265]) that we begin to realize that this wordplay on bottoms as grounding and bottoms as bottomlessness (holes), serves a greater artistic purpose. In a clever corrective to Hugh Kenner, who pointed out the similarities between the second law of thermodynamics and a principle of construction in Beckett's plays – their tending to a dissipation of energy, or rather, a non-convertibility of energy – Suvin goes on to invoke the third law of thermodynamics, 'absolute zero can only be approached asymptomatically, i.e. getting ever closer to it without ever reaching it', characteristic also, for him, of Beckett.[130] Soyinka's key departure from Beckett is here. The play's general (though qualified) movement is downwards into the cellar, and it is a movement into the illusionism of a certain kind of staged theatre.

Specifically, the cellar becomes the stage for ritual climax, which is to say, as is orthodox in Soyinka's usage of ritual in his plays, its rhythm becomes one of *acceleration*. Nilaus Gessner once offered a typology of forms of disintegration in Beckett's plays, including double-entendre, repetition of synonyms, forgetfulness, arguing that these convey the persistent breakdown, or indeed absence, of the dialectical

---

[130] Suvin, *To Brecht and Beyond*, 212.

exchange of thought.[131] In a world of interruption or collapse, inconsequentiality or mere successiveness, the draining of meaning from time becomes the *focus* of tragedy. Here, the disintegrations and interruptions which characterize the Mendicants' speech in the opening parts of the play will be gathered up and drawn together in the final scene; there do they receive form, are they shaped and guided and made to run into a dénouement, a pure formal fiction, as if empty stage ('cellar') and directionless or perspectiveless language need and await each other; as if, quite terrifyingly, the non-expository intelligence of 'play' is always susceptible to the effacement of the distinction between illusion and reality, if only it receives the right form.

We have, through Beckett's Winnie, hinted at the literary uses of the *Gloria patri*: the intensification of claustrophobia, the foreclosure of salvation, the embarkation into the absurd – and such, no doubt, is part of Soyinka's purpose in *Madmen and Specialists*. 'As', however, has a further (and, I think, more interesting or important) role than this, and it derives from Wallace Stevens' astonishing poem 'An Ordinary Evening in New Haven'. The final lines of part XXVIII read:

> A more severe,
> More harassing master would extemporize
> Subtler, more urgent proof that the theory
> Of poetry is the theory of life,
>
> As it is, in the intricate evasions of as,
>
> In things seen and unseen, created from nothingness,
> The heavens, the hells, the world, the longed-for lands.[132]

---

[131] Cited in Martin Esslin, *The Theatre of the Absurd* (London: Eyre and Spottiswoode, 1962), 62.

[132] Wallace Stevens, "An Ordinary Evening in New Haven XXVIII," in *The Palm at the End of The Mind: Selected Poems and a Play*, ed. Holly Stevens (New York: Vintage Books, 1972), 349. The opening strophes of part XXVIII read: 'If it should be true that reality exists / In the mind: the tin plate, the loaf of bread on it, / The long-bladed knife, the little to drink

There are two moments in which Bero berates the Old Man's evasiveness – 'No more evasions.' (262); 'Again you are being evasive' (263) – and these are held as prelude to Old Man's more provocative evasions through 'as':

BERO: What is As? Why As!

OLD MAN [*gasps but tries to smile. He cranes up to look him in the face.*] In a way I should be flattered. You want to borrow my magic key. Yours open only one door at a time.

BERO: [...] WHY AS! [...] What is As?

OLD MAN: As Was, Is, Now, As Ever Shall Be. (263)

Stevens is concerned with the movements which obtain between mind and reality, the search for the momentary concord between the two which the poem, or art, might hold. Soyinka, I think, reworks the principle of 'intricate evasions' away from formal artistic considerations into a moral context – or rather, an absurd context in which moral considerations are fatally weakened. Rather than seeking the poem's more urgent proof – 'the theory of life, as it is, in the intricate evasions of as,' the necessary oscillations between reality and mind – he imagines a situation in which those 'intricate evasions' give way, ultimately, to the fatal effacement of a supreme fiction, to *as* being taken for *is*.

We have jumped to the end of the yarn, and must take a step back to proceed more slowly. Close on the start of the second part of *Madmen and Specialists*, Goyi recounts his 'treatment' in hospital after the war. The 'hospital' is not to be taken unequivocally as a place of rehabilitation. It held

---

and her // Misericordia, it follows that / Real and unreal are two in one: New Haven / Before and after one arrives or, say, / / Bergamo on a postcard, Rome after dark, / Sweden described, Salzburg with shaded eyes / Or Paris in conversation at a café. / / This endlessly elaborating poem / Displays the theory of poetry, / As the life of poetry.'

'only nurses who couldn't tell a man's end from their own,' (247) a dirty joke which doubles more profoundly, again through the word 'end', in the suggestion that somehow they are all lost together, that those offering treatment are themselves, just as much as their patients or wards, beyond remedy or release, whether they know it or not. Goyi continues, in what is a remarkable passage:

> GOYI: Hey, listen, and let me tell you, it was the cleverest thing I ever thought all those sweet times we spent with the Old Man. With him saying this and saying that to us and me on my side – couldn't turn on my back and couldn't turn on my belly – and the sun would come up one day and I wouldn't see it again until it comes up the next. One thing he told us – remember that day? – he told us the earth goes round and round, which if you remember was just too much for someone like me to swallow. So, the following morning when the sun came round again, I said to myself well, I suppose the Old Man must be right. I don't know what makes the world go round but I do know what goes round the world. It's wind. And I broke it loudly and felt better. (247)

The image of an injured man immobile and facing a window or hole through which he is forced to try to imagine earth spinning round him, himself as the centre of a spinning disk, while another – the teacher, the Old Man – fills his head with 'this and that'; that summoning of a cosmic frame for Goyi, at once eternal and dead, turning and inert, a 'sweet time' which leads to nowhere but incomprehension, is moving. The final joke's potential bathos, albeit prepared in Goyi's words just before the speech quoted ('F' stands for Farts), is just about held in check because the world's turning is placed in the embrace of wind, which could have associations with sophistry or endless formal rearrangements, and the words of the Mendicants have hitherto acted to undercut any sense that words are stable, their meanings continuous. (Is this, too, another chiming association with bottoms?) The broader point is this: that what epistemologically would be unacceptable (the idea that the mind is an empty receptacle awaiting information), in literature in general, and here in particular, can be a rich starting-point for exploring the discontinuities between thought and experience, the motions of the mind which feels no corrective pull from reality. Bero has previously described his father's teaching, of which Goyi, then, is a result:

> BERO: Father's assignment was to help the wounded readjust to the pieces and remnants of their bodies. Physically. Teach them to make baskets if they still had fingers. To use their mouths to ply needles if they had none, or use it to sing if their vocal chords had not been shot away. Teach them to amuse themselves. Instead he began to teach them to think, think, THINK! Can you picture a more treacherous deed than to place a working mind in a mangled body? (242)

The two concluding sentences express both Bero's own fascism (he associates intelligence with physical strength) *and* – and here we should discern the author's own voice – the dangers inherent not in thinking as such, but in thinking, thinking, thinking (words, words, words), in applying thought to anything, in generating things (illusions) from nothing.

'The theory of poetry is the theory of life, as it is, in the intricate evasions of as,' writes the poet Stevens; which is to say that life as it is, is life *between* as and is, the necessary and continuous search for balance between the two. I have spoken of how, in Soyinka's play, we are dealing not merely with the interaction between mind and reality, but also with the basic moral distinction between right and wrong as upheld in the distinction between real life and mind; and as corollary, the things we *do* against the things we *say*. As we argued in our discussion of *The Road,* Soyinka is perfectly capable of using language to generate a desire in the audience for resolution. Yet while in *The Road* he uses the foreclosure of the model of apocalypse to subject the word 'Word' to breakdown, here he is working through *syntax,* using evasion against positivist truth.

'As' is a syncategorematic word, meaning a word which cannot serve as the subject or predicate of a proposition; or more simply, a word which has no meaning in and of itself. Its enthronement as self-sufficient or meaningful in and of itself induces in Bero the acute desire for some sort of resolution, distilled in definition; for some sort of clear *referent.* Bero the positivist wants as and is to be the same thing, to relegate anything standing beyond as non-existent (which also explains why his language is so poor or dead or unintelligent, so unresponsive to the 'motives of metaphor', as Stevens again might have had it). Soyinka has observed well the grammatical function which has become something of a working rhetorical principle among the Mendicants: the 'pivot', the endlessly spinning *tourniquet* of words, until we are not sure whether there are any fixed terms which we might compare, until we are not sure whether there is any fulcrum to hold things in relation, and this is what must most frustrate the positivist, who eventually cries, after definition: 'You know As, the playword of your convalescents, the pivot of whatever doctrine you used to confuse their minds, your piffling battering ram at the idealism and purpose of this time and history. What is As, Old Man?' (263) The sentence's rhythm is quickening, but it quickens not into conclusiveness, but rather finds itself back at the start, at the bottom of the wheel, forced to recognize the insufficiency of its own findings, forced, just like Beckett's Winnie, to begin or try again.

It is with the first mention of 'illusion' in the play, with talk of humanity, which Aafaa had skipped as he ran through the alphabet ('G, As is Godhead. I is next.' [247]), that we begin to hear the acceleration in rhythm, a quickening of intent:

BERO: Take a look at your companions – your humanity.

OLD MAN: I recognized it. A part of me identifies with every human being.

BERO: You'll be disillusioned soon enough.

OLD MAN: I do not harbour illusions. You do.

BERO: [*genuinely astonished*]: I? You say that of me? I, of all people? (264)

Bero's astonishment before the very *notion* of his being susceptible to illusion might be typical of positivists, but more significant is the hidden sense in which Old Man and the Mendicants might themselves be the illusions, the transitive object of the verb 'harbour', held in clandestine captivity by Bero. Bero's positivism or impulse to be Queen of Fact or ruler of reality (two Stevens epithets) is weakened as Old Man progressively ensnares him in the illusion of a play within the play. In other words, the illusions which Bero harbours, he who seeks to stand above and beyond, now move to engulf him, and, for a moment, we no longer know who is bettering whom, though the broader frame we never forget.

Against Bero's leaden remark 'Your old games won't help you. Forget that line' (264), Old Man's riposte possesses the improvisatory intelligence of the actor: 'Throw me a new line then. Feed the drowning man a line.' 'Line', for Bero, is a shorthand for 'line of questioning', but Old Man's response expands it retrospectively, so that we, the audience, now understand it as the words an actor might say, his or her lines. We cannot miss Old Man's satisfaction at this drawing in or initiation, the simple satisfaction of a teacher before the student's slow apprehension – [*turning to the others*] See? He's getting good. [...] [*pleased*] You're getting very good, very good.' (264) When we eventually come to talk of 'character', Bero seems fully trapped in the net of illusionism, or better, of illusion-based theatre – 'Or... is it merely in character? Is that it? Your peculiar little specialization. Perhaps that's it. So. When do you start?' (265). The entire exchange tends towards that old teaching ideal of confronting the student with his ignorance, Old Man forcing Bero to recognize his vulnerability, his non-omnipotence, the existence of things outside of his control.

When Old Man speaks the words 'Smoke. Smoke-screen. That's what it all is. [...] The pious pronouncements. Manifestos. Charades. At the bottom of it all humanity choking in silence' (265), he is yet a man perfectly capable of making basic moral distinctions – truth from falsity – a man, indeed, with the moral imagination to hold this distinction in an intelligent metaphor, the smoke-screen being a distraction, but a fatal one for the human constituency. This sharp moral distinction, we might be tempted to conclude, is continuous with the *reductio ad absurdum* he employed (before the action of the play) with classical (and perverse) rhetorical rigour, to demonstrate the self-contradictions which characterize the warmongers' justification for war – the way they hitch unity to massacres, torture and killing, the way they preach solidarity and coherence amid bodies and lives torn asunder – all arguments to which a contemporary Nigerian, particularly those of the defeated Biafra, would be sensitive. And yet if we are to talk of deconstruction seriously, we must not stop at what could (and no doubt should) be thought of as the re-creative wordplay of punnery ('the dog in dogma, tick of a heretic, the tick in politics' [275], and so on), but must also pause to consider *inconsistencies* of argumentation; in other words, we must be quite careful to distinguish a logical demonstration (*reductio ad absurdum*) from the impulse of a deconstructive method, whose basic principle is that we can never control all the meanings of the words we use.

Such is the ambivalence of Old Man, his 'deconstructive wit' constantly susceptible to its own unintended supplements, be it in his mouth or the Mendicants'. Take for instance, the astonishing reworking of Old Man's song of what Wilfred Owen called 'the old lie' – *dulce et decorum est pro patria mori* – that it is sweet and proper to die for one's fatherland. Under the Old Man (though prior to the events of the play), the old lie had become 'pro patria mourir dulce et decorum' (261): the omitted 'est' replaces the logical connection between dying for one's fatherland and sweetness and properness, with mere contiguity – so that death and sweetness are now associated, as in flesh. Yet that was then, and this is now. Here, the Old Man is no longer in control of his wordplay:

> CRIPPLE: Pro patria mourir.
>
> MENDICANTS:... mourir mourir mourir...
>
> CRIPPLE: Dulce et decorum...
>
> MENDICANTS:... quorum quorum quorum...
>
> OLD MAN: Corum, stupes, not quorum.
>
> MENDICANTS: Corum corum corum, not quorum.
>
> OLD MAN: Decorum, Dulce et decorum...
>
> MENDICANTS: ... quorum quorum quorum...
>
> OLD MAN: God damn you. Can you learn nothing? – corum, not quorum.
>
> GOYI: No quorum, no quorum, that's the damned trouble.
>
> CRIPPLE: Yes sir, you've banged the hammer on the nail.
>
> OLD MAN [*turning to Aafaa.*]: Will you tell me what these idiots are talking about? (261)

The Mendicants, his students, integrate his song into a wider deconstructive economy, the decorousness of 'decorum' running into 'quorum', or rather the absence of a 'quorum', meaning the absence of a guarantee of the validity of proceedings. It is important, too, that Cripple should reverse the idiomatic 'hitting the nail on the head' ('you've banged the hammer on the nail'), not simply because we are here moving towards the unlatching of words from context, but also because it picks up on the earlier wordplay of *'Rem Acu Tetigisti'*.

With this in mind, I would like to turn to the final scenes, and patiently inspect Old Man's words:

> OLD MAN [*He rises slowly*]: As Is, and the System is its mainstay though it wear a hundred masks and a thousand outward forms. And because you are within the System, the cyst in the System that irritates, the foul gurgle of the cistern, the expiring function of a faulty cistern and are part of the material for re-formulating the mind of a man into the necessity of the moment's political As, the moment's scientific As, metaphysic As, sociologic As, economic, recreative, ethical As, you-cannot-escape! (271)

What seems like an apodictic point – there is, as they say, no escaping the system – is complicated in that long second sentence, which establishes a principle of reciprocity between conflicting poles, effaces the distinction between apposition and opposition. Crucially, that 'you' becomes expressive *both* of the system's ill-functioning *and* its reformulation: the logic is that of the parasite. This notion of sinister renewal is clarified in and through language, beginning with what we might call the most sophisticated of toilet humour. Cyst derives phonically from system, quite obviously, but the intransitive usage of the word 'irritate' should prevent us from interpreting the phrase in a limiting orthodox sense – 'the cyst that irritates *the System*' – should rather encourage us to keep open its possibilities. The phonic crushing of 'cyst' and 'system' into 'cistern' is clever because 'cyst', etymologically, comes from the ancient Greek word for 'bladder', so brings together cyst and cistern in sound *and* meaning; and even if we wished to rest on transparency of image, to save an unequivocal sense of inside against outside or System against subversive assailant we could not, for a foul gurgle is symptomatic of waste just as much as it is a prelude to flushing away. Even that awkward expression 'expiring function' expresses this ambivalence, that a perfect function depends for its activity on its house, here in the cistern.

The most exquisite ambivalence of Old Man's speech, however, is saved for last, at the very moment we hope to return to safety. The motion from active to passive in the second sentence – from the active 'irritates', through the noun-verb 'gurgle' to the present participle 'expiring' – translates into grammatical mood that ambivalence between active irritation and passive tool held in the idea of being 'part of the material for re-formulating the mind of man'. The meaning of the phrase is not 'you re-formulate the mind of a man', but rather depends on the senses which 'material' inhabits, both the plastic sense of 'material from which something is made or reworked', and the sense of 'necessary tools'.

It is obviously tempting to assume that the referent of 'you' throughout the speech is the group of Mendicants, not least because the Old Man begins by responding to Aafaa's question: 'why risk putting us here together?' (271) This would also seem coherent with the logic of breaking down and reconstitution which has characterized their rhetoric hitherto, itself indissociable, perhaps, from their bodily breakdown (or 'non-integrality'). I have argued, however, of *The Lion and the Jewel*, the *Jero* plays and *The Road* – and shall go on to argue in subsequent chapters – that directness of address is difficult to sustain in longer speeches, be it through motives of drift, or self-address, or else generic dictate. Here, it seems to me, 'you' must not be taken as holding one referent, but must be seen, rather, as a cipher, its referent subject to oscillations, derivative of ambiguities of voice:

OLD MAN: And what can you pit against the priesthood of that constant deity, its gospellers, its enforcement agency? And even if you say unto them, do I not know you, did I not know you in rompers, with leaky nose and smutty face? Did I not know you thereafter, know you in the haunt of cat-houses, did I not know you rifling the poor-boxes in the local church, did I not know you dissolving the night in fumes of human self-indulgence simply simply simply did I not know you, [...] Simply simply, do I not know you Man like me? Then shall they say unto you, I am chosen, restored, re-designated, and re-destined and further further shall they say unto you, you heresiarchs of the System arguing questioning querying weighing puzzling insisting rejecting upon you all shall we practise, without passion– (272)

The crucial point comes in the ambiguity between conditional clauses and direct speech: the way in which, following the conditional 'even if', which syntactically introduces a conditional clause, we suddenly switch into direct speech, whose length and *crescendo* make us temporarily forget our conditional starting point. As corollary, we move from the formal or abstract usage of 'you', where it means something like 'one', to direct address, to Old Man's biographical involvement and investment, for the addressees become the agents most directly responsible for oppression as clarified in Bero, to whom that impassioned and we are to suppose personalized question – 'did I not know you in rompers, with leaky nose and smutty face?' – is aimed.

Eventually, we are reminded that we are, after all, still in a conditional clause. 'Then shall they say unto you' picks up on the earlier conditional (the sense is: 'Even if you say..., then shall they say...'), but the same motion holds, the conditional immediately submerged in direct speech. Only here, *the Mendicants and the Old Man do not emerge*. The conditional is not re-established, the hypothetical safeguard of syntax melts away, leaving their ventriloquism to spin on unqualified.

I have argued, as to the first part of the speech, that the basic parasitical bind of sustenance and weakness or strength and poison, is expressed in language and syntax, and ambivalence of imagery and address. Here, the words 'you heresiarchs' can be taken *either* as the Old Man's aside which ends with 'rejecting', *or* as the vocative which re-opens 'their' direct speech. This is astonishingly skilled writing, for it perfectly captures an insoluble ambiguity of voice – who is speaking? Old Man or the System? is this imitation or the real thing? Far from enacting the arguing and questioning and querying worthy of the cyst, the Mendicants rather take up the voice of 'them', pick up the thread of that 'upon you all shall we practise, without passion' and so seem to inhabit, at this moment, the closing down of questioning, the reformulation of material of 'you'. And here it is that we begin to intimate the difference between ventriloquism as play and ventriloquism as the usurpation of the real: how it enacts in voice and language, when harnessed and given direction or purpose, that effacement of the distinction between illusion and reality, between forgery and the real thing. The word 'practise', finally, repeated as in a loop, speaks both to acting and rehearsals (those coming from Latin languages say 'repetitions') and, in its associations with the doctor's place of work, the 'surgery' where currently we stand, to cutting and incisions, the real administrations of the knife.

I stated earlier that longer speeches tend to weaken direct address, and went on to argue that, in the speech of the Old Man, Soyinka seems to be playing around with this in switches of perspective, and the weakening of the conditional. In terms of basic dramaturgy, this slight weakening of address is indicated by the Old Man standing up; and so, in a sense, Aafaa's subsequent speech has, formally at least, the same sense of standing on its own – '[*As the Old Man slowly resumes his seat, Aafaa rises, speaking.*]' (272) A summary of Aafaa's speech would give something like this: from the schisms of the priesthood, between those of this earth (the political) and those not of this earth (the spiritual), man, deprived of metaphysical guarantee, turned inward ('The loyalty of homo sapiens regressed into himself'), sought to resolve the problem of his mortality ('his little tick-tock self'), a parasitic ('self-ticking') and self-indulgent ('self-tickling') and self-defeating ('self-tackling') enterprise, the assertive hubris of the 'lone usurper of the ancient rights and privileges of the priesthood' (273). Only, in the midst of Aafaa's speech, there opens up, it would seem, a glaring contradiction:

> AAFAA: the loyalty of homo sapiens was never divided for two parts of a division make a whole and there was no hole in the monolithic solidarity of two halves of the priesthood. No, there was no division. The loyalty of homo sapiens regressed into himself... (272)

The contradiction, I think, works on the homophony of 'hole' and 'whole', a particular instance, here in English, of a general principle of many (every?) language(s): that of serendipitous homophones. (As ever, the measure of the artist is what he does with these possibilities.) In a well-known essay, David Willbern once catalogued the iridescence of the word 'nothing' in Shakespeare's *King Lear,* its cognates and synonyms and surrogates, to explore the dialectical theme of knowledge and negation, or the incorporation of different senses of 'nothing' into the 'positive nothing' which was the 'global' theatre.[133] What is useful here, beyond the culturally-

---

[133] David Willbern, "Shakespeare's Nothing," in *Representing Shakespeare: New Psychoanalytic Essays,* eds. Murray M. Schwartz and Coppelia Kahn (Baltimore; London: The John Hopkins University Press, 1980), 244-263.

bound (though no less rich for it) senses which obtain in Willbern's analysis,[134] is the doubleness of 'nothing': nothing both as absence, zero, void, lack, cipher, as *hole* and given meaning only by context ('like Polixenes' 'cipher... standing in a rich place', in Willbern's felicitous formulation), *and* as positive, fullness, 'the opportunity, indeed the imperative, to create "something" – some meaning or sense: a name for absence', 'a version, however malignant, of the generativity that linguistic or dramatic production *ex nihilo* involves.'[135] That is, hole as *whole*.

In Soyinka's play, we have, even before the final scenes, heard two fleeting and suggestive puns which move in this sense. 'I don't like the whole business', says Goyi, where the standard idiom 'whole business' is undercut by the quite concrete reference to Old Man's inter(n)ment in 'that underground place' (231), 'that hole' (232) where we now stand. And later, as the Old Man entangles Bero, re-creation from nothing: 'Prod. Prod. Probe. Probe. Don't you know yet what I am? [*Dramatic whisper*] Octopus. Plenty of reach but nothing to seize on. I re-create my tentacles, so cut away.' (262) The more suggestive sense of Aafaa's speech, I think, is that divided loyalty makes a *hole*, where there is no *whole* in the two halves of the priesthood, where there is no sacred order to guarantee the meanings which once held.

When we return to the surgery following the exchange between Si Bero and the old women, we build towards, as Nuttall has put it (again in the context of *Lear*), 'the exponent power of zero',[136] the sense that we are gathering and sliding

---

[134] Most obviously in Willbern's psychoanalytical musings: 'The image of the stage as pregnant enclosure [...] lies at the basis of Shakespeare's conception of theatrical space as generative – and destructive – female interiority.' *Ibid.*, 257.
[135] *Ibid.*, 249.
[136] Nuttall, *Shakespeare the Thinker*, 302.

into a huge hole. It is the climactic moment in which our not knowing whether language holds us to anything – deconstruction's methodological and epistemological ambivalence – is clarified through plot, as Old Man proceeds to attempt to 'operate' on Cripple:

> OLD MAN: [...] oh how dare you raise your hindquarters you dog of dogma and cast the scent of your existence on the lamp-post of Destiny you HOLE IN THE ZERO OF NOTHING!
>
> CRIPPLE: I have a question.
>
> OLD MAN [*turns slowly towards the interruption.*]: It's the dreamer.
>
> CRIPPLE: I have a question.
>
> OLD MAN: Black that Zero! [*Aafaa, Goyi and Blindman begin to converge on the Cripple.*]
>
> CRIPPLE: I have a question.
>
> OLD MAN: Shut that gaping hole or we fall through it.
>
> CRIPPLE: I have a question. [*The Mendicants chorus 'Practise' as they beat him.*]
>
> OLD MAN: Stop him cold, stop him dead! Let me hear the expiring suction of an imperfect system.
>
> CRIPPLE: My question is... [*Aafaa snatches one of Goyi's crutches. In the background the sound of Bero breaking down the door. Aafaa brings down crutch on Cripple's head.*] (275)

Again, we must point to the homophony, here of the Old Man's concluding address 'you hole in the zero of nothing!' For, consistent with our argument hitherto, the dressing down of hubris through insistence on nothingness also holds presence, the presence of the 'whole', the sense that, in the midst of nothingness stands something. I have said address, but in truth the Old Man's frenzied voice only receives clarification or focus, a receptacle for its overspilling meanings, in Cripple. Observe how Soyinka preserves the dramatic notion that Cripple here is merely playing a part, a part that he has played before, a part for which he is so suited by being the dreamer, the one who projects beyond. We must here recall Cripple's earlier dream of miracles (another genre in the desire for release or resolution which subtends the Mendicants' existence):

> CRIPPLE: I... dream he tells me to get on that table. He says, I could not attend to you before but there were other things... one thing at a time, certain things are more important than others. So he operates on my back and in another moment he's finished, wipes his hands and says. . .
> AAFAA: Arise, throw off thy crutches and follow me.
> CRIPPLE: [*lowering his eyes as if in abashment.*] Yes, more or less the same words. But just as I want to get up, I wake up from the blasted dream! (248-9)

And, in turn, the violence of Aafaa's response, the cynic's desire to cheat the reception of life, to cheat those imaginative projections we might embrace or use, in favour of a reasoned apprehension, a pre-emptive sense which says that because something has happened before, and so it shall happen again, the present therefore counts less:

> AAFAA: Miracle, Miracle! That's all we ever get out of your smelly mouths. Because you blackmailed one Christ into showing off once in a while you think all others are suckers for that kind of showmanship. Well, you've met your match this generation. Turn left, turn right, turn right about again, you'll find everyone you meet is more than a match for you. (249)

The central point – even allowing for something fundamentally dissatisfying in Aafaa's remorseless cynicism – is this: that he is, *at this moment,* perfectly capable and willing to uphold the distinction between wish-fulfilment or dreams or hypotheticals on the one hand, and reality on the other.

I have said that Soyinka preserves the dramatic notion that Cripple is playing a part. I should have said: Soyinka preserves the ambiguity that Cripple *thinks* he is playing a part, such as he has played before. How swift is Aafaa in condemning a dream of bodily restitution as charlatanry, as in the quote above for instance, yet how willing he is to furnish proof that this generation has indeed met its match, in the final scene, by collaborating in Old Man's 'operation' on Cripple! What is so striking, and terrifying, for me, on every reading of the play as it hurtles to its climax, is the way in which Old Man's talk of 'nothing', his voice now fully blended into that of the System, becomes a challenge to which Cripple's Mendicants are prepared to respond, as if that reminder of truth's necessary partiality – the 'gaping hole' or the questioning mouth – is, here, enough to engage them in a fiction, a spectacle which casts into the hedge the distinction between the two senses of 'practise'. Our chapter title is an obvious reference to William Wordsworth's line 'We murder to dissect'. [137] Wordsworth was talking of the motions of the intellect, the misshaping which meddlesome minds, or theory, minister to beauteous things. Soyinka's *Madmen and Specialists* is a play on the murderous dissection of language, which leads, or almost leads, to real murder:

> *As he shouts, the Old Man snatches the Surgeon's coat from where it is hanging, puts it on, dons cap, pulls on the gloves and picks up a scalpel.*
>
> OLD MAN [*at the top of his voice.*]: Bring him over here. [*He dons mask.*] Bring him over here. Lay him out. Stretch him flat. Strip him bare. Bare! Bare! Bare his soul! Light the stove!

---

[137] William Wordsworth, "The Tables Turned," in *Lyrical Ballads and Other Poems, 1797-1800*, ed. James Butler and Karen Green (Ithaca; London: Cornell University Press, 1993), 108-9.

[*They heave him onto the table and hold him down while the Old Man rips the shirt open to bare the Cripple's chest.*] [...]
OLD MAN: Let us taste just what makes a heretic tick.
(274-5)

Perversely, in this the darkest of Soyinka's plays, it is Dr Bero, the violent and despotic son, who interrupts his father's turned ritual (he shoots him dead). The surviving characters are cast adrift in a world in which nothing of the old order survives.

I have called this the darkest of Soyinka's plays, though it is essential to recall that we leave *Madmen and Specialists* not with a sense that there is no difference between good and bad, but rather with a *sharpened* sense of the difference between the two. An alertness, that is, to the fact that we protect the way in which we speak to protect the way in which we think, lest, like the Old Man and the Mendicants, we lose sight and control of our own humanity. At the same time, this important point is not quite capable of providing *consolation*. At the end of the play we are, like Si Bero, like the old women, left to look on through the smoke, speechless, listening to the terrible spinning words of the Mendicants' liturgy of 'As'. This gesture of looking on is a gesture of helplessness, symptomatic of their diminished possibilities of action. And perhaps it should be taken as the characteristic stance of a new historical moment; a stance coherent with the paradox which has us burn our most precious possession so as not (yet) to fall into destruction. A *silent* stance, reduced to ineffectuality.

In fact, Soyinka had been alive to the theoretical problem of onlooking and impotence, and the dramatic and linguistic possibilities therein, at least a decade before the completion of *Madmen and Specialists*. Such possibilities, focussed on a character who stands apart, looking on as a juridical procedure progresses (or unravels), are the subject of the next chapter.

III

The Blind Spot of Justice, or What Does The Onlooker Say?

> I experience the feeling that if ever I found myself in a fox-hole or its equivalent, engaged in a life-and-death struggle, and found some photographer so calmly pointing his objective, uninvolved camera in my direction, I would probably shoot him out of sheer annoyance at what, after all, is a grossly superior stance. It is, I concede, a rather ambiguous subject altogether, and there can be no last word on the subject.
> — Wole Soyinka, "Between Self and System: The Artist in Search of Liberation" (61)

Judith Shklar once argued that inajustice merits a substantive place in our considerations of justice, by forcing us into sceptical interrogation of the philosophically weak (though publicly necessary) distinction between injustice and misfortune.[138] In a discussion of Charles Dickens' *Pickwick Papers*, she observes that even the omniscience of the narrator, which provides the reader with information more complete than he or she would have in life, is itself not sufficient to resolve the ambiguities of injustice, which we might complacently have attributed to the characters' own misjudgements, their limitations of situation:

> Dickens and his readers, who like God have created all these people, are omniscient. We know everything and

---

[138] Judith N. Shklar, *The Faces of Injustice* (New Haven: Yale University Press, 1990), 8-9.

we are so remote from the events that we can be totally impartial. This is never possible in real life as the great skeptics have reminded us all along. [...] Yet we go right on acting as if we knew as much about those whom we judge as God does. In the event, it is not easy to decide who was and who was not unjust, even with all the unnaturally complete information at our disposal.[139]

Shklar's point is that we are, in life, prepared to assume the transparency of justice despite our obvious and varied human limitations; and that literature, in the realm of imaginative expression, can help against this tendency, precisely by multiplying perspectives, artificially nearing us to omniscience the better that we might understand that, even there, in that unnatural clarity, we still cannot, at times, decide easily. Her example reminds us of the sceptical lesson of literature, its ability to hold and test various situations against each other; the way in which it says to us – 'Even with all this information, even with that formal omniscience which you now enjoy, just you dare to try to assume that the answers are going to be any easier!'

Scepticism has always been useful against the pretensions of theoretical distance, and Soyinka is quite sensitive to the various complexities attending to what we might call the moral implications of distance. The epigraph to this chapter expresses this quite well both in message – the absence of empathy which distance can entail, the trading of theoretical understanding for the deeper human compassion – and in its open conclusion, in its acknowledgement that distance is a paradoxical notion. It remains, however, a theoretical reflection. In this chapter, I am rather concerned with the ways in which Soyinka stages onlookers, and the *language* he deems appropriate for these characters, for looking on is not a particularly dramatic stance. In the previous chapter discussion of *The Road*, we suggested that the flatness of

---

[139] *Ibid.*, 9.

Kotonu's language is connected to his suspension between a former world (coast-to-coast driving) and a new, unimagined one; that his imminent lapse into apathy can only find expression in non-poetry.

In this chapter, I am concerned with the ways in which Soyinka's sceptical literary interrogation of justice procedures in *The Strong Breed* (first published in 1964), *A Dance of the Forests* (completed in 1960; first published in 1963) and *The Bacchae of Euripides* (1973),[140] might take on resonance and complexity through the staging of isolated onlookers, or characters which stand apart (Eman; Obaneji/Forest Head; Tiresias and the Old Slave). The antimonies of a posture of distance embrace the distinction between looking on and being amid, between the spectator and the actor, between acting and action, between theory and practice. More particularly, I am interested in the *language* Soyinka deems proper to a stance which is not immediately dramatic; a language which, in the onlooker, always seems on the verge of dropping away into isolation, emptiness, or drift. As a coda to the chapter, I will conclude by relating the language of the onlooker in such sceptical interrogations of justice, to Soyinka's reception of Léopold Sédar Senghor, and Senghor's language of forgiveness, in *The Burden of Memory, The Muse of Forgiveness*.

---

[140] James Gibbs' account of the first productions of *The Strong Breed* is equivocal. It attributes the first production of *The Strong Breed* to Derek Bullock and Chris Groves at Ibadan, in 1966, only to suggest that a production also took place in Afikpo, in 1964. See Gibbs, "The Masks Hatched Out," 186. I have followed the versions in *Wole Soyinka: Collected Plays 1* for each play.

1

The Strong Breed: Tranquil Recollection Versus Present Circumstance

Philip Brockbank has written well of the moral imperatives which underscore *The Strong Breed* and Eman's actions;[141] my reading of the play is to be taken as a more muted thread within this stronger moral tapestry. 'The Strong Breed', announces an alternate emphasis in the title, 'breed' as verb rather than noun, but Soyinka is diligent and attentive in showing that strength, first of all, is loneliness, isolation, an almost inhuman aspiration to self-sufficiency, quite apart from any pull to belonging. The paradox is that of plenitude as lack, fulfilment as loneliness; of voluntarist assertions of control over emotions or attachments or human exactions, an aspiration to transcendence (or inhumanity, if you will) – 'Think carefully before you say any more. I am incapable of feeling indebted to you. This will make no difference at all', says Eman (*SB*, 123) – the better to serve a deeply human purpose.

Formally, the carrier-ritual, an annual rite of cleansing for the village community, whatever the specific rules governing the carrier's selection, presupposes shared rules; in practice, such shared criteria can be subject to slippages, to unlatching or weakening. It is just such a weakening or confusion of

---

[141] Philip Brockbank, "Blood and Wine: Tragic Ritual from Aeschylus to Soyinka," in *Perspectives on Wole Soyinka: Freedom and Complexity*, ed. Biodun Jeyifo (Jackson: University Press of Mississippi, 2001), 78-9. First published in *Shakespeare Survey*, Vol.36, No.1 (1983), 11-20.

criteria – a juridical model which is formally the same will alter according to practice – which offers Soyinka an opportunity to explore the psychology and ambiguities inhering within self-sacrifice, an opportunity to insinuate, that is, its antinomies. Here is Eman, the young man who has refused to succeed his father's carrier duties in his home village, and who now finds himself a stranger in a new village, in talk with his companion Sunma, over a game of 'ayo':

> EMAN: Let me continue a stranger – especially to you. Those who have much to give fulfil themselves only in total loneliness.
>
> SUNMA: Then there is no love in what you do.
>
> EMAN: There is. Love comes to me more easily with strangers.
>
> SUNMA: That is unnatural.
>
> EMAN: Not for me. I know I find consummation only when I have spent myself for a total stranger.
>
> SUNMA: It seems unnatural to me. But then I am a woman. I have a woman's longing and weaknesses. And the ties of blood are very strong in me.
>
> EMAN [*smiling*]: You think I have cut loose from all these – ties of blood.
>
> SUNMA: Sometimes you are so inhuman.
>
> EMAN: I don't know what that means. But I am very much my father's son. (125-6)

The underlying notion is paradoxical, or ambiguous: the greater humanity is inhumanity. In the abstract, the idea of the love of a stranger coming more easily to someone might be held apart from life for idle consideration, something to consider but not to live by, but here, we have the memory of Eman's playing with the mute Ifada and the Girl, against the backcloth of Sunma's desperation, as if, just perhaps, he were more comfortable amid the helpless or unknown or speechless than with the exacting and engaging yokes of adulthood. The language with which Eman fleshes out the word 'love' takes on what in this context can only be considered a curious sexual resonance, in both the word 'consummation' and the notion of being 'spent', which bespeaks a draining of energy. This is, perhaps, all the more inhuman or superhuman as the sexual sense is communicated to Sunma with whom actual sexual consummation – 'I am not trying to share your life. I know you too well by now' she has just acknowledged (125) – now seems off the horizon. At this stage we do not really know what consummation might entail for Eman, apart from that it does not entail sex, and we must not, I think, justify it too quickly in the name of what is to come, for that is to elide the reactions of Sunma, the human reaction: if Sunma dutifully puts her 'longings and weaknesses' down to her being a woman, the audience need not.

This is, in truth, the climax of meticulous preparation. The opening exchanges of the first scene have enmeshed psychology, through Sunma's frustration and rhetorical *pique*, with the deeper thematic of the carrier-ritual, the senses of self-sacrifice in a land of strangers:

> SUNMA: Why do you continue to stay where nobody wants you?
> EMAN: That is not true.
> SUNMA: You are wasting your life on people who really want you out of their way.
> EMAN: You don't know what you are saying.
> SUNMA: You think they love you? Do you think they care at all for what you – or I – do for them?
> EMAN: *Them?* These are your own people. Sometimes you talk as if you were a stranger too. (120)

It is a dangerous game of cat and mouse, in which both may suffer injury. Observe how Eman's two weak responses – the defensive though unargued first and the equally unargued though now patronizing second – are quickly abandoned as he seizes on what is Sunma's weakness, her desire to form a human bond with him, even at the expense of belonging in her own community, expressed in her attempt to stand beyond, to separate her 'I' from 'them'. Sunma wishes to place herself beyond the carrier-ritual of her village, to respond to the challenge of Eman's 'as if', for, says she, 'they are nourished in evil and unwholesomeness in which I have no part.' (121) Eman, however, even if he seems willing to let her affirmation pass, continues to insist on his own apartness from Sunma, to refuse her implicit invitation: 'I reproach you with nothing. But you must leave me out of your plans. I can have no part in them.' (121)

This broadens into a more sustained psychological study of detachment, in which Eman's desire to remain apart is tested, held open and vulnerable to the exactions of situation, his spirit moving from distress, to pity, to confidence:

> SUNMA [*desperately*]: Two days Eman. Only two days.
>
> EMAN [*distressed*]: But I tell you I have no wish to go.
>
> SUNMA [*suddenly angry*]: Are you so afraid then?
>
> EMAN: Me? Afraid of what?
>
> SUNMA: You think you will not want to come back.
>
> EMAN: [*pitying*]: You cannot dare me that way.
>
> SUNMA: Then why won't you leave here, even for an hour? If you are so sure that your life is settled here, why are you afraid to do this thing for me? What is so wrong that you will not go into the next town for a day or two?
>
> EMAN: I don't want to. I do not have to persuade you, or myself about anything. I simply have no desire to go away.
>
> SUNMA [*his quiet confidence appears to incense her*]: You are afraid. You accuse me of losing my sense of mission, but you are afraid to put yours to the test.

EMAN: You are wrong Sunma. I have no sense of mission. But I have found peace here and I am content with that.

SUNMA: I haven't. For a while I thought that too, but I found there could be no peace in the midst of so much cruelty. Eman, tonight at least, the last night of the old year.

EMAN: No Sunma. I find this too distressing; you should go home now. (121)

I said from distress to pity to confidence, but the movement is more like from distress to pity to confidence and then back to distress once more, though by this time Eman has recognized his returning to the bottom of the wheel to distil it into descriptive language ('I am distressed').

It is, I think, important that we feel that slight chill of paradox regarding Eman, within what we come to understand as his moral imperative, from the start, from these opening exchanges: his apparently self-sufficient insistence on not having to do anything for anyone rather than seeing the importance of doing something for others precisely *because* one does not have obligations or the impulse to persuade, is as rhetorically weak as it is ironic, given what is to come, and bespeaks an inability to communicate verbally what he feels he knows; his ingenuous insistence on continuity when Sunma's behaviour points to something deeper and his odd determination not to understand that a sudden change in behaviour might bespeak something beyond itself, beyond mere erraticism, means that he does not seem to register Sunma's mention of cruelty, the cruelty specific to that very day, the last night of the old year. (That question only comes later, and is striking precisely in its belatedness: 'I am not blind Sunma. It is true I would not run away when you wanted to, but that doesn't mean I do not feel things. What does tonight really mean that it makes you so helpless?' [125])

What I have called the first scene is underscored by the

narrowing timeframe of the lorry's departure. Dramaturgically, this is an economical means of staining the present with foreboding, as well as endowing the words exchanged between Sunma and Eman with an extraordinary tonality and hue, the sense that the words spoken now have meaning which goes beyond common usage. It is a technique that Soyinka has used in the major key of *The Lion and the Jewel*, as Baroka wrestles in body with his servant and rhetorically with Sidi, flipping both, one after the other, though in different senses; and it is one he will return to, in a far more sophisticated sense, through the exploitation of drum-music in the tragedy of *Death and the King's Horseman*.

Just prior to the lorry's departure, we witness and feel Sunma's unnerving and desperate acuity, or loss of inhibition, her placing her cards on the table in order to elicit from her interlocutor any reaction, improbably but just possibly the one she longs for:

> SUNMA: Sometimes I think you believe that doing anything for me makes you unfaithful to some part of your life. If it was a woman then I pity her for what she must have suffered. [*Eman winces and hardens slowly. Sunma notices nothing.*] Keeping faith with so much is slowly making you inhuman. (*SB*, 122)

When the lorry's horn signals the foreclosing of escape, the puncture and draining of hope, Sunma is left to ask – to herself – persuasion now redundant: 'What happens now?' (122)

The psychological miniatures that we have discussed in this first scene form a low promontory from which to contemplate the broader waters of justice. This holding together of affirmation and withdrawal, strength and emptiness, possible (though by no means easy) in familiar instances (Sunma is one person, and Eman can handle her responses), is less simple when we are placed in situations in which we are unaware of or do not share others' motivations, in which our own reactions suffer greater testing. This is well conveyed, I think, in the discussion between Oroge, one of the leaders of the cleansing rite, and Jaguna, Sunma's father:

> OROGE: He took the beating well enough. I think he is the kind who would let himself be beaten from night till dawn and not utter a sound. He would let himself be stoned until he dropped dead.
> JAGUNA: Then what made him run like a coward?
> OROGE: I don't know. I don't really know. It is a night of curses Jaguna. It is not many unprepared minds will remain unhinged under the load. (132)

We are obviously not to be satisfied by Oroge's response to Jaguna's question. (I think the last sentence carries an error, and should read: 'It is not many unprepared minds will remain *hinged* under the load', 'an unhinged mind' connoting one which has lost control. It does, however, strike me as symptomatic of what Soyinka is seeking to convey in Oroge's speech and thought: negatives strung together, cautiously, with calculation, the sense of nuance and questioning which is in fact no questioning at all.) Rather, we hear between Oroge's conditionals and Jaguna's question, even without the slight, something that we cannot fully reconcile: wilful submission and flight, preparedness to die under blows and vulnerability, expressed already in self-address, or self-persuasion, as Eman crouches against a wall: 'I will simply stay here till dawn. I have done enough' (131).

I have given full range to the first exchanges between Sunma and Eman because I wanted to draw attention to Soyinka's intelligence in using psychology, and the point of view of the carrier, to enter into the juridical mechanism: the tensions within transcendence, the paradox of inhumanity, the strength of standing perhaps beyond human understanding; I wanted to resist, that is, receiving too quickly the notion that Eman is inscribed in a carrier-line from his father, which he eventually comes to assume, albeit with unknown results for the new community, that this notion should somehow govern the way in which we understand his person, spent not by himself or on his own terms, as in his own words, but, perhaps, just as much by others and on their terms.

It is worth spending a little time on the Old Man's 'prediction' to his son, Eman (132-4). The exchange begins with father speaking to son in general truths, the sort of apodictic passing-on proper to fatherhood:

> OLD MAN: Ours is a strong breed. It is only a strong breed that can take this boat to the river year after year and wax stronger on it. (133)
>
> No woman survives the bearing of the strong ones. Son, it is not the mouth of the boaster that says he belongs to the strong breed. (133)
>
> Forgive me then if I say that your grief is light. It will pass. (133)

It is only after Eman states that he still does not understand, it is only after Old Man responds that he still has ears to hear, that we eventually come to Old Man's 'prediction', the clarification of general truths as to Eman's situation, their sharpening into warning:

> OLD MAN: You only go to give to others what rightly belongs to us. You will use your strength among thieves. They are thieves because they take what is ours, they have no claim of blood to it. They will even lack the knowledge to use it wisely. Truth is my companion at this moment my son. I know everything I say will surely bring the sadness of truth. (134)

In the previous chapter, we observed, of *Madmen and Specialists* (1970), that the contrast between the old women's language and their harried realization of the change in present circumstance, constitutes an important undercurrent in the play. In *The Strong Breed*, an early play, Soyinka had already exploited a similar sort of cross-rhythm. I would like to suggest how this works through two separate imaginative projections which follow the flashback quoted above. The first sees a young Eman, as he learns of the corruption at the heart of his training to pass into adulthood, in the form of his lecherous tutor; and as he takes the difficult decision to leave his village, entrusting Omae, the girl he loves, to his father (136-142); the second projection comes at the play's climax, as a tired and thirsty Eman desperate for water, flees the strangers' ritual in which he has offered to replace Ifada, a young dumb child, as carrier (144-5). I have called these scenes 'imaginative projections'. In truth, the movement between the opening flashback and the final projection is the movement from tranquil recollection – formal discussions as to the nature of tradition between father and son – to the progressive encroachments and pressures of present circumstance, in Eman's (and our) mind and understanding. In other words, the clarity that memory provides in the scene between Eman and his father (132-5), is gradually submerged amid the quickening and gathering uncertainties of the carrier-ritual in a strange land.

In the first instance (136-142), then, the present Eman participates, vocally, *'as carrier'* (136). This is neither a disembodied recollection, nor a fully-involved imagining, so to speak, but rather a vision which expresses two voices at once, which clarifies an ambiguity of perspective – on the one hand, the factual, the historical, the voice of precedent; on the other, a concentrated intensity of self-questioning and present search for meaning, framed by a ritual among thieves. When Eman speaks the words to Omae 'I am becoming a man. For the first time, I understand that I have a life to fulfil' (138), we hear *both* the historical Eman and the *present* Eman, the young boy not yet disabused of the corruption at the heart of ritual preparation, the young man skirting or approaching the full consequence of what fulfilment might come to involve.

By our second instance (144-5) – and this is important for the understanding that we might have of Eman's own understanding of what he is doing – we are no longer in the technical frame of the flashback, nor with one foot in the present and the other in recollection, but rather, in an imagining, a dream or vision or illusion. Brian Crow has argued that Eman, rejects a

> traditional wisdom and practice that he regards as irrelevant to his own experience, only to follow ironically in his father's footsteps as carrier – as the old man had himself predicted – as he [Eman] accepts the full implications of his individualistic quests.[142]

Crow's point usefully draws our attention to the ambiguities attending the transmission of understanding through precedent. One precise expression of what he calls Eman's ironic following in his father's footsteps, it seems to me, comes in a moment so obvious that we might easily miss it, like the purloined letter hid in plain sight. The final vision ends with Eman running after his father and not being able to reach him, lost, yet seeking company and solace and instruction – and this is expressed, in the vision, quite exactly by Eman following his father's footsteps:

> *He makes to hold him. Instantly the old man breaks into a rapid trot. Eman hesitates, then follows, his strength nearly gone.*
>
> EMAN: Wait father. I am coming with you... wait... wait for me father... (145)

---

[142] Brian Crow, "Soyinka and the Romantic Tradition," in *Before Our Very Eyes: Tribute to Wole Soyinka*, ed. Dapo Adelugba (Ibadan: Spectrum Books, 1987), 156.

The difference between 'following' and 'following in', between a literal and a metaphorical sense, is clarified (but not resolved) in what follows, *'a sound of twigs breaking'*, and *'a sudden trembling in the branches. Then silence.'* Perhaps those twigs are not voiced only under the feet of the oncoming ritual party, but also under the feet of Eman, running under the imperatives of his vision; perhaps the stage direction even allows for the possibility that it is Eman's running after his father, here by the forest stream, the strength of the idea of following in his father's footsteps, of conflating 'following in' and 'following', that is prelude and confirmation of the fated moment of fulfilment. The last we hear of Eman is in that weak imperative, the trailing word 'father'.

These ambiguities, ultimately guaranteed by an underlying firmness of moral imperative – the villagers returning subdued and guilty having seen Eman's body hanging from a tree, the words having died in their throats –, survive any reading. If, in pointing to the tentative moral advance achieved through Eman's sacrifice, for example, we do not also feel the full force of the violence of Eman's death, earlier hinted at – the Girl's instruction to Ifada ('You may hit harder than that. As long as there is something left to hang at the end.' [119]) and Oroge's intimation ('[he] is the kind who would let himself be beaten from night till dawn and not utter a sound.' [132]) – we lose the reminder of the physical pain involved in transcendence, involved in strength. Notions of acceptance of quests, of the redefinition of inherited wisdom, rely on the clarity of knowledge and apprehension, the clarity of individual choice and will; a clarity which, within this terrible illusion and its fatal overspill, are held just enough in abeyance for us imaginatively to enter ambiguous enrichment. The economy of ambiguity which Soyinka achieves in *The Strong Breed* and Eman comes through the economy and small scale of the carrier-ritual. Yet the same point of interest – the language proper to an onlooker, proper to distance – animates the larger and far more ambitious play *A Dance of the Forests*, in which a sceptical interrogation of justice procedures is yoked to an onlooking god, both spectator and actor in a trial he organizes. We now proceed to analyse how this works.

2

A Dance of the Forests: Foreknowledge, or the Language of Emptiness I

It is quite easy to assume that prescience alone in a writer is a literary quality, that a literary work, like the voice of the prophet, acquires resonance through the historical fulfilment of its forecasts. Zodwa Motsa, responding to James Gibbs' (dispensable) slight to *The Invention* (1959; first published 2005), among the first plays written by Wole Soyinka, is of the opinion that 'the play's merits lie in its content, embodying Soyinka's prophetic power as a playwright.'[143] Yet why should we assume that correct prophecy amounts to more than just that – correct prophecy? And, conversely, that incorrect (unfulfilled?) prophecy might somehow diminish a work of literature? The first assumption, and what I have taken to be its corollary, carry the unfortunate (and I think unnecessary) risk of reducing literature to the information it brings, to what it is talking about – what, for instance, do we do with the work once the 'prophecy' has been fulfilled, other than look on helplessly as our satisfaction at a series of correspondences wanes? (Literary canons, on the other hand, would be shaken up with prophetic acuity as defining criterion.)

Motsa's edition is curious in this regard, for her introduction is preceded by Abiola Irele's divergent discussion of the same point. For in Irele's foreword, such moments are of relevance

---

[143] Zodwa Motsa, Introduction to *The Invention* and *The Detainee* by Wole Soyinka (Pretoria: University of South Africa, 2005), 6. Gibbs, she relays, had called it 'terrible'.

and literary interest, first and foremost, insofar as they anticipate future *dramatic* attempts to render continuing moral and aesthetic preoccupations, both in Soyinka's subsequent production (*Kongi's Harvest* [1965; first published in 1967], *Madmen and Specialists* [1970; first published in 1971], *The Man Died* [1972], *The Shuttle in the Crypt* [1972]) and beyond (Athol Fugard's *Sizwe Bandi is Dead* [1972]). Where *The Detainee* evinces 'acuity of premonitions', confirmation or fulfilment comes not just in the fact of Soyinka's later arrest, say, but in the aesthetic enlargements which he will later provide.[144]

A better place to start on prescience would, I think, be the memorable essay which Wilson Harris has dedicated to *The Road*, entitled 'The Complexity of Freedom'.[145] For our purposes, the essay is important in at least two senses. Firstly, it preserves the distinction between, on the one hand, the challenges which confront the artist at particular moments of crisis, or re-birth, or renaissance, those of seeing or hearing or responding to perspectives that lie half-buried, or half-exposed, in and under a traditional unfree order (the age's tendency to suppress heterogeneity in favour of order's unfreedom, as Harris might say); and, on the other hand, the specific aesthetic challenge of expressing these intimated or half-identified perspectives and forms, with and through and against the very tools available from the same tradition. Such, for Harris, is the renaissance which we might perceive in early Picasso, in Henry Moore, in Conrad. His examples are important insofar as they concretely address how the artist might express truths hitherto suppressed through strength of imagination and skill, not as radical rupture or *ex nihilo* creation, but rather as gaining

---

[144] Abiola Irele, Foreword to *The Invention* and *The Detainee*, xi.
[145] Wilson Harris, "The Complexity of Freedom," in *Perspectives on Wole Soyinka*, ed. Jeyifo, 51-61. First published in *Wole Soyinka: An Appraisal*, ed. Adewale Maja-Pearce (Oxford: Heinemann, 1994), 22-35.

strength from both belonging and departure, gaining cogency to the extent to which they draw on traditional tools to extend possibilities. This is what Harris intends by the 'complexity of freedom', the simultaneous confession of a bind with the intimation of its loosening.[146]

Secondly, and more specifically, this preliminary discussion flows and narrows into *The Road,* and into the question of 'foreknowledge'. Taking Professor's injunction 'One must cheat fear, by fore-knowledge' (*TR,* 227), Harris provides the crucial clarification, pushing us to meditate on the *resemblance* between the two which, he writes, 'remains open in the strangest alertness to the unexpected nature and texture of events.'[147] For Harris, if I have understood correctly, to cheat fear, fear being the quality of a doomed culture, is to perceive through the 'cracks', to hold a quality of alertness against a prevailing order's 'weight of persuasion', a quality which 'begins to reach out to a new undreamt-of order of life beyond each sentence of death.'[148]

The word 'crack' which I have quoted Harris as using is not arbitrary. Harris is himself reworking Professor's conspiratorial suggestion to Kotonu:

> PROFESSOR: When a man has one leg in each world, his legs are never the same. The big toe of Murano's foot – the left one of course – rests on the

---

[146] 'There is no decision or originality of gesture and freedom of movement that can be authentic unless as it arises to consciousness it confesses to how it is still masked, in some degree, by the very conditions from which it arises, by past education or propaganda, past or present insecurities and anxieties, by the historical restriction it partially breaks. And as it so confesses it points intuitively to the reality of freedom, the complexity of freedom, as an unfathomable decision that varies with the cloak of age or biased history it unravels.' Harris, "The Complexity of Freedom," 53.

[147] *Ibid.,* 57.

[148] *Ibid.,* 55.

slumbering chrysalis of the Word. When that crust cracks my friends – you and I, that is the moment we await. That is the moment of our rehabilitation. When that crust cracks... (*TR*, 187)

There is perhaps no better metaphorical pairing to understand the shaping of Harris' article than that 'crust' and 'crack', our relative freedom from the age's weight of persuasion being defined by whether we can pierce that crust, in art and interpretation as in life, and see through the cracks; and it is here, too, that we see that reciprocity of artist and critic of which we spoke in the introduction. There are two moments in *A Dance of the Forests* (1960) and *The Bacchae of Euripides* (1973) in which Soyinka uses the word 'crust' (or a cognate) to suggest a deadening of perception within a present order or motion of habit – recall Shklovsky on how habit swallows a man's wife or his fear of war[149] – and both are expressive of an artistic intention directed towards exploring the resemblance or difference between cheating fear and foreknowledge, between renewal and the weight of familiarity; to holding their resemblance open. In *A Dance of the Forests*, Forest Head, in solemn peroration, opines that his secret, his eternal burden is 'to pierce the encrustations of soul-deadening habit, and bare the mirror of original nakedness – knowing full well, it is all futility.' (*ADF*, 71) While in *The Bacchae of Euripides*, Tiresias, in a newly-intercalated scene with Dionysos, observes that 'Something did begin. Perhaps those lashes did begin something. I feel... a small crack in the dead crust of the soul. Listen! Can you hear women's voices? Strange, just then I almost felt my veins race.' (*BE*, 244)

We must now come to *A Dance of the Forests*, and Forest Head's prescience. It should be obvious by now that I think the literary importance of its being written for the

---

[149] See above, 81.

Independence celebrations of October 1960 comes not only in its acuity of prognosis, as admirable as that undoubtedly was and yet remains, but also, and no less importantly, in the fact that the question of foreknowledge, of familiarity, of prospect itself, becomes a structural principle and indeed suggestive moral problem in the play. For one paradox or even contradiction at the heart of this play, as we shall come to argue, relates to the dramatic possibilities of staging a trial, under the guidance of a deity who appears to be omniscient. The direction of the play moves both to elicit greater awareness in humankind, yet there is a persistent and subtle questioning of familiarity, of permanent recognition, of deadened perception, in matters of human justice, which is expressed in the staging of Forest Head, and in the disruptions of his planned trial, his lines of order.

Darko Suvin once remarked of Brecht's ideal onlooker – the Judge or the Wise Fool – that he is he 'to whom all familiar things are unfamiliar because he looks for the unrealized potentialities in each stage of human development – man of blessed classless Future'.[150] The ideal onlooker is a logical expression of what Suvin identifies as Brecht's dramaturgical angle of vision, the *look backward* from an imagined Golden Future of justice and friendliness to his (and our) cold world and dark times.'[151] Yet the angle of vision, to borrow Suvin's phrase, is different in Soyinka, exists within, if I may say, a more complex coordination of the spatial and the temporal. 'The action is cyclic, yes, but is it claimed anywhere that society returns precisely to its original phase?' observes Soyinka of what is often called a 'cyclical' notion of history;[152]

---

[150] Darko Suvin, "The Mirror and the Dynamo: On Brecht's Aesthetic Point of View," *TDR*, Vol.12 No.1 (Autumn 1967), 60.
[151] *Ibid.*, 57.
[152] Respectively: Wole Soyinka, "Notes on *Idanre*" in *Idanre & Other Poems* (London: Methuen & Co. Ltd., 1967), 87-8; "Who's Afraid of Elesin

but such a notion in a Yoruba context in general, and in Soyinka's imaginative sensibility in particular, bespeaks a strong coordination of forward movement on spatial enlargement. Soyinka's angle of vision, then comes from within, must look at once in several directions, embrace different orders, and this exigency of moral and historical imagination receives expression in Forest Head, the Father of the Forest, and he to whom all things, or so it would seem, are *familiar*.

In an early reading of the play, Abiola Irele writes that Forest Head, representing the Supreme Deity, 'also acts as a kind of objective judge of human condition, and it is through him that the essential point of the play is put across clearly'.[153] Oyin Ogunba once made a similar point, again concentrating on a divine (Irele's 'objective') viewpoint, here predicated on Aroni's opening speech:

> when he presents the past and the present and looks ahead to the future he does so as a being to whom the whole of human history has been divinely revealed. [...] If Soyinka is speaking through Aroni it is because, like him, he grasps the essentials of human history in terms of a cycle of cause and effect or crime and its attendant punishment.[154]

This reading risks ignoring the substantive difference which should obtain between dramatic *language* and prefatory *summary*, the latter invariably unable to contain its object. In Ogunba's identification of Soyinka's voice with Aroni, in his attribution of the play's presiding message to both (that 'if' is

---

Oba?" [1978] 73. For a detailed discussion, see Fioupou, *La Route*, 160-2. Fioupou, because from Katrak, reveals a note on the manuscript of *Idanre* held at the British Museum, part of which, they relay, reads: 'I know of nothing more futile, more monotonous and boring than a circle.' Cited in Fioupou, *La Route*, 120; for the original reference, see Katrak, *Wole Soyinka and Modern Tragedy*, 66, 103 n.10.
[153] Irele, "Tradition and the Yoruba Writer," 61.
[154] Ogunba, *The Movement of Transition*, 70.

not a conditional, but means something more like 'Soyinka chooses to speak through Aroni because...'), we lose both the challenges of staging 'omniscience', and more particularly, the suggestive exploration of omniscience's limitations in matters of human justice, as enacted in the play. (I am not questioning the cultural underpinnings of Ogunba's characterization of Aroni, but rather, what Ogunba sees Soyinka as doing with those.)

Let us consider Aroni's 'testimony' more closely, then, recalling that in subsequent plays, as we shall see with *Death and the King's Horseman*, 'prefatory' comments must not be taken as transparent upon the work, but rather as discreetly pointing to the fragile threads over which the work is stretched.[155] Here, the fiction is a fiction of summary, so to speak, and as such, we should be interested just as much in the elisions and omissions and connections as we are in the open account of what happened:

> [The living] drove them out. So I took them under my wing. They became my guests and the Forests consented to dance for them. Forest Head, the one who we call Obaneji, invited Demoke, Adenebi and Rola to be present at the dance. They followed him, unwillingly, but they had no choice. [...] It was not as dignified a Dance as it should be. Eshuoro had come howling for vengeance and full of machinations. His professed wrongs are part of the story. (*ADF*, 5)

We should, I think, retain a few points: how the dance is 'not as dignified [...] as it should be', how it deviates from whatever plan it was supposed to follow or structure to take, and how, so runs the implication, this is attributable to Eshuoro's desire for vengeance; and how, at the same time, these 'machinations' are themselves part of the story, how, in pushing us beyond the dignity of the Dance, they focus

---

[155] See below, 264-5.

attention on the Dance itself, its inadequacies or the inadequacies of its planned staging or mechanisms; and how, consequently, that loss of 'dignity' (for whom?) is perhaps not a loss at all, but rather, just possibly, an enrichment or enlargement – the submitting or cracking of simple knowledge into partiality, into imbrication, beyond even the rationalized plans of the deity; into, that is, a wider fabric, or a more complex, human freedom.

In an astute comparison between this play and Shakespeare's *The Tempest,* Biodun Jeyifo has argued that 'Soyinka shows great originality in his conflation of both this pristine West African judicial-administrative ritual matrix and, in the persons of Forest Head and his servitor, Aroni, elements of the absolutist-monarchical paradigm of Prospero's trial of his enemies in *The Tempest.*'[156] What I find rich, implicitly, in the rapprochement between Prospero and Ariel and Forest Head and Aroni, and more broadly, between the two plays, is how forms of schematic allegory are deployed by Shakespeare and Soyinka – the one with its paradigms of grace, purity, chastity, as standing over nature, 'rough magic', incivility; the other with its deformed birthings as heralding imminent trouble – the better to dramatize and render what cannot be assimilated or incorporated into ordered correspondence.[157]

---

[156] Jeyifo, *Wole Soyinka,* 130.
[157] Is it but a happy coincidence that, in the case of *The Tempest,* it was George Wilson Knight, Soyinka's (somewhat maverick) teacher at Leeds in the late 1950s, who instituted an influential break with schematic allegorical readings of the play? See Frank Kermode, Introduction to *The Tempest* by William Shakespeare (London: Methuen, 1954), lxxxiii-v. Frank Kermode has the following interesting remark on the crucial role played by Antonio in Shakespeare's play, in *ibid.,* lxii: 'A world without Antonio is a world without freedom; Prospero's shipwreck cannot restore him if he desires not to be restored, to life. The gods chalk out a tragicomic way, but enforce only disaster. The rest is voluntary.'

Here, the organization of the first part is, as Forest Head (who has been masquerading among the humans as Obaneji) later reveals, to 'force them [i.e. the human characters] into an acceptance of my aloofness' (45), which is, in turn, a way of preparing the humans for the trial of the Dance of the Forests. Obaneji/Forest Head, then, seeks to move the human characters to disgust at his apparent lack of human understanding, through the paradox of almost total knowledge with almost total emptiness, plenitude of information going with lack of compassion. What better voice to adopt, to this end, than the language of a pedantic bureaucrat ('[...] I work as a filing clerk for the courts. Senior clerk, mind you' [16]), the modern exemplar of the diminishing of the moral imagination that distance can induce in us, the treating of large numbers of human individuals as if they were numbers or abstract entities?

In this sense, Obaneji's imitated criteria of 'knowledge' and 'rightness' are perfectly apposite, are the believable words of the bureaucratic agent:

> I know about people even before I've met them. Know their whole history sometimes. And against my will, I find that all the time, I am guessing which name belongs to who. You don't know how unnerving that can be, especially when one is so often right. (16)

This is knowledge as statistics, as an aggregate of information, rather than as experiential; the subsequent slippage – 'Take one lorry I was examining only yesterday – the records that is –' (17) – in which records are taken for the real thing, is a symptomatic expression of just such an idea of knowledge.

In the first part of the play, the main human characters – Demoke, Adenebi and Rola –, we were saying, are submitted to a practice trial by a disguised Forest Head, the better to bring them into acknowledgement of their crimes, and, so goes the implication, the better to prepare them for the Dance. Each seeks to avoid acknowledgement of his or her crimes, before the underlying motivation is eventually teased or forced out. The clearest instance comes with Adenebi, the council orator of the human community. Obaneji/Forest Head's (merely adoptive?) impermeable familiarity with death and suffering, his disguise of impassivity, constitutes a highly ironic and critical *imitation* and mirroring of Adenebi's own state of consciousness at fiddling the books in the bureaucratic office, to Adenebi's face:

> ADENEBI: Have you no feeling for those who died? Are you just an insensitive, inhuman block?
>
> OBANEJI: I didn't kill them. And anyway, we have our different views. The world must go on. After all, what are a mere sixty-five souls burnt to death? Nothing. Your bribe-taker was only a small-time murderer; he wasn't even cold-blooded. [...] No, you cannot really punish the man. After all, how was he to foresee the consequences of his actions? How was he to know that in two months from the deed, the lorry would hit another, overturn completely, and be set on fire? (19)

Adenebi's indignation is expressive not of moral persuasiveness, but rather of hypocrisy; better yet, the measure of his hypocrisy is the measure of his indignation, for he himself has been guilty of bureaucratic 'oversight', with terrible consequences for human life. In other words, Forest Head's aloofness elicits an exemplary expression of human hypocrisy, holding up hypocrisy's sanctimony against its underbelly of venality, through the weak though apparently logical rationalizations meant to attenuate injustice (implicit in Adenebi's acceptance of the bribe is his acknowledgement of infraction, which in turn suggests an understanding of the potential dangers involved in infraction). Obaneji/Forest Head's stance, as Forest Head later observes, is a mirror which holds the language of hypocrisy in relief.

The historian only confesses ('I have always lived in mortal terror of being lost.' [39]) after having offered a generously non-critical first version, like the would-be employee who lists his faults at interview as perfectionism or diligence ('I have a weak heart. Too much emotion upsets me. This is the era of greatness. Unfortunately it is to those who cannot bear too much of it to whom the understanding is given...' [11]). For even before we arrive at this confession, we have seen the run of Adenebi's 'understanding'. Consider, for instance, the brief exercise in direct and indirect speech, which cleverly effects the motions between recollection, immersion in recollection, and eventual or reluctant stepping out once more:

> ADENEBI: Well, in addition I said;... no, you said, and I took it up, that we must bring home the descendants of our great forebears. Find them. Find the scattered sons of our proud ancestors. The builders of empires. The descendants of our great nobility. Find them. Bring them here. If they are half-way across the world, trace them. If they are in hell, ransom them. Let them symbolize all that is noble in our nation. Let them be our historical link for the season of rejoicing. Warriors. Sages. Conquerors. Builders. Philosophers. Mystics. Let us assemble them round the totem of the nation and we will drink from their resurrected glory.
>
> OLD MAN: Yes. It was a fine speech. But control, at some point was lost to our enemies. (31)

The ambiguity begins early, with that 'Find them', which could be reported speech (following on from 'you said that we must'), or direct speech, a reinvesting of the moment in the imperative ('Find them!'). This ambiguity is resolved, I think, by the time we reach 'Bring them here', where the imperative purpose cannot be missed, and this motion is confirmed with the jussives 'Let them', which, syntactically, cannot go with reported speech. In other words, in but a few sentences, Adenebi has cast off the shackles of the present moment to relive his speech, itself a glorification of the past. The Old Man's attempts to recall him to the demands of the present are repeatedly averted until the final wistful 'Mali. Songhai. Lisabi. Chaka... but who did we get?' (32), the ellipsis and the entrance of Agboreko closing the moment. When his sycophancy is finally routed, it is done so at length: the sudden isolation in darkness, without the audience needed to hold and sustain the fictions of order he speaks:

> *He looks round, half-dazed but becomes suddenly active on discovering that he is alone. Runs around shouting names, then turns to run into the headlamps, stops suddenly and stands with raised arms, screaming. There is a crash, the noise stops suddenly, and the lights go out. Adenebi's scream being heard above it and after, stopping suddenly as he hears his own terror in the silence.*
>
> ADENEBI: [...] I have always lived in mortal terror of being lost. (38, 39)[158]

We have spoken of the 'transparent organization' of the first part of the play. This is Forest Head's own description, in conversation with Aroni:

> FOREST HEAD: Oh, they made amusing companions. It was really their latent violence which frightened me. I did not know what I would do if it involved me.

---

[158] I am not quite convinced of the tone of Adenebi's final confession ('I have always lived in mortal terror of being lost' [39]), its sounding out of register with what has come before, too sudden or abrupt in effect to justify. Perhaps we should think of it as preparation for the pathological crucible of self-loathing in *The Interpreters* which is poor old Joe Golder, as he stands with his feet in a circle of emptiness singing of distant home, 'cradled in grief, mangled-soul bared'. See Wole Soyinka, *The Interpreters* (London: Collins, Fontana Books, 1965), 247.

ARONI: They appear tame enough now.

FOREST HEAD: So tame in fact, I could send them home. But they forget too easily.

ARONI: They had no suspicion of you?

FOREST HEAD: Only uncertainty. I threw dark hints to preserve my mystery and force them into an acceptance of my aloofness. It held them all except the woman. (*ADF*,45)

Aloofness is not without its own ambiguities, however, and Soyinka is, I think, quite careful to suggest a few moral ambiguities in Forest Head's distance, and his rationalizations of distance – critical distance which comes at the price of human empathy and understanding, as inhumanity; excessive distance as provoking indifference or snobbishness or loftiness or condescension; ignorance of the real presences of people.[159]

Let us consider, then, the acknowledged exception to what Forest Head calls, rather grandly, 'dark hints to preserve mystery' (45): Rola, the courtesan. Indifference or stated impassivity or silence do not exist in a vacuum, but rather become expressive and communicative when in human context, when silent or impassive or indifferent *before* or *to* something. And this is what Obaneji seems not to like, or understand, in his interactions with Rola: the sense that his attempts to 'force acceptance of his aloofness' are perhaps rightly met, by his human companions, and Rola most particularly, with resistance, *despite* everything that we know about their own hypocrisies and crimes and failings, and it is a measure of the difficulty of the play that we are expected to hold these together and distinct. The most cogent expression of this comes in sex, a great leveller of pretension or role-

---

[159] For a brilliant series of discussions on the moral implications of distance, which I have not hesitated to draw on, see Carlo Ginzburg, *Occhiacci di legno: Nove riflessioni sulla distanza* (Milan: Feltrinelli, 1998).

playing: instances of chastity going with all-knowing smugness abound in literature, and it is of course the drawing in through sex that is most commonly employed as a device to undercut such pretensions to standing apart, the loftiness of moderation. Consider this edited instance of the exchange between the one hollowed of sensitivity and the other stripped of sentimentality, two nuances of emptiness:

> ROLA: How would you like to be killed?
>
> OBANEJI: Oh. I shall have to think a minute or two over that... Let me see...
>
> ROLA: Why don't you confess it? You are the type who would rather die in your bed. You look it.
>
> OBANEJI: You say that as if one should be ashamed of it.
>
> ROLA [*contemptuously*]: No. I suppose there are things which do crawl into a hole to die.
>
> OBANEJI [*laughs softly*]: And you? [...] *Rola swings round suddenly, embraces him and tries to kiss him.* [*Struggling*]: Please... please... let me go. [...] please keep your distance in future. I have a particular aversion to being mauled by women.
>
> ROLA [*furiously*]: I suppose you weren't born by one. [...] Who do you think you are anyway, looking perpetually smug and pushing people around?
>
> ADENEBI: I hope you like what you've started. After all you asked the question. You should not complain if you get an unexpected answer.
>
> OBANEJI: You are wrong there. It was not unexpected. It was only the method of reply for which I wasn't prepared.
>
> ROLA [*looks at him with withering contempt*]: No wonder you were not prepared. I don't suppose you have ever in your life dared to hold a woman in your arms...

OBANEJI: Please... please... let us change the subject.

ROLA: You started it. And anyway who are you to think that we will only talk of whatever happens to please you? I am getting sick of the way you step back when it seems you are about to get splashed, especially as you swing your feet about as much as you do... (20-1)

Obaneji's soft laughter is quickly undermined in surprise, which in turn triggers that slightly misogynistic expression 'mauled by women'. The central question, articulated around the emotional poles of smugness and fury, is weakly addressed by Obaneji's neat distinction between method of reply and reply, for the two are only dissociated at the risk of losing the deeper truth. This is the lesson of literature, of art, certainly, and I find it interesting that Obaneji should express himself thus, just when thrown off balance.

There is another possible suggestion that Obaneji knows the reply but ignores its method, whether it comes as kiss, punch or tickle. This comes with the Chimney of Eroko. On the surface of things, Obaneji's apparently admiring talk of the Chimney or polluting lorry, as we have seen, provides a way of bringing Adenebi a little closer to himself, of trying to enforce upon him the experience or at least the representation of what he elides in official history and speeches, the terror of being robbed of those supportive beams. What for Obaneji is a simple ruse, however, is invested with quite a different tonality and consequence in the Old Man's rehabilitation of the Chimney of Eroko. 'We asked for statesmen and we were sent executioners' (29), he opines, and his reaction is to flush out those executioners whom Aroni and Forest Head have sent. The result, in turn, is the flushing out of the forest creatures from their homes, under the poisoned cloak of petrol fumes. What began as a simple inversion, a welcome of accusation rather than a welcome of celebration, an attempt to control and submit humans to a form of understanding, begins to spill over into and harm the realm of the forest. Perhaps control is not so clearly defined, as once it was.

I earlier implied that we should resist attributing to Obaneji/ Forest Head a single role, such as that of Objective Judge. It seems to me that we are better served if we see in him instead a figure which changes under dramatic pressure, under the pressure of being in situation, so to speak. Again, it seems to me that this is part of the sceptical intelligence of Soyinka's specific understanding of the 'cyclical'. The basic conceit that Soyinka has chosen here, intelligently I think, is that of aloofness, a posture which claims to stand outside the action the better to observe, and it is precisely by *situating* this posture, by *integrating* it into various orders of meaning, by *staging* its claims to objectivity, to omniscience, rationalizations of order, that he can better probe its assumptions. This, it seems to me, explains the importance of Soyinka's discreet though insistent qualification of Obaneji's control, prepared in the first part of the play. From there, aloofness will be projected onto the wider canvas of the procedures of justice. If Soyinka is making a point on the ways in which an external point of view can be used to show us up to ourselves, to show our own representations of ourselves as precisely that, he is also, through the staging of foreknowledge and ambivalences of distance, discreetly suggesting the kinship between familiarity, or wilful standing apart, or an external point of view, and the loss of a deeper, human, understanding.

I am arguing that Soyinka deliberately insinuates – as in the conclusion to the essay 'Between Self and System', quoted in the chapter's epigraph – that standing apart is, dangerously, only ever one step away from moral abdication, that contemplation might just subside into mere contemplation, if it never steps into action. You will recall the play's first scene, a sort of *précis* or condensation of character: Adenebi runs off, terrified of the 'real presences' of the dead; Demoke equivocates, both undecided and reasonable; Rola is all openness and contempt. And of Obaneji, this: '*Obaneji stops and looks thoughtfully at them. The Dead Man, listening hard, goes quickly towards him. Obaneji withdraws, looking back at the pair.*' (7) We are unsure at the start whether this thoughtfulness is interesting, or whether, in truth, he is a sphinx without a secret – this feeling is never fully dispelled, indeed ensures a tension basic to his role.

Obaneji/Forest Head enacts, and voices, such an attitude of impermeability and distance throughout the play:

> OBANEJI: Unfortunately I have seen so much and I am rarely impressed by anything. (10)
>
> OBANEJI: I know too much... about people... far too much. When I saw them all, actually rejoicing – that much is true at least – most of them did experience joy... but you see... when they laughed, I was looking down their throats.
>
> ROLA: And what did you see?
>
> OBANEJI: Only what I know already. (16)
>
> OBANEJI: I have seen so much. It simply doesn't impress me, that's all. (19)
>
> OBANEJI: He needn't speak. Why does he? Why do you all? I want nothing, asked nothing. (26)
>
> FOREST HEAD: I take no part, but listen. [...] [*Goes to his seat, impassive.*] (64)
>
> FOREST HEAD: I merely sit and watch. (69)

Where, in the first part of the play, his responses may be shaped for the preservation of disguise, in the second part, disguise is no longer necessary. Although the Forest Father's non-intervention is an important guarantee, within the play's logic, of humanity's free will, it *also* sounds to us like self-address, which, proper to threatened control, chimes close to self-persuasion or self-reassurance, like the muttering father who tells himself that all is well as the shortcut bears the family to destinations unknown. It suggests to us, that is, that foreknowledge and self-awareness are not the same thing; that foreknowledge's blind spot, indeed, is the self. The implication, in idea as in language, is that foreknowledge leads to emptiness. And this, in turn, can but imply a blind spot at the heart of the dance itself.

At the end of the play, these pieces are gathered up into Forest Head's final speech, a self-portrait of the motions of foreknowledge and emptiness:

> FOREST HEAD [*more to himself*]: Trouble me no further. The fooleries of beings whom I have fashioned closer to me weary and distress me. Yet I must persist, knowing that nothing is ever altered. My secret is my eternal burden – to pierce the encrustations of soul-deadening habit, and bare the mirror of original nakedness – knowing full well, it is all futility. Yet I must do this alone, and no more, since to intervene is to be guilty of contradiction, and yet to remain altogether unfelt is to make my long-rumoured ineffectuality complete; hoping that when I have tortured awareness from their souls, that perhaps, only perhaps, in new beginnings... (71)

We have seen how certain important (and canonical) speeches might cleverly express equivocation: Professor's opening words on the miracle, say, or Old Man's climactic ambiguity of voice. In the earlier *A Dance of the Forests*, as the climactic speech comes, we should be attentive to what Wilson Harris enjoined upon us through his reading of *The Road*: a quality of alertness to the resemblance of foreknowledge, and the superior cheat. We have been arguing that Obaneji/Forest Head enacts the ambivalence of standing apart, and the paradoxical (or contradictory) language of his speech moves in that direction: he is to 'torture' awareness from human souls, in his own slightly portentous phrase; but he himself is diminished by the moral ambivalences which perpetual familiarity or recognition imply. The clever word 'unfelt' – *not* 'unfeeling', which we would expect – preserves a physical texture, and conveys empathy only in rationalist or calculating terms. 'Weariness' and 'distress' are not complementary motions of the spirit, the one connoting lofty boredom, an absence of empathy, and the other suggesting a real and exacting emotional response; but the possibility of the two being balanced has surely been undermined by the condescending or paternal 'fooleries' with which the speech begins.

What follows is an apodictic summary of his own condition ('Yet I must persist, knowing that nothing is ever altered'), followed by a more detailed self-diagnosis. (With an eye to a critical edition, I would suggest that the second hyphen has the function of a comma, both the 'piercing of encrustations' and the 'knowing full well all is futility' being in *apposition* to secret and burden.) It is here that self-diagnosis gives way, for the first time in Forest Head, to the *temptation* of exposition, to the temptation of thinking through his empty condition to its full consequences. And his irresolution or continued oscillations are held in the awkward repetition of 'yet'. What does that final ellipsis convey? Merely the hope of new beginnings for humans, through awareness? or also the unshakeable remaining sense of his 'long-rumoured ineffectuality', against the corollary hope that it might be stayed or deferred, that his *own* renewal somehow depends on attaining human awareness?

Some will object that I am focussing excessively on the principal deity, at the expense of the humans, but what always strikes me, as we come to the trial, is precisely that the humans are almost entirely passive, until the key scene with Demoke; that they are placed before an allegorical parade (they briefly participate when masked), which begins to widen and complexly spin out of control, into a profusion of signs and orders of meaning. Such a widening, whilst preserving the thread of its central moral concern – essential to Soyinka's basic purpose of warning, the ground bass of justice – threatens to weaken the planned lines of order, the rationalized dignity, as it opens out into acknowledgements of various competing claims of justice; into acknowledgements, that is, of complexity, of a complexity greater, perhaps, than imagined at first. In other words, within and against the structural cyclical notion of 'approximate duplications', to paraphrase the (officialist) Crier (*ADF,* 45), of approximate repetitions in history, what we actually have is competing claims and procedural orders of justice and revenge pushing against the frame of the initial conception.

This is expressed, in the second part, as the tension and movement between order and chance, as anthropomorphized in Forest Head and Eshuoro (a sort of *portmanteau* god bringing together Eshu and Oro), receives full structural and symbolic elaboration in the trial. I use the terms 'order' and 'chance' quite deliberately. It seems to anticipate that sudden evocative expression of Yoruba metaphysics succinctly captured in the novel *The Interpreters*:

> of the parting of the fog and the retreat of the beginning, and the eternal war of the divining eyes, of the hundred and one eyes of lore, fore- and after-vision, of the eternal war of the first procedure with the long sickle head of chance, eternally mocking the pretensions of the bowl of plan, mocking lines of order in the ring of chaos (*TI,* 226).

In the play's second part, we are confronted both by the basic strength and truth of allegory, and led, through the cunning preparation of Rola's mocking Obaneji's impotence, to a wider judgement on judgement, and the question: is the original trial under the pair Forest Head-Aroni able to respond to the challenges of this brave new world? The overall intention, that is, must be to preserve the frame ('Do not deny that all goes as you planned it. [*Eshuoro goes out.*] But only because it is my wish. And so we must all be content.' [60]), but to feel it stretched and pressured from within. The artistic intention, that is, will be respected to the extent to which we hold *both* of the gods' claims together, that sense of basic moral duty, as conveyed in allegory (the trial of 'the lesser criminals, pursuing the destructive path of survival [...] hiding their cowardice in sudden acts of bluster' by placing them before the terrible issue 'born when they acquire power over one another, and their instincts are fulfilled a thousand-fold, a hundred thousand-fold' [69]), *and* the indissociable sense that things are more complex, that not everything can be integrated into such perspectives. Crucially, these claims, in turn, are held against the fundamental *human* concern, to suggest how the sense and expression and constant balance between deeper harmony and contingency, which we understand formally, might overwhelm us as we stand before it, how this sense easily and quite terrifyingly disarms and then bludgeons us, and how that, just possibly, is the expression of truth.

The qualification of the trial, the invitation to a judgement on judgement, is catalysed through the 'machinations' and howlings with which Eshuoro swells and complicates the official allegory as planned by the Forest Father; machinations which, we recall, 'are also part of the story'. So, to Eshuoro:

> ESHUORO: Have you seen how they celebrate the gathering of the tribes? In our own destruction. Today they even dared to chase out the forest spirits by poisoning the air with petrol fumes. Have you seen how much of the forest has been torn down for their petty decorations? [...] Where the humans preserve a little bush behind their homes, it is only because they want somewhere for their garbage. Dead dogs and human excrement are all you'll find in it. The whole forest stinks. Stinks of human obscenities. And who holds us back? Forest Father and his lame minion, Aroni. They and their little ceremonies of gentle rebuke. (41)

Eshuoro cannot explain why the humans chased out the

forest spirits, but he does perceive that this is in step with their increasing predations upon and destruction of Nature, impunity emboldening daily insult (the accrual of garbage, waste-depository) into daring obscenity; and, accordingly, he stresses that redress is urgently needed. The very sense of Forest Head's own trial, which we may hitherto have assumed to be justifiable, is here called into question from the outside, so to speak, in being reduced to 'another mild lesson' (41), which hints, beyond personal affront, that there might be precedent for the ineffective staging of justice. (Notice too, that 'lame' is both descriptive and just possibly an indictment of ineffectuality.) The return of humans 'supposedly wiser' after the 'little feast' comes to the crux of Eshuoro's interrogation: are such trials an illusion of justice, their enactments vulnerable to forgetfulness, rather than the source of the enduring truths which come through suffering and experience?

Eshuoro's broad sense of wronging both enfolds and gains sustenance from the more particular sense of personal outrage he feels at the hacking of his limbs, the gouging of his eyes and roots, his bearing naked to the world, 'the desecration of [his] forest body' (42), which lead to his call for vengeance ('I'm telling you today must be a day of reprisals. While they are glutted and full of themselves that is the time. Aroni's little ceremony must be made into a bloody sentence' [41]). Revenge, in other words, is not reducible to personal redress, but is also a channel or catalyst for the wider claims of a wronged community; contingency's justification moves beyond private wronging. 'Since when was the forest so weak that humans could smoke out the owners and sleep after?' (42), he asks Murete, the tree-imp. And we must hear Murete's response, consistent with his individualism or looking out for himself, just as much as with his plain-talking, as being one ambiguously poised between correct diagnosis and wilful avoidance (ingenuousness?) – it is difficult to tell which: 'No one has complained much. We have claimed our own victims – for every tree that is felled or for every beast that is slaughtered, there is recompense, given or forced' (42).

Let us come to the trial; or rather, the first part of the trial. The overture, what we might call the officialist version, relies on an historical re-enactment which, precisely against the vibrancy of what we have seen in the first part, feels stilted, less historical – allegorical, even? – trying to over-determine the sense we are to receive through reducing language to the voicing of ideas, and little else. And allegory as more or less direct correspondence, as we know, is unlikely to move humans. The Historian is hardly subtle in his dark arts ('We were so near to the greatness of Troy and Greece... I mean this is war as it should be fought... over nothing... do you not agree?' [51]); the soothsayer trades in insinuating enigma for obsequious commonplace ('It does not depend on you, Mata Kharibu. It is in the nature of men to seek power over the lives of others, and there is always something lower than a servant' [54]); and the Warrior, whose welcome we are here to celebrate, is content to disburse banal platitudes – 'Unborn generations will, as we have done, eat up one another' (49) he observes, as if this were useful to us in the present, beyond being a mere caution against naïve optimism or self-induced blindness to present suffering.

This is no doubt a little provocative, but the complex symbolism of the later trial surely gains relief and strength precisely against this flatness of language. Eshuoro's response to the stilted 'spectacle' we have just seen – 'What have you proved?' (58) – is therefore a good, pointed question, despite the harshness of his expression. Eshuoro's indictment gains strength not from his dialogue with the Forest Father, but rather in how he comes to inhabit Forest Head's questions from within the spectacle or trial.

This, in turn, ensures that the compass of the trial embraces not simply Forest Head's original plan, nor his subsequent welcoming of the dead, but stretches rather into questions not easily dismissed, which is to say, questions with bite in the *present,* which the general or formal dimensions of foreknowledge seem to dismiss too quickly: the turning and spinning of Forest Head's anodine 'I knew you', of the dance 'to quiet your spirits torn loosely by the suddenness' (61). (This interruption has been prepared by Rola's silencing Obaneji/Forest Head as he indulges in lyrical invocations of his own immemorial knowledge:

> OBANEJI: Do you realize, I even knew your ancestors. I knew...
>
> ROLA: And you, I suppose you have no ancestors. You are merely the dust that came off a moth's wing.
>
> *Obaneji appears to be shut up by this. There is an uncomfortable silence.* [24])

What of the human characters in all this? I think that the crucial point in the discussions of point of view, in the widening symbolism which works within and against any simple allegory, lies precisely in the fact that 'awareness' is, as we have been intimating, a stepping into greater complexity, which corresponds neither to Forest Head's planned Dance, nor Eshuoro's machinations. Eshuoro, disguised as the Figure in Red, goes to play *'sesan'* with the Half-child, who, appealing for help in vain, is eventually defeated. We see and hear the following:

> *They vanish. The Figure in Red goes resolutely to Forest Head and confronts him. Forest Head appears hesitant, even reluctant. Eventually, he gestures brusquely to the Interpreter.*
>
> FOREST HEAD: Unmask them. The Half-child has played out his game and lost. Let them see the rest with their natural eyes, their human sight. (69)

A spatial mode, as Achebe so perceptively saw and imagined in Yeats' gyre, can well be exploited to express a subtle or sudden broadening of perspective, a coming into an awareness of the limits of one's understanding, and we should feel, with the humans now unmasked, that sense; we should see and feel and live it with them as, amid the yelling triplets, the thickening and exponential symbolism, they can but *'again cluster together'* (71), an expression of solidarity as they prepare to step into a new sense of things. This I take to be the clearest moment of submission to a trial, a testing or exaction, during which the only way not to perish is to cluster together with others whose sight is as limited as your own but who are human nevertheless.

The final exchanges of the play, an emergence from ritual tension and climax, deliberately and simply oppose formal and experiential knowledge. The desire of Agboreko and the Old Man, the one a proverb-spinner and the other leader of the human community (and father to Demoke), to enter into knowledge without experience, to buy it on the cheap, meet with Demoke's elliptical and non-expository response: 'We three who lived many lives in this one night, have we not done enough? Have we not felt enough for the memory of our remaining lives?' (73) And Rola's chastened silence, it would seem, marks the halting first moments of the new community of the changed. There is in this play, then, a sense in which true suffering into truth, true passage into understanding, leaves us speechless, without words, incapable of articulating what it is we have undergone. And this, I find, is true to the important moments of life: the sense that our moral or emotive vocabularies are always lagging behind the largeness of event; the truths that we feel in our gut and marrow, yet to which we can but failingly gesture towards with our words. A little over a decade later, Soyinka makes of this possible rupture between words and understanding the dramatic climax of his play *The Bacchae of Euripides*.

3

The Bacchae of Euripides: Foreknowledge, or the Language of Emptiness II

Isidore Okpewho approaches Soyinka's 1973 adaptation of Euripides' *The Bacchae* from the outside, as it were, 'as a translation of culture, not of text'.[160] Although Okpewho is thereby able to offer a number of stimulating correspondences, his method ultimately cannot avoid eliding a number of specifically literary facets of the play, eclipsing what is written in what is written about. Where he indicates, for example, a possible instance of Soyinka borrowing from Yoruba cult-lexicon; where he connects the interplay between knowing and not knowing or naming and not naming to cult practice in West Africa – and for that we must be grateful; he fails to go on to ask the key question: what is its function *in this play*? Instead, he observes that the interplay 'may justly be read as a metaphor for the stresses that frustrated the political and intellectual life of late fifth-century Athens',[161] and leaves it at that.

We would, I think, be better served by assuming that Euripides first, and Soyinka second, is concerned not with the interplay between knowing and not-knowing as a metaphor for something else – what I understand to be Okpewho's reading – but for what we might come to understand about

---

[160] Isidore Okpewho, "Soyinka, Euripides, and the Anxiety of Empire," in *African Drama and Performance*, eds. John Conteh-Morgan and Tejumola Olaniyan (Bloomington: Indiana University Press, 2001), 55.
[161] *Ibid.*, 62.

different types of knowing, held together in fine balance and contrast through plot, against an historical background. William Arrowsmith's useful discussion, included in one of the editions which Soyinka relied on for his own adaptation,[162] helped identify a few changing forms which *sophia* assumes in Euripides' work – the 'wisdom' of ripe old age; the narrow professional expertise of the sage and seer; mere cleverness or intellectual sophistry; and, finally, the animal cunning of the practised hunter. He continues:

> over the surface of these meanings of *sophia* the action plays endlessly, testing one *sophia* against another, matching opponents in a steady rage of exposure that in the end inverts all roles and pretensions and leaves the stage, desolate and bleak, to the suffering survivors confronted with the inexorable, pitiless necessity that Dionysus is.[163]

I would like to consider just a few threads in the respinning of this web of *sophia* or 'knowledge' in Soyinka's adaptation, concentrating on Tiresias and the Old Man, and culminating in the music of communion.

Forest Head, in *A Dance of the Forests*, has played a paradoxical role – that of teasing out awareness against familiarity, all the while being himself condemned to familiarity through foreknowledge. In *The Bacchae of Euripides*, Tiresias' foreknowledge, for Euripides a pretext to probe the limitations of calculating expertise, is placed under increased scrutiny by the innovations which Soyinka introduces. Tiresias' dilemma, if I may put it this way, grows out of Forest Head. The clue comes in two short moments in each play. Firstly, Rola tugging Obaneji's beard as she mocks him in song:

---

[162] William Arrowsmith, Introduction to *The Bacchae* by Euripides in *Euripides V*, eds. David Gene and Richard Lattimore (Chicago; London: Chicago University Press, 1959), 145-146.
[163] *Ibid.*, 146.

ROLA [*teasing quite bitchily, makes a sudden dart and pulls at his beard*]
He'll die in his bed but he'll die alone.
He'll sleep in his bed but he'll sleep alone.
He'll wake in the morning and he'll eat alone.
So good up in heaven he sang praises alone. (*ADF,* 21)

This is an acute anticipation of Forest Head's later talk of loneliness, unfussedly spoken for what it is: singing, eating, sleeping, the human pleasures, are human pleasures the richer for being shared. Beyond the psychological motivations which frustrate Rola and which render her more vulnerable and hostile before others' judgements, we also understand with her that there is something mildly annoying in Obaneji's stance of self-sufficiency, well conveyed in the tugging of the beard. In *The Bacchae of Euripides*, we watch the following (partial) exchange between Dionysus and Tiresias:

DIONYSUS [*He moves close to Tiresias, tugs gently at his beard*]: Poor Tiresias, poor neither-nor, eternally tantalized psychic intermediary, poor agent of the gods through whom everything passes but nothing touches, what happened to you in the midst of the crowd, dressed and powdered by the hands of ecstatic women, flagellated by sap-swollen birches? What sensations coursed through your withered veins as the whips drew blood, as the skin of the birches broke against yours and its fragrant sap mingled with your blood. You poor starved votary at the altar of soul, what deep hunger unassuaged by a thousand lifelong surrogates drove you to this extreme self-sacrifice. (*BE,* 243-4)

The suddenness of Rola's grab and tug is here displaced into the suddenness of Dionysus' rhetorical ascent, for which we are prepared neither by Euripides' original, nor by any precedent here, for the god has not spoken in such terms yet. Dionysus would seem to be bludgeoning Tiresias into a reminder of the limits of his specific form of *sophia*, the calculating expertise of the seer as opposed to the more complex enrichments of experiential knowledge, of which the extreme expression, we are to suppose, is the dionysiac expression. (The cumulative and accelerating vocatives we may recognize as a general stylistic tick of Soyinka, in a mode of accusation. We have seen it in the false ritual context of *Madmen and Specialists;* we shall see that it surfaces in *The Man Died,* clearly of the same historical moment; and we will see it later again, for instance, in the oneiric prose of Sipe's dream in *Ìsarà,* before Otuyemi and Reverend Beeston.[164])

Tiresias' premeditated responses to Dionysus are rehearsed, not receptive or responsive to felt experience. Why take the risk of submitting to flagellation, given your rank as high priest of Thebes? What if you had been flogged to pieces? enquires Dionysus. Tiresias responds: 'Then I shall pass into the universal energy of renewal... like some heroes or gods I could name.' (243) The not-so-subtle comparison with Dionysus and the mythic logic of breaking down or disintegration

---

[164] On *Madmen and Specialists,* see above, 132-5; see also *The Man Died,* 81: '[...] truth, the truth is *that* truth of their arrest following upon hints of your generous confession. That is Truth. We have re-created truth and truth is now defined in our image. Each man who loses liberty or life is added to the score of your betrayal. What will you say? How will you say it? Who will believe you? Who will *want* to believe you? Who will *think* of believing? Truth, my dear friend, is the thousands who have vanished since we fixed your interfering little mind!'; and finally *Ìsarà,* 60, 69: '[...] you just wait and see, and you, Otuyemi, must therefore remain and bear witness to history fulfilling itself and be content to be recruited into the army that would lay siege to the fabulous kingdoms of wealth [...] Don't think we didn't know you had been laughing up your sleeve these many years, but we found you out, didn't we? Issuing us only bowdlerised dictionaries while you kept the one with the secret of the tongue and clamped the Sixth and Seventh Books of Moses under your bed so we could not learn the secret. I can do without you, Beeston, I tell you I can do without your type.'

followed by re-assemblage is but an analogy, and a poor one at that, for Tiresias is not comparing like with like, experience with experience; and this it is that provokes Dionysus' sustained accusation. Indeed, ultimately forced into revealing his true motivation, Tiresias confesses – in what feels like a development or filling out of the potential in Forest Head's peroration – only here Tiresias' emptiness or hollowness acquires some pathos because he is a human denied his humanity; his burden is not one of condescension or wearisome duty, but rather preserves the full sense and weight of the *curse,* from which he seeks relief. The high-minded rhetoric of Forest Head's conclusion, which speaks of feeling as an obligation, is quite different from Tiresias' yearning to suffer, in which we should be able to hear, I think, the ancient Greek *pathos,* through the Latin *patio,* the meaning of undergoing or enduring or experiencing something with intensity, whence Tiresias' sensual emphasis:

> TIRESIAS [*cornered. Finally.*]: Yes, there was hunger. Thirst. In this job one lives half a life, neither priest nor man. Neither man nor woman. I have longed to know what flesh is made of. What suffering is. Feel the taste of blood instead of merely foreseeing it. Taste the ecstasy of rejuvenation after long organizing its ritual. When the slaves began to rumble I saw myself again playing that futile role, pouring my warnings on deaf ears. An uprising would come, bloodshed, and I would watch, untouched, merely vindicated as before – as prophet, I approach death and dissolution, without having felt life... its force... (243-4)

The seer's agenda, then, is double: reformist (to defuse the slaves' discontent through the enactment of ritual); and personal (to take upon himself the role of symbolic carrier, in order to crack the crust of familiarity in which foreknowledge has him encased). Here, however, he is trying to have his cake and eat it, to use illusion both to defuse the slave revolt, *and* to accede to a different or deeper experience or fulfilment, to *feel*. Dionysus has no difficulty in showing this up in rhetoric, at first, and then in inducing Tiresias to dance, which will prove to be the second interrupted dance of its kind, the second prelude of things to come. (The first comes with the vestal virgins, and constitutes a sort of *ars poetica* of the trance, or the surrender of inhibition; following their initial 'liturgical' response, rehearsed or prepared and so lifeless, they relax into immersion. We might here recall Soyinka's own insistence on his understanding of Euripides' play being the theatre's celebration of the theatre. The staging here is clearly an attempt to show the ways we might enter into a dionysiac state, the comparison with mere illusionism being used both thematically, and as a reflection on the genre itself. No doubt this triggered the rather ambitious dimensions of his review of the first production at the National Theatre in London, which he attributed not merely to a failure in production, but rather to a society's inability to understand revolution.[165]) This second interrupted dance, we were saying, comes with Tiresias himself, and easily outmanoeuvres the seer's belated invocation of the tricks of illusionism – the cracking of the crust after Dionysus *'lays hands'* (*BE*, 244) on his shoulders, the entrancement, the moving into rhythm; and then the falling away, to defer fulfilment a little longer.

Through the strong lines of ideological review, then, new shoots of complexity begin to grow. Brecht used to love Shakespeare because of the complexity of his expositions, how no one got off the hook, and I sense a similar creasing in the alterations Soyinka makes to the chorus from Euripides' play, complementary rather than contradictory to Soyinka's insistence that his adaptation belongs under the rubric of 'theatre as community, as idiom of liberation and renewal',[166]

---

[165] See Wole Soyinka, "Between Self and System," *Essays*, 40–61.
[166] Soyinka, "Between Self and System," *Essays*, 47.

to a struggle against a lack of renewal. Take, for instance, the shedding of the alternation between what, in the ancient Greek, as Arrowsmith conjectures, could be a contrast between conviction and possession, attributable perhaps to Euripides' desire to preserve the Bacchantes' ability to separate their humanity from the god, which later becomes important dramatically as they sympathize with Agave.[167] Soyinka's chorus, it would seem, is on the contrary all aspiration to possession, to merging and loss of individuation, well-expressed by the leader's enthusiastic yielding to the power of life, by his talk of the seminal flood, alliances, bonds, great unions, 'the end of separation between man and man' (*BE*, 265), without an evident check or balance or note of restraint. (Consider also the accumulation of synonyms of verbs of ecstasy: shake, retch, melt, swarm, take, swell, grow, move, strain, groan, clutch, thrust, burst, breathe, blow [274-5]. Such verbs are perilous to use for, depending on the production, they could easily collapse into a sort of Mills-and-Boonish genre. The risk of bathos is immense.) In other words, the newly emergent political solidarity as stimulated through Dionysos is also – and this, according to sensibility, will appear paradoxical or effective or contradictory – a stepping beyond the pale of humanity, in 'immortal communion' (272).

This is part of the significance of the expansions of ritual celebration to which Brian Crow has called our attention.[168] Perhaps we are supposed to feel slightly '*overpowered*' by all this, to recall the important stage direction of *The Trials of Brother Jero*[169] – the force of religious ecstasy and something a little darker, which underscores collective abandon. Certainly such a sense, at least in part, seems to be present in the note of

---

[167] Arrowsmith, Introduction to Euripides' *Bacchae*, 152.
[168] Crow, "Soyinka and the Romantic Tradition," 160.
[169] See above, 54.

zealotry which inhabits the voice of the slave leader and which we might see, borrowing from that telling stage-direction which follows on the final unifying of slaves with Bacchantes, as informing the later *'fanatic front'*. In this perspective, it is interesting that Soyinka is careful to qualify Dionysus' victory ('It is not entirely a noble victory' [294]), just as Aroni has qualified Forest Head's dance ('It was not as dignified a dance as it should be' [*ADF*, 5]), the slight hiatus or break between a victory not entirely noble and the uptake of fanaticism undermining the latter at the foundations. The Slave Leader has form in this regard, of course, and we might recall that important early exchange between him and the other slaves:

> SLAVE LEADER: You hesitant fools! Don't you understand? Don't you *know?* We are no longer alone – slaves, helots, the near and distant dispossessed! This master race, this much vaunted dragon spawn have met their match. Nature has joined forces with us. Let them reckon now, not with mere men, not with the scapegoat bogey of a slave uprising but with a new remorseless order, forces unpredictable as molten fire in mountain wombs. To doubt, to hesitate is to prove understanding.
>
> SLAVE: There is such a fault as rashness.
>
> LEADER: When the present is intolerable, the unknown harbours no risks.
>
> ANOTHER: I don't know... why make ourselves conspicuous. Let the free citizens of Thebes declare for this stranger or against him.
>
> LEADER: Whose interest will direct their choice? Ours?
>
> SLAVE: No, but... *The slaves look away from one another, uncomfortable but afraid. After an awkward silence, the Leader sighs in defeat.* [...] *They follow him out guiltily.* (*BE*, 240)

This is more than the jubilant exultation of the imminent

coming of solidarity. Its slight sense of recklessness or abandon, though morally guaranteed by the pain and outrage at the massive human suffering under the House of Pentheus, is expressed in the unqualified welcoming not of controlled redress, but of what he calls 'a remorseless order' with all its terrible unpredictability, the anticipation of something whose actual instancing he cannot know. The hesitations of the group against their leader, in turn, are not mere pusillanimity but rather reasonable reservations – as long as they can imagine something worse, as long as, that is, the present is tolerable even though terrible, risk still carries its dissuasive force – and are in no way assuaged by the leader's assurance that when 'the present is intolerable, the unknown harbours no risks'. At the same time, these are reasonable reservations which, all the same, ensure continued enslavement. I mention these doubts because they in fact persist after the final union of 'the near and distant dispossessed', despite what the stage directions, now seemingly back within the neat perspective of ideological review, call the *'casting off of the long vassalage in the House of Pentheus.'* (294)

This doubt or questioning, as we know, eventually gives way, in the slaves, to participation. At the same time, it seems to be taken up in the character of the Old Slave – an innovation upon Euripides – initially chosen as carrier in the rites of Eleusis, adjudged dispensable by both the royal household he serves (a dogkeeper sacrificed to herald royal renewal) and by a lowly herdsman ('He's old enough to die.' [236]). Soyinka uses the Old Slave to suggest that watching on – 'It is enough to concede awareness of the inexplicable, to wait and watch the unfolding...' (292) – is itself just as susceptible to a language of equivocation and ambivalence. As Dionysus completes his dressing-up (and down) of Pentheus, the Old Slave asks a question whose central notion we have seen in both *A Dance of the Forests* and *The Road* – a variation on cheating fear by anticipation:

> OLD SLAVE: What does it mean life? Dare one hope for better than merely warring, seeking change, seeking the better life? Can we control what threatens before the eruption? Defeat what oppresses by anticipation? Can we? Dare we surrender to what comes after? It is enough to concede awareness of the inexplicable, to wait and watch the unfolding... (292)

Can we defeat what oppresses by anticipation, avoid experience and consequence and issue through a sort of perpetual and canny prolepsis? The quotation clarifies the opposition between rhetoric (words) and reality (events), of which the Old Slave becomes a dramatic expression. In a basic sense, his questions are meaningful only to the extent to which they inform his behaviour, his active participation in life; to the extent to which, that is, they allow him to form general ideas, to sift and sort and judge according to principle – this, and this alone, is the condition of their not being condemned to 'undoing'.[170] The movement of the play, however, has the Old Slave buffeted from one position to the next, his thinking reactions the mere sum of events, his resolutely empirical intelligence incapable of making the creative connections. In *The Road*, through Professor, Soyinka offered a critique of the attempt to bypass experience (death) to get to essence; in *The Bacchae of Euripides*, through the character of the Old Slave, Soyinka is offering a critique of the *inability to get past experience*, a critique of an empirical stance which can only see events as unconnected, isolated, singular. I would like to consider a series of Old Slave's reactions, to events of different type throughout the play:

> OLD SLAVE: He is nothing. A trickster. Windbag. A commonplace illusionist. [...] breeder of false cravings (272)

---

[170] See above, 28-9.

> He stands at the gate of retribution, the tyrant. Shall I pity him? I do not know. (290)
>
> It is enough to concede awareness of the inexplicable, to wait and watch the unfolding... (292)
>
> Headlong he runs to his death, the gods do humble us with death lest we forget we are not such as gods are made of. I say accept, accept. Humility is wise, is blessed. There are great things unfathomable. The mind cannot grasp them. (296)
>
> We know full well that some must die, chosen to bear the burden of decay, lest we will all die – [...] And yet, this knowledge cannot blunt the edge of pain, the cruel nature of this death. Oh this is a heartless Deity, bitter, unnatural in his revenge. (300)
>
> AGAVE: Look at the prize. Is it noble?
>
> OLD SLAVE: It is royal, Agave. Where did you find it? (301)
>
> He knows the way to a death-hunt of the self. (301)

On Dionysus' arrest and imprisonment, the Old Slave switches abruptly from a brief dream of salvation, to self-recrimination (272); he moves from watching on torn and undecided and incapable of decision, as Pentheus is bewitched by Dionysus (290), to an orthodox expression of surrender, the acknowledgement of his limited human understanding before the gods (292); after another expression of orthodoxy, which holds Pentheus' death as proof of humility's lowly wisdom, as the mime builds to its gullet-piercing conclusion (296), he proceeds to shed humility, retracting his former confession (300); his sympathy for Agave is shaped into ironic participation in her disabusal (301); and his final words leave us with the description of what Dionysos' *sophia* seems to have dwindled into, little more than the cunning of an animal (301).

'What does it mean life?' he has asked. Without general ideas, without an intelligence which enables connections, without *principles*, life is simply the aggregate of its disparate events. And the language which befits such an attitude is, appropriately, chameleonic, bent and ordered according to occasion. And so if the Old Slave's point of view never remains anchored in any one stable standpoint in the play; if it is always resistant to assimilation into one exclusive perspective; it is not simply to ensure the theoretical point that there are different ways of perceiving any one event, but at least as much, indeed perhaps even over and beyond, an angle of vision *ultimately diminished* by the very fact of its being amenable to various competing claims, by the very fact of its easy or identity-shorn ventriloquism.

Philip Brockbank once cleverly observed that, in this play, Soyinka 'gets even closer than Euripides to the pathos and absurdity of human ordinariness'.[171] Pentheus, following his first exchange with Tiresias, slaps the Old Slave to the ground for his insolence – the simple language proper to a slave, in his words – before exclaiming: 'Something is wrong with the old men of this city. It affects freemen and slaves alike.' (263) We are of course supposed to feel the cruelty and unjustness of Pentheus here, but his exasperation at Tiresias should also resonate, despite ourselves, with what we have seen in the previous scene – that is, the old men's ordinariness evinced in the extended exchange with Kadmos. This has been prepared: there has earlier been some enjoyment on the author's part, as Tiresias wilts and collapses under the stroke of the lash, the slaves unable or unwilling to preserve the distinction between ritual and reality (241) – after all, people have died for the tyrannical state that Tiresias claims to protect, as he says, for the purposes of a friendship; and further, as we have seen, his disarming and confession in the rhetorical joust with Dionysus.

With Kadmos, however, the 'absurdity of human

---

[171] Brockbank, "Blood and Wine," 86.

ordinariness' is expressed in a few, interrelating ways. The (slightly camp) banter, the pratfalls, what we might suspect to be an intrusive concession to the hand that fed him, the National Theatre in London, are in fact an important part of the scene's intention. They provide stark contrast to the solemn and rehearsed description of dionysiac rites ('He has broken the barrier of age, the barrier of sex or slave and master. It is the will of Dionysus that no one be excluded from his worship.' [255]). More importantly, their private frivolity casts into relief the deliberateness or the public register, which temporarily surfaces, and in between the two we do not feel that there is any necessary connection. This is where the importance of old age lies. We have read Tennyson's 'Ulysses', and know that the dullness of a pause, of making an end, might successfully be countered by some work of noble note, an ultimate striving. With Kadmos, however, we are never afforded the assurance that he remains a part of all that he has met. His epithet 'sower of dragon's teeth' comes hard upon talk of 'trad or trendy' crowns, of difficult join for the audience; perhaps it is this sense of the 'inarticulate' that triggers the following reflection about his past:

> KADMOS: From a life which constantly rejuvenated my bones I sat down and became an administrator. An administrator Tiresias! Then an old-age pensioner – on the court list. I who slew the dragon and bred a race of warriors from his teeth. (254)

In Soyinka's play, the line 'Where shall we tread this dance of life, tossing our white heads to the drums of Dionysus' (254), reworked from Arrowsmith's Euripides ('Where shall we go, where shall we tread the dance, tossing our white heads in the dances of god?' [1.183-4]), has its lyricism greatly qualified by pratfall, and Kadmos' subsequent talk of staging a *coup d'état* comes perilously close to the realm of childishness, of ingenuousness, the flipside of renewed energies.

In his discussion of 'contact' and 'discontinuity' on the ancient Greek stage – that is, the sliding scale of alertness which an individual has with his surrounding as a whole, or to other individuals on the stage – Donald Mastronarde has shown how technical spatial innovations, alterations in the conventionalized exploitation of separate areas of theatre-space, for instance in entrances and exits, came to offer new dramatic possibilities. For example, by the end of the fifth-century BC, as Euripides was writing, a newcomer on stage could speak in 'isolation from contact' as he or she approached the main scene of action; he or she could preserve 'partial vision', coming into contact with only part of the scene; or again, and more suggestively, there could be a lack of contact despite what appears to be direct address.[172] One of Euripides' most effective exploitations of partial contact, of discontinuity, comes at the end of his *Bacchae*. Dionysus' weak response to Cadmus' criticism of the harshness of his judgement – 'I am a god. I was blasphemed by you. – Gods should be exempt from human passions. – Long ago my father Zeus ordained these things.' (1.1346–1348) – issues from on high, and, as the scene continues, as the grieving humans seek to console one another, Dionysus falls out of contact:

AGAVE: I pity you, Father.

CADMUS: And I pity you, my child, and I grieve for your poor sisters. I pity them.

AGAVE: Terribly has Dionysus brought disaster down upon this house.

DIONYSUS: I was terribly blasphemed, my name dishonoured in Thebes.

AGAVE: Farewell, Father.

---

[172] See Donald J. Mastronarde, *Contact and Discontinuity: Some Conventions of Speech and Action on the Greek Tragic Stage* (Berkeley, Los Angeles; London: University of California Press, 1979), particularly chs.2 and 5.

CADMUS: Farewell to you, unhappy child. Fare well.
But you shall find your faring hard. (1.1373-1380)

With the god speaking above, in epiphany, the gulf separating the gods from the humans is rendered spatially, and given psychological coherence in the spatial terms of the Greek stage.

In Soyinka's *Bacchae*, in response to the seer's yearning to 'feel the taste of blood instead of merely foreseeing it' (*BE*, 243), Dionysus has earlier stated: 'Tiresias will know ecstasy' (244). (It is striking that Tiresias has used the dissonance between 'feeling the taste of blood' and fore*seeing* the feel of the taste of blood – for how do we pass from seeing to touching? – to express his isolation from sensual endowment.) As we approach Soyinka's ending, we must ask not simply what 'ecstasy' means – and by extension, communion – but also, how it is expressed. Unlike Euripides' ending, Soyinka's play does not end with Agave's emergence from ecstasy into grievous clarity under an open sky. No longer is a pathos-ridden lament before Necessity – 'Why us? – Why not?' – the closing moment, no longer is consolation only to be had in human compassion. Rather, those words form the prelude to the new ending; which is to say that one structural difference between tragedy and communion rite, between Euripides' *Bacchae* and Soyinka's adaptation, comes in the extension of the former beyond suffering into truth.

I think we would do well to retain Mastronarde's spatial terms. In Soyinka's adaptation, the god is no longer represented on high, his fading or even petulant voice ignored by the parting humans who, immersed in their own grief, gain what little consolation they can from solidarity; no longer is the god looking on from above – the path away from all true communion, cut off from earth, as Professor might have said (*TR*, 158); nor is he figured, given physical expression on the stage. (Indeed, his final physical appearance comes as he warns the Bacchantes of Pentheus' imminent arrival [*BE*, 294].) Rather is Dionysos' presence expressed in music, *'welling up and filling the stage with the god's presence.'* (307) – which is to say, that the characters, variously emergent from what they take to be the final dionysiac expression, are suddenly immersed in a different form of presence. This sense of being immersed and lost in a presence, expressed through music, which tends in all directions, has been prepared from the opening scenes, with the slave leader's calling 'Evohe-e-e-e!': *'The sound is taken up by echoes from the hills. It roves round and round and envelops the scene. All heads turn outwards in different directions, listening. A mixture of excitement and unease as the sound continues, transformed beyond the plain echo to an eerie response from vast distances.'* (239)

This does not mean that consolation is easy, or that we understand just what it is that we are coming into. The conjunction of blood and wine of the final scene has tended to dominate our readings of the play. It seems to me, however, that eliding the function of music in this final scene is to elide an essential point: the fact that communion, 'ecstasy', in this context, lies beyond our ratiocinations, our rhetorical calculations, our human linguistic expertise. Communion, or 'ecstasy', is, it would seem, a sudden sense of bewildered immersion which *music,* and music alone, can best provide for and express. This may be difficult to understand in the abstract,[173] and it is no doubt quite a considerable dramaturgical risk to tie such a crucial moment to music; but I do not think that it is, for that, any less important an innovation upon

---

[173] We might think of Soyinka's words in "The Fourth Stage", *Essays*, 31: 'Language in Yoruba music [...] transcends particularization (of meaning) to tap the tragic source whence spring the familiar weird disruptive melodies. This masonic union of sign and melody, the true tragic music, unearths cosmic uncertainties which pervade human existence, reveals

Euripides' own spatial solutions; and nor do I think, lastly, that we should be deaf to the possibilities which music can bring, in nearing us, just possibly, to something *'dream-like'* (307), a deeper awareness beyond our discursive capacities.

---

the magnitude and power of creation, but above all creates a harrowing sense of omni-directional vastness where the creative Intelligence resides and prompts the soul to futile exploration. The senses do not at such moments interpret myth in their particular concretions, we are left only with the emotional and spiritual values, the essential experience of cosmic reality.'

Coda

The Burden of Memory: Of Senghor, and the Language of Forgiveness

> What is Hecuba to him, or he to Hecuba?
> – Wole Soyinka, *The Burden of Memory,*
> *The Muse of Forgiveness* [174]

In this coda, I would like to consider a curious thread in Soyinka's characterization of Léopold Sédar Senghor, against (and, I hope, in complement to) what we have seen in the discussion of the previous chapter: how might the language of music, in a *theoretical* context, be related to the language of justice? The underlying assumption is that we would do well to remain constantly attentive to the conditions of Soyinka's reception of 'Negritude', lest we cede too quickly, despite the advantages of historical perspective we may entertain, to the temptations of reducing the entire movement to a few philosophical premises; we would do well, that is, to recall how 'Negritude' was distilled (and, I would add, rendered, or made partial) into and through Léopold Sédar Senghor, how the language employed, which claimed as its sole alibi the object of Negritude, was aalso, perhaps primarily even, depending on the instance or impulse, a response to Senghor, which is to say, a response to whichever creative and intellectual and artistic responses were elicited and provoked in Soyinka by

---

[174] Wole Soyinka, *The Burden of Memory, The Muse of Forgiveness* (Oxford; New York: Oxford University Press, 1999), 106.

listening to and reading Senghor.[175] The discussion comes with the late lecture series which he delivered at Harvard University in 1995 during his Abacha-exile (1994–1998), subsequently published as *The Burden of Memory, The Muse of Forgiveness*. The general and difficult moral problem which is the subject of *The Burden of Memory, The Muse of Forgiveness* concerns the ways in which human societies, and more particularly their procedures of justice, can deal with massive human rights violations. The Argentine political philosopher Carlos Santiago Nino has usefully clarified this bind between mechanisms of justice and their moral aspect using the (Kantian) philosophical notion of 'radical evil' – that is, 'offenses against human dignity so widespread, persistent, and organized that normal moral assessment seems inappropriate.'[176] His study is intended as a corrective to Hannah Arendt's cooption of the notion, in her discussion of the Nuremberg trials, her sense that we 'are unable to forgive what [we] cannot punish and that [we] are unable to punish what has turned out to be unforgivable.'[177] In other words, the idea that radical evil stands beyond punishment and forgiveness, and therefore the possibilities of human power. Soyinka's reflection, which becomes, as we

---

[175] Abiola Irele's scholarship, contemporary to Soyinka's literary output, has provided consistent evidence of Negritude's complexities, and should further warn us against limiting our understanding of Soyinka's reception of the movement to a few philosophical premises. See Abiola Irele, *The African Experience in Literature and Ideology* (London: Indiana University Press, 1981); *The African Imagination: Literature in Africa and the Black Diaspora* (New York: Oxford University Press, 2001); and *Négritude et condition africaine* (Paris: Editions Karthala, 2008), which includes an interesting preface by Olabiyi Yai. The publication dates of the last two should not obscure the fact that their individual chapters often date from decades earlier.

[176] Carlos Santiago Nino, *Radical Evil On Trial* (New Haven; London: Yale University Press, 1996), vii.

[177] Quoted in *ibid.*, viii.

shall see, a foray into the moral universe of forgiveness, is book-ended by two contemporary responses to the 'radical evil' of apartheid and the transatlantic slave trade. He asks:

> How on earth does one reconcile reparations, or recompense, with reconciliation or remission of wrongs? Dare we presume that both, in their differing ways, are committed to ensuring the righting of wrongs and the triumph of justice?[178]

And his response, which we are never allowed to forget or elide, is clear: reconciliation or remission lacks those two ingredients essential to justice, the moral element of remorse and the material element of reparation.

This is, of course, consistent with any number of literary instances throughout the chronological run of his work. There is a simple example of the uses of forgiveness in *The Trials of Brother Jero* in which Amope, initially surprised by her husband Chume's keen negligence of the precarious balance upon which complaint depends – silence as passive, rather than the silencing which a beating suggests – begins to call on those around her:

> AMOPE: [Chume's] going to kill me so come and bear witness. I forgive everyone who has ever done me evil. I forgive all my debtors especially the Prophet who has got me into all this trouble. Prophet Jeroboam, I hope you will pray for my soul in heaven...
>
> CHUME: You have no soul, wicked woman.
>
> AMOPE: Brother Jeroboam, curse this man for me. You may keep the velvet cape if you curse this foolish man. I forgive you your debt. Go on, foolish man, kill me. [*warming up as more people arrive.*] Bear witness all of you. Tell the prophet I forgive him his debt but he must curse this foolish man to hell. (*TBJ*, 166)

---

[178] Wole Soyinka, *The Burden of Memory, The Muse of Forgiveness*, 23-4.

This riff on forgiveness we readily understand, the readiness with which it might be invoked under expediency; but, at the same time, and this is the essential counterpoint, that even expediency does *not* yield to unconditional offer, but still predicates forgiveness on reciprocity, which in this comic instance, lies in Jero's cursing the foolish husband to hell.

In the altogether more complex ethical context of *The Burden of Memory*, Soyinka is able to draw upon historical examples. The ANC's political decision to institute the Truth and Reconciliation Commission in *de jure* post-apartheid South Africa enacts a few perplexing ambiguities which can never be resolved; which are, indeed, inevitable where recompense is precluded from the workings of justice. In the commission's stagings, the onlooker can never be sure whether she or he is before a mere illusion of justice, the formal staging of its motions, or actual justice, whether before a (perverse and outrageous) game of shadows or mimicry, or a genuine prelude to reconciliation; like the slaves lashing the old seer Tiresias, we cannot tell ritual and reality apart. Ultimately, then, the exposition of Truth or information is not enough; Truth 'as the justification, as the sole exaction or condition for Reconciliation' (*TBM*, 13), requires a complement in matters of justice, despite the undeniable importance of the exposition of fact, and its therapeutic aspect against civic alienation. Truth alone does not set us free.

At the same time, a constitutive rhythm of these lectures, heuristic, exploratory, is the constant departure from this basic stance, the inhabiting of alternatives. Jean Starobinski, in a skilful monograph on Montaigne, sought to trace Montaigne's 'movement' from an initial observation of pessimistic philosophy's repudiation of illusory appearances; from an originary stance which accepted the existence of artifice and dissimulation all around him; to this (negative) stance's logical consequences, paradoxically expressed in Montaigne's writing project – that is, a constant search for balance between two poles, which 'finds paradox, and can from that moment on no longer find rest.'[179] Here, the terms are different, but the principle of a constant search for balance issuing from the consequences of an originary (here positive) *prise de position*, is the same: from recompense as a constitutive element of justice, Soyinka constantly reaches out to powerful contemporary instances of non-retributive justice, instances which cannot be dismissed, which demand acknowledgement.

We earlier spoke of Soyinka's attraction to conversions.[180] Conversion, we suggested, provided a humorous way of undermining the curious pretensions of alienated Africans to deny their cultural heritage, to block up their ears and eyes and minds. The ensuing lack of assurance, Nuttall's oscillatory constant, provides a simple technique for staging their susceptibilities, the vulnerabilities of voluntary memory. In such a perspective, Senghor is out of the ordinary, in Soyinka's eyes, precisely because he evinces *no* oscillatory constant. This is cleverly expressed in *The Burden of Memory*, regarding Senghor's view on the destiny of Negritude, a view, says Soyinka,

> that underwent various degrees of refinement in an outpouring of poetry, essays, and near-obsessive private conversations, but retained its core creed. Indeed, as Senghor grew older and memory impaired, it became a common and rather sad experience for his associates, young or old, to encounter him at an event, or at his home, and immediately find themselves drawn into the same discourse in Paris or Stockholm at the very point at which it terminated five, ten, sometimes fifteen years before in Dakar or Tunis. [...] That discourse, unsettling in the precision with which Senghor would resume it with you from a ten-year suspension, as if it had been interrupted only yesterday, is summed up in his

---

[179] Jean Starobinski, *Montaigne en mouvement* (Paris: Gallimard, 1982), 7.
[180] See above, 30.

contribution to the Second Congress of Black Writers and Artists in Rome [...] (135-6)

This passage, it would seem, works to weaken the structural hierarchy between reality and the dream, to superpose them, to suggest homology. This eternally spinning and inhumanly unchanging fiction of 'unsettling precision' (how would Soyinka know, unless he too had memorized the speech?), focused in the present in that slightly unreal situation, the televised recording of his French garden, shrouds Senghor here, I think, in a light senility, freezes him in an embrace with an idea which he once had, but which has, for some time since, had him. Is it not the greatest of accusations, the most acute of elbow-jabs, that in a reflection on memory, on memory as necessary to securing lasting renewal, Senghor should be portrayed, here, as trapped in perpetual feedback, a tireless self-address, still, after all these years, impermeable to history?

Prudence or a certain modesty or clerkly scepticism, however, is in order before swift clutching at Soyinka's renderings of 'Negritude', and wherever there is a failure to define the contours of the object, particularly in polemical instances, we would do well to ask ourselves, as with the grand political announcement, what else is going on. One of the most strikingly obvious points is the following: that of all the most resolute critics of the movement, it is Soyinka who returns to it most often, he who seems most unwilling to accept its irrelevance. In 1963, all youthful zing, he remarks that it 'is futile now to knock negritude; it is far more useful to view it as a historical phenomenon and to preserve the few truly creative pieces that somehow emerged in spite of its philosophical straitjacket.'[181] Three decades later, we read the following:

> Even then, however, in those early days, there was a niggling suspicion in the mind, indeed, one that was often

---

[181] Soyinka, "From a Common Backcloth," 8.

implicit in the very language and focus of rejection in the turbulent sixties, that it was not so much the message that was contested as the messenger himself, both as medium and mediator. (*TBM*, 96)

One suggestive means of linking historically the early literary and critical writings to this reflection, three decades later, comes, I think, in that core creed which Soyinka has cited Senghor as citing, concerning the destiny of Negritude, its historical role as being 'leaven for the exhausted dough of European humanity' (135); that is to say, 'Negritude', or Senghor, as sacrifice, as sacrificial gesture. With Eman in *The Strong Breed*, we saw Soyinka's skilled working of the figure of sacrifice and, more to our purposes here, of sacrifice as consummation, as expressive of the sort of love which transcends the human. Philip Brockbank writes beautifully of certain 'antinomies of tragic response' on the part of the sacrificial victim which have literary precedent – whether in Euripides' Iphigenia 'recoiling from the cruelty and arbitrariness of premature death [...] yet attracted, under the pressure of necessity, by its apparently sublime significance'; or Soyinka's Eman and Elesin, in the concurrent expression of willingness and unwillingness, in the evasions and ambiguities available to the artist within the formal mould of sacrifice, the singing of the dying-into-life process and a dissenting form which cries out against it.[182] The ambivalence of Negritude's destiny, then, is precisely the ambiguity of the meaning of transcendence, of sacrifice.

And it is just such an 'antinomy of response' which Senghor holds and clarifies, in life as in poetry, and that Soyinka here uses to enter and explore that alternative universe, a universe of forgiveness, the 'theology of accommodativeness', which assures passage between aesthetic and moral concerns. Senghor's sacrificial gesture, his offering up of the black race as

---

[182] Brockbank, "Blood and Wine," 82.

the object of sacrifice, to assure the redemption of its oppressors, is expressed in the poetic imagery of 'Prayer for Peace' in *Hosties Noires*, as well as, for Soyinka, 'much of Senghor's poetic advocacies' (*TBM*, 116), an 'informing urge' which always tends towards forgiveness, to the remission of sins (98). And yet what we have earlier called the paradox of inhumanity ensures a constant tension. On the one hand, the transcendence of forgiveness as a gesture which is inhuman because striving to do away with human memory, with human experience, with human desire for vengeance or even simply recompense – 'Senghor's inhuman heart of forgiveness – yes, inhuman, because near super-human, transcendental' (113-4) – and, with Senghor, we always suspect, a gesture that is slightly perverse in its expression.[183] And on the other, the question as to whether this faculty which Senghor displays might also be a source of admiration, whether this harder price, this price harder to come by than the paths of vengeance, might, in its transcendence or inhumanity, show up *our own* ordinariness or weak moral imagination, and thereby provide us not with an example to flee, but an example to which we might rightfully aspire.

Perhaps, then, the 'narcissism' which Soyinka had spoken of in 'And After the Narcissist?', three decades ere, so different in tone, is, nonetheless, of the same universe as this one of transcendence and inhumanity and remission, for all, it would seem, are dependent on a certain forgetfulness, on an unloosing of the burden of memory (memory understood as historical complexity and understanding), the momentary peace which that can bring.[184] What

can we claim is truly left of the autonomy of Negritude,

---

[183] Soyinka, *The Burden of Memory*, 107: 'When laudatory lines by the victim enhance such claims, it resounds like a poetic kiss of absolution on the ring of the whiphand.'

[184] Wole Soyinka, "And After the Narcissist?" *African Forum*, Vol. 1, No.4 (Spring, 1966), 53-64.

of the repleteness of its conceptual being, if indeed, as Senghor proclaimed, its destiny was to be leaven for the exhausted dough of European humanity? (*TBM*, 135)

One way of trying to answer this might come, I think, with the subtle word 'repleteness', with the notion of plenitude, and it is to three examples that I turn by way of conclusion to this chapter.

We see the word 'replete' in Soyinka's attack on academic formalism, mediated through Barthes' *Mythologies*, where it is used as part of his armoury to express a paradoxical notion: 'the paradox of music', writes our author, 'is that it exploits the incompletion of *langue* to transcend language. It is truly a form "in solution", even at its most replete'.[185] Music's elliptical nature, he continues, 'paradoxically projects the existence of this replete, structural reality.'[186] Music, then – and the rhetorical purpose of this point, a polemic or moment of contestation, does not in any way diminish the idea – derives its capacity to express fullness, from its constitutive incompletion, from the fact that it never aspires to the hermetic or bound formalism of theory; its condition, that is, to express and project completion just as it must then gesture beyond itself, just as it must then intimate that, for all our involvement, for all its fullness, the plenitude is but momentary.

In *Aké*, published in 1983, there is an episode which we might entitle 'The Rock and the Guava Tree', which begins thus:

> Even the baobab has shrunk with time, yet I had imagined that this bulwark would be eternal, beyond the growing perspectives of a vanished childhood. Its girth has dwindled with time and the branches now give only a little shade. (*Aké*, 63)

---

[185] Wole Soyinka, "The Critic and Society: Barthes, Leftocracy and Other Mythologies" [1982], *Essays*, 111.
[186] *Ibid.*, 111.

The technical ambiguity of this opening is quite striking. We begin with a present perfect, the narrator considering the baobab as it stands before him, and the pluperfect moves us further back in time, back to a former imagining which now stands corrected. The temporal dissonance comes with the present participle 'growing' against the past participle 'vanished', for either the narrator had imagined that the tree would stand undiminished by time within his childhood ('beyond the growing perspectives of childhood'), *or* once that childhood had vanished ('beyond the perspectives of a vanished childhood') – but not both. Perhaps the logical contradictions here, as expressed through tense, speak to what the Empsonians used to call a 'fundamental division in the writer's mind', though Empson's seventh type of ambiguity, as Yemi Ogunbiyi found out in a different context (and presumably Empson well knew), is best reserved for authors departed.[187] The more seductive (and respectful?) line, which I prefer, is that the passage bespeaks the narrator's desire to recapture and relive that imperviousness to time which he felt as a child before the reductions administered through understanding, just as it simultaneously expresses, through the dissonance in tense, the impossibility of the enterprise.

Indeed this sense of wishing to forget the diminutions administered by explanation, the loss of shade provided by the branches, is illustrated in miniature in the two episodes subsequently narrated. The first, the case of the rock which comes to be called Jonah, in which the young protagonist had experienced moments of solitude and privacy, sinking

---

[187] See William Empson, *Seven Types of Ambiguity* (Middlesex: Penguin, 1930), ch.7. Yemi Ogunbiyi's Empsonian impudence – 'The kind of ambiguity I refer to here relates to that statement or statements so fundamentally contradictory that they reveal a basic division or even contradiction in the author's mind' – is slapped down in Soyinka's "The Critic and Society," *Essays,* 104-5.

'through its broad back into deep immobility' (64), only for that sense to be lost as it is drafted into the teacher's story:

> It did not sound wholly improbable but it did belong in a world of fables, of the imagination, of Aladdin's lamp and Open Sesame. Whereas before... I experienced the passing of a unique confidant, the loss of a replete, subsuming presence. (64)

This is a complex idea beautifully expressed: the coming into awareness, into the correspondences of knowledge (or 'knowledge') as the experience of loss, as the receding of a full presence. And again, in the presence of the guava tree, 'its indefinable assurance of swallowing time, making it cease to exist.' (65) These two episodes reproduce the gesture of that opening technical ambiguity: the recovery through memory of an anterior harmony or plenitude, as we briefly enter that moment of past repletion, although all the while, we can never forget that we are in retrospect, and stand among the receding shadows.

Our final example comes with the Nimba mask of the Baga, which 'threatens and encroaches on the viewer's sense of adequate being, leaving no route for the individual except to weld his ego into the security of that community of being'; a mask whose 'infolding aesthetic' and envelopment of its people 'in the plenitude of its womb' leads, 'despite the threat to individuation, despite the abundant tyranny of this mass', to a final experience of 'lofty serenity, a quiet, enfolding haven to all who participate in what would otherwise be an insupportable burden of thought-procreation'.[188] Here, before and within the dance of the Nimba mask – or rather, Soyinka's imagining and revitalizing of the dance of the mask, enshrined or encased in immobility, offered up to the gaze of the

---

[188] Wole Soyinka, "The External Encounter: Ambivalence in African Arts and Literature" [1985], *Essays*, 163, 164.

museum-goer — we are held, in danger and security, under tyranny and protection, our individuation threatened and reaffirmed, in a harmony which is momentary, constantly toppling over or under 'exponential' threat, as Soyinka quotes William Fagg as saying of African sculpture,[189] something like the very principle of harmony, its momentariness.

The Burden of Memory, The Muse of Forgiveness concludes with a recollection. The Sosso-bala, instrument and symbol of the Mandingo empire, is played — in its first ever outing — in Paris, at UNESCO, for Senghor's ninetieth birthday celebration — the lyric poet who celebrated the instrument, in turn celebrated. The music's harmony, writes Soyinka, 'enfolded the gathering in a mantle of humanity that excluded none', was a 'dirge of ancestral severance' and yet 'filled with evocation of a quiescent triumph that is an extract of human resilience, of a shedding of individuation into a tide of universal affirmation of a humane oneness.' (*TBM*, 193) He continues, and I must quote in full:

> Perhaps it is within this territory that lodges the impulse of forgiveness, since oneness eschews distinctions and makes war and peace, creativity and destruction, guilt and innocence, Negritude and tigritude, Senghor and Depestre, all facets of an irreducible humanity and thus steers that dichotomized, even fragmented entity toward a resolution within an anterior harmony. [...] such glimpses and echoes of the possibilities of harmonization do surface periodically as consolation, and can open up horizons for a humanized vision. Within such a context, the Sosso-bala becomes an unsolicited metaphor for the near intolerable burden of memory, a Muse for the poetry of identity and that elusive 'leaven' in the dough of humanity — forgiveness, the remission of wrongs, and a recovery of lost innocence. (193-4)

---

[189] *Ibid.*, 164.

The 'territory' of which Soyinka speaks – and that spatial sense well expresses the musical moment, I think; the way in which it is a presence – is a moral space precisely to the extent to which it enfolds, includes, resolves difference in the renewing movement of return to 'an anterior harmony', to the extent to which it enables us to come back together once more, despite it all. Forgiveness here is no longer 'the leaven of European humanity', but rather the leaven of humanity *tout court*. And yet observe how those final words of the Nimba quote – 'an insupportable burden of thought-procreation' – foreshadow the terms of this conclusion ('the near intolerable burden of memory'), for both speak, just like music's ellipsis, or the receding of the branches, or the exponential dance, of how that unity or harmony or communion which comes through remission is, by definition, but fleeting, a momentary concord or respite only, a brief reprieve from the pressures of knowledge, of history, of individuation; both make it clear that the consolations of remission are dependent on our acknowledgement of its passing.

IV

The Language of Being and Non-Being

> Descartes, on the other hand, would probably become an American citizen if he should return.
> — Chinua Achebe, 'The Writer and his Community'[190]

We now turn to more specific concepts of individuation, as expressed in literature, in tragedy, to the craft and resource which the tragic artist might bring to render such concepts. Soyinka's essay 'The Fourth Stage: Through the Mysteries of Ogun to the Origin of Yoruba Tragedy', first published in 1973, begins not with a definition of tragedy, but rather with the acknowledgement of the limits of any definition, the way definitions might gesture towards something real and felt, and in the same motion fall short:

> of all the subjective unease that is aroused by man's creative insight, that wrench within the human psyche which we vaguely define as 'tragedy' is the most insistent voice that bids us return to our own sources. There, illusively, hovers the key to the human paradox, to man's experience of being and non-being, his dubiousness as essence and matter, intimations of transience and eternity, and the harrowing drives between uniqueness and Oneness.[191]

---

[190] Chinua Achebe, "The Writer and his Community," in *Hopes and Impediments: Selected Essays 1965-1987* (Oxford: Heinemann, 1988), 34.
[191] Wole Soyinka, "The Fourth Stage: Through the Mysteries of Ogun to the Origin of Yoruba Tragedy" [1973], *Essays*, 27.

Beyond the quite irresistible 'illusively' (elusively?), which rather casts doubt over the whole enterprise to come, this passage expresses in the slightly grand register to which we have become accustomed in definitions of tragedy – 'Few artistic forms have inspired such extraordinarily pious waffle', notes Terry Eagleton in general terms,[192] and he is right – a concrete and important literary problem: in what ways does tragedy test our fundamental conceptions of existence ('man's experience of being and non-being'), probe them, and break them down, even ('the harrowing drives')?

We have come to learn that Soyinka's conceptions of being, against a Yoruba backcloth, derive from Ogun; and that Ogun means assertion, venturousness, virility, daring, to say no more. Yet there is a quite important side of Ogun which we neglect at our peril; an introspective side, held in the *oriki's*[193] beautiful and terrifying salutation to the 'lone being, who swims in rivers of blood.'[194] The aim of this chapter is to explore, as concretely as possible, what might be a few implications for *language* in these two divergent and complementary threads, in two separate contexts. In approaching *The Man Died* (1972), Soyinka's prison memoirs, we might ask ourselves what happens when a philosophy which depends on assertion and experience and venturing forth is curtailed and pressured and broken down by terrible solitude, by literal poverty. Secondly, we will proceed from a discussion of a few (West-)African conceptions of being as

---

[192] Terry Eagleton, *Sweet Violence: The Idea of the Tragic* (Oxford: Blackwell Publishing, 2003), 16.
[193] The word *'oriki'* is most commonly translated into English as 'praise-song'. For a full and nuanced discussion of the rhetorical range of *oriki* in a concrete Yoruba context, see Karin Barber's *I Could Speak Until Tomorrow*: Oriki, *Women, and the Past in a Yoruba Town* (Edinburgh: Edinburgh University Press, 1991).
[194] Soyinka, "The Fourth Stage," 28.

addressed by Kwasi Wiredu and Chinua Achebe, to Soyinka's *Myth, Literature and the African World,* a series of lectures which Soyinka gave in the department of anthropology at Cambridge University, in the academic year 1973-4 (first published in 1976). In our discussion, we seek to link the Yoruba conceit of the 'world' as a journey, and the dangers associated with Ogun's archetypal journey, to those which inhere, too, in a certain strand of Yoruba oral poetic resource.

1

The Man Died: Solitude

John Agetua's early anthology of responses to Soyinka's prison autobiography[195] is quite lively: Soyinka-the-narrow-Yoruba-jingoist (Adamu Ciroma), Soyinka-the-potentially-notable-writer-whose-work-we-only-praise-greatly-at-the-risk-of-inverse-racism (O'Brien), Soyinka-the-skilled-manipulator (Peter Enahoro), Soyinka-the-garrulous-author-who-has-no-iota-of-respect-for-truth (Sobo Sowemimo). A conciliatory note is struck by Abiola Irele, when he remarks that over and above Soyinka's petulance, motivated perhaps in part by a desire to provoke,

> it is probably unfair to insist on a certain order of limitations in a book whose obvious purpose is less a detached analysis than the expression of a general mood of dissidence and the declaration of a moral stand.[196]

This has the right elements, I think, but in seeking to accommodate and attenuate the content of Soyinka's outbursts, glides by an essential structural principle of the book. We come closer with Kole Omotoso's reading, which places emphasis on the continuation and elaboration, in the prison account, of Soyinka's 'basic concern for physically and mentally strained and constrained humanity'.[197] For a

---

[195] *When the Man Died: Views, Reviews and Interviews on Wole Soyinka's controversial book,* ed. John Agetua (Benin City: Bendel Newspapers Corporation, 1975), 11; 14; 15; 23.
[196] *Ibid.,* 8.
[197] *Ibid.,* 18-19.

constitutive part of the book's meaning, it seems to me, comes quite exactly in the literary techniques which come in to play, as the limitations to which the protagonist is subjected tighten and intensify.

In truth, what I have called 'Soyinka's prison autobiography' lacks a key nuance, and that nuance is both of genre, and, as corollary, of point of view. The full title of the prose account is *The Man Died: Prison Notes of Wole Soyinka*. This neatly expresses, I think, the *two* generic dictates under which he wrote and organized the work: that of autobiography – 'a retrospective prose narrative written by a real person concerning his own existence, where the focus is his individual life, in particular the story of his personality', as Lejeune's influential definition of the 'autobiographical pact' once had it[198] – *and* that of the diary, that is the 'recording' of private experiences and reflections more or less as they arise – the scribbling between the lines of Paul Radin's *Primitive Religion* or his own *Idanre*, various 'fragments of plays, poems, a novel and portions of the prison notes which make up this book.' (*TMD*, 9) My sense is that, at certain particularly charged moments of the account, these two are brought together, superimposed even, so that we cannot quite be sure as to whether we are reading the private account of the self more or less as it undergoes experience, a form of self-address, or whether we are before retrospective recollection, the public appeal to justice. This generic and temporal ambiguity is focussed in the present tense.

One fairly straightforward example comes in the first part of the title. The phrase 'The man died', which appears a few times over the course of the account, does not inhabit one meaning – despite the emblematic significance which that

---

[198] Philippe Lejeune, *On Autobiography*, trans. Katherine Leary (Minneapolis: University of Minnesota Press, 1989), 4.

solemn sentence 'The man dies in all who keep silent in the face of tyranny' has come to take (13) – but rather is nuanced according to context. Its first appearance comes in the first chapter, the 'letter to compatriots', which stands outside the retrospective narrative of the prison experience (it is dated 14 December 1971) – the necessary remove for the constitutive generic appeal to justice to hold; indeed it comes in an explanation as to why it was adopted as title. Soyinka receives a cable that very morning, we read, with those simple words, 'The Man Died'; the words trigger associations in his mind:

> I was struck first by the phrasing. It sounded weird, yet familiar. Its familiarity was that of the ending to a moral tale, a doggerel – 'the dog it was that died', a catechumenical pronouncement, the eyes of a surgeon above the mask, or the surprise of a torturer that misjudged his strength. I heard the sound in many different voices from the past and from the future. It seemed to me that this really is the social condition of tyranny – the man died, a dog died, the matter is dead.
>
> The man dies in all who keep silent in the face of tyranny.
>
> The dog of this immediate death was a journalist, Segun Sowemimo. (13)

How to express the death of a man, at a time in which enough death has been seen and lived for lifetimes over, in which death has become familiar, and that very familiarity perplexing? It is the uncanniness of the expression ('weird, yet familiar') that slaps Soyinka hard and cold. I, in turn, am struck by the psychologically convincing way in which his mind grasps at situations and registers which might house and hold and explain the phrase, but which end up merely suggesting open pathways, from ditty to rote-liturgy to medical routine-pronouncement to the final and most complex torture situation (who is speaking? an onlooker, perhaps? or somebody discussing what to do following the fatal inadvertence?); and by the way in which this private imagining is textured by voice, voices heard within, in memory, through the channels of the imagination. As the passage continues, the word 'death' and its cognates cast a light of different shade and hue, the better to gesture towards our more complex and historically darkened understanding of what death and deadness and dying has come to mean, following the genocidal massacres, the torture, the imprisonments, the war. Notice how the phrase-ending 'the matter is dead', which constitutes the climax of the sentence, recalls an old association: dog and man collapsed into the impersonal or bureaucratic category of 'general file', life reduced to matter. And more, how there is a sense that Soyinka is momentarily stepping into the voice of tyranny itself, the voice of shrugging indifferentiation, as the definite article, which speaks to identity, passes into the indefinite article, the sense that this is just one among many so why care? – 'dog' is taken up shortly afterwards, as we shall see – and that 'matter is dead', the final word of the administration as it eschews acknowledgement of its perpetrations.

I have spoken of voice, because the sense of internal dialogue, of self-address structured as dialogue, whether loud or inconspicuous, has some importance in the account, and we should be alive to its importance. Indeed, those sentences which Soyinka quotes of George Mangakis, at the time imprisoned in Greece, and Soyinka's own gloss, should be taken extremely seriously in our attempts to understand parts of the account, the undertows of the prose: '[...] we need somebody else's mind in order to keep on working terms with our own. We also need moments devoid of thought', remarks Mangakis, and Soyinka follows: 'I testify to the strange, sinister by-ways of the mind in solitary confinement, to the strange monsters it begets.' (12) Here, it is just that unstated ventriloquism which triggers a sudden stridency and outrage, the reaction of the human to the inhuman – 'The man dies in all who keep silent in the face of tyranny'. 'Death' now has a less physical pallor than what has come before, as the general sense is now moving in the problematic moral direction of 'passive injustice', of those who sit on and watch and later say they could do nothing, or knew nothing. And yet there is still time for a final sudden change in perspective. For immediately afterwards, that strident aphorism flows into the brutal reminder of what could and did happen, the man who died, Segun Sowemimo, beaten to death because he was adjudged *not* to have kept silent in the face of tyranny, because of an 'imagined slight' (13) against a Military Governor of the Western Region. The subtle angles of perspective result in a greater moral density, a more complex expression of the many facets death has come to take on, in the grievous wake of the Nigerian civil war.

There is one last appearance of the phrase. It comes at the end of an episode in which Soyinka, encrypted in solitary confinement, has heard the hollowed voices of winnowed women singing, the urgent cry of a new-born, and – death in life – the rhythmed groaning and unrelenting pulse of an inmate who is yet on the threshold of death:

> It is close to dawn when the sound stops. Abruptly. No weakening ever, neither faltering nor a rallying intensity. I know it is over. My body is straining for the lightest sounds. One man has got up, he is gone near the silence to enquire. Others sit up in their beds, a few join the first by the bed. A minute later I hear the murmuring of prayers. The prayers continue until the doors are open. A warder steps in, pauses, shouts for his superior.
>
> Soon it is that hour when 'all the dead awake'. As the key turns in my lock I ask the warder what became of the suffering man.
>
> 'The man died,' he said. (200)

A retrospective account might use the present tense's gift of urgency (or 'vividness', as we were taught at school), without letting the reader forget the retrospective angle of vision. Here, however, such a possibility cannot account for the incredible effect of that small break between penultimate and final sentence, the key which turns in the lock, and the perfect tense of reported speech ('he said'), because we can never quite be sure whether that present tense belongs to a moment of imprisonment, or the post-prison recollection. Perhaps we are supposed to hear in that break a huge silence in time between the warder's response and the prisoner's record, on the one hand, and the writing of report on the other; a reminder, that is, that the words on the page before us issue from the same source under different stresses, at different moments of reflection and experience, from different angles of vision, and that we might hold together experience and the experience of memory, for the enlargements of our moral imagination.

I wish to pursue this method of commentary, as I come to what I consider the most complex of moments in the account, in the perspective that is ours. The book's presiding chronological movement, despite its digressions, possesses a paradoxical weight; what we feel, from the momentum of the first part, to be a forward movement in time,[199] becomes a

---

[199] Jean Starobinski once conceived of autobiography along a sliding-scale ranging between Emile Benveniste's poles of third person *histoire* and first-person *discours:* at one end, the *histoire* or narration of the reported 'facts', at the other, the *discours* of the monologue of the narrator's present thoughts, independently of the reported facts. The first section of *The Man Died* (chs.1-8) is very much on the side of *histoire*, the 'reporting of "facts"'; and this is attributable to the fact that the autobiographer is there concerned with presenting a version of truth over and against the various versions of the federal government, to establish Truth before Justice, so to speak. See Jean Starobinski, *L'Œil vivant II: La relation critique* (Paris: Gallimard, 1970), 114-5: 'Un coup d'oeil sur des autobiographies récentes (Michel Leiris, Jean-Paul Sartre) nous montre toutefois que les caractères du discours (énonciation liée à un locuteur qui écrit je) coexistent avec ceux de l'histoire (emploi de l'aoriste). S'agirait-il d'un archaïsme? Ou bien n'aurions-nous pas

movement into stasis, to a dead and eternal present, into an order of time drained of meaning. The Soyinka of this period is perfectly alert to the difficulties of representing passage, the movement from one order to a different order (as we have seen, for example, with *Madmen and Specialists,* of the same historical moment as *The Man Died*). The chronological movement is accompanied by slowing movement on spatial retrenchment; that is, we move from an interrogation room, to a Minimum Security Prison, to a Maximum Security Prison, to solitary confinement.

Within this chronological movement, chapters 9 to 12 form the crucial structural pivot; the turn comes with the prisoner's burial or screening or interment within a state propagandist fiction (chapter 9), his realization that a perfectly formal and inhuman fiction makes of him, an innocent man, something other, further usurps his being, already physically incarcerated, in words – observe the terms in which he characterizes this: '"Confession – foiled escape – wail of humiliation." [...] A beautiful logic all its own. A masterpiece of credible fantasy' (80); that is, it brings home to him the most terrible sense of dangerous and oppressive fictions – the fact that they might be taken as transparent upon life. These chapters, culminating in the sustained reflection of chapter 12, constitute a small structural frame within the broader account, and focus our attention on the protagonist's crucial and tense and desperate psychological reflection, as he is confronted by the terror of his fate, and thrown back desperately on his own fundamental conceptions of being.

At certain charged moments, we were saying, Soyinka's

---

affaire, dans l'autobiographie, à une entité mixte, que nous pourrions dénommer *discours-histoire?* [...] La forme traditionnelle de l'autobiographie tient le milieu entre deux extrêmes: le récit à la troisième personne et le pur monologue.' There is a useful summary in Cohn, *Narratives of Consciousness,* 188-9.

usage of the present tense does not allow us resolutely to adopt the point of view of retrospect but rather maintains a complex oscillation or ambivalence between different temporal points of view, through which we might experience a greater psychological complexity which holds both experiencing self, and a consciousness recollecting retrospectively. Chapter 11 begins with the description of the kernel of a recurrent dream, recounted in the present tense, here deployed in its iterative sense.[200] In message, it attempts to express the awareness of moving into greater solitude, the moment in which we come into that awareness ('It is the silence that strikes me first and slowly I realize that work has ceased.' [85]), and this is why it involves a slight movement of retrospect – it is, paradoxically, with change that we come into a sharper awareness of a past condition or circumstance; something like what Kierkegaard used to say about the human condition, how we are condemned to live forward and understand backwards. Notice the different tenses which animate the passage:

> Later I recognize the physical landscape. It is one of the threads that have gone into the weaving of that metaphysical web which holds men dead in their tracks with the frightening certainty of having returned to a point in a cycle. The landscape of Shaki conjured up long-buried images of the Dutch lowlands where years ago, as a student, I once joined in building new houses for victims of a flood disaster. I recall the pure uncomplicated giving and camaraderie and I know what gave birth to the earlier nostalgic sadness. The rest is horror, the long fall in the abyss, night after night the awful silence... (85-6)

That adverbial 'Later' introduces an ambiguity into the moment of narration: how much later does this recognition take place? In solitary confinement, for example? Or only

---

[200] For uses of the present tense in English, see above, 79.

later, *now*, which is to say, at the moment of writing? With the perfect tense 'conjured' we have the sense that we are in the autobiographer's present, that we are before a retrospective diagnosis of the well-spring of the dream. Yet what of that 'I recall'? Is that the issue of his present consciousness, pen in hand? If so – and I like to think so – it gains further relief from the great technical feat of the final sentence, of being able to hold *both* the experiential sense of the present tense, as if we are reading what the prisoner is experiencing, *and* the sense that we are reading, also, what the autobiographer is coming to experience *again*, through memory.

These technical possibilities receive their fullest expression in chapter 12. If we take this chapter, as might be tempting, as an isolated manifesto – Soyinka using threads of African and Western philosophy, say, to explore or express self and community[201] – we lose both the pathos of situation *within* the chronological narrative of the account, and the enriching ambiguities and enlargements which come from its rubbing up against a retrospective angle of vision. The chapter opens with a long description in the past (imperfect) tense, before switching quite abruptly into the perfect, set into stark relief in a new paragraph: 'Time vanished. I turned to stone. The world retreated into fumes of swampland.' (87) And then, immediately, the distance of that tricolon of verbs in the perfect tense vanishes before the use of the present perfect: 'I have been here before. I have passed through this present point again and again.' (87) The point is simple: the chapter has

---

[201] Werner Sedlak's reading, for instance, trades in detailed analysis and commentary for generality, and thereby drains the moment of urgency. See his "Prison Memoirs by African Writers (Ngugi, Pheto, Soyinka): The Cultural Unity and Complexity of Resistance," in *Fusion of Cultures?* eds. Peter O. Stummer and Christopher Balme (Amsterdam: Rodopi, 1996), 183-193.

begun retrospectively the better to give the reader the sense of entering into temporal ambiguity.

If this sounds too abstract, the subject-matter of the third paragraph should help. In the final paragraph of the previous chapter, we read of the 'threads that have gone into the weaving of that metaphysical web which holds men dead in their tracks with the frightening certainty of having returned to a point in a cycle.' (86) Here, we are witness not to the formal description, but come to inhabit the cycle at the moment of alignment, as well as the protagonist's attempts to understand this moment. There is no doubt that we are supposed to feel that this is the prisoner's present experience, though to this end we have both a fiction of privacy (why bother with the exposition of '*I try hard* to stay the moment, to come to terms with it and if possible, mark it in a place, a time.' [87; my italics], if only addressing himself?) and the more convincing sense that the prisoner is working things out for himself, as they come to him:

> It resolves itself, in so far as anything has resolved itself today, lightly on the rims of consciousness. A knowledge of where I have been till this moment, knowing it for a phase to which I will never return, yet aware also that this ritual of transition is a perpetual one and that the acquisition of experience in fording the pass does not lessen its overwhelming sadness. (87-8)

The prisoner, then, is seeking rationally to come to terms with this continuous return and departure, its human meaning for him. The ebb and flow within this sentence – knowledge, recognition, departure, rational rejection, experience, sadness – announces the movement of the rest of the chapter. The paragraph ends – 'I try to feed some muscularity into the marshmallow of sensations.' (88) –, and therein moves into the particularity of the *now*. A staying of retrospect? Or a sudden swing into the private records of the diarist, writing an imagined dialogue? Or is the point, rather, that at certain points, we cannot tell, an enriching, rather than frustrating, ambiguity? We must now come to this rhythm of 'ebb and flow'. I have been arguing that there is an important sense in which we do not receive the pathos of this chapter if we ignore or simply fail to perceive the ambiguity between confinement, the closing down of imaginative renewal, of horizons, on the one hand, and on the other, the assertions or eternal truths or ratiocinations to which indignation and righteous suffering understandably give rise – and this recalls the grip on the prose which comes as a consequence of those limitations of which we earlier spoke, the way in which limitations shape and structure and animate the words, the choice of words, their specific expression:

> I have quarrelled too often even with the ego-centred interpretations to which the existentialist self gives rise. Any faith that places the *conscious* quest for the inner self as goal, for which the context of forces are mere battle aids is ultimately destructive of the social potential of that self. Except as source of strength and vision keep inner self out of all expectation, let it remain unconscious beneficiary from experience. Suspect all conscious search for the self's authentic being; this is the favourite fodder for the enervating tragic Muse. *I do not seek; I find.* Let actions alone be the manifestations of the authentic being in defence of its authentic visions. (88-9)

Instead of taking this as a philosophical or artistic declaration or manifesto, placed *sub specie aeternitatis*, or privileging *content*, I hear in this rather the strength of *temptation* of what he will come to call the tragic lure, the inward turning into and loss in consciousness. That is to say, I take it as a *response* shaped by a silent but insistent challenge. Deliberate rationalist expression is working incrementally through aphorism, through self-directed imperative, to act as bulwark against temptation; and this, shortly afterwards, flows into a string of assertive definitions, repeated assertion used to shore the self.[202] Wonderfully, however – and here we see once more the constitutive chapter-movement of ebb and flow – this quickly gives way to a question ('Do I or do I not recognize the trap?') and the *mise en scène* of his search, amongst whatever sources he has to hand – a high-stake game of expediency played according to the rules of the place, rather than a general airing of views –, of quotations which move in this sense and direction. In other words, far from being a 'reflection', an abstract standing outside of time, or even a reflection within prison but shorn of urgency, we here have a sort of desperate *bricolage,* an expedient intellectual exercise in which he must continuously remind himself of the

---

[202] Soyinka, *The Man Died*, 89: 'Tragedy is possible solely because of the limitations of the human spirit. There are levels of despair from which, it rightly seems, the human spirit should not recover. To plunge to such a level is to be overwhelmed by the debris of all those anti-human barriers which are erected by jealous gods. The power of recovery is close to acquisition of superhuman energies, and the stagnation-loving human society must for self-preserving interest divert these colossal energies into relatively quiescent channels, for they constitute a force which, used as part of an individual's equipment in the normal human struggle cannot be resisted by the normal human weapons. Thus the historic conspiracy, the literal brain-washing that elevates tragedy far and above a regenerative continuance of the promethean struggle.

'To survive, but to survive in a transmitted form, full of nebulous wisdoms, corrupted and seduced by sagehood homage, carefully insulated from intimacy with the affairs of men, that kind of bribery which Oedipus first snatched at, blinding himself physically to eradicate in entirety the route to socially redemptive action – this is the preference of all establishment. Against all questioning and change, against concrete redress of the causative factors of any crisis, society protects itself by this diversion of regenerative energies into spiritual in-locked egotism. To ensure that there is no reassertion of will the poetic snare of tragic loftiness is spread before him - what greater sublimity than the blind oracular figure, what greater end to the quest for self than graceful acceptance, quiescence and senescence!'

fundamentals so as not to fall into the temptations of self-absorption, and, while there, something more perilous: 'When? Where? I neither remember nor care. I recall only that I once made a note of it to use in what a student called my special anti-literature seminars.' (90) This is not tranquil reflection – indeed self-persuasion is never to be had completely – but rather the desperate shoring that a man administers unto himself when under attack from the 'waves of negations' that engulf him, the 'mob hatred', he writes, 'that I distinctly hear even in this barred wilderness.' (90)

This last sentence introduces voice and hearing, another texture in this recording of consciousness, and, in my view, retrospectively illuminates that preceding cumulative rhythm of definitions, confirms our intimations of menace, against which the rational construction is to hold firm. (What are the 'combative voices'? Where are they heard? What is their relation to memory?) These voices that he imagines, and which to us are unheard though must be felt, shape and condition the arc of his thought; in other words, the prisoner's initial 'rational rejection' is in fact a response to another, silent run of voices, its searches for and expressions of coherence in fact symptoms of the pressure under which his consciousness labours – strident affirmation of order in fact a sign of underlying disorder. Observe that this affecting of his peace comes after the apparently heartening concluding sentence of chapter 10 ('They would wreak vengeance on those who lay within their power but that source of pleasure could not now be expanded nor could it be based on a fantasy of betrayal.' [84]), and so represents, starkly and unmistakeably, a recrudescence of fear ('I know why you reach me, you mindless mob. I see myself consigned to a living death, denied that affirmation.' [91]). The prose tissue, the blood of its sentences, their organization and structure, come to take on the motions of the mind.

The central and almost crippling problem exercising that mind is the redundancy to which a philosophy of action, and its attendant presuppositions, must be placed in a situation of absolute poverty. Strident affirmation as to action, individual responsibility, and even suffering into truth, which itself depends on the knowledge that he and truth will emerge, must, at best, be rhetorical attempts to buttress the self; at worst, they will be just so many words. In an important sense, the truth of this chapter, in my eyes, comes not only in its affirmation in the face of death, to 'make even dying a triumph, an ultimate affirmation' (91), though that is an essential part of the autobiographer's testimony. What the focus on the present account within the retrospective recollection enjoins upon us is a reading method which reintegrates our favourite lines back into the chemical process in which they are involved – for even that episode of Hermias of Aternias is itself woven back into the deeper rhythm of the chapter's organization, the ebb and flow between rationalist rejection and the hearing of voices, between voluntarism, and its evanescence into the involuntary.

To continue:

> Morality, and therefore actions which come from a moral inspiration create the only 'authentic being', they constitute the continuing personality of the individual and cannot be substituted by absolving palliatives. The gap in my guts, the hurtful hiatus that threatens to suck my egoist essence into its own void is the evasion of that moral imperative; the despair comes from a knowledge that I cannot now carry out this sole affirmation nor can I envisage, in this barren encirclement, the possibility of a rational substitution. (95)

This sentence is slightly more complex than it appears, I think. The first sentence is a definition, and seems to belong to the 'general truth' category of the present tense; only, as we have just stated, a philosophy of action depends for its relevance on the *possibility* of action – even taking into account the temporary bulwark it might provide against waves of dangerous thoughts – a possibility which here, in barren encirclement, is receding. And so the lasting force of that definition is, in fact, in his concrete situation, conditional upon a missing premise. For the only knowledge he has here which obtains, it seems to me, is precisely the knowledge into which he is slowly entering through this pained reflection; the knowledge, that is, not merely that he is attempting to find rational substitutions to assuage his boundedness, but that, progressively, the very sense of *envisaging* rational substitution for action is falling away. Against stridency, then, he finally comes back to the reality of his situation, expressed powerfully as he digests his own words used against him, just as he must, himself, digest what has happened to him, acknowledge the reality of his present circumstance, repeat it, ruminate over it – a nasty but necessary prelude to the pursuit of the self's protection in solitary confinement.

The acknowledgement of present circumstance seems immediately to relapse into an embittered accusation ('Your contemptuous insight into the minds of a hysteria-manipulated mob has rendered you immune to further confrontation – this is your purpose and I acknowledge its present success.' [95-6]), but if we take this as a parting swipe, the prelude to acceptance, it becomes perfectly understandable psychologically. Notice, too, that associative cluster in the prisoner's mind between hysteria and mobs and voices:

> the mob hatred that I distinctly hear even in this barren wilderness (90)
>
> You, outside of these walls, whose hysteria I confess penetrates my proud defences (90)
>
> I know why you reach me, you mindless mob (91)
>
> I ought truly to have contempt for this world of zombies. I shall, but you have yet to create them. I think that

finally, you cannot. True, the voices which I hear are not the voices I seek to hear. (96)

(Perhaps an instinctive reaction might baulk at the same epithet being used both of criminals and civil society, though, given the massacres of civilians in 1965 and 1966, the indistinction has its own partial damning truth.) In each of the sentences there is the sense that voices reach him against his will, are both beyond rational substitution and issuing from himself; that his mind-bound solitude is the staging for the chapter, the wrestling between acknowledgement and evasion of present circumstance. The ambiguity or movement is preserved throughout, I think, until we come to the final paragraphs, where it receives a form of resolution.

At the start of chapter 10, the prisoner, in 'a moment of enforced calm' (80), has attempted creative self-identification with his oppressors. This passage into enforced calm – away from the echoes of voices in the streets and markets, the 'whispers in corridors', 'glances in gatherings', 'the rain of spittle and contempt', the 'target of pointed fingers', the 'giggle in the dark', the 'wise nods of geriatric consciences', the mockery (80) – looks forward to the anti-penultimate paragraph of chapter 12, and gestures to the close of that miniature structure within the book's wider organization, of which earlier we spoke:

> Instead I see hands thrown up in horror. I see furtive slinks of shame in the streets, in dark corners of homes. I smell hate, evil, fright and capitulation. But it is your smell, the smell of irredeemable corruption that travels with you and clings to all over whom your breath of lies has blown. And I hear a fresh wind coming up from beyond the boundaries of expediency. (96)

In the former, a movement 'out of', emergence, creative self-identification conditional upon a moment of enforced calm; in the latter, no such movement, but rather voices that he hears despite himself, visions he sees, derivative of an ambience, communicated through 'smell' – though of abstract nouns, of corruption, just as one smells a rat, or fear. Is that 'fresh wind', the apocalyptic register, the summoning of a *deus ex machina*, thereby stained with suspicion, further to the strength of that previous confession – that he cannot envisage, 'in this barren encirclement, the possibility of a rational substitution' (95)? What to make of that weak connector 'And', which does not suggest a logical passage between corruption's spread and its eventual decline? What to make of those visions of shame and cowardice against the paragraph's opening – 'I ought truly to have a contempt for this world of zombies. I shall, but you have yet to create them. I think that finally you cannot.' (96) – the distinction between reality and his visions? All of these possible meanings are there, I think, and gain moral strength precisely in the motions of their reflection.

There is a famous sentence which usually drifts free of its context: 'For me, justice is the first condition of humanity.' (96) I think of that sentence – it should now be clear – as the hard-won droplet which comes after the long and tense experiment; not the simple sententious or righteous affirmation, not only the retrospective declaration of someone who has survived to tell of the real witnesses, those who did not make it (the 'submerged', as Primo Levi might have said[203]), but also the result of a torrid and tormenting psychological process in the experiencing present, triggered, as we have seen, by his burial in a state fiction, and rendered pressing by his imminent deeper and more literal burial:

> Listen to what Adolfe Joffe wrote to Trotsky before his death by suicide. 'Human life has meaning only to that degree and as long as it is lived in the service of humanity. For me humanity is infinite.'
>
> For me, justice is the first condition of humanity. (96)

---

[203] See Primo Levi, *I sommersi e i salvati* (Torino: Einaudi, 2007 [1986]).

We have been arguing that the underlying rhythm of the chapter is one of ebb and flow, as rational affirmation and moral stridency, underpinned by a philosophy of action, give way, as they must in the literal poverty of prison circumstance, to other forms of understanding, beginning with acknowledgement; and that we lose the pathos and, perhaps, even meaning, if we lose that movement upon which the chapter is constructed. Finally, we suggested that the retrospective beginning obeys the dictates of autobiography, the better to cast us into generic ambiguity between autobiography and diary. The end of the chapter preserves and concentrates this ambiguity, beautifully, for here it is turned not to ebb and flow, the puncturing of will and voluntarism by clamouring voices, but rather the expression of a principle to which the protagonist has come following a terrible psychological battle, an expression which is rich and morally enlarging precisely because the present tense preserves *both* the synchronic tension, *and* – to the extent that that synchronic experience guarantees and justifies the moral lesson – sustains the present-tense-as-general-truth, the authenticated experience of subsequent recollection.

* * *

In the essay entitled, significantly, 'The Credo of Being and Nothingness', Soyinka recounts a mental exercise in which he used to indulge as a child, which involved trying to understand the Christian myth of creation and, more specifically, the void or emptiness of the beginning: 'I found myself impelled by curiosity to experience the absolute state of non-being, of total void – no trees, no rocks, no skies, no other beings, not even I.'[204] Shortly afterwards, in the same

---

[204] Wole Soyinka, "The Credo of Being and Nothingness" [1991], *Essays*, 231.

essay, the author relates the experiencing of nothingness to this world's demotion to a mere dependence or 'staging-post', the eclipse or conquest of time, and the *segue* into his experience in solitary confinement feels perfectly natural: the contesting of the element of Time in the negation of existence, a graduation from childhood 'under prison conditions, into even deeper illumination into the profundities of nothingness.'[205] The tone in that last sentence is one of gentle provocation, the essay's central subject being that of religious intolerance, but there is an important sense which we might preserve here for our reading of *The Man Died*.

There may be certain situations in which we are confronted with a real curtailment of freedom, what Frank Kermode, drawing on Wallace Stevens, might have called a real 'poverty', rather than the figurative one which is our common lot,[206] and such, most surely, is solitary confinement. There the movement, as we have tried to suggest, is not between self-assertion and communion, for there is no (or hardly ever any) communion to be had, no renewal of resource in the voices of peers. Rather the movement of the protagonist's self in the solitary confinement of the Kaduna of *The Man Died*, is a movement which is both turned inward, and not reducible to consciousness; a realm of the self which stands beyond existential self-exploration (the tragic lure), and simultaneously, in its ideal expression, beyond the intrusions of reality, of the outside. The more interesting question, however, is how this notion of nothingness is deployed, in the prison account, as a *structural* principle, once we enter solitary confinement. This forms the concluding observations of my discussion.

Of the many intellectual exercises which the protagonist sets himself, as related in *The Man Died*, the following one is

---

[205] *Ibid.*, 233.
[206] Kermode, *The Sense of an Ending*, ch.6.

particularly striking:

> I set about the only choice, but with deliberation. I begin to relive the entire sequence of events even in time-span though not always quantitatively exact. In fact, hardly ever. Thoughts, even memory, flash through the mind with a regal contempt for the crucifying ache of planning, waiting, executing, waiting, concluding and recommencing in active time. Again and again I effect a brake: you have all the time in the world, fool. A few months reliving a few months past means a few months obliterated in an empty future. It will, I slowly acknowledge, become the pattern of existence. Only control it Kronos. (*TMD*, 132)

This is the template of a Borgesian fiction, in which a fictional structural homology becomes a surrogate for the reality we had considered primary, displaces it, and eventually reorders a hierarchy of relations. In Borges' 'Funes el memorioso', Funes, following a fall from his horse, acquires the inhuman perfection of a faultless memory, to go with the all too human imperfection of a paralysed body. To forget, remarks the narrator, is to form general ideas, to elide detail, to synthesize; never to forget, to preserve the full perception, so to speak, of every moment, is to lose this capacity of transcendence, of going beyond, and, further, to lose the distinction between past and present, between things seen and things no longer seen. Borges achieves a sort of formal perfection here, but not without what might be called a slight (and characteristic) perversity, born of a consistent and studied provocation of reality, or experience – so it is that his narrator can remark, tucked away in parentheses, 'that the least important of his memories was more detailed than our perception of a moment of physical pleasure or physical torment.'[207] The difference is in condition. Funes is, in a sense,

---

[207] Jorge Luis Borges, "Funes el memorioso," in *Ficciones*, 134 (my translation).

an involuntary prisoner of the inhuman richness of his memory; for Soyinka, a prisoner in real poverty, the task is to exercise the will to achieve a condition of nothingness; and the prisoner's failure, the constant return to reality or piercing of his defences despite his efforts of will, become the very structural principle of the book's representation of solitary confinement.

The prisoner's exercising of the will when in solitary confinement tends towards a form of impenetrable immobility, within which, nonetheless, a limited and controlled activity remains. (This is clearly an idea to which Soyinka is attracted, as we might see in the spider as cipher in *The Road*, and shall yet again read many years later, when he writes, as preliminary to Ben Okri's writing in 'exile', that the embrace of an anchor in alien territory and the simultaneous remove from that milieu, requires 'erecting a creative barrier, sometimes half-hearted but sufficient to distance itself from complete absorption'; that it is both a reflection and deflection of present reality.[208]) I think the logic of the prisoner's attempt to insulate himself in a 'capsule of individualist totality' (*TMD*, 91) lies here: the erection of a barrier, a bulwark against complete absorption, here understood as self-absorption, the calamitous loss of self paradoxically entailed in narcissism, which is itself a recognition of the alien territory of this reality; to preserve the distinction between 'the area of will-power' and 'the drugged immersion in rainbow-tinted ether.' (252) The rhythm of solitary confinement in *The Man Died*, then, becomes that of the motion towards nothingness, on the one hand, against, on the other, a constant return to reality, a penetration of that defence, of those barriers – a failing not so

---

[208] Wole Soyinka, "EXILE: Thresholds of Loss and Identity," in *Anglophonia/Caliban 7*, ed. Christiane Fioupou (Toulouse: Presses Universitaires du Mirail, 2000), 63.

much of the will, but rather a reminder that the will is not enough before the predations of the involuntary: of memory, of situatedness, of context, of imagination.

I want to end with what I find to be one of the most moving moments of the book. In the essay 'And After The Narcissist?' (1966), half-submerged under the stridency of tone, Soyinka expresses a beautiful idea. He is careful to nuance the senses he gives to 'action', showing that it is coherent with an inward movement. This inward movement, writes Soyinka, should suggest a realm within the mind which, implicitly, stands beyond mere consciousness:

> what we constantly seek when [the poem] claims its right to be static is the movement that accompanies introspection, a movement within the image, shall we say, not merely a crescendo of passions. A pause even into the heart of image which has left the poet's lips gently or been violently wrenched from him. It is at such moments that the poetic self is suspended and the phrase, the concept, lives on its own, freed from all subordination to the poet's self-interest.[209]

In other words, immobility is perfectly legitimate as poetic intention, but that immobility must itself hold and express a paradoxical movement and pause, the poet's submission to poetry, the surrender of self-interest which comes in that moment of concord. This ideal moment of concord, in which the prisoner and poet expresses the suspension of the poetic self from within the deepest inward isolation, that affirmation of life at the moment of death, which is freed from self-interest, which issues from protective isolation, is the structural sense I give to the poem 'I anoint my flesh' (*TMD*, 256) of the greatly winnowed poet, as his fast lengthens.[210] It gains strength not merely through its poetry, through words, but also, dare I say primarily, through its generic house, through the subtlety

---

[209] Soyinka, "And After the Narcissist?" 63.

with which this affirmation of life at the jaw of death is intensified by its being, in the terms of the earlier essay, a suspension of the poetic self; how its poetic truth derives precisely from its severance from self-interest.

The bind of self-sufficiency and emptiness has been implicit, with different emphases, in many of our discussions hitherto: with Lakunle in *The Lion and the Jewel*; with Professor in *The Road;* with Eman in *The Strong Breed,* Obaneji/Forest Head in *A Dance of the Forests,* and Tiresias in *The Bacchae of Euripides*; and, now, with Soyinka-prisoner, battling against literal poverty and 'the tragic lure' in the solitary confinement of Kiri-Kiri. Philosophically, self-sufficiency might suppose an existential conception of existence. The most emblematic (and catchy) declaration of an existential conception of the self which, it would seem, implies or even advocates self-sufficiency, comes with Descartes. It is with a few African responses to the *cogito* – culminating with Soyinka's discussion of tragedy in *Myth, Literature and the African World,* and its implications for the rhetorical resource proper to tragedy – that the following discussion is concerned.

---

[210] The poem also appears, of course, in the collection *A Shuttle in the Crypt* (London: Methuen, 1972), 19. The important point, however, is the structural role it occupies in *The Man Died.*

2

Myth, Literature and the African World: Using and Abusing the *Cogito*

Cartesian epistemology is haunted, into the marrow of its catchphrase, by scepticism, defined, in Western terms, as the challenge to the very possibility of human knowledge. We might recall the fact that the *cogito* itself is subject to breakdown and declensions, which speak to Descartes' own equivocations. Bernard Williams once astutely observed that the *Regulae* offer existing and thinking as two *separate* propositions, and that even the *Méditations Métaphysiques* do not propose thinking as something of which Descartes is certain, but rather only the proposition 'I am, I exist'.[211] In turn, part of the animating tension of the *cogito* of the *Discours de la Méthode* as it responds to the challenge of scepticism – Descartes is writing after the translation of Sextus Empiricus' *Outlines of Pyrrhonism,* after Montaigne, after Charron, after La Mothe le Vayer – becomes, then, what the content of that 'sum' is, whether it can be inferred from thinking, or whether it depends on a general premise stating that whoever thinks, exists. If it does form part of a syllogism with a suppressed major premise ('Whatever thinks exists. I think. Therefore, I exist), the inference of being from thought becomes a purely conceptual claim, elides experience, and therefore becomes susceptible to sceptical analysis. (And even this is a point subject to some equivocation: Descartes denies that it comes

---

[211] Bernard Williams, *Descartes: The Project of Pure Enquiry* (Sussex: The Harvester Press, 1978), 73.

with a suppressed major premise in the *Second Replies,* and yet seems to qualify or change or modify this position in *Principia* I.10.[212])

Williams goes on to analyse what he calls the Cartesian reflection's 'perspective of consciousness', and the assumption that 'the standpoint of consciousness, is *in itself* enough to provide the basis for the coherent individuation of items which can be basically characterized from the third-personal, objective, point of view.'[213] The only way to step out of mind, in this project of pure enquiry, to proceed from his own existence to something other than himself, to emerge from pure thought itself, comes in his God, and once God leaves, there is a problem.

I would like to contrast this project of pure enquiry with philosopher Kwasi Wiredu's well-known analyses of concepts of being in Akan,[214] for many of his conclusions, or lines of

---

[212] See, respectively, René Descartes, *Secondes Réponses,* in *Oeuvres et Lettres* (Paris: Gallimard, 1953), 375-6: 'Mais quand nous apercevons que nous sommes des choses qui pensent, c'est une première notion qui n'est tirée d'aucun syllogisme; et lorsque quelqu'un dit: *Je pense, donc je suis, ou j'existe,* il ne conclut pas son existence de sa pensée comme par la force de quelque syllogisme, mais comme une chose connue de soi; il la voit par une simple inspection de l'esprit. Comme il paraît de ce que, s'il la déduisait par le syllogisme, il aurait dû auparavant connaître cette majeure: *Tout ce qui pense, est ou existe.* Mais, au contraire, elle lui est enseignée de ce qu'il sent en lui-même qu'il ne se peut pas faire qu'il pense, s'il n'existe.'; and *Principes* I, 10, in *ibid.,* 575: 'et lorsque j'ai dit que cette proposition: *Je pense, donc je suis,* est la première et la plus certaine qui se présente à celui qui conduit ses pensées par ordre, je n'ai pas pour cela nié qu'il ne fallût savoir auparavant ce que c'est que pensée, certitude, existence, *et que pour penser il faut être* [my italics], et autres choses semblables;'

[213] Williams, *Descartes,* 100.

[214] Akan is predominantly spoken in Ghana. There is also a considerable Akan-speaking population in Ivory Coast.

investigation – clarified against Descartes, and, given the Frenchman's quite extraordinary shaping influence or hold over Western philosophy, stretching to the present – are to our purposes here. Wiredu's seductive essay analysing the critique of Descartes' conception of mind by Akan-born Anton Wilhelm Amo – Amo's opposition to ascribing the feeling of sensations to the mind, *despite* his acceptance of the tenets of the dualistic philosophy of mind – ends with an appealing speculation: 'May it not be that some recess of Amo's consciousness was impregnated by the concept of mind implicit in the language and thought of the Akans?'[215] A difference in concepts of mind is enriched by his various discussions of Akan conceptions of being. Within the conventional possibilities of the Akan language, argues Wiredu, existence is necessarily spatial, locative, situated, bespeaks an empirical conception which precludes expressions of absolute nothingness just as it does a standpoint of pure consciousness; in Akan, says Wiredu, the verb 'to be', can only be predicative or adverbial, for being is syncategorematic, which is to say, it has no meaning by itself, it depends on other parts of speech. This in turn would suggest, still according to Wiredu, that an existential concept of being, in which being is defined without recourse to principles beyond self – he cleverly notes that because the word 'exists' does not shout about its spatiality, 'it has been possible in English to speak as if existence is not necessarily spatial without prohibitive implausibility'[216] – cannot be expressed in conventional Akan. (Pragmatic philosophy, in one sense, is perhaps then merely a congenial

---

[215] Kwasi Wiredu, "Amo's Critique of Descartes' Philosophy of Mind," in *A Companion to African Philosophy*, ed. Wiredu, 204.
[216] Kwasi Wiredu, Introduction to *Decolonizing African Religions: A Short History of African Religions in Western Scholarship* by Okot p'Bitek (New York: Diaspora Africa Press, 2011), xxiv.

philosophical tradition for Wiredu, insofar as it is premised upon subjective location as a constituent element in determining truth.)

I am not discussing whether this is a correct rendering of the possibilities within conventional Akan, upon which I am unable to judge. (Nowhere does Wiredu assert that one mode of conception is, *a priori*, superior to the other – though he is quite careful not to rule this out. Rather he is making the commendable point that we must first strive to understand the substantive differences in order to be able to have a conversation.[217]) In this context, rather, I am interested in the ways in which the *cogito* becomes a sort of foil for Wiredu against which to develop and clarify conceptions of being from within Akan culture, in the realm of philosophy; a sort of peg which, now burdened by developed sustained philosophical analysis and critique, breaks or falls off to the ground. And, by implication, how we might see a similar attempt in two leading Nigerian responses, those of Achebe and Soyinka, as they talk of Igbo and Yoruba conceptions of being, and the tragic treatment proper to such conceptions.

Before we get there, however, I would like briefly to consider a work which clarifies the direction of this chapter, the sense that conceptions of being shape conceptions we have of the world or worlds which we inhabit, and in turn come to bear upon the artistic solutions we deem apposite for such renderings. In Cheikh Hamidou Kane's novel *L'Aventure ambigüe* (1961),[218] Samba Diallo, the protagonist, reflects upon

---

[217] *Ibid.*, xviii: '[...] it may possibly be that these African languages are inadequate and are in need of a supplementation in this regard. On the other hand, it may be that this existential concept of being is a semantically defective concept, notwithstanding its great currency in Western metaphysics.'

[218] Cheikh Hamidou Kane, *L'aventure ambigüe* (Paris: Julliard, 1961).

the orthodox history of Western scepticism (as it represents itself to itself), what he calls its 'ontological accident', clarified and held in the distance between Descartes and Pascal. Here is Diallo:

> [...] ne sentez-vous pas comme le projet philosophique n'est plus tout à fait le même chez Pascal et chez Descartes déjà? Non qu'ils se soient préoccupés de problèmes différents, mais qu'ils s'en soient occupés différemment. Ce n'est pas le mystère qui a changé, mais les questions qui lui sont posées et les révélations qu'on en attend. Descartes est plus parcimonieux dans sa quête; si, grâce à cette modestie et aussi à sa méthode, il obtient plus de réponses, ce qu'il apporte nous concerne moins aussi, et nous est de peu de secours.[219]

Samba Diallo is nothing if not a good and serious student at the Sorbonne – in the early 1960s as now, respectful of philosophical orthodoxy. What he (correctly, in my view) identifies as Descartes' modest parsimony is expressive of the eclipse of philosophy before epistemology, that characteristic turn of the European seventeenth century, yet I am more interested in what is suggested implicitly; for, in an important sense, the contrast between Descartes and Pascal is also a contrast between conceptions of space: a conception of being as syncategorematic, so to speak, against a conception of meaning as indissociable from a constant search for balance, for organization, around a given point in space.

In his classic monograph *Du monde clos à l'univers infini*,[220] Alexandre Koyré once examined the spatial and cosmological implications of Descartes' epistemology: the displacement of the Aristotelian conception of space, its intraworldly hierarchy of values – the sublunary region, the incorruptible celestial

---

[219] *Ibid.*, 126.
[220] Alexandre Koyré, *Du Monde clos à l'univers infini*, trans. Raissa Tarr (Paris: Gallimard, 1973).

spheres, and so on – by an indefinite, infinite universe, in which everything exists on the same ontological level. The geometrization of space, which conflated space (understood as homogenous extension) with the real space of the universe, led to a rejection 'of any consideration based on notions of value, perfection, harmony, [...] and lastly, the complete devaluation of Being, the total divorce between the world of values and the world of facts.'[221] The key Cartesian word is 'étendue' ('extension' or 'extensiveness'). Matter being identical to space, the world becomes all extension:

> la nature de la matière, ou du corps pris en général, ne consiste point en ce qu'il est une chose dure, ou pesante, ou colorée, ou qui touche nos sens de quelque autre façon, mais seulement en ce qu'il est une substance étendue en longueur, largeur et profondeur.[222]

By means of contrast, we would do well to turn to Michel Serres' brilliant identification of the central principle in Pascal's varied intellectual investigations. In strictly scientific terms – in geometry, arithmetic, infinitesimal calculus, physics and mechanics – writes Serres, there is a constant theme, modified according to purpose:

> [...] de la théorie de l'équilibre à celle du mouvement, de la géométrie pure à la cosmologie, de la science de la vision à la vision du monde et du destin humain, tous ces exemples ont au minimum en commun la *recherche d'un point fixe*. Dans tous les cas, ce point est la *référence* sans laquelle nulle loi ne saurait être établie, nul désordre apparent soumis à la droite raison, nulle définition précisée; et, plus généralement, aucune mesure, aucune proportion, aucun ordre.[223]

The constant search is for a fixed point, moving and subject

---

[221] *Ibid.*, 11-12 (my translation).
[222] Descartes, *Principes* II, 4, in *Oeuvres et Lettres*, 612-3.
[223] Michel Serres, *Le Système de Leibniz et ses modèles mathématiques* (Paris: Presses Universitaires de France, 1968), 657-8.

to constant pressure or tension or forces acting upon it; a point which is the reference without which no law can be established, no definition refined; and this search is also characteristic in Pascal, of man's condition. That is, his condition, his being, is expressed in terms which are still just about felt as spatial – the agony of Pascal's tone, of course, indicating the direction things were taking.

The premise of *L'aventure ambigüe* was conventional even at the time, under a Negritudinist wing – and this despite the protagonist's (or author's) caution regarding the word Négritude: 'J'avoue que je n'aime pas ce mot et que je ne comprends pas toujours ce qu'il recouvre.' (154) A quick list of tropes might include the inexorable change within the protagonist under foreign influence ('Il nous apparaît soudain que, tout au long de notre cheminement, nous n'avons pas cessé de nous métamorphoser, et que nous voilà devenus autres.' [125]); the anguish of a sort of hybridity *raté* ('Il n'y a pas une tête lucide entre deux termes d'un choix. Il y a une nature étrange, en détresse de n'être pas deux.' [163]); or the doubting of the reality of the original African culture, despite protestations to the contrary, the loss of assurance before the encroaching extensiveness of the West, always a give-away ('L'exemple toujours vivant de son pays était là, pour lui prouver, dans ses moments de doute, la réalité d'un univers non occidental.' [169]). This is an anguished Samba Diallo, his belated prayer sounding rather like interrogation, accusation, saddened observation:

> Ils disent que l'être est écartelé de néant, est un archipel dont les îles ne se tiennent pas par en dessous, noyées qu'elles sont de néant. Ils disent que la mer, qui est telle que tout ce qui n'est pas elle y flotte, c'est le néant. Ils disent que la vérité, c'est le néant, et l'être, avatar multiple. [...] Et Toi, Tu bénis leur errement. Tu lui attaches le succès comme l'endroit à l'envers. Sous le flot de leur mensonge qui s'étend, la richesse cristallise ses gemmes.

Ta vérité ne pèse plus très lourd, mon Dieu... (139)

We sense the rhythm of his thought here, uncontrolled, associative, searching, everything that the coercively (and, Soyinka might have said, sadistically) securing Word of the *maître* was not. Samba Diallo's words gain force and pathos precisely because they are neither reducible to his former conceptions, nor amenable to the newer (Western existentialist) conceptions of the encroaching present. 'Nothingness', for instance, is no longer simply a constant injunction to our common humility before God, no longer bespeaks only a conception of existence grounded in hierarchies beyond and above self; nor is it yet reducible, however, to existentialist notions of man (and woman's) originary isolation, as islands prised away from a common base, their common constituency submerged, hidden, forgotten. Consistent with such an anguished reflection, his words float, unrelated, ill-defined, themselves cast out into drift like the islands of a vanished archipelago.

One key aspect of the novel's *expression* is the importance which the Cartesian shibboleth 'étendue' comes to assume, precisely as Samba Diallo's dilemma increasingly resembles the conventional existentialist poles of being and nothingness. The fullest and most condensed expression comes with the madman's account of that other world to the *maître*, in a sudden moment of stillness and insight. The asphalt road, the concrete pavement – 'L'asphalte... Mon regard parcourait toute l'étendue et ne vit pas de limite à la pierre. [...] ici, le gris clair de la pierre, ce noir mat de l'asphalte. (101) – become cogent expressions of grey, homogenous extension or extensiveness. Like a dried artery funnelling nothing but the metallic circulation of cars ('La marée des conques sur l'étendue de l'asphalte courait à ras.' 102), the road is 'une étendue parfaitement inhumaine, vide d'hommes, [...] une étendue interdite à sa chair nue' (102). The imagery swells:

> J'ai vu les mécaniques. Ce sont des coquilles. C'est
> l'étendue enroulée, et qui se meut. Or, tu sais que
> l'étendue n'a point d'intérieur; elle n'a donc rien à perdre.
> Elle ne peut pas se blesser, comme la silhouette, mais
> seulement se dérouler. Aussi, elle a refoulé la silhouette,
> peureuse, elle, en se blessant, de perdre l'intérieur qu'elle
> contient. [...] Cette étendue se meut. Or, tu sais qu'elle
> était la stabilité même qui rendait apparent le mouvement,
> comme son miroir. Maintenant, elle a commencé à se
> mouvoir. Son mouvement est plus achevé que la
> progression saccadée de la silhouette hésitante. Elle ne
> peut tomber, où tomberait-elle? Aussi, elle a refoulé la
> silhouette, peureuse, elle, en tombant, de perdre le
> mouvement. (103)

The opposition comes in the lissome movement of extensiveness, held by the road and the cars, in the dimensionlessness of extension, its absence of hierarchy, as against human sense and touch and colour, human meaning, vulnerable and stumbling and weak like a thin silhouette but keen to protect what it has, to protect that movement which it bespeaks. And yet the historical movement which the madman discerns, is the overwhelming of that stumbling silhouette, its disappearance into the 'étendue enroulée', into the movement of inertia.

This is Samba Diallo walking down the Boulevard St. Michel in Paris, not too long afterwards:

> Je marche. Un pied devant, un pied derrière, un pied
> devant, un pied derrière, un... deux... un... deux... Non!
> [...] Je pense à mon gros orteil droit. Il n'y a rien, que
> mon gros orteil droit. Sinon, leur rue est vide, leur temps
> encombré, leur âme ensablée là-dessous (140-1)

This picks up on and actualizes the madman's terms in the present – Diallo's waning assurance, his silhouette's pained movements – and traces a horizon of loss, in which the jerked movements of the silhouette will cease, before remorseless extension. (It takes flesh through Kane's conscription of an episode in Rilke's *Notebooks of Malte Laurids Brigge,* which Diallo thinks of as he tries to walk. Rilke's narrator walks up the wide and empty Boulevard St. Michel, with the wind up and smells and cries and bells rising in the street; he notices people reacting to somebody, though he knows not whom; he eventually sees this person and begins to follow him, intrigued by that person's apparent attempts to dodge obstacles in the street, though which obstacles he cannot see; the man's irregular movements – hopping, collar-straightening, bowing – are, so the narrator comes to realize, sudden movements passing through his body like shots of pain which translate his fear of being among people.[224]) In this perspective, Abiola Irele has succinctly expressed Diallo's fate as integration 'into the cosmos, that is – nothingness'.[225] for where a conception of being collapses into itself, into individualism, into the mind with nothing beyond, it forms coherent expression with the cosmology it implies, a world in which men and women are exiled in appearance, in solitude.

Chinua Achebe quotes Diallo's reflection on Pascal and Descartes in his 1984 essay 'The Writer and his Community', describing it as one of his personal highlights in what he regards as a fine novel.[226] In Achebe's essay, Kane's novel performs two divergent roles. Through Diallo's reflection, it well captures

---

[224] Rainer Maria Rilke, *The Notebooks of Malte Laurids Brigge,* trans. William Needham, ebook.

[225] Abiola Irele, "In Praise of Alienation," in *The Surreptitious Speech: Présence Africaine and the Politics of Otherness 1947-1987,* ed. V.Y. Mudimbe (Chicago: University of Chicago Press, 1989), 203.

[226] Achebe, "The Writer and his Community," 34: '[...] don't you feel as if the philosophical plan were already no longer the same with Descartes as with Pascal? It is not the mystery which has changed but the questions which are asked of it and the revelations which are expected from it. Descartes is more niggardly in his quest. If, thanks to this and also to his method, he obtains a greater number of responses, what he reports also concerns us less and is of little help to us.'

what Achebe thinks regarding the sceptical and individualist turn of Western intellectual history and society which took place in the seventeenth century (Descartes 'made the foundation of his philosophical edifice including the existence of God contingent on his own first person singular! *Cogito ergo sum.* I think therefore I am!'[227]). And yet, at the same time, it clarifies Achebe's continued conception of being, of existence, as dependent on and sustained by hierarchy, principles beyond the self – a conception, that is, in which the individual receives constant enlargement and undergoes perpetual circumscription and limits from what is felt to be a cluttered space around him; in which fulfilment is defined not as 'uncluttered space or an absence of controls', but rather as 'a presence – a powerful demanding presence limiting the space in which the self can roam uninhibited; [...] other-centred, a giving or subduing of the self [...] to something external to it.'[228]

Tragedy presses down on the joints of our most fundamental assumptions, probes and tests our conceptions of existence (fulfilment as other-centred, existence as spatially located, the mutual constitutions of the individual and community) and senses of cosmology until, perhaps, they break down. This, no doubt, had already constituted Achebe's laboratory in *Things Fall Apart* (1958) and *Arrow of God* (1964), his two earlier tragic masterpieces. We saw, with Descartes and Pascal, how a brief history of ideas might offer us a moving contrast between two radically different conceptions of being, the passing of one conception before another; in the same way, a literary history might helpfully clarify two different novelistic responses to a common set of problems, in the way they draw on conceptions of being. The challenge is gestured

---

[227] *Ibid.*, 35.
[228] *Ibid.*, 36.

towards in Achebe's exchange with the American novelist John Updike who observes, of Ezeulu and *Arrow of God*, that 'having created a hero [most Western novelists] would not let him crumble'.[229] Achebe's response is worth quoting in full:

> Of course a Westerner would be most reluctant to destroy 'in a page or two' the very angel and paragon of creation – the individual hero. If indeed he has to be destroyed, it must be done expansively with detailed explanations and justifications, not to talk of lamentations. And he must be given as final tribute the limelight in which to speak a grand, valedictory soliloquy![230]

The challenge of the tragic novel, that is, becomes the challenge of representing the hero's destruction, without the 'grand, valedictory soliloquy'; becomes the representation of both the individual assertions valued in Igbo cultures and its simultaneous circumscription; the dance between the two. And I think that one way of understanding Achebe's artistic response comes in his endings.

Thomas de Quincey once wrote a memorable essay on *Macbeth*, in which he wondered why, every time he watched the play, he reacted with such perplexity at hearing the knocking at the gate following Duncan's murder; in which he wondered how the effect, which reflected back 'on the murder a peculiar awfulness and a depth of solemnity',[231] actually worked. It is just when a transitory vision dissolves, he concludes, the moment 'when the suspension ceases, and the goings-on of human life are suddenly resumed', that our human awareness of the suspension of time, of activity, reaches its fullest and most affecting. No summary, however,

---

[229] *Ibid.*, 38.
[230] *Ibid.*, 38.
[231] Thomas de Quincey, "On the Knocking at the Gate in *Macbeth*," in *Miscellaneous Essays* (Boston: Ticknor, Reed, and Fields, 1851), 2.

does justice to De Quincey's prose, which I prefer to quote in full:

> Hence it is, that when the deed is done, when the work of darkness is perfect, then the world of darkness passes away like a pageantry in the clouds: the knocking at the gate is heard; and it makes known audibly that the reaction has commenced: the human has made its reflux upon the fiendish; the pulses of life are beginning to beat again; and the re-establishment of the goings-on of the world in which we live, first makes us profoundly sensible of the awful parenthesis that had suspended them.[232]

De Quincey was exercised by the momentary thwarting which art could administer to time's mere successiveness, and his subject-matter here is just one instance of that – the suspension of ordinariness which allows us to enter fully a murderous and momentary world, and of which we only receive a full awareness as the pulses of life begin to beat once more. Achebe's intention is of course not to make sensible the 'retiring of the human heart and the entrance of the fiendish heart',[233] but rather works in the other sense, the sense of a falling apart, a loss of integrity. I use that word carefully:

> HUMPTY DUMPTY [*rather scornfully*]: When I use a word it means just what I choose it to mean – neither more nor less.
>
> ALICE: The question is whether you can make words mean so many different things.
>
> HUMPTY DUMPTY: The question is, which is to be master – that's all.[234]

---

[232] *Ibid.*, 15.
[233] *Ibid.*, 14.
[234] Lewis Carroll, *Through the Looking-glass* in *Alice's Adventures in Wonderland* & *Through the Looking-glass* (London: Academy Editions, 1974), 193.

Humpty Dumpty, balancing on the wall, might come to know how putting things together again, how regaining integrity, is harder after the fact, even with all the king's horses and all the king's men. Achebe liked to use the word 'anarchy' to suggest this placing of words to different and unsanctioned senses, of course, yet it is, in my view, the qualifier 'mere' of W.B. Yeats' poem 'The Second Coming', which sits as epigraph to his first novel, which goes to the heart of his sense of an ending.[235] It is not only that, in his two tragic masterpieces, Achebe has perfectly understood the literary uses of over-determination, the multiplication of possibilities beyond necessity as an intellectual and literary response to the grievous geographical enlargements which colonialism brought. For despite and perhaps even because of this, we always pursue the byways proposed, though our emphasis each time will change. Rather, it is the abruptness of the endings – in *Things Fall Apart* the switch into colonial perspective, in *Arrow of God* the madness of Ezeulu ('Perhaps it was the constant, futile throbbing of these thoughts that finally left a crack in Ezeulu's mind.'[236]) – which functions as the knocking at the gate. Only here, what comes is not the *re-establishment* of the goings-on of the world, but rather the sense that everything that we have seen and lived before, even with its over-determinations, is itself now a form of parenthesis, awful because unrecoverable; and that feeling, that sense which holds both the terror of irremediable loss *and* the illusion of formal continuity, is the sense of 'mere anarchy'.

* * *

Descartes, for Wole Soyinka, is most obviously mediated through Senghor's unfortunately catchy misreading of (the

---

[235] See above, 14.
[236] Achebe, *Arrow of God*, 229.

deliberately Alexandrine?²³⁷) 'La raison est hellène, l'émotion nègre'. The idea that Negritude was conditioned and determined and circumscribed by its adoption of a flawed major premise which derives from Descartes²³⁸ will become something of a commonplace across Soyinka's later critical prose. In 1982, for instance, he writes of 'the "Cartesian response," [...] or more familiarly, "Negritude" [...] To Descartes' "I think, therefore, I am," they responded on behalf of the black man: "I feel, therefore I am." Rationalism is essentially European, they claimed; the black man is emotive and intuitive.' Or later, in 1985, this:

> The philosophers had proved the principal culprits, since it is the mission of philosophy not merely to frame, but to phrase the world. Thus, rejecting the endocentric parameters which had, to the satisfaction of those philosophers, placed even Jacobus Capitaen, Gulielmus Amo, Francis Williams, etc. outside intellectual history they chose Descartes as the scapegoat of their own complementary rejection and declared: 'I feel, therefore, I am.'

And again, in 1991: 'need I remind you that Leopold Sedar Senghor took on Descartes and his thesis of rational [racial?] exclusivity by proposing his negritudinist credo of: "I feel, therefore, I am."'²³⁹

---

²³⁷ This, at least, is Souleymane Bachir Diagne's tongue-in-cheek – or even mildly facetious – suggestion. See his interesting *Léopold Sédar Senghor: l'art africain comme philosophie* (Paris: Riveneuve éditions, 2007), 56.

²³⁸ For a full version of what this syllogism might be, see Marcien Towa, *L'idée d'une philosophie négro-africaine* (Yaoundé: Editions Clé, 1979), 17: 'Le syllogisme du racisme peut s'énoncer ainsi: L'homme est un être essentiellement pensant, raisonnable/Or le nègre est incapable de pensée et de raisonnement. Il n'a pas de philosophie, il a une mentalité prélogique, etc./Donc le Nègre n'est pas vraiment un homme et peut être, à bon droit, traité comme un animal.'

²³⁹ Respectively: "Cross-currents: The 'New African' After Cultural

Yet, moving back towards *Myth, Literature and the African World* (1973-4; first published in 1976), there is arguably a more suggestive lead, in the way in which an existential conception of existence is qualified. A pith-helmet-crowned Descartes is 'engaged in the mission of piercing the jungle of the black pre-logical mentality with his intellectual canoe' (*MLAW*, 138), a phrase it is difficult to transcribe without laughing; the Frenchman is depicted as attempting to reduce the cosmic (or spatial) logic of being 'to a functional particularism of being'; and finally, is himself reduced to 'syntactical proportions' (recall Wiredu), the severance and abstraction of that free-hanging '*sum*' or '*je suis*' corrected and invested by the clear-eyed African standing before him, who invents the following grounding epithet: 'white-creature-in-pith-helmet-in-African-jungle-who-thinks and, finally, white-man-who-has-problems-believing-in-his-own-existence.' (*MLAW*, 139) The journey here is not one of exploration, but becomes, quite simply, a slap from reality, a reminder of the spatiality of his existence. The corrective to this – and it works in a few ways – comes in the conception of life as a journey.

George Steiner's work *The Death of Tragedy* is a tale diagnosing the decline and decadence of what is, he says, the highest Western art form. It stems from an orthodox account in Western intellectual history – the diminishing of sensibility administered to our creative imagination through a sceptical turn in the seventeenth century.[240] Its angle of vision, to rework Suvin,[241] looks back on a golden and receding past of artistic sensibility, amid a denuded present, our dark and cold times; and as is proper to a thinker attracted to decadence, that dark

---

Encounters" [1982], *Essays*, 125; "The External Encounter," *Essays*, 171; and "The Credo of Being and Nothingness," *Essays*, 245.

[240] See, for example, Paul Hazard, *La crise de la conscience européenne: 1680–1715* (Paris: Gallimard, 1968).

[241] See above, 159.

and cold present seems futureless, projects no horizon beyond the present's 'étendue'.²⁴² One structure of *Myth, Literature and the African World*, is the usage of this (Western) sceptical arc the better to formulate and describe a conception of 'world', which channels the potential of Yoruba poetic resource into tragedy.

We know the explicit points of contention between Steiner and Soyinka off by heart: how Steiner, whose great studies seem to depend on an annoying, prescriptive and apparently irrepressible desire to limit the range of great artistic achievement to the things he knows how to talk about, thinks that tragedy – 'that representation of personal suffering and heroism' – is not universal, but distinctive of the western tradition;²⁴³ and how he sees the rational understanding of electricity, which comes with Benjamin Franklin, the fading fury of lightning's reach between heaven and hell, its receding from the tragic stage.²⁴⁴ But beyond the explicit content of the

---

²⁴² George Steiner, *The Death of Tragedy* (London: Faber and Faber, 1961). Chinua Achebe, in implicit contrast, would later characterize the importance and availability of mythic resource to the African writer, via Japan's example of the possible symbioses of technological development and historical cultural practice. See "What's Literature Got To Do With It?" in *Hopes and Impediments*, 110: 'In one sense then it was travelling away from its old self towards a cosmopolitan, modern identity, while in another sense it was journeying back to regain a threatened past and selfhood. To comprehend the dimensions of this gigantic paradox and coax from it such unparalleled inventiveness requires not mere technical flair but the archaic energy, the perspective, the temperament of creation myths and symbolism.' 'Archaic energy' is quite a grand phrase for a writer like Achebe to use, but can easily be decanted into the more concrete sense of an artist who moves in a world in which mythic symbolism is readily available and meaningful.
²⁴³ Steiner, *The Death of Tragedy*, 3.
²⁴⁴ *Ibid.*, 194. The specific example is pilfered from Marx's *Grundrisse:* 'Let us take e.g. the relation of Greek art [...] to the present time. It is well known that Greek mythology is not only the arsenal of Greek art, but

argument, I am struck by one specific expression. Steiner remarks that Milton was the last poet to move and work and imagine within the 'ancient hierarchic world image', and his characterization of the importance of *Paradise Lost* seems to me good enough to quote at length:

> His refusal in *Paradise Lost* to choose between the Ptolemaic and the Copernican accounts of celestial motion is a gesture both serene and sorrowful; serene, because it regards the proposals of natural science as less urgent or assured than those of poetic tradition; sorrowful, because it marks the historical moment in which the forms of the cosmos recede from the authority of humanistic judgement. Henceforth the stars burn out of reach. After Milton the mythology of animate creation and the nearly tangible awareness of a continuity between the human and the divine order – that sense of a relationship between the rim of private experience and the hub of the great wheel of being – lose their hold over intellectual life.[245]

The difference we feel moving within that metaphor 'world',

---

also its foundation. Is the view of nature and of social relations on which the Greek imagination and Greek mythology is based possible with self-acting mule spindles and railways and locomotives and electrical telegraphs? What chance has Vulcan against Roberts and Co., Jupiter against the lightning rod and Hermes against the *Crédit Mobilier?* All mythology overcomes and dominates and shapes the forces of nature in the imagination and by the imagination; it therefore vanishes with the advent of real mastery over them... From another side: is Achilles possible with powder and lead? Or the *Iliad* with the printing press, not to mention the printing machine? Do not the song and the saga and the muse necessarily come to an end with the printer's bar, and hence do not the necessary conditions of poetry vanish?' See Karl Marx, *Political Writings, Vol.3: The First International and After*, ed. David Fernbach (New York: Random House/Vintage Books and Monthly Review Press; London and Harmondsworth: Penguin Books and New Left Review, 1974), 110-111.

[245] Steiner, *The Death of Tragedy*, 320.

between the Ptolemaic and the Copernican, is expressed movingly as Satan travels back towards earth and Eden in Book II of *Paradise Lost*: the 'serenity' with which Milton includes heaven and hell within the confines of the physical universe, the 'sorrow' as those distances have become so vast as to place those confines beyond our sense of space, as one world recedes beyond our imagination.[246]

There is an irresistible sense in which Soyinka's skeletal Ogun narrative riffs on Milton's rendering of Satan's return journey to earth.[247] In Milton's poem, none but Satan 'could be found/So hardy as to proffer or accept/Alone the dreadful voyage' (1.424-5), and he it is that for the general safety despises his own (1.481-2); and so he who is 'the adversary of God and man' (1.629) crosses the 'unfounded deep', 'the void immense' (1.829), 'the hoary deep, a dark/illimitable ocean without bound,/Without dimension, where length, breadth, and height,/And time and place are lost' (1.890-4); or again, the 'wild abyss,/The womb of nature' (1.910-11); eventually arriving, 'shrouds and tackle torn' (1044), though safe; before Sin and Death pave 'after him a broad and beaten way/Over the dark abyss' (1.1026-7).[248] In Soyinka's *Myth, Literature and the African World,* Ogun must 'journey across the void' (*MLAW*, 28), an 'impassable barrier'

---

[246] See Stephen Prickett, "The Bible in Literature and Art," in *The Cambridge Companion to Biblical Interpretation*, ed. John Barton (Cambridge: Cambridge University Press, 1998), 170-1.

[247] Christiane Fioupou has conjectured as to a possible link between the sudden metaphysical ascent of the penultimate chapter of *The Interpreters* and the opening sentence of *Paradise Lost*, held in the anaphora of 'Of'. "Salut à toi Saint Atunda... Grand iconoclaste dès la genèse: récits de création, traditions yoruba et réappropriations littéraires," paper delivered for the conference 'Avatar des commencements: récits de genèse', Université de Toulouse-Le Mirail, December 4, 2012.

[248] John Milton, *Paradise Lost,* ed. Alastair Fowler (London; New York: Longman, 1968).

(28) having arisen between gods and the world of men; the god 'plunge[s] through the abyss' (29), is 'torn asunder in cosmic winds' (30), only to rescue himself 'from the precarious edge of total dissolution' (29) through the strength of his will. Ultimately, it is this strength of will which enables him to clear the primordial jungle separating the gods from men, and to forge a bridge for his companion-deities to follow. What might this mean?

A number of things, I think. Firstly, that the imaginative sympathy which Soyinka has with Greek tragedy and Shakespeare, or the serene part of Milton, assured through contemporary Yoruba ritual and festival, might be thought of as attributable to a single span of imagination. Eric Gombrich liked pointing out that, in terms of human and artistic evolution, 3000 years is a short time,[249] and there is an important sense in which the imaginative creations of a chronologically distant past remain within the same imaginative span of certain cultures, at given moments. In the context of Soyinka scholarship, it is a point which Philip Brockbank has made persuasively:

> Little is to be gained by considering Shakespeare in relation to the theatre of our own time unless we recognize that the continuing traditions of tragedy have primordial as well as literary sources, and that its literary history of some twenty-five hundred years in the western world is, in an anthropological perspective, quite brief. [...] It is not merely that Shakespeare and the Greeks

---

[249] See, for example, E.H. Gombrich, *Art and Illusion: A Study in the Psychology of Pictorial Representation* (London: Phaidon, 1960), 96: 'No lesson of psychology is perhaps more important for the historian to absorb than this multiplicity of layers, the peaceful coexistence in man of incompatible attitudes. There never was a primitive stage of man when all was magic; there never happened an evolution which wiped out the earlier phase. What happens is rather that different institutions and different situations favour and bring out a different approach to which both the artist and his public learn to respond.'

have had an influence upon Soyinka; it is rather that influences – current and flowing-in from the remote past – are by his work made more accessible to us in plays that have gone before.[250]

Secondly, that being in its most fundamental, tragic acceptation and expression, strongly coordinates spatial situatedness and forward movement, in the conceit of the journey, the breaking down and disintegrations which we might undergo in life, and which require great will and endurance to recover and rebuild ourselves from. And this is held and guaranteed in the key Yoruba modulation of the meaning of 'world' from 'standard' (English?) English. For the Yoruba word *'ayé'* conflates 'life' and 'world', senses which in standard English might be kept apart. As Jacob Olupona has observed in his study of Ile-Ife and Yoruba religious practice: 'Life in this world is symbolized as a journey that ends with a return to one's home – *Ayé l'àjò, bí ó tilè pé pé, a ó relé* [The world is a journey, and no matter how long we stay abroad we will return home].'[251]

In the perspective of a writer seeking tragic tools from contemporary ritual, this conflation of world and life in the journey suggests two things: firstly, in line with the *symbolic* constitutions of space in ritual, the chorus and poetry and music form the stage, the cosmic envelope, so to speak. Soyinka has the following to say of choric participation in such a ritualist sense of space:

> The so-called audience is itself an integral part of that arena of conflict; it contributes spiritual strength to the protagonist through its choric reality which must first be conjured up and established, defining and investing the arena through offerings and incantations. The drama

---

[250] Brockbank, "Blood and Wine," 77-8.
[251] Jacob Olupona, *City of 201 Gods: Ile-Ife in Time, Space, and the Imagination* (Berkeley; Los Angeles; London: University of California Press, 2011), 34.

would be non-existent except within and against this symbolic representation of earth and cosmos, except within this communal compact whose choric essence supplies the collective energy for the challenger of chthonic realms. Overt participation when it comes is channelled through a formalised repertoire of gestures and liturgical responses. The 'spontaneous' participant from within the audience does not permit himself to give vent to a bare impulse or a euphoria which might bring him out as a dissociated entity from within the choric mass. (*MLAW*, 39)

Secondly, there is a constant tension between protagonist and chorus, between journeyer and world, and this constant search for balance, held in the ritual in the 'balletic tension' (31) of the stave, its aggressive ore and restraining fronds, must, in the writer's tragic resource, find a different form of expression. This, I think, comes in a certain facet of Yoruba oral poetry. Abiola Irele once defined what he called the 'experience of literature' as 'the reminder it provides that the use of language for imaginative purposes represents a fundamental component of the symbolic structures by which the individual relates to society and by which society itself relates to its universe of existence.'[252] A key constituent of this symbolic structure comes in the ways it expresses just this dance between the mutual constitutions of 'world' or human constituency (not limited to the living) and protagonist, in the dance of coercion or restraint, and self-assertion. It is a point of which Olabiyi Yai, another who has spent much of his intellectual life reflecting upon the endowments which specific oral rhetorical conventions bring to our understanding of the workings of literature, has posed the following trenchant question:

> Is it an exaggeration to find in it [oral poetics] the display – at the level of artistry – of dialectical and political relationships between the dream of an unrealisable

---

[252] Irele, *The African Imagination*, 27-8.

absolute freedom of the individual and the lived experience of an integrative social matrix? This social matrix is as reassuring as it is coercive.[253]

Here, the constitutive tensions of the motions of oral poetry enact the constitutive tensions of society's conceptions of individual and collective being. And with this, it is to the experience of *Death and the King's Horseman* that we now turn.

---

[253] Olabiyi Yai, "Issues in Oral Poetry: Criticism, Teaching and Translation," in *Discourses and its Disguises: The Interpretation of African Oral Texts*, eds. Karin Barber and P.F. de Moraes Farias (Birmingham: Centre of West African Studies, African Studies Series 1, 1989), 65.

V

Death and the King's Horseman: Rhetoric and Insinuating Possibility

> This book is concerned with the problem of how men actually think. The aim of these studies is to investigate not how thinking appears in textbooks on logic, but how it really functions in public life and in politics as an instrument of collective action.
> — Karl Mannheim, *Ideology and Utopia*[254]

> It may be worth noting that the Yoruba verb 'jẹ', 'to be' – denoting the possession of intrinsic qualities [...] also means 'to answer'. Thus it is suggested that one's intrinsic nature is called into being by being addressed.
> — Karin Barber, *The Anthropology of Texts*[255]

> Do me credit.
> — Elesin Oba, *Death and the King's Horseman* (21)

1

The Couple Pilkings

I would begin with the colonialists. It seems to me that too swift a diagnosis of Simon Pilkings' motivations obscures both

---

[254] Karl Mannheim, *Ideology and Utopia: An Introduction to the Sociology of Knowledge*, trans. Louis Wirth and Edward Shils (San Diego; New York; London: HBJ, 1985), 1.

[255] Karin Barber, *The Anthropology of Texts, Persons and Publics: Oral and Written Culture in Africa and Beyond* (Cambridge: Cambridge University Press, 2007), 128.

the meaning of ideology and, more importantly, its literary working-out, the ways in which our understanding of the functioning of ideology in a colonial context are, through *Death and the King's Horseman* (first published in 1975), clarified and enlarged. Biodun Jeyifo has written that, like

> the much-discussed hollow, self-serving 'benevolence' of the reformist claims of the imperialist ban on the institution of 'sati', widow-burning, in colonial India, Pilkings is motivated to intervene in Elesin Oba's suicide and thus 'contain' the institutional matrix which sustains it because it stands beyond, and confounds, the spheres of his secular, political-administrative authority.[256]

This is impeccable – the joke about the sun never setting on the British Empire (because God does not trust them in the dark) does not come from nowhere – but it is also clear that Pilkings himself is not *exclusively* motivated by hollowness, or self-serving indulgence, or (presumably) hypocritical benevolence; nor *exclusively* by the need to control and usher in everything into the pale of his administrative authority. If we fail to pause over the ways in which ideology works, the way in which men and women actually think in public and in politics, as signalled in Karl Mannheim's quote in the first epigraph to this chapter, we risk losing the deeper moral critique which comes specifically through literature, and which is not, ultimately, reducible to historical analysis.

In a discussion of the ideology of law in eighteenth-century England, the English historian E.P. Thompson memorably observed that in order to maintain hegemony, the law cannot be evidently unjust, as that way 'it will mask nothing, legitimate nothing, contribute nothing to any class's hegemony.' He goes on to point out that 'even rulers find a need to legitimize their power, to moralize their functions, to feel themselves to be

---
[256] Jeyifo, *Wole Soyinka*, 59.

useful and just', before making the essential point: that immersion in the logic of a particular ideology of law might lead practitioners to take this ideology on good faith, to be wrapped up and ravished by its own claims about itself; and that for sustenance and maintenance, those upholding and enforcing the law must consider it, broadly speaking, as morally justified, appealing even.[257] There is a keen expression of colonial ideology, how thinking really functions, in Jane and Simon Pilkings' discussion of ritual suicide:

> JANE: You know this business has to be stopped Simon. And you are the only man who can do it.
>
> SIMON: I don't have to stop anything. If they want to throw themselves off the top of a cliff or poison themselves for the sake of some barbaric custom what is that to me? If it were ritual murder or something like that I'd be duty-bound to do something. I can't keep an eye on all the potential suicides in this province. And as for that man – believe me it's good riddance.
>
> JANE [*laughs*]: I know you better than that Simon. You are going to have to do something to stop it – after you've finished blustering. (*DKH*, 31)

This is a convincing enactment of how law as ideology works. I am always struck by Jane's confidence that Pilkings is *bound* to action. What binds him is not just the administrative threat of sanction by his superiors, not just the fear of independent Yoruba political institutions beyond the pale, but that word 'duty', which steps into that moralizing of functions of which E.P. Thompson wrote. And what the exchange brings out extremely effectively is that what Pilkings cannot but feel as a moral duty – we are to assume that Jane's

---

[257] E.P. Thompson, *Whigs and Hunters: The Origin of the Black Act* (London, Harmondsworth: Peregrine Books, 1977), 263.

confidence derives from precedent (the fawning 'You are the only man who can do it' [31] is directed to swell her husband's head by recalling him to his past exploits) - is indeed a burden, but for him as for her (though not for us), yields the deeper satisfaction of helping-the-natives-do-the-right-thing-despite-themselves. The challenge, then, is to show how Soyinka's dramatic intelligence is applied to a specific and concrete expression of paternalist hypocrisy.

In order to begin to understand the Pilkings couple, we will first need briefly to imagine the ways in which community was construed and imagined and reinforced, across the British Empire. Benedict Anderson offers us a *tableau vivant* - he calls it 'grimly amusing', an idiomatic phrase generally used with the word 'spectacle' - of petty-bourgeois and bourgeois men and women using the colony to play, in his words, 'aristocrat off centre court: i.e. anywhere in the empire except at home.' The *dramatis personae* of these scenes of 'aristocratic' life include, *mutatis mutandis,* the 'bourgeois gentilhomme speaking poetry against a backcloth of spacious mansions and gardens filled with mimosa and bougainvillea, and a large supporting cast of houseboys, grooms, gardeners, cooks, amahs, maids, washerwomen, and, above all, horses.'[258]

Anderson speaks of colonial life, even in its domestic drabness, as some sort of spectacle or staging, yet he also directs us towards the wider historical motivations for this classically middle- or lower-middle class wish-fulfilment: namely, the colonial empire's expanding bureaucratic apparatus, which increasingly depended on recruiting from among the middle classes. Hannah Arendt, in an earlier essay, had conjectured that European colonies allowed a man to escape a society in which he would have to forget his youth if

---

[258] Benedict Anderson, *Imagined Communities: Reflections on the Origin and Spread of Nationalism* (London; New York: Verso, 1993), 150-1.

he wanted to grow up, to pursue untrammelled the boyhood ideals of the public school system, ultimately preventing, thereby, 'their converting the ideals of their boyhood into the mature ideas of men.'[259] A sort of Peter Pan-esque stayed childishness, understood by Arendt as curtailed or interrupted moral development – what J-M. Barrie expressed in the 'lost boys'.[260] (Arendt seems a little unconcerned by what all that preserved 'innocence' wrought across the world.)

In Anderson, the historical reason of an expanding bureaucracy and the wish-fulfilment of the middle classes in imitating the rituals of a dying landed class; in Arendt, the 'moral' sense of preserving boyhood ideals, at the cost of those ideals: both are useful in that they are attentive to the meaningful dislocation between metropole and colony, the way in which that distance, geographical and temporal, shapes and informs and sustains colonial ritual. What, we ask ourselves, is the first appearance of the Pilkings couple in Soyinka's play? Dancing a tango by an aged gramophone; their shapes dancing in and out of the shadows; wide windows and a verandah. And the standing apart of Amusa.

James Gibbs once performed the useful service of cataloguing the responses to the 1991 production of *Death and the King's Horseman* at the Manchester Royal Exchange Theatre, in England. Leaving aside the historical ignorance and casual racism of many of the journalists and academics under review (tribal fables and drum-bashing and cups of

---

[259] Hannah Arendt, "The Imperialist Character (On Kipling)", in *Reflections on Literature and Culture*, trans. Susannah Young-Ah Gottlieb (Stanford, California: Stanford University Press, 2007), 171.

[260] See J.M. Barrie, *Peter Pan or The Boy Who Would Not Grow Up* (London: Hodder and Stoughton, 1928). Are we perhaps to hear in 'Pilkings' – (plain?) Jane and (simple?) Simon – that hint of the pickle, the sense of interrupted preservation which Arendt alluded to?

jungle-juice), the most persistent thread is their concern before the 'caricaturing' of the colonial agents. Grevel Lindop, for instance, writing in the *Times Literary Supplement*, observes that they were 'just sufficiently caricatured to remind us that we are seeing the colonial administrator through African eyes.' For Michael Schmidt, writing for the *Daily Telegraph*, the achievement of the actor Dormandy, playing Pilkings, lay in turning 'a caricature of a part into a rounded character', adding that Soyinka's 'less than certain grasp of English characters' was 'generally too unsubtle to be credible'.[261] There are considerable constraints in review-writing in newspapers – ideological, obviously, but more pressingly, constraints of space – but it seems to me that, if I may be allowed to extrapolate from Gibbs' selection, there is no consciousness of the dislocation between home and colony as being a specific and historical problem, which in turn merits its own mediations in literature.

The Tunisian and Jewish writer Albert Memmi, in his diagnostic *Portrait du colonisé, portrait du colonisateur*, wrote memorably of how the colonialist's attempt to sustain a life within a picturesque or tourist décor inexorably declined, under pressure from surrounding historical circumstance, into the reconstitution of the smells and sounds of childhood, a faux-pastoral shield from moral consciousness. Memmi goes on to inscribe this into a broader relationship, that of the image the colonialist has and needs to have of the metropole, the source and guarantee of his own staged grandeur:

> [Le colonisateur] exige qu'elle mérite sa confiance, qu'elle lui renvoie cette image d'elle-même qu'il souhaite: idéal

---

[261] See James Gibbs, "Neglected Masterpiece: Responses to a UK Production of a major Wole Soyinka play," in *West Africa*, 1-7 April 1991, 471-473. For a discussion of 'caricature' in *Death and the King's Horseman*, see Soyinka's interview with Henry Louis Gates Jr., "Post Mortem for a Death," in *Art, Dialogue and Outrage: Essays on Literature and Culture* (Ibadan: New Horn, 1988), 342-344.

> inaccessible au colonisé et justificatif parfait de ses propres mérites empruntés. Souvent, à force de l'espérer, il finit par y croire un peu. Les nouveaux débarqués, la mémoire encore fraîche, parlent de la métropole avec infiniment plus de justesse que les vieux colonialistes. [...] Le colonialiste semble avoir oublié la réalité vivante de son pays d'origine. [...] Il est remarquable que, même pour des colonisateurs nés en colonie, c'est-à-dire charnellement accordés, adaptés au soleil, à la chaleur, à la terre sèche, le paysage de référence reste brumeux, humide et vert.[262]

Notice the fading arc of that decline into pastoral illusion, which comes with old age and (wilfully?) slack memory. The freshness of experience at 'home', we are to imagine, loses itself in time, as words and linguistic conventions *from* the colony displace those of the metropole, and the schemata of pastoralism displace those of realism. I find that final sentence remarkable in the way it spells out for us the strength of illusion, and representational schemata, over experience, in the colonialist's representations of 'home'; how it shows, perhaps, that a 'home from home' is, for the colonialist, a fiction fighting disabusal before both metropole and colony.

I have briefly discussed Anderson, Arendt and Memmi not because their ideas exhaust the range of experience of colonialists across British and French empires, which is obviously not the case. Rather, they seem to me useful starting points in approaching Soyinka's representation of the colonial agents who inhabit the world of *Death and the King's Horseman*. The starting point for representing Simon and Jane Pilkings comes not so much in representing them 'through African eyes' – although Amusa arriving and observing the tangoing shapes certainly has that satirical function – as in the fact of showing that government in the colonies, and the agents who

---

[262] Albert Memmi, *Portrait du colonisé. Portrait du colonisateur* (Paris: Gallimard, 1957), 80.

enforced and maintained government power, were themselves shaped by a sort of interrupted history, in which formalism – the reduction of reality to illusion, substance into fiction – became an operative principle.

A key instance comes in the poverty of the colonial agents' English. This is *not* merely an individual poverty, as if with a little more Quintilian or Puttenham, a little more Dickens and Tennyson, each could arrive at the desired level of eloquence. As Memmi suggests, we are born into or inherit a repertoire of words and phrases and tournures, which shapes and conditions the words we can choose. (In this sense, the old hand represents something of a language-horizon.) Take Soyinka's intelligent exploitation of standard Western anthropological categories in the exchange between Amusa, the Yoruba and Muslim police sergeant, and the Pilkings:

> JANE: Oh Amusa, what is there to be scared of in the costume. You saw it confiscated last month from those *egungun* men who were creating trouble in town. You helped arrest the cult leaders yourself – if the juju didn't harm you at the time how could it possibly harm you now? And merely by looking at it?
>
> AMUSA: Madam, I arrest the ringleaders who make trouble but me I no touch *egungun*. That *egungun* inself, I no touch. And I no abuse 'am. I arrest ringleaders but I treat *egungun* with respect. (*DKH*, 25)

Jane's argument is logical, though the premise is flawed, for the phrase '*egungun* men' conflates two incompatible entities (an *egungun* masquerade among the Yoruba is an ancestral spirit, not a man and an ancestral spirit.)[263] Indeed I hear in that '*egungun* men' Jane's desire to have her cake and eat it, to

---

[263] Soyinka summarizes the probable origins of *egungun*, and its subsequent evolution into *agbegijo* and *alarinjo* theatre (amongst others), in "Theatre in African Traditional Cultures," *Essays*, 135. The classical formulation

suggest to Amusa a respectful recognition of the status of the *egungun*, her 'understanding', just as she denies it in language. By contrast, Amusa's Pidgin expresses precision, and upholds the necessary distinctions. And even in a realm of language in which he is not entirely at ease, such as administrative-ese, Amusa's language still preserves precision:

> AMUSA: I have to report that it has come to my information that one prominent chief, namely, the Elesin Oba, is to commit death tonight as a result of native custom. Because this is criminal offence I await further instruction at charge office. Sergeant Amusa. (26)

This is reported speech, which should suggest to us that Amusa is performing some sort of simultaneous translation for his superiors (in rank alone), into a language which he thinks they will comprehend. This explains the periphrasis of 'prominent chief', which would be obvious to anyone local, and the concessions to the legal hegemony of the British agents – 'Because this is criminal offence' is stronger than 'as a result of native custom'. The apodictic thrust, however, cannot resolve that 'commit death', a hendiadys which perfectly expresses the demanding ambiguities of the ritual already enacted in the play's first scene: we hear in that 'commit' something of the pledge, the full implication to a communal project, an absolute engagement taken out on behalf of community; yet it also triggers associations with suicide, or what England and Wales still criminalized as 'self-death'. (And

---

of the relationship between *egungun* and *alarinjo* theatre came in Joel Adedeji's article "'Alarinjo': The Traditional Yoruba Travelling Theatre," in *Theatre in Africa*, eds. Ogunba and Irele, 27-49. The article stemmed from Adedeji's unpublished PhD thesis *The Alarinjo Theatre: the Study of a Yoruba Theatrical Art from its Earliest to the Present Times* (University of Ibadan, 1969).

notice too how it straddles the discourses of sin and crime.) The Pilkings work together to resolve the profusion encapsulated in the phrase 'commit death' into generality – the sort of casual abstraction which we can imagine colonialists picking up during their postgraduate training at Oxbridge[264] – ironing it out from committing death, to committing murder, to committing ritual murder, and finally sealing it in a diptych of clichés, which neatly marry glibness and paranoia: 'You think you've stamped it all out but it's always lurking under the surface somewhere.' (26) And yet Soyinka is careful to show that the colonialist can fall short of imaginative engagement whilst remaining capable of intimation of the limits of his or her understanding. The cleverest dramatization of hearing something and not having the ears to hear comes with Simon Pilkings' reaction to 'those bloody drums', as he seeks to establish which measures to take to anticipate the death problem. We watch on, as what he first hears as 'noise-making', after a moment's reflection, becomes something else:

PILKINGS: It's different Jane. I don't think I've heard this particular – sound – before. Something unsettling about it.

JANE: I thought all bush drumming sounded the same.

PILKINGS: Don't tease me now Jane. This may be serious. (27)

---

[264] Anthony Kirk-Greene, *On Crown Service: A History of HM Colonial and Overseas Civil Services 1837-1937* (London; New York: I.B. Tauris Publishers, 1999), 23; ch.3. Training for the colonial service passed from the two-term Tropical African Service to a full academic year in 1928; to the Colonial Administrative Service course in 1932; and to the major rebranding of 1946, with the Devonshire course. Until the institution of the Devonshire course, learning was widely and thinly spread, primarily academic, and tended to ignore contemporary political developments in the colonies. See Anthony Kirk-Greene, *Symbol of Authority* (London; New York: I.B. Tauris, 2006), ch.3.

That something else is 'a sound', or a noise with 'nuance', but which nonetheless remains impermeable to Pilkings. Jane's teasing reminds him and informs us that this is an improvement on past performance, but the overall dramatic effect is simply to suggest gradations of interpretative poverty.

These are fairly simple instances of not being able to imagine meanings beyond which conventional uses of language provide for – the conventions here being those of the administration of a region in this colony – yet the crudest or most stark example of this comes with the aide-de-camp, the wonderfully named Bob, a palindromic name which suggests a sort of perpetual violent feedback:

> AIDE-DE-CAMP: Sir, there's a group of women chanting up the hill. [...] What do we do about the invasion? We can still stop them from here. [...] They're not many. And they seem quite peaceful. (72)

This would be an amusing dramatization of the limits of Bob's language being the limits of his world – what relation in his own mind is there between the word 'invasion' and a few women peacefully chanting? – if we had not already heard his trigger-happy racism, which reminds us of the festering aggression stalking that word 'stop'.

I earlier distanced myself from the notion that the Pilkings were the colonial administrators 'seen through African eyes', as being analytically limited. I think we would be better served if we saw these two characters, who are not to be conflated, as a reworking of a colonial literary tradition. This is to say that Soyinka is not only working within a Yoruba or Nigerian or West-African tradition of representing the colonial agents, but also within and against an English literary tradition which represents the height of tragedy *for the colonial agent* either as an inability to understand, or as some sort of intractable moral dilemma.

Soyinka's 'Author's Note' (*DKH*, 6-7) is, in truth, one of

the first *commentaries* on the play's production, and might be seen as a corrective to interpretations which fail to acknowledge the care he takes to diminish and reduce and subvert a colonial literary tradition. If one 'of the more obvious alternative structures of the play would be to make the District Officer the victim of a cruel dilemma', writes Soyinka, nonetheless no attempt 'should be made in production to suggest it.' His well-known line about the catalytic function of the colonial agents in the same 'Author's Note' ('The Colonial Factor is an incident, a catalytic incident merely' [7]) is, among other things, a way of suggesting a formalist literary history, the fact that here the tropes and commonplaces of one genre are emasculated and mocked, reduced to size.[265] It is a matter of technique: the risk lies in granting too much attention to the colonial agents, as if their individual psychological uncertainties or prevarications were the justified focus of our concern and sympathy. The greatest expression of this comes in Simon Pilkings' relationship with Olunde, the medical student recently returned from Britain, and son to the King's Horseman; it is there, I think, that we see Soyinka working out a powerful representation of ideology, in his colonialist who puts the paternal into paternalism.

Simon Pilkings is striking because he assumes that he is an exception to the rule of exclusion. There is a memorable

---

[265] See also Soyinka's discussion of Ousmane Sembene's *God's Bits of Wood* [*Les Bouts de Bois de Dieu*], in *Myth, Literature and the African World*, 120: 'As with most writing that concerns itself with the process of an organic revolution, the colonial agents, though they form an important component of the conflict, are paid only grudging attention. Their appearance is reduced in scale to enlarge the positive emergence of the indigenous. Though their presence and actions lay the ground for the conflict, they are reduced to the proportional relations of catalysts; their fate is of no interest to the author except in so far as it may by contrast illuminate the virtues of the new vision of society.'

exchange in which Jane attempts to bring her husband to acknowledge his exclusion from the local Yoruba community:

> SIMON: He was rather close you know, quite unlike most of them. Didn't give much away, not even to me.
>
> JANE: Aren't they all rather close, Simon?
>
> SIMON: These natives here? Good gracious. They'll open their mouths and yap with you about their family secrets before you can stop them. Only the other day...
>
> JANE: But Simon, do they really give anything away? I mean, anything that really counts. This affair for instance, we didn't know that they still practised that custom, did we?
>
> SIMON: Ye-e-es, I suppose you're right there. Sly, devious bastards. (*DKH*, 29)

I love the way in which Soyinka conveys the impression that Jane is quoting Simon to Simon, that she is voicing deference without sacrificing truth, as the objective of true deference must always have been. The exchange is framed by Simon Pilkings' two contradictory statements, and the passage between the two succinctly expresses his paranoia. From his opening summary declaration that the 'natives' are free with their 'secrets', he arrives, under Jane's prompting, at the more insidious (for him) sense that there is a world beyond ('Sly, devious bastards'). It is clever too to have Joseph on stage during the exchange, for, in the outrageous lack of contact, this well conveys the ways in which colonized people might only be meaningful, for colonialists, insofar as they represent puzzles or intellectual riddles to be cracked, or inferiors to respond to orders. This exchange is later echoed in the village girls' parody of British colonial language, which discreetly demonstrates that such exchanges are not random or exceptional, but rather symptomatic and widespread. Part of

the girls' play reads thus:
— He's loyal?
— Absolutely.
— Lay down his life for you what?
— Without a moment's thought.
— Had one like that once. Trust him with my life.
— Mostly of course they are liars.
— Never known a native tell the truth.
— Does it get rather close around here? (38)

If we have been listening carefully, we will recall Simon Pilkings' insulting 'compliment' to Amusa ('Oh, Amusa, what a let down you are. I swear by you at the club you know – thank God for Amusa, he doesn't believe in any mumbo-jumbo.' [24]), the club being the arbiter of colonial taste. More subtly, the link between the particular example (the scene between Jane and Pilkings) and the general rule (the basis of the girls' parody) works through the word 'close', which builds a bridge between the two. In the scene between the Pilkings (29; quoted above), the word 'close' had been used to express the classical colonial fear that the natives hold an impenetrable secret, that they are always keeping something back. In the language of the girls' parody, the word 'close' reappears under a different though related meaning – the less common meaning of stifling heat, with its hint of menacing claustrophobia – and if we miss the association, we miss the parody's cogency.

The less obvious and far more important function in my eyes, however, is the extremely quiet and persistent way in which Soyinka has Pilkings assume, throughout the play, that he continues to benefit from the confidence of Olunde. Pilkings' sentence 'Didn't give much away, not even to me' (29), implies not merely that there was a measure of cooperation in spiriting Olunde away, but that he lends it meaning beyond the mere fact of Olunde studying medicine in England; that this fact comes to assume, for him, a number of values. Aristotle is said to have said that a key moment in the complex tragic plot was the moment of anagnorisis (recognition, or discovery), a character's major movement from ignorance to knowledge, in which he or she comes to know the real nature of things.[266] What might seem to us like Simon Pilkings' peripatetic moment is prepared by Olunde's support for the ritual, despite his education in England as a doctor, the trope which saw the colonial subject turned into the colonialist's image. At the moment in which 'that very sensitive young man', who is 'going to make a first-class doctor' (28) utters the words that any intervention against his father's participation in the ritual would be a 'calamity', we are not surprised – are perhaps also (perversely?) gratified – by his shock. In truth, however, Soyinka is responding to the convention in colonial literature of making, as he puts it, a tragedy of a moral dilemma, by making of the moment of recognition a *false* moment of recognition, by staging a dummy anagnorisis; for, and this is brilliant because it shouts out tragic convention just as it goes on to ignore it, Pilkings *persists* in thinking that things can go on as they were before, as if this is a mere problem readily subject to resolution, a glitch liable to smoothing; he *persists*, that is, in his ignorance, in his former state, does not move from ignorance to a form of even qualified knowledge, despite his open-mouthed inarticulacy ('You... said what?' [58]).

This is the deeper meaning and powerful irony shadowing Pilkings' attempts to report Olunde's speech to a father now imprisoned by the District Officer: a divested father, but a father nonetheless:

> PILKINGS: Your son, anyway, sends his consolation. He asks for your forgiveness. When I asked him not to despise you his reply was: I cannot judge

---

[266] Aristotle, *Poetics,* trans. Stephen Halliwell (Chicago: University of Chicago Press, 1998), chs. 16 and 24.

him, and if I cannot judge him, I cannot despise
him. He wants to come to you to say goodbye and
to receive your blessing. (63)

I think we should assume that 'sending consolation' is a paraphrase, or mistranslation, of what Pilkings himself assumes Olunde to have meant, for Olunde, as we later learn, well knows that no consolation can be had. The next sentence is more complicated: is this directly reported speech (OLUNDE: I ask for his forgiveness)? Pilkings' own imputation? (Stepping outside the play's world, we might recall that the word 'forgiveness' is usually, as we have seen, submitted to sceptical interrogation within Soyinka's moral vocabulary.) Perhaps we might conjecture that Pilkings' usage of the word 'forgiveness' in fact betrays his intention to pass over the insoluble harm done to justice with a vague and no doubt empty category.

From here, we move briefly from the ambiguities of report – reported speech or paraphrase? – to quotation, Olunde's voice coming through strongly despite his intermediary. But then – as if that quotation is the only instancing of Olunde's voice Elesin might be afforded – we move back into report. And here we cannot miss the fact that, despite all his misunderstandings up to this point, despite what we might have hoped to be a powerful anagnorisis and the attenuation of ignorance into a form of knowledge, Pilkings can continue along the old lines, with his old assumptions and suppositions intact. For he assumes that the word 'goodbye' denotes a simple hand-waving as the boat leaves the harbour, a return to England, to studies, to medicine (abstracted of its war-torn terrain); he assumes that to 'receive blessing' is to reconcile, to patch up differences, so that each can go on his merry way; and so cannot hear in that goodbye the hint of a more terrible *despedida*, a profound parting of ways. It is essential, then, that we hear

Olunde's voice straining among the echoes and empty corridors of Pilkings' speech.

It gets worse. There is something of an awful pride in Pilkings, pride at having re-established a certain order, an order recognizable to him, in which the old hierarchies of understanding are not so much re-aligned as harried back into place, held down over the gaping cracks. As Elesin Oba asks Pilkings whether his son Olunde is to return to Britain, the irony inhabiting Pilkings' response is terrible:

> PILKINGS: Don't you think that's the most sensible thing for him to do? I advised him to leave at once, before dawn, and he agrees that is the right course of action. (64)

The word 'sensible' – a good word which betokens a completely inapposite pragmatism – is allied to leaving, whose association with death Soyinka has carefully prepared over the run of the play, though Pilkings has not heard this. (It is, of course, the structural underpinning of the ritual.) The adverbial 'at once' merely lends bite to the irony – and indeed beyond, insofar as it suggests Olunde's own logic: that if he acts quickly, something might yet be salvaged. If we suspect a certain pride in Pilkings in having taken charge of the situation, in having disbursed good advice, it comes through more insistently as he repeats the verb 'advise' shortly afterwards: 'As soon as the town is a little quieter. I advised it.' (64) Only his is not advice – Olunde is not passive or following something he had not already thought – and his meanings are not those of Olunde. Recognition is nothing of the sort; transforming Olunde into his image is a dream which must fail. But not even the tired voice of Simon Pilkings' last words which try to buy moral superiority on the cheap – 'Was this what you wanted?' (76) – only to meet with firm rebuttal, is the final expression of a will to ignorance. That will be reserved for the moment in which he goes to close the eyes of the once-King's

Horseman, to drawing the curtains, so to speak, to provide himself a neat sense that an end has come with death, and that it should fall to him to provide the suitable gesture of respect. Iyaloja, mother of the market, cries 'Let him alone!', likens him to a pauper and a stranger; and from Simon Pilkings no more do we hear.

***

A 'hermetic universe of forces or being', writes Soyinka in *Myth, Literature and the African World*, is 'the most fundamental attribute of all true tragedy, no matter where geographically placed.' (*MLAW*, 49) He gives the example of *King Lear:*

> [T]he world of the court, the world of Old Man Frost in the disordered community of wind and heather is rounded and entire. The relationship of seemingly disparate entities such as Court and nature is established through character transition – Lear, Kent, Edgar and Clown, out from one and into the other environment and back again; then the progressively vixenish daughters in near physical transformation. (50)

Each 'world' is complete in itself, and can either open up into smaller 'worlds' complete in themselves, or be integrated into other 'worlds'. The aggregate of these worlds, it would seem, would be the universe. The key point when considering *Death and the King's Horseman* is the nature of the articulations between 'worlds', or communities; and this becomes useful in a literary discussion because one of the key achievements in Soyinka's tragedy is the testing of senses of community – in war, in ritual, in law – through language, through different conventionalized ways of apprehending and creating the world, which are brought up, so to speak, against each other, or drawn into the others' shadow. At this most basic level, Soyinka's innovation on Duro Ladipo's Yoruba-language play

Oba Waja ['The King is Dead'] (which deals with the same historical event), his integration of the son of the King's Horseman into events of global (geographical) resonance through the War of 39-45,[267] invests *Death and the King's Horseman* with a different historical rhythm, creates, as we shall come to see in our discussion of the British monarchy's ceremonial, its own rule-generating force, its own specific dictates, its own order of time proper to that realm of human life.

Biodun Jeyifo has observed that

> in the course of the dramatic action of the play, we come to see that he [i.e. Simon Pilkings] is the representative of a social power that is nearly as feudal, nearly as shaped by expressive, ceremonial codes constructed around pre-modern patriarchal-aristocratic values as the culture of the 'subject race' over which he rules.[268]

Leaving aside the intriguing adverb 'nearly', I wish to clarify here just what that phrase 'social power' might fruitfully come to mean in *Death and the King's Horseman*, through a brief historical contextualization of staged rituals of power across the British Empire.

The 'minor reasons of dramaturgy' which Soyinka almost blithely refers to in his 'Author's Note', which has the play set back a few years into the historical moment of the war,

---

[267] In Act IV of Ladipo's play, the Horseman's son, Dawudu, is sipping beer in a highlife bar in Ghana when he learns of his father's death. See Ulli Beier's English adaptation in *Three Yoruba Plays: Oba Koso, Oba Waja and Oba Moro by Duro Ladipo* (Ibadan: Mbari Publications, 1964), 83:
  A GHANAIAN: O what a pity, the king of Oyo is dead. You son of Nigeria, a king has died in your country. Look at the news. The Alafin of Oyo is dead – did you know that man?
  DAWUDU: Stop music! Stop! This is bad news indeed!
  CHORUS: This king who died, is he your father?
  DAWUDU: No! But my father too, must die today.
[268] Jeyifo, *Wole Soyinka*, 159.

clarifies the divergence between the pastoral idyll of the colonialists' imagined community, and the carnage at 'home' – the aerial bombings, the execution of prisoners, the starvation, the sacrifice of lives without sufficient reason. Soyinka is careful to show just how remote the war, the suffering, the deaths, actually are from Jane's imagination; how it is reduced to just another dramatic illusion among many. It is depressing that it holds importance for her – consciously – only insofar as it intrudes upon the *ennui* of her existence. This is the full reach of her childishness – the war, the massive loss of life, as nothing but a sort of inconvenient memory of home, of reality:

> JANE: Ah yes the war. Here of course it is all rather remote. From time to time we have a black-out drill just to remind us that there is a war on. And the rare convoy passes through on its way somewhere or on manoeuvres. Mind you there is the occasional bit of excitement like that ship that was blown up in the harbour. (*DKH*, 51)

The first sighing phrase 'Ah yes the war' well expresses the head-shaking enactment of sadness which abstract and studied sympathy produces. The word 'rather' can be both an intensifier and a qualifier, and here it is a clever way of maintaining the ambiguity in Jane's mind as to the meaning behind the purely formal responses to the danger which drills imply. And a sense of being lost, or of not understanding one's relation to what is going on, is held and conveyed in the looseness of her deixis, 'somewhere'. This is preparation for what is to come. As the agon between Olunde and Jane intensifies, we are struck by Jane's glib because rehearsed line, which resonates in full contradiction to her previous unguarded talk of the war's remoteness, her talk of how, here in her colonial enclosure, she could scarcely remember that a war was actually going on:

OLUNDE [*waves his hand towards the background. The Prince is dancing past again – to a different step – and all the guests are curtseying as he passes*]: And this? Even in the midst of a devastating war, look at that. What name would you give that?
JANE: Therapy. British style. The preservation of sanity in the midst of chaos. (53)

I have argued in general that colonialists require a specific image of the metropole – pastoral, idyllic – in order to sustain their illusions and ideology in the colony. This is true of Soyinka's colonialists. The 'minor reasons of dramaturgy' legitimate the drafting in of the Prince into his critique – an extremely important means of exploring British royal ceremony, which is to say, the symbol at the heart of colonial ideology. (Anthony Kirk-Greene, the official historian of the British colonial service, has written of the trope of the royal visit in the memoirs of Governors 'fortunate enough to have been involved and maybe rewarded with a glimpse, a word, perhaps a decoration in the sovereign's own order after months and months of preparation.'[269]) It should probably be stressed – lest we take this as fortuitous, or accidental, or not-so-important – that this is an invention or a liberty Soyinka deliberately chooses to take with history: Edward VIII, in the years between 1919 and 1925, travelled to the dominions, to India, the West Indies and parts of British Africa. His younger brother, as Duke of York, travelled to East Africa (1924-5) and Australia (1927), and as George VI to Canada (1939) and South Africa (1947). At no time, to my knowledge, did a British prince travel to Nigeria in the 1940s.

For all the talk of the 'invention of tradition' on the African side following Hobsbawm and Ranger's edition of the same name, and particularly Ranger's essay on the invention of

---

[269] Kirk-Greene, *Symbol of Authority*, 120.

tradition in colonial Africa,[270] David Cannadine's studies on the invention of British royal ceremonial from the early nineteenth century up until the present date, part of which appeared in the same volume, seem to me more suggestive in this context.[271] Cannadine divides the development of British royal ceremonial into four phases: the inept management and uninventive royal ritual proper to a localized and diversified pre-industrial society (1820s-1870s); the heyday of invented tradition, heralded with Victoria's becoming Empress of India, which saw the resuscitation of old ceremonials, expertly staged (1877-1914); Britain's period as lone European monarchy, following the collapse of the European royal houses after the war of 1914-1918 (1914-1953); and the arrival of television and televised ceremonial, as Britain's power declined. Of interest here, are the first three periods, particularly insofar as they relate to English and British politics, and the power of the royal family.

Cannadine's studies demonstrate that, *domestically*, the invention of royal ritual and its attendant ceremonial enhancements depended in large part on the monarch's being excluded from politics, which is to say, within the political history of England and Britain, on the monarch's respecting parliament's exclusive right to govern. The disorienting change brought about by industrialization, observes Cannadine, created the obvious conditions for a 'preservation of anachronism', 'the deliberate, ceremonial presentation of an impotent but venerated monarch as a unifying symbol of permanence and national community'.[272] From 1914 to 1953,

---

[270] E.J. Hobsbawm and Terence Ranger, eds., *The Invention of Tradition* (Cambridge: Cambridge University Press, 1983).

[271] David Cannadine, "The Context, Performance and Meaning of Ritual: the British Monarchy and the 'Invention of Tradition', c. 1820-1977," in *ibid.*, 101-165. The following summary of British royal ritual is indebted to Cannadine's research.

[272] David Cannadine, "Splendor out of Court: Royal Spectacle and Pageantry in Modern Britain, c. 1820-1977," in *Rites of Power: Symbolism, Ritual,*

Britain underwent more substantive and far-reaching change: full adult suffrage and the demise of the great aristocratic families, notes Cannadine, 'left the Crown increasingly isolated in London society.' And the anguish and animosity which both the General Strike and Great Depression engendered, as well as the wars of 1914-1918 and 1939-1945, led to the presentational necessity: 'a politically neutral and personally admirable monarchy', 'the most effective aspect of which was its restrained, anachronistic ceremonial grandeur.'[273]

What, however, of Empire? Royal events, such as Victoria's Golden and Diamond Jubilees, or, from 1904, Empire Day on the anniversary of Victoria's birthday, became imperial events. Processions with banners and flags; religious services; the unveiling of statues or memorial halls; all sought to stress history and hierarchy and unity, as secured and guaranteed in the crown. 'By these interconnected pageants and mutually reinforcing ceremonials,' remarks Cannadine, 'the British Empire put itself on display, and represented itself to itself, more frequently, more splendidly, more ostentatiously and more globally than any other realm.'[274] The powerful fiction of national identity easily forgot or effaced what Benedict Anderson has reminded us in one of the more amusing footnotes of *Imagined Communities*, as to the – from a nationalist perspective – 'foreign' basis of today's ruling family:

> It is nice that what eventually became the late British Empire has not been ruled by an 'English' dynasty since the early eleventh century: since then a motley parade of Normans (Plantagenets), Welsh (Tudors), Scots

---

and *Politics Since the Middle Ages*, ed. Sean Wilentz (Philadelphia: University of Pennsylvania Press, 1985),215.

[273] *Ibid.*, 224. We should no doubt be perplexed that people continue to praise the British royal family for its restraint.

[274] David Cannadine, *Ornamentalism: How the British Saw their Empire* (London: Penguin Books, 2001), 111.

(Stuarts), Dutch (House of Orange) and Germans (Hanoverians) have squatted on the imperial throne. No one much cared until the philological revolution and a paroxysm of English nationalism in World War I. House of Windsor rhymes with House of Schönbrunn or House of Versailles.[275]

In Soyinka's *Death and the King's Horseman*, we are privy to one instance of imperial power 'representing itself to itself', its *'tawdry decadence'* (45) hanging in relief against what we know of the misery and death of the ongoing war. There is no doubt in my mind that Soyinka expects of the audience an awareness of this history, of contemporary events in Europe, for this gives traction to the staging of royal ceremonial, to its obscene ripening.

The overture to the Prince's appearance in Act IV has the colonial couples in fancy-dress, and the local police brass band complete with white conductor. As so often in Soyinka's work, we would do well to dwell not just on the 'direction' in stage direction, but on the specific words he uses. (Nabokov said he could not write theatre because he saved all the best stuff for the stage directions, the only place he could flex his writing muscles.) Couples are *'ranged'* as paintings or stills, and *'gaze'* (45), the word of the lovelorn, at the door through which the prince is to enter. If I were to direct this scene, I would pay considerable heed to that *'At last, the entrance of Royalty'* (45), giving full scope to their gazing, to the wait, allowing the full force of that badly played 18th-century Thomas Arne number 'Rule Britannia!' to reduce it all, for us, to pitiful illusion: *'Britain rules the waves!'*, though that was then and this is now; *'Britain never never never shall be slaves!'*, though the couplet slave-wave has a nasty historical ring, here in Nigeria as elsewhere; *'Rule Britannia!'*, because that is the image, as

---

[275] Anderson, *Imagined Communities*, 83 n1.

Memmi says, which the colonialists so needed for their own mission, to bask in the radiated glory of an overripe anachronism. Perhaps the 'European costume' of the Prince and the Governor is an atavistic or nostalgic nod to a golden European aristocratic age, when power went with ceremony or fêted pomp (grime lurks within the party, fêted sounds with fetid); perhaps European costume means French seventeenth-century dress, the costume of the *société de cour* which Norbert Elias so illuminatingly analysed, that extreme expression of power through style as exercised by Louis XIV.[276] What is intelligent, in any case, is that the division between power and performance, between action and acting, is here attenuated; that there is no sense of weakening of performative codes – the footman is liveried, but still delivers the letter; the Resident still instructs Pilkings within his seventeenth-century attire, and his clichés and idiomatic banalities – 'Nose to the ground'; 'don't let things get out of hand'; 'Keep a cool head' (47) – which carry the weight of hierarchy, are felt to be a perfectly adequate expression.

I must now come to Jane Pilkings. One of her more obvious functions is to make us cringe at the misogyny which she has so readily taken upon herself ('Darling, why are you getting rattled? I was only trying to be intelligent.' [26]; or again: 'Shut up woman and get your things on.' – 'Alright boss, coming.' [34]). There is an important sense in which this is most cogently expressed in her attempts to be stupid, to suppress her intelligence or play the role of incomprehension, which means we risk no longer being able to distinguish between the charlatan and the real deal. Consider, for instance, her description of events at the harbour to Olunde:

JANE: I don't quite understand it really. Simon tried

---

[276] Norbert Elias, *La société de cour*, trans. Pierre Kamnitzer (Paris: Calmann-Lévy, 1974).

to explain. The ship had to be blown up because it had become dangerous to the other ships, even to the city itself. Hundreds of the coastal population would have died. (51)

Formally, this is not at all difficult to understand, even if certain pieces of information are lacking; and Jane is by no means the 'simpering fool' of Mrs Higgins in Soyinka's early play *The Invention* (1959).[277] Indeed, the point Soyinka seems to be making through her in his play is one about poverty – a poverty of understanding which easily co-exists with basic intelligence, indeed informs and shapes the expression of intelligence, in a colonial situation.

At the most simple level, this might simply be a question of not understanding the language of the place. In his 1936 essay 'Shooting an Elephant', George Orwell applies his rare intelligence to a situation which is almost purely negative – not the negativity of satire, the dismantling or stripping of illusion and cant to clear the terrain, but the negativity of paranoia and violence and hatred, in which Orwell, deployed as a policeman in the Indian Imperial Police in Burma in the 1920s, is himself enmeshed. This is the scene in which he describes a football match in which he is involved, which, rather than being a moment of pastoral relief from the responsibilities of governance, becomes something else:

> When a nimble Burman tripped me up on the football field and the referee (another Burman) looked the other way, the crowd yelled with hideous laughter. This happened more than once. In the end the sneering yellow faces of young men that met me everywhere, the insults hooted after me when I was at a safe distance, got badly on my nerves. The young Buddhist priests were the worst of all. There were several thousands of them in

---

[277] Wole Soyinka, *The Invention*, in *The Invention and Detainee*, ed. Motsa, 20.

the town and none of them seemed to have anything to do except stand on street corners and jeer at Europeans.[278]

The tempering honesty of that almost ingenuous idiom 'got badly on my nerves' is overwhelmed in the laughter which is heard as 'hideous'; in 'the sneering yellow faces'; in the paranoid intimation of being the butt of a joke; in the sense that this could happen again and again, that the rules here are different.

But it might also reach a little further than that. I have argued that Simon Pilkings' false anagnorisis expresses Soyinka's exploitation of tragic convention to render paternalist ideology. In fact Jane is the first to be confronted with disabusal. (In French neo-classical theatre it was a considerable event for somebody to sit down, a gesture associated with not having control over one's passions. I like to think a similar principle is in operation here - I might even have Jane sit down on the floor – '[*sits down open-mouthed*]: You... you Olunde!' [52]) Yet her reaction is not put to the purposes of Simon's false anagnorisis, but becomes rather the occasion for Soyinka to explore her sense of exclusion from a world beyond – something of a trope in colonial literature; Orwell had it, though he also had the humanity to self-diagnose – that paranoia which holds that there is always a secret or mystery or joke or threat behind everything, and which never allows for a sense of belonging. Again, Benedict Anderson's reflection on language in a colonial situation is illuminating:

> What limits one's access to other languages is not their imperviousness but one's own mortality. Hence a certain privacy to all languages. French and American imperialists governed, exploited, and killed Vietnamese over many years. But whatever else they made off with,

---

[278] George Orwell, "Shooting an Elephant" [1936], in *Shooting an Elephant and Other Essays* (London: Seeker and Warburg, 1950), 1.

the Vietnamese language stayed put. Accordingly, only too often, a rage at Vietnamese 'inscrutability', and that obscure despair which engenders the venomous argots of dying colonialism: 'gooks', *'ratons'*, etc.[279]

Before the colonialist's exclusion from other languages, the 'certain privacy' of those languages which he or she can never fully bypass, each will bring his or her own solutions: the rage at 'inscrutability', the racism and violence of the Bobs of the colonial world, or – and this, I think, is truer of Jane – the attempt to 'understand', which nonetheless remains an attempt to understand, as Soyinka puts it in a different context, the otherness of the other: 'I accept, indeed, I insist that the question "What am I?" was, in fact, a quest for the totality of the species. In short, it stood for: "What are we? Who are we? Why are we?" – not "What is the otherness of – that one?"'[280] Or indeed, the otherness of the other's mind on the condition that the immediate context of indirect rule is spirited away, abstracted.

Jane Pilkings moves in this circumscribed realm, in a poverty which no amount of intelligence is able to step out from, try as it might. The truth of her qualified disabusal comes here, in her understanding that there is a certain communal pressure towards racism in such colonial situations, a pressure or presence that is felt at one's back, like wind to the sails, driving and pushing to places where one does not necessarily wish to go. So that towards the end of the diptych of exchanges with Olunde, she seems to stand out from Bob, with his inherited language of bold racism into which he has seamlessly been woven and which, one imagines, he will pass on in turn; and qualified, because she is still trying to get at some hidden mystery behind it all, to get beyond that sense of exclusion

---
[279] Anderson, *Imagined Communities*, 148.
[280] Soyinka, "The Credo of Being and Nothingness," *Essays*, 243.

she feels without conceding that it comes from her own situation as a colonialist, and the run-of-the-mill European fantasies about Africa:

> JANE: Please, I promise not to keep you. It's just that... oh you saw yourself what happens to one in this place. The Resident's man thought he was being helpful, that's the way we all react. [...] I feel a need to understand all I can. [...] No. It has to be more than that. I feel it has to do with the many things we don't really grasp about your people. At least you can explain. (*DKH*, 56)

Perhaps, finally, the premonitory phrase which comes later – 'Oh you poor orphan, what have you come home to' (60) – represents a sort of negative concession by the author; a moment of unassisted insight which expresses in words as solemn as we might reasonably believe from a colonial Englishwoman, the gravity and sense of the situation; a *negative* insight, that is, but an insight all the same, and which receives final relief against her husband's unwavering paternalist illusions.

I should probably insist once more that Soyinka is careful not to make Jane's sense of exclusion tragic, is careful to create a reasonably intelligent character who is subject both to the limitations of her situation, and her own active participation in that situation. It is important in the message of the plot that she should not be persuasive – recall the terms of the 'Author's Note', that it was not by chance that he avoided dialogue which would encourage an interpretation of the District Officer, and by extension, his wife, as victims of a cruel dilemma. We have already seen the inadvertent contradictions into which Jane is drawn in order to justify the Prince's visit; she does not fail to attempt to belittle Olunde's argument through condescension; her own categories are peculiar to say the least – 'However cleverly you try to put it, it is still a barbaric custom. It is even worse, it's feudal!' (53), where we are left wondering as to the paradigmatic value she attaches to each, and the logic of the hierarchy. More suggestively, take the climax of the first half of the exchange, following on from the drums which would seem to announce the death of the King's Horseman:

> JANE [*screams*]: How can you be so callous! So unfeeling! You announce your father's own death like a surgeon looking down on some strange... stranger's body! You're just a savage like all the rest. (55)

Jane has lost control at this moment, and is at her most unguarded and vulnerable, and the irony is mordant. The human condemnation she offers of Olunde takes the name of the most skilled of doctors, in the name of which her husband had Olunde sent to England, and on account of which she cannot understand his reversion to 'barbarism', that is, the sanctioning of his father's suicide. The savagery, then, comes of the severances and interruptions of empathy which derive from the constant need for objective or theoretical distance, precisely what the old racist trope denied to the African: savagery as sensual immersion, savagery as surgical distance. And, lastly, the continuities and discontinuities to which a single word can be put:

> JANE: But don't you think your father is also entitled to whatever protection is available to him?

> OLUNDE: How can I make you understand? He *has* protection. No one can undertake what he does tonight without the deepest protection the mind can conceive. (53)

'Protection' derives from 'protectorate', for Jane, and is orthodox in terms of imperial ideology: the colonial power providing protection in the form of 'Law' to people who had hitherto been without law, integrating them into a wider legal community, a *Pax Britannica*, sanctioned by the British

Crown. Not for nothing would Olunde's passport have carried the mention 'protected subject', without a trace of irony.

Olunde's response, however, does not preserve an easy opposition. We earlier spoke of the chronotope of meeting, and, as is typical of Soyinka's dramaturgical intelligence in this play, it seems that there is rarely a moment of oneness or ease or serene balance. Soyinka, as writerly critic, has paused over moments of agon, in discussions of Kane's *L'aventure ambigüe* and, indirectly, in Ayi Kwei Armah's *Two Thousand Seasons*. In speaking of the 'well-matched contest' between Monsieur Lacroix and Sambo Diallo's father, le chevalier, in Kane's novel, Soyinka is attentive to the pressure which the very fact of contest brings out in the latter, pushing him to excess:[281] 'Diallo's mission, his destiny, is defined in staggering pan-ethnic terms with a sonorous invocation of cosmic arbiters that sounds excessively impassioned.' (*MLAW*, 81) There is a slight ambiguity, for it is not clear whether Soyinka is attributing to Kane a technical flaw, that of a sudden and unguarded inhabiting of character by authorial wish-fulfilment, or whether he is pointing to the novelist's intelligent rendering of the excesses to which vulnerability in rhetorical combat might push us. (The latter, in my view, is correct. Soyinka's

---

[281] For the passage in question, see Kane, *L'aventure ambigüe*, 91: 'Ne vous forcez pas, monsieur Lacroix! Je sais que vous ne croyez pas en l'ombre. Ni à la fin. Ce que vous ne voyez pas n'est pas. L'instant, comme un radeau, vous transporte sur la face lumineuse de son disque rond, et vous niez tout l'abîme qui vous entoure. La cité future, grâce à mon fils, ouvrira ses baies sur l'abîme, d'où viendront de grandes bouffées d'ombre sur nos corps desséchés, sur nos fronts altérés. Je souhaite cette ouverture, de toute mon âme. Dans la cité naissante, telle doit être notre oeuvre, à nous tous, hindous, Chinois, Sud-Américains, nègres, Arabes; nous tous, dégingandés et lamentables, nous les sous-développés, qui nous sentons gauches en un monde de parfait ajustement mécanique.'

sentence might shed its ambiguity if it held, for example: 'Samba Diallo's mission, his destiny, is defined *by his father* in staggering pan-ethnic terms...') In his reading of Armah, in any case, he shows that he is aware of the chief lure in such literary instances. In upbraiding Armah's 'gleefulness', and the 'reckless ascendancy of the vengeance motif' in his novel, Soyinka criticizes the emotion unchecked in the author's voice and sluicing into character and prose, rather than emotion unchecked in, say, a character's voice, and deliberately staged as such. In one sense, Soyinka's treatment of Olunde might be thought of within the formal trope of the agon between colonial agent and colonized 'subject': for through the rhetorical pressures to which Olunde is subject before Jane Pilkings, Soyinka tantalisingly insinuates the dangers into which formal perfection in argument might just lead us.

The following lines are a masterful exercise in the rhythms of thought:

> OLUNDE: You white races know how to survive: I've seen proof of that. By all logical and natural laws this war should end with all the white races wiping out one another wiping out their so-called civilisation for all time and reverting to a state of primitivism the like of which has so far only existed in your imagination when you thought of us. I thought all that at the beginning. Then I slowly realized your greatest art is the art of survival. But at least have the humility to let others survive in their own way. (*DKH*, 53)

Olunde's talk of the white race's 'art of survival' seems like a variation on what Kane's La Grande Royale describes as the trick of the French – 'L'art de vaincre sans avoir raison';[282] and there were no doubt any number of conversations and ruminations to that purpose across colonized lands. The key

---

[282] Kane, *L'Aventure ambigüe*, 48.

point, however, is in the expression and articulation which the idea receives in Olunde's mouth. We opened with a discussion of a line in Achebe's poem 'Beware, Soul Brother', which I always find beautiful and impressive in its acute control of the rhythm which must come with the usage of long sentences; and there are many instances across Soyinka's oeuvre in which punctuation is shed for effect.[283] Here, however, the effect is, I think, more complex, for we feel the rhythm not as unleashing or exponential but rather as the momentary release of longing, which recognises itself as such, and then hits the brakes. The length of the sentence beginning 'By all...', particularly given the rhetorical control that Olunde has hitherto evinced, might make us suspicious that we have here fallen into a tirade or rant or even 'gleeful' envisaging of the 'white race's' downfall. The next sentence, however, quickly defuses this sense, not by showing that it was misplaced, but by showing us that that was what Olunde *used* to think; that we have just heard a self-quotation from a past self. In other words, the temporality of the passage moves from conclusion ('You white races know how to survive') to superceded opinion of the past ('By all logical and natural laws...') before spelling out that the two are separated by a moment of learning or coming into understanding ('Then I slowly realized'). This contrasts – favourably for Olunde, it would seem – with the market women's bravado, before Amusa's challenge to Elesin Oba's authority ('The chief who calls himself Elesin Oba' [35]):

> WOMAN: You ignorant man. It is not he who calls himself Elesin Oba, it is his blood that says it. As it called out to his father before him and will to his son after him. And that is in spite of everything your white man can do. [...] Tonight our husband and father will prove himself greater than the laws of strangers. (35-36)

---

[283] We briefly discussed the vocative and accusatory register above, 204-5.

It is, however, difficult to avoid thinking that it is precisely Olunde's control, his assurance, or rather his *assumption* that all will continue as he had foreseen, that we must not miss. Perhaps we have given Olunde's response to Jane's charge of callousness too easy-a-ride, for it is quite rich in implication, particularly given what we have seen in our earlier discussion of foreknowledge. Is it possible to cheat the pain of the death of a loved one in foreknowledge, as Olunde suggests? Does the fact that I know a loved one's time to be numbered, even if this heralds a moment of honour and celebration, allow me to skirt the pain of his or her passing? Might it make me insist more on formal duties or regularity and rules as a way of avoiding the recognition of what has happened, or is happening, an insistence on ritual and duty and role over and against personal intrusion?

> OLUNDE: And anyway, my father has been dead in my mind for nearly a month. Ever since I learnt of the King's death. I've lived with my bereavement so long now that I cannot think of him alive. On that journey on the boat, I kept my mind on my duties as the one who must perform the rites over his body. I went through it all again and again in my mind as he himself had taught me. I didn't want to do anything wrong, something which might jeopardise the welfare of my people. (57)

This 'getting used to the thought', a more solemn variant of Lakunle's 'getting to like the thought'; this assumption of familiarity with something that has not yet happened, lightly colours the entire exchange, intimates – nothing more – a curious dissonance between the risk of the ritual, its necessary and attendant dangers of failure, and the sense of casualness with which Olunde presumes his father will assert his will.

I have just written 'intimates – nothing more'. One of the most exciting aspects of the language in Soyinka's *Death and the King's Horseman* comes in the sudden vistas opened up through the circulation of poetic metaphor, in the King's

Horseman's ritual, just as quickly as they pass away. This circulation of metaphor operates through the rhetorical tools available to Soyinka through Yoruba oral poetry.

2

Give and Pull

Karin Barber, because from Biodun Jeyifo, once noted of Yoruba popular travelling theatre that the two-dimensional disposition of the action always threatened 'to burst out of the frame'.[284] The suggestion is that the rhetorical skills and verbal mastery which was a central feature of this form of theatre, its interest in neologism and punnery in the Yoruba language (as opposed to the polyglottism of Ghanaian and Togolese concert party plays), was felt to be coherent with two-dimensionality on stage precisely because register and style were felt and experienced as compensatory, as giving of depth. Soyinka, from his earliest essays, has been concerned with the interaction between drama and its specific physical environment, the mutual influencing that might take place between each, and the changes to which each is subjected under historical pressure.[285] His most explicit reflection comes,

---

[284] Karin Barber, John Collins and Alain Ricard, "Three West African Popular Theatre Forms: A Social History," in *West African Popular Theatre*, eds. Karin Barber, John Collins and Alain Ricard (Bloomington and Indianapolis: Indiana University Press; Oxford: James Currey, 1997), 48. For the relevant mention of stage-alignment, see Biodun Jeyifo, *The Yoruba Popular Travelling Theatre of Nigeria* (Lagos: A Nigeria Magazine Publication, 1984), 13-14.

[285] See, for instance, Soyinka's early essay "Towards a True Theatre" [1962], *Essays*, 3: 'Theatre, and especially, a "National Theatre", is never the lump of wood and mortar which architects splash on the landscape.' Or two decades later, in "Theatre in African Traditional Cultures," *Essays*, 134: 'We must not lose sight of the fact that drama, like any other art

I think, in the 1982 essay 'Theatre in African Traditional Cultures,' where he discusses various mutations that African theatre has undergone. There he conjectures that 'contemporary drama, as we experience it today, is a contraction of drama, necessitated by the productive order of society in other directions.'[286] The concrete pressures of history as they impact upon drama and, more specifically, as they *contract* the scope of drama, was clearly instanced in 'Victorian Lagos', to borrow Echeruo's well-known phrase;[287] a phenomenon of which Soyinka, in a polemical context, writes: 'it was not the Shakespearean stage which "malformed" – during a particular period – the African colonial theatrical venturousness, but the Victorian. As a decidedly antiproscenium stage-artist, I hope to see fewer of these mind-constrictors left in the world.'[288]

Harold Bloom, in a Western literary context, characterizes Shakespeare's individual genius as a complete fusion of rhetoric, psychology and cosmology in his greatest plays, which in turn necessitates a criticism which is not separately rhetorical, psychological or cosmological.[289] Yet this, as Soyinka sees and realizes in *Death and the King's Horseman*, is readily available in *resource* from Yoruba poetic and festival practice. In that play, he is representing a ritual within, if such

---

form, is created and executed within a specific physical environment. It naturally interacts with that environment, is influenced by it, influences that environment in turn and acts together with the environment in the larger and far more complex history of society. The history of a dramatic pattern or its evolution is therefore very much the history of other art forms of society.'
[286] Soyinka, "Theatre in African Traditional Cultures," 138.
[287] See M.J.C. Echeruo, *Victorian Lagos: Aspects of Nineteenth Century Lagos Life* (London; Basingstoke: Macmillan, 1977).
[288] Wole Soyinka, "Who's Afraid of Elesin Oba?" *Essays*, 68.
[289] Harold Bloom, *The Anxiety of Influence: A Theory of Poetry* (New York; Oxford: Oxford University Press, 1997 [1975], xxvi.

were the context of production, a contracted space (the consequence of that 'productive order of society in other directions'), and so the specific challenge is to reinvest and expand the contracted space with a greater economy and concentration of poetic language, to compensate for the retrenchments and contractions brought about by the advent or imposition of new theatrical forms, through the administrations and dimensions of metaphor. 'Poetic drama', remarks Soyinka, 'being largely metaphorical, [...] expands the immediate meaning and action of the protagonists into a world of nature forces and metaphysical conceptions.' (*MLAW*, 43)[290]

The representation of ritual in *Death and the King's Horseman* works through dramatic economy: verbal and metaphorical 'richness' are not expressed, I think, through lexical enlargement, so much as through the textures that can be had through control and limitation and nuanced repetition. Indeed perhaps none of Soyinka's dramatic works provides such a useful propaganda tool for the importance of literary studies, of slow reading, of not assuming the transparency of words on the world, than this play, for the nuance in metaphor is extremely difficult to hear on a naïve listening – and even on

---

[290] The following discussion would no doubt benefit from a sustained dialogue with Akinwunmi Isola's Yoruba-language translation of *Death and the King's Horseman*, *Iku Olokun-Esin* (Ibadan: Fountain Publications, 1989). A useful starting point would be Dan Izevbaye's discussion of Isola's translation in "Elesin's Homecoming: The Translation of The King's Horseman," in *Research in African Literatures*, Vol. 28, No.2 (1997). There, Izevbaye writes: '[...] Akin Isola's translation of *Death*, takes as its point of departure the idea that the play is essentially Yoruba, especially in its use of language. [...] Isola's translation is not conceived as merely a textual communication between two cultures. It seeks to return a text to what its translator sees as its cultural origin. *What it actually achieves is the location of a hybrid text in a literary culture to which it only partly belongs, since it is also partly the product of English literary history.*' (my italics)

repeated listening, if unaccompanied by sustained reflection. One point of ingress in apprehending this sense of feedback, of indulgence followed by greater coercion, freedom snapped back into obeisance, is the usages to which certain recurring metaphors are placed, the very texture and hue of dynamism. It is here that the challenge of hearing well is most acutely felt, and most intellectually and emotionally understood, and, it seems to me, Kermode's reminder to us that we should think of hearing as a 'technical skill possessed' is salutary.[291]

Quintilian, one of the first rhetorical systematizers of the Western rhetorical tradition, sees little sense in metalepsis, a derivation of metonymy. It signifies nothing in itself, he writes, merely affords a passage to something else, and thereby remains of that limited category of use 'where one thing is to lead to another'. He gives the example of the passage or intermediary step between two *equivalent* expressions: 'The most common example of it is – *cano* "to sing" is equivalent to *canto* "to reiterate", and *canto* equivalent to *dico* "to say"; therefore, *cano* is equivalent to *dico*.'[292] Roman Jakobson, a few millennia later, made the point that the literature on metonymy in the Western critical tradition has nothing like the richness of the critical literature on metaphor.[293] He observes that metaphor, which works through substitution and reliance on contextual knowledge for ease of equivalence, thereby provides the researcher with more homogeneous means of interpretation.[294] This, however, is dependent upon the textual tradition within which the researcher is working –

---

[291] Kermode, *Shakespeare's Language*, 4.
[292] Quoted in Richard Lanham, *A Handlist of Rhetorical Terms* (Berkeley; Los Angeles; London: University of California Press, 1991), 99.
[293] Roman Jakobson, "Two Aspects of Language and Two Types of Aphasic Disturbances," in *Selected Writings II: Word and Language* (The Hague; Paris: Mouton, 1971), 258.
[294] *Ibid.*, 245.

'text', following Karin Barber, as not conferred by or limited to writing, but understood rather as utterance, oral or written, 'that is woven together in order to attract attention and to outlast the moment', its 'recognisable existence as a form'[295] – and it seems to me that the Yoruba are in a quite formidable place to demand of us an attention to metonymy, a motion suggesting passage to something *without,* as does Quintilian, *reducing that moment of suggestion to equivalence.*

A formidable case for metonymy as the underlying motion of Yoruba poetics has been made by Olabiyi Yai. Yai has been at pains to demonstrate the aesthetic principle that Yoruba art-forms engage reality through departure rather than mimesis, that 'Art is an invitation to infinite metonymic difference and departure, and not a summation for sameness and imitation.'[296] In the context of Soyinka's oeuvre, Christiane Fioupou's collaboration with Yai, which resulted in the (Yoruba) transcription and (English, then French) translation of a few *ese Ifa* or Ifa divination verses directly concerning the road,[297] provides beautiful cultural instances of the enmeshments between the road and the journey – the threat of destruction or loss among byways, and the simultaneous sense in which experience or 'venturing forth' or the journey is the only option: 'the man seeks fortune on the road, for there is no other way' – [298] and the rhetorical possibilities which

---

[295] Barber, *The Anthropology of Texts*, 2.
[296] Olabiyi Yai, "In Praise of Metonymy: The Concepts of 'Tradition' and 'Creativity' in the Transmission of Yoruba Artistry over Time and Space," in *The Yoruba Artist: New Theoretical Perspectives on African Arts,* eds. Rowland Abiodun, Henry J. Drewal and John Pemberton III (Washington; London: Smithsonian Institution Press, 1994), 113.
[297] Fioupou, *La Route,* 345-356. Yai recorded them, retranscribed them in Yoruba and had them translated into English in 1985, when Professor of Yoruba at what was then called the University of Ile-Ife.
[298] For the fuller quotation see *ibid.,* 350: 'Ainsi, Orunmila dit que parmi les quatre cents dieux et les deux cents dieux, la route est l'aînée de tous

inhere in oral poetics.

Ifeanyi Menkiti has written a memorable account of African personhood as a form of risk-laden moral journey, which, in theory, seems quite apposite in its premises to *Death and the King's Horseman*.[299] In Menkiti's account, then, the individual only acquires the status of full personhood through the

---

car si un homme est très puissant, ou s'il possède une sagesse particulière, quels que soient ses projets, c'est une nécessité pour lui d'emprunter la route qui l'amènera à sa destination. Dans son cas, c'est grâce à la route qu'il voyagea, de par la nature même de ce qu'il cherchait, la recontre était inévitable. Lorsqu'un homme cherche fortune, il prend la route, il n'y a pas d'autre moyen. Nul ne peut s'égarer dans la forêt et y trouver fortune. Ils dirent tous d'un commun accord que c'est la Route leur aînée à tous.' Abiola Irele's notion of 'signposts', in his formal characterization of orality's principle of impermanence and instability, is useful here, too. See *The African Imagination*, 34: 'The point is that an oral text is almost never fully determined beforehand, given once and for all, as in the case of written literature, which strives to endow the text with the permanence of the material object. An oral text is actualized in oral performance and is thus open and mobile; what can be abstracted as the verbal content of a given work is perpetually recreated, modified as the occasion demands, and given new accents from one instance of its realization to another.' In his study of Fela Kuti, Tejumola Olaniyan has written of the importance of the cultural notion of 'perambulation' or *'irin iranu'* – aimless drift or purposelessness – for the Yoruba, which finds expression through notions of paths and byways. Yoruba culture, he writes, is 'perpetually apprehensive about the nature of paths and directions: Are they purposive and do they advance the journey or are they purposeless and impede it? The stories of creation the culture tells itself are replete with momentous journeys by this or that deity or ancestor, between this or that place. It is perhaps for this reason that roads and directions carry much symbolic significance for the Yoruba, for they are the stage upon which the drama of life is played; the journey of life taken.' See Tejumola Olaniyan, *Arrest the Music! Fela and his Rebel Art and Politics* (Bloomington and Indianapolis: Indiana University Press, 2004), 98, 100.

[299] Ifeanyi Menkiti, "On the Normative Conception of a Person," in *A Companion to African Philosophy*, ed. Wiredu.

community, which plays both a catalytic and prescriptive role in his or her transformation. In placing transformation beyond the individual, he diminishes the role of individualist epistemology in the making of personhood – 'the approach to persons in traditional thought is generally speaking a maximal, or more exacting, approach, insofar as it reaches for something beyond such minimalist requirements as the presence of consciousness, memory, will, soul, rationality, or mental function' – instead conceiving of life as a journey, conditioned by the end of 'moral arrival'. His conclusion could not be more apposite:

> Since triumph and failure have their consequences, and the consequences cut beyond the life cycle of the assignable individual, affecting others in the community as well, it follows that societies, both large and small, are in need of recognizing that they are caught up in an inextricable dance with their component individuals.[300]

What is dramatically intelligent in *Death and the King's Horseman* is that the ritual becomes a miniature laboratory for exploring just this conception, as enacted in and through language – yet the conceit of the journey is subjected to an extreme paradox, and, consequently, to an extreme intensification or condensation of the dangers of being and non-being, so to speak, for the fullness of both individual and communal flourishing or eudaimonia depends on the passing of the individual. I am interested in metonymy, as I was saying, not for its help in passing between two terms, which still makes of the middle term an equivalence, a substitution; but rather in the insinuating and unresolved possibilities it opens up and suggests through language. Astonishingly here – and this is specifically Yoruba, I think – it is the enmeshment between the structural conceit of the ritual – that is, the journey – and

---

[300] *Ibid.*, 326.

the formal rhetorical resource which inhere in certain facets of oral poetry, in the 'byways' they open up, which allow us fully to comprehend the threat of loss attendant on the blurring or retreat of signposts, on the falling away of the path we thought most trodden.

A discussion of the relationship between protagonist and chorus ought not do away with the risks involved in their mutual constitution of being. This mutual constitution is not conferred by grace or arrived at through epistemology, but is rather something gained or earned and constantly sustained, an enterprise fraught with difficulty and the risk of failure. The chorus, in turn, is a community looking out for its own continuity and protection, conscious of the fact that it depends on the protagonist, just as the protagonist is nothing without the chorus.

Herbert Cole once observed of African festival, in a passage which Soyinka would later quote, that although dependent on life-sustaining rituals, it is 'an elaborated and stylised phenomenon which far surpasses ritual necessity.'[301] Here, cleverly, we enter the play just as the emphasis on necessity, within the ritual, is being tightened; we enter, that is, at the mouth of the narrowing path, at the closure of rhetorical indulgence before improvisation, harried by the imperatives of the moon's gate. Soyinka suggests this passing into 'necessity' in a few ways, though interruption, the most subtle, is quite effective. We saw in our discussion of *The Bacchae of Euripides* the ways in which continuity and discontinuity can be exploited on stage for dramatic effect, or to create space for psychological texture. What is instructive for today's scholars in the case of Euripides, as Mastronarde has argued, is the way in which interruption or uncomfortable joints cannot be ascribed to a definite cause, but rather leave open

---

[301] Quoted in Soyinka, "Theatre in African Traditional Cultures," *Essays*, 138.

the possibilities of cause to 'textual corruption, to psychological or dramatic motivations, or to an actual misinterpretation by one character of what the other is saying.'[302] The lesson that there are different types of interruption is useful here. Let us look closely at the syntax of the following interruption:

> PRAISE-SINGER: The cockerel must not be seen without his feathers.
>
> ELESIN: Nor will the Not-I bird be much longer without his nest. (*DKH*, 11)

That 'nor' constitutes a slightly awkward interruption at the level of syntax, for there is neither continuity in subject nor in mood of verb (passive to active). This is the first moment of syntactical discontinuity between Elesin and his human constituency, and to me suggests not the general point that he inclines to excess, but the more simple and particular point that he already has this digression in mind, that it is *not* an 'improvisation', if by that we only mean an imaginative springing from the verbal sources of what has just come before. This lengthy expression is permitted, indeed encouraged, for hitherto the tightening is only beginning.

Our emphasis here comes on the conative function of language –[303] the importance of eliciting a response or reaction, whence the frequency of address. The deeper sense, as suggested in Karin Barber's words quoted in the chapter's

---

[302] Mastronarde, *Contact and Discontinuity*, 84.

[303] For a discussion of the importance of the conative function of language in the context of the translation of African oral poetry, which embraces Yoruba *oriki*, see Olabiyi Yai, "Seuils pour repenser la traduction des poésies orales africaines," in *Anglophonia/Caliban* 7, 225-237. The specific term 'conative function' comes from Roman Jakobson, who distinguished six elements necessary for communication to occur. See his "Linguistics and Poetics," in *Style in Language*, ed. T. Sebeok (Cambridge, Massachusetts: M.I.T. Press, 1960), 350-377.

epigraph, is that Yoruba conceptions of being, as enacted in this ritual, are dialogic.[304] Perhaps the most simple instance, though it announces a later and far more ambiguous instance, comes with the Praise-singer's archetypal history:

> PRAISE-SINGER: In their time the great wars came and went, the little wars came and went; the white slavers came and went, they took away the heart of our race, they bore away the mind and muscle of our race. The city fell and was rebuilt, the city fell and our people trudged through mountain and forest to found a new home but – Elesin Oba do you hear me? (10)

Address must not lose its tension, which is to say its bind with its addressee, and it is precisely in longer fragments of speech that this risk seems greatest. The Praise-singer's question implies that he himself senses that he has lost address, which is to say that he intimates the attenuation of his addressee's attention, and so the history is interrupted. Such must be the rhythm, a rhythm always attentive to the risk of inertia and autonomy of language, its inclination to isolation and non-commonality.

---

[304] Olabiyi Yai has argued that the etymologies kì (to perform oríkì verbally), and gbé and yà (to carve), imply mutual provocations, 'to provoke and be provoked,' which he conceives as part of an underlying Yoruba aesthetic tending to difference and departure, whose prime trope is metonymy. See "In Praise of Metonymy," 113. Following the Fon linguist Georges Guédou and the Fon sage Yesi, he has elsewhere discussed different categories in the classification of oral genres in Fon. Interestingly, within this classification, 'didactic narratives' are characterized by the fact that they 'must generate another discursive reaction from their addressees. They are invariably marked by the word gbè (voice).' See his article "The Path is Open: The Herskovits Legacy in African Oral Narrative Analysis and Beyond," PAS Working Papers Number 5 (Program of African Studies, Northwestern University, Illinois, 1999), 17.

There are other striking negative instances, moments of discontinuity, moments in which the tension between speaker and addressee is felt to slacken or indeed vanish, in which the context of address is suddenly transcended or made to vanish. 'Proverbs are the horses of communication; when communication is lost or elusive, proverbs are summoned to find or illuminate it', runs the commonly cited Yoruba proverb.[305] There is one moment in which Elesin, running towards his peroration as he anticipates sex, for want of a better expression, abandons the commonality which proverbs suppose, in sudden lyrical ascent: 'I shall leave that which makes my going the sheerest dream of an afternoon.' (20) This comes from nowhere, and disappears just as soon as it has come; it gains its subtle strength from what we have called the lexical economy of the play, the circulation and recycling of key metaphors, for these metaphors gain their force from their concreteness, their materiality, their referents in daily life, in ways that a dream, and a 'sheer' one at that, cannot. On hearing that phrase, no image is conjured, no image seen or understood; instead do we fall quite suddenly into a hole – which is of course exactly the poetic effect that Soyinka is seeking – a moment of still disarming.

A quite different sort of interruption comes with Iyaloja, as she gets used to the thought of Elesin's later request – and this must resonate with the example we earlier saw of the Praise-singer:

> IYALOJA: It is those who stand at the gateway of the great change to whose cry we must pay heed. And then, think of this – it makes the mind tremble. The fruit of such a union is rare. It will be neither of this world nor of the next. Nor of the one behind us. As if the timelessness of the ancestor world and the unborn have joined spirits to wring an issue of the elusive being of passage... Elesin! (22)

---

[305] For a detailed discussion, see Rowland Abiodun, "Who Was the First to Speak? Insights from Ifá Orature and Sculptural Repertoire," in *Orisa Devotion as World Religion*, eds. Olupona and Rey, 52-3.

Those little words 'And then' institute a distinct order of thought, signal the sudden arrival of a new thought, and as such, weaken direct address into something which hovers between direct address and self-address. This is the speech of a tantalising and unprecedented thought, not the filling, to borrow Irele's terms, of 'the outline of a verbal structure [...] as reference points for the development of ideas and images, as suggestive signposts in the narrative or prosodic movement of a discourse that is still in the future.'[306] Iyaloja's sentence 'Nor of the one behind us' is an afterthought which carries historical resonance, we feel its being born as she speaks it. Most suggestively of all is that 'As if', the only instance in which Iyaloja trades in metaphor for the idiom in English which most clearly heralds a fictional imagining, the difference between reality and illusion. (In fact, in the entire play, I have only found three instances of simile as against metaphor in the Yoruba-source poetry. The first comes in an early context with the Praise Singer, an unhurried context: 'Your name', he sings, 'will be like the sweet berry a child places under his tongue to sweeten the passage of food. The world will never spit it out.' [10] The second, however, seems to me more important, as the Praise Singer attempts to bring Elesin Oba back to the matter in hand, quickly to recall simple distinctions: 'Elesin-Oba why do your eyes roll like a bush-rat who sees his fate like his father's spirit, mirrored in the eyes of a snake?' [18] Perhaps simile in this instance, as opposed to metaphor, is a momentary stepping out of the performative, translates a slight unease which cannot be held in metaphor. It is, in any case, quickly resolved once more into the subsequent praise-epithets. The third, as we shall see, comes with the first of Elesin's later 'confessions'.) It becomes exquisite, therefore, that Iyaloja is brought back to full alertness by her intimation

---

[306] Irele, *The African Imagination*, 34.

that she has lost address, which is to say the attention, of her addressee. We see here how the byways or insinuating possibilities of drift are given resonance through plot, for how much more risk-laden is this moment than that of the Praise-singer's earlier interruption?

Generally speaking, however, the operative principle is one of holding possibilities open through a few recurring metaphors; the objective, to force us into hesitations, apprehension, as if at a crossroads deciding which direction to take. Indeed, importantly, the meta-rhetorical proverb on horses and proverbs being used to retrieve meaning is implicit, perhaps, under or within the broader imagery of ropes, tethers and reins, and ultimately, perhaps, from the underlying risk of excess leading to drift, the isolations of meaninglessness which stand beyond coercion and control. This is how I read the opening lines. More than a simple illustration of a stage direction – *'He is a man of enormous vitality'* (9) – it announces *ab initio* the danger of outrunning or stepping beyond into drift, which the chorus and the Praise-singer must seek to rein in through language-address: 'Elesin o! Elesin Oba! Howu! What tryst is this the cockerel goes to keep with such haste that he must leave his tail behind?' (9) A little later, there comes an exquisite moment of homophony:

ELESIN: You all know what I am.

PRAISE-SINGER: That rock which turns its open lodes into the path of lightning. A gay thoroughbred whose stride disdains to falter though an adder reared suddenly in his path.

ELESIN: My rein is loosened. I am master of my fate. (14)

The thrust of the message moves in the way of control. Elesin's sturdy monosyllabic invitation is readily accepted in the imagery of the firm-striding horse, which image is in turn taken up in the word 'rein'. Perhaps our alertness is awoken by that classical expression of hubris – 'I am master of my fate' (14) – but this has already been prepared, I think, in the word 'rein'. The loosening of the rein intimates both the narrowing of time, and the sense of his preparedness to ride on alone, but it also provides just enough for the shadow of an earthly meaning, for if time is narrowing his earthly 'reign' is loosened too. There is an irresistible sense in which this *might* elicit a brief melancholy or contemplative sadness in Elesin, which he then suppresses in that assertive expression of mastery and control. Again, this is quiet and quick – the melancholy or reflectiveness or passivity of the line is immediately snapped back into a positive declaration of intent – and (I must again stress) comes as nothing more than a possibility.

Reins are linked to rhetoric, then; and cords, in a far more suggestive enlargement, are linked to cosmos:

> ELESIN: We cannot see the still great womb of the world – No man beholds his mother's womb – Yet who denies it's there? Coiled to the navel of the world is that endless cord that links us all to the great origin. If I lose my way the trailing cord will bring me to the roots. (18)

If we consider this in isolation, we could make the following formal observation: that Soyinka, through Elesin, projects the tensions of mutual constitution as enacted hitherto in poetry, the give and pull of the rope, the elasticity and tension of address, interruption and imperative, onto a cosmic scale, the sense that Elesin's being and personhood is intrinsically linked to and perhaps even derivative of a broader or older origin, to which he will be brought back for safety and refuge should he drift too far. It is precisely this formal possibility that renders the speech, in context, more dramatic, for it comes just after Elesin has snatched a glimpse of the beautiful young girl. And it constitutes, in turn, a first rhetorical gesture towards his request to Iyaloja, a first motion of preparation, which must advance its cause as far as possible whilst its audience remains unaware of the deeper intention. In this perspective, the conditional evocation of loss ('If I lose my way') becomes a subtle or cunning proleptic pleading for indulgence, on this day of all days.

It is perhaps inevitable that, in the give and pull between individual and community, the possessive should be deployed to express the oscillations of self-assertion and community dependence. Elesin speaks of his 'friend and master' following his Not-I Bird skit, and the moving sense in which their reign (rein?) was shared and predicated on the trust they elicited in the community is well-expressed through the fluid alternation between various forms of the first-person singular and plural:

> ELESIN: Where there was plenty I gorged myself. My master's hands and mine have always Dipped together and, home or sacred feast, The bowl was beaten bronze, the meats So succulent our teeth accused us of neglect. We shared the choicest of the season's Harvest of yams. How my friend would read Desire in my eyes before I knew the cause – However rare, however precious, it was mine.
>
> WOMEN: The town, the very land was yours.
>
> ELESIN: The world was mine. Our joint hands raised houseposts of trust that withstood the siege of envy and the termites of time. (14-15)

In displaying cohesion, these alternations – my, mine, our, us, we, (and, from an external perspective, yours) – suggest quite movingly the ways in which Elesin's 'reign' depended on another, and the survival of both on their constant and wider acknowledgement of something beyond, and reciprocally expressed in trust. And yet shortly after, following the all-important glimpse of the off-stage object, the first-person singular has come apart just enough to suggest independence, is insistent just enough for us to hear or intimate

Elesin's going-solo, the undercurrent of self-interest:

> ELESIN: How can that be? In all my life as Horseman of the King, the juiciest fruit on every tree was mine. I saw, I touched, I wooed, rarely was the answer No. The honour of my place, the veneration I received in the eye of man or woman prospered my suit and played havoc with my sleeping hours. And they tell me my eyes were a hawk in perpetual hunger. (18)

The only reference to his master and friend now comes as reminder to the women of hierarchy, of the entitlement proper to rank, and the erstwhile moving alternations are here displaced onto a first-person singular in relief – 'I saw, I touched, I wooed'. (And we might even conjecture as to the purely phonic way in which Soyinka intrudes this 'I' upon us in the homophony of 'eye'/'eyes'.)

This insinuating suggestion is given import by the run of what has come from the moment Elesin sees the beautiful young woman, or girl. These are the lines to introduce the modulation:

> ELESIN: The world I know is good.
>
> WOMEN: We know you'll leave it so.
>
> ELESIN: The world I know is the bounty of hives after bees have swarmed. No goodness teems with such open hands even in the dreams of deities.
>
> WOMEN: And we know you'll leave it so. (17)

We should be alive to the possibility here that 'world' for Elesin is also something more akin to 'immediate circumstance', the better to hear the dissonance in the women's sense of 'it' or 'world' – ostensibly the same referent – which is in fact more turned towards their own spiritual safety; alive, also, to the possibility that the word 'good', for Elesin, might connote something more akin to the serendipity or happy circumstance which those in positions of hierarchical privilege might allow themselves to indulge in, the better to hear the dissonance with the women's cautionary response 'leave it so', meaning 'leave it morally safe' for the community. The women's subsequent repetition is striking: its slight impatience and concern (in that 'And') anticipates the Praise-singer's imminent exclamation ('all these questions!' [18]), and does not seem to pick up directly on Elesin's preceding sentence (does the 'it' refer to the world or to goodness?), as if they are more concerned with reining Elesin in, as if they intimate a slight coming apart between community and Elesin, the same words being put to slightly different usage.

This seems to receive confirmation in Elesin's own words shortly after:

> ELESIN: I like this farewell that the world designed, unless my eyes deceive me, unless we are already parted, the world and I, and all that breeds desire is lodged among our tireless ancestors. Tell me friends, am I still earthed in that beloved market of my youth? (18)

Elesin is passing off the world's design as his own – the word 'design' also connotes the purpose or intention which lurks behind an action or speech – which somewhat undermines the idea that world or community and personhood are mutually constitutive, and here directed to the same goals. Better still, he introduces the notion of 'earthing' through a rhetorical question of whose response he is assured, to challenge and recall the women and the Praise-singer to their continued responsibility towards him.

I must pause over this. This, it seems to me, is an extremely bold working by Soyinka upon his own *formal* description of the relationship between protagonist and 'choric vessel and earthing mechanism' which obtains in tragic ritual, as expressed in *Myth, Literature and the African World* (*MLAW*, 33). For it is precisely at the moment of the most intense and moving 'envisioned coherence', to borrow Abiola Irele's rich notion,[307] the moment at which 'Elesin stands resplendent in rich clothes', the women dancing around him, that *'his attention is caught by an object off-stage'* (*DKH*, 17), a *'beautiful young girl'* (18). Structurally, then, the emotional impulse towards a representation of cohesion and oneness is simultaneously expressed and undercut, and it is precisely the intensity achieved in the expression of coherence that will ensure the irony and pathos held and announced in the wandering eye. The effect, then, is to stage the communal presence, to provide lines of sight which stretch beyond its own imagination – in short, the difference between the ritual and the representation of ritual. Rather than the descriptive and theoretical cogency of *Myth, Literature and the African World*, we must rather turn to the essay 'New Frontiers for Old' (1990) for the definitive sense of what I mean, that nostalgia which gains force only because it is chilled from without:

> [...] the experience of colonization involves seemingly contradictory but indeed complementary motions: for instance the sensibility of entrapment, not only physical entrapment but entrapment within a recollected but receding idyll. Simultaneously it is the shattering of barriers, a brutal thrust into an extended world from within whose expanded reality, the rendering even of the prior experience now takes form and resonance. And of course, we do not speak here of a purely physical distension. However determinedly rooted the colonized remains within the same circumscribed anterior world,

---

[307] Irele, *The African Imagination*, 57: '[Achebe's use] of a parable art in the novel – of the folktale as a kind of metafiction that mirrors and refocuses the text in order to insist upon the moral function of art – becomes a personal statement of an envisioned coherence, which (as he is fully aware) the lived referent of his own work does not begin to approximate. In his instance, the notion of art as parable of life reflects a desperate imaginative effort to subdue a refractory present.'

the dynamics of that physical reality have changed irreversibly.[308]

I would add more. It seems to me that Soyinka is daring us to deliver ourselves unto a moment of nostalgia by undercutting it with what risks appearing the most bathetic of motivations, Elesin's getting his leg over one last time, as it were; that our author is saying, 'Go on, I dare you to celebrate this moment!' Perhaps a ritual which might be so easily weakened, the implication goes, and by such an act, should be felt to be awry, itself overly ripe.

Shortly after the wandering eye, there emerges a riff involving the 'world' and 'knowledge':

> ELESIN: But, if you say this earth is still the same as gave birth to those songs, tell me who was that goddess [...] Iyaloja, who is she? I saw her enter your stall: all your daughters I know well. (19)

We need here to recall that the market can double in Yoruba culture symbolically for the world, or community[309] (this explains Elesin Oba's infecting his market retinue with his humour and energy, and the very real meaning of the vocative he gives the women, 'breath and giver of my being' [16]). The unknown girl's entering the market, therefore, is for Elesin to see the continuation of the world's dynamics just as he prepares to leave. The pain of this he signals by casting the earth and its songs he knows, the daughters of the

---

[308] Wole Soyinka, "New Frontiers for Old" [1990], *Essays*, 226.

[309] See, for example, Henry Drewal, "Introduction: Yoruba Art and Life as Journeys," in *The Yoruba Artist*, eds. Abiodun, Drewal and Pemberton III, 195: 'When the Yoruba say 'the world is a marketplace' *(ayé l'ojà)*, they intentionally choose a metaphor that wonderfully captures the dynamics surrounding transactions, the pushes and pulls, the actions and reactions, the negotiations involved in living life, which is for the Yoruba the utilization of/serious play with *ase*, the power to act and accomplish.'

stall he knows so well, into the past tense, the order of past knowledge – 'And that radiance which so suddenly lit up this market I could boast I *knew* so well?' (20; my italics) – as if the girl is indeed something which illuminates everything else.

Wonderfully, Elesin Oba makes another quick adjustment of what has come before, stating 'The world I know is the bounty of hives after bees have swarmed.' (20) Now, the association of 'world' and 'honey' has a tonality altogether different from his former commemoration of the bounteousness of his life, a speech set in the past tense of someone reconciled to his destiny, a man who had learned to get used to the thought: 'Who says the mouth does not believe in "No, I have chewed all that before?" I say I have. The world is not a constant honey-pot.' (14) The metaphor of world is re-invested, renewed – and psychologically this is extremely convincing: the formal declaration of one's control, and its sudden collapse before the parading evidence of continuing life; the confounding of that idea that it is the same to *say* that there is nothing new under the sun as it is to live and move as such – the honey-pot is renewed, and with it, knowledge of the world.

That word 'knowledge', as the translators of the King James Version of the Bible well knew, declines into conceptual or formal knowledge on the one hand, and experiential knowledge on the other, and it is to the latter that Elesin Oba now quarries. 'Shall I step burdened into the unknown?' he enquires, after one of the rare moments in the play in which chorus and protagonist are separated, divided even, Elesin making of his passage from formal to experiential knowledge, so to speak, the condition of the community's survival. This receives extension from his usage of imagery of renewal – 'Let seed that will not serve the stomach on the way remain behind. Let it take root in the earth of my choice, in this earth I leave behind.' (21) – ultimately confirmed in Iyaloja's subsequent development:

IYALOJA: Not we, but the very earth says No. The sap in the plantain does not dry. Let grain that will not feed the voyager at his passage drop here and take root as he steps beyond this earth and us. Oh you who fill the home from hearth to threshold with the voices of children, you who now bestride the hidden gulf and pause to draw the right foot across and into the resting home of the great forebears, it is good that your loins be drained into the earth we know, that your last strength be ploughed back into the womb that gave you being. (21-2)

The transfiguration that the Praise-singer observes in these words of Iyaloja is, I think, a result of the strength and beauty of her reworking of imagery, but notice how this is swiftly qualified in Iyaloja's own subsequent 'Elesin, even at the narrow end of the passage I know you will look back and sigh a last regret for the flesh that flashed past your spirit in flight' (22), which surprises us in how it remains in the *present* and *future* tenses, as if even this hasty marriage will not assuage his regret for missed opportunities; and, a few exchanges later, in her exchange with Elesin: 'You wish to travel light. Well, the earth is yours.' (23) In a short space, the metaphor of 'earth' has been punctually pared down, probed and pressurized, as Iyaloja's complete reconciliation (22) gives way to ill-assurance, to the fear that she has yielded too great a concession. The sequelae of this concession are the subject of the final part of this chapter.

All this hangs together. To analyze the rhetoric of the ritual *a posteriori* is to risk not hearing its language as it is spoken and as it resonates and circulates, is to risk not receiving the rich and insinuating possibilities which are so intrinsic a part of Soyinka's dramatic intention. In such a context, analysis, which must come after the fact, so to speak, is incommensurate with its object if it does not, as it unfurls, call attention to the balance it has destroyed and recreated in the name of criticism.

3

Death, and the King's Horseman

In a reading of *Arrow of God*, Soyinka writes that 'we know Ezeulu is not afraid of death – and death in Achebe's world is not simply the curtailing of existence, but may embrace a more terrible loss of the self.' (*MLAW*, 91) In *Death and the King's Horseman*, Elesin Oba observes early, with aphoristic conviction:

> ELESIN: Life has an end. A life that will outlive fame and friendship begs another name. What elder takes his tongue to his plate, licks it clean of every crumb? He will encounter silence when he calls on children to fulfill the smallest errand! Life is honour. It ends when honour ends. (*DKH*, 15)

My sense is that the final part of *Death and the King's Horseman* is Soyinka's attempt to represent death as 'not simply the curtailing of existence'. In this perspective, one structure of the play, encouraged by the prospective movement ending in failure or non-fulfilment, becomes the dramatization of non-being; we are introduced, so to speak, to the other side of the veil, the world of consequence where our fundamental conceptions of being have been pressured and broken down. Years later, Soyinka will make an influential point on the structure of Shakespeare's *Antony and Cleopatra*, and more particularly on the structural relationship between two different moments, a beyond which renders all precedent reality merely contingent. The historical conflicts have concluded – 'it becomes clear that our playwright has already

315

inscribed *Finis* on the actual historic conflicts of power and passion'[310] – but the final act of the play is an excursion into death.

In the preceding chapter we discussed the importance of endings in Achebe's *Things Fall Apart* and *Arrow of God*, how they lend us a sudden clarity of what we have just experienced and lived, just as that experience passes into parenthesis; and how, paradoxically, the depth of that awareness can only be felt as life takes up again, as the old successiveness of time resumes.[311] There is a profound moment in Wole Soyinka's *Aké* in which the narrator recalls his attempts to understand the passing of his sister, Folasade:

> There was no CHANGE after Folasade's departure, none whatever. I daily expected a cataclysm of unthinkable proportions but it never happened. If the house had picked itself up by the roots and floated skywards, I would have shown no surprise, but nothing happened. The normality was almost overbearing and I began to suspect a conspiracy between our parents to ensure that this time when CHANGE would be so reasonable, even necessary, it did not happen. (*Aké*, 98)

Each reader may decide whether he or she agrees with the premise or trope that *children* rather than adults are always seeking to allegorize – the house floating skywards, change being painted on the walls in capital letters – in order to reach understanding. Within the fiction's movement, however, a movement of individuation expressed through the emergence and refinement of consciousness,[312] the reflection is convincing:

---

[310] Wole Soyinka, "Shakespeare and the Living Dramatist" [1983], *Essays*, 158.
[311] See above, 243-5.
[312] See, for example, Jeyifo, *Wole Soyinka*, 93: 'What *Aké* is about is the process of individuation of the future author from the earliest years of very dim, unformed consciousness of a distinct selfhood to the emergence of a remarkably strong sense of his own uniqueness against the backdrop of family, hometown, nation and the world.'

the inability to understand that part of the desolation of death of those who form our world comes precisely in the fact that things do go on, in that sense of overbearing normality which exists despite the breach opened up in life's fabric.

In *Death and the King's Horseman*, the effect which snaps us into awareness of the present, the community's irremediable loss, the passing of a world into parentheses, comes in Pilkings' attempted ventriloquism, his imitation of what he imagines to be a Yoruba idiom. And as we saw with his tragic attempts to relay Olunde's message, the effect gains traction from the fact that proximity in words reinforces what seem like incommensurable moral and poetic imaginations:

> PILKINGS: It is a beautiful night.
> ELESIN: Is that so?
> PILKINGS: The light on the leaves, the peace of the night...
> ELESIN: The night is not at peace, District Officer.
> PILKINGS: No? I would have said it was. You know, quiet...
> ELESIN: And does quiet mean peace for you?
> PILKINGS: Well, nearly the same thing. Naturally there is a subtle difference... (*DKH*, 61)

Pilkings is quickly floundering, his attempts at ingratiation easily unpicked; and by the end of this short exchange we hear the intellectual phoneyism of someone slightly annoyed at being caught out ('Naturally there is a subtle difference'). Elesin's distinction between quiet and peace is an important one, in this sense, when we remember that the (Arabic-derived) word 'alaafia', often translated into English as 'peace', in Yoruba usage holds the broadest of connotations, enfolding health and success and prosperity, something closer to a profoundness of well-being. Pilkings' central concern is to worm his way back into Elesin's good books by offering him consolation where his people offer him none, but again here, the word is invested with what we feel to be a radically different sense:

PILKINGS: If you don't want my consolation...

ELESIN: No white man, I do not want your consolation. (64)

Consolation cannot be bought on the cheap, garnered through duping or the expediency of tone; as we remarked in the introduction, no consolation is to be had, in life as in art, without a sufficiently strong acknowledgement of reality, of things as they stand; as Olunde has already pointedly asked Jane, 'What can you offer him in place of his peace of mind, in place of the honour and veneration of his own people?' (53) Yet still Pilkings persists, and Soyinka's inhabiting of a voice seeking ingratiation is expert. In Pilkings' 'I wish to ask you to search the quiet of your heart and tell me – do you not find great contradictions in the wisdom of your own race?' (64), the deployment of 'quiet' has become more subtle, allied as it is with 'heart': quietness of the heart has precedent in the slightly trite English poetic catchphrase of the beating heart ('Be still thy beating heart'), and perhaps, by association, in the Christian metaphysical sense of 'stillness'. (A later example of practised imitation of colonial pastoral or lyrical tropes comes with Dr Mackintosh's programme notes in Soyinka's *Ìsarà*: 'Imagine a river flowing... the wind gently swaying the willows... sunlight glinting on pebbles as a trout threads a silvery path through the ripples...' Though there, 'the black heads dropped, one after the other, sank onto their chests' [47]. Lakunle, of course, allowed Soyinka to test his pen early on – his heart bursting into flowers [*TLJ*, 7], romance as the sweetening of the soul with fragrance offered by the stricken heart [8], and the like.) The phrase 'wisdom of your own race' sounds both *faux*-reverential and too much like a quote from a colonial novel, one by Fenimore Cooper say, to take it as anything but just that, a quote or imitation of what Pilkings imagines to sound dignified to the Yoruba ear.

The most terrible instancing of the discontinuity of meaning in the employment of the same word comes not with Pilkings, however, with whom no moment of shared language has existed, but rather with Iyaloja on her return, surrounded by the drums which have fallen silent. The economy of the play's metaphorical imagery, as we have seen, is here allied to the audience's memory for effect, for it is memory, the memory of words and their purposive and tense movements of the representation of ritual which holds these two moments together, and ensures the audience's understanding of the breaking of unity, the full meaning of irreversibility, that there can no longer be continuity, that from one side to the other there has come a sudden darkness which we cannot wish away or traverse. It is precisely to the extent that the spatial enlargements conveyed through the language of the drums have now been lost – the spatial resonance with which human speech is extended and expressive potential enlarged, as Abiola Irele once wrote[313] – that the 'repetitions', the refrains, move us into an understanding of the irreversible and irremediable.

The most subtle expression of death in language comes, I think, with the shift between two conceptions of existence – one which conceives of personhood as indissociable from community, no matter how extreme or paradoxical certain structural expressions of this may be, as with the play's ritual; and the other which appears to belong to a more existential conception, which expresses personhood as beginning and ending with the individual. What before was carefully expressed, as we have seen, as mere possibility, important

---

[313] Irele, *The African Imagination*, 27: 'In the African context one might mention the constant recourse to surrogates (the use of drum language is a notable example) and to other nonlinguistic symbolic schemes, which serve both to give spatial resonance to human speech as well as to extend the expressive potential of language.'

reminders of what *might* happen, the dangerous yet nonetheless untaken byways which oral poetry holds and recognizes as part of its own constitution, here forms the stage. Again, I must insist that this is no use unless the artist, Soyinka in this instance, finds the rhetorical means with which to express it, the generic framework which might lend cogency and force to the particular expressions of the idea. This generic framework, it seems to me, comes through our shift from a performative realm in which shared conventions support and uphold what Abiola Irele has appositely called the 'empowering function of the word',[314] into a casuistical regime, in which Elesin has become defendant, retrospectively going over the different probable causes which led to his (in)action. This is reminiscent of what Stanley Cavell, speaking of tragedy in the Western literary tradition, has called the 'tragic fact', the sense that what 'has become inevitable is the fact of endless causation itself, together with the fact of incessant freedom. And what has become the tragic fact is that we cannot or will not tell which is which.'[315]

I have spoken of casuistry because of its etymological link to the courtroom, through the *casus* or case. The courtroom, which is the prison here, is the home of death not just because it represents physical confinement where once all had been moving towards 'openness and light'; not because he who was once Elesin Oba is held in a room of things of broken use where once slaves were chained before being shipped into slavery or death; and not, the final cruel joke, because he is forcibly separated from Iyaloja by a thin white line, the term used, by colonialists, to describe the fragility of what separated them from the colonized masses; but rather because here the new discourse is an individual-bound one, full of self-

---

[314] *Ibid.*, 19.
[315] Cavell, *Disowning Knowledge*, 89.

justifications and equivocations and 'intricacies', no longer purposive or forward-moving and deriving strength from a constituency beyond itself, but rather cast adrift in the loneliness of retrospect. The existential concentration is the result of a collapse in the order of language, a fleeting sense of which we heard in the closing moments of the first act:

ELESIN: I refuse to take offence.

IYALOJA: You wish to travel light. Well, the earth is yours. But be sure the seed you leave in it attracts no curse.

ELESIN: You really mistake my person Iyaloja.

IYALOJA: I said nothing. Now we must go prepare your bridal chamber. Then these same hands will lay your shrouds.

ELESIN [*exasperated*]: Must you be so blunt? (23)

Of Eman in *The Strong Breed* we saw how he struggles to maintain serenity in distance, drawn in as he is, despite himself and the rational controls he erects by his all too human attachments. The same is true here, psychologically, as Elesin moves from his self-persuading fiction of being above the fray, to the childish or falsely ingenuous protestation of innocence, and on again to guilt-ridden frustration before Iyaloja's refusal to listen, to pick up the thread of his fictions. The substantive dramaturgical expansion upon The *Strong Breed,* however, comes from the fact that this is a parenthesis in the ritual, each personal pronoun standing in relief against the ideal enactment of mutual constitution; and the implications are metaphysical. It is almost as if, in this final act of *Death and the King's Horseman,* Soyinka is staging what he elsewhere calls the shrinking of tragic art's cosmic scope, the diminution of morality into an intellectual conundrum, into an 'extraction of the intellect, separated from the total processes of being and human continuity.' (*MLAW,* 36)

On the night I attended Peter Badejo's 2010 production of

Death and the King's Horseman at the National Theatre, London, Elesin's infamous lines 'That is my wife sitting down there. You notice how still and silent she sits? My business is with your husband' (*DKH*, 66), were met with the nervous chuckles and outraged gasps that we might expect from such a bald statement of sexist condescension. There is, however, a dramatic observation that can be drawn from the young bride's silence which works against Elesin Oba, and is rather subtle. For one of her functions, it seems to me, is to constitute a sounding-board for Elesin, a technique formally commensurate with the one we saw in *The Man Died*, a sort of false audience against which Elesin tries to lift himself up rhetorically from his fall. She provides the moral alibi of witness which Elesin needs to pass off self-address as sincere confession. With the assurance that she will not offer recrimination, nor abandon him to loneliness, the voices dying away altogether, the full loss of the heavy tread of all the people at his back, to paraphrase Achebe on Ezeulu's loneliness;[316] with the assurance, that is, of her mere presence, he offers the following disguised self-address:

> ELESIN: My young bride, did you hear the ghostly one? You sit and sob in your silent heart but say nothing to all this. First I blamed the white man, then I blamed my gods for deserting me. Now I feel I want to blame you for the mystery of the sapping of my will. But blame is a strange peace offering for a man to bring a world he has deeply wronged, and to its innocent dwellers. Oh little mother, I have taken countless women in my life but you were more than a desire of the flesh. I needed you as the abyss across which my body must be drawn, I filled it with earth and dropped my seed in it at the moment of preparedness for my crossing. You were the final gift of the living to

---

[316] Achebe, *Arrow of God*, 218, 286.

their emissary to the land of the ancestors, and perhaps your warmth and youth brought new insights of this world to me and turned my feet leaden on this side of the abyss. For I confess to you, daughter, my weakness came not merely from the abomination of the white man who came violently into my fading presence, there was also a weight of longing on my earth-held limbs. I would have shaken it off, already my foot had begun to lift but then, the white ghost entered and all was defiled. (65)

It is a casuistical confession, for it is not a description of what he did, opening himself up to judgement from an addressee (is this silence what later earns Iyaloja's contempt?), but simultaneously a confession *and* mitigation through explanation or justification. Or better yet, in literary terms, a yielding of description before the temptation to narrative, story-telling, which is all we have left following absolute failure. This explains the tension between the message of confession, and its form and tone; the transparent words, and the truth in the undertows.

And so he begins with a logical confession of blame wrongly attributed, with an acknowledgement of responsibility shirked, the proleptic interception of the weakness of the blame argument, coming as it does from the guilty mouth. It is important not to pass over the fact that this speech follows Elesin's preliminary attempt to come to terms with his failure (the white man, abandonment by the gods). All the same, despite this apparent recognition that blaming others is no substitute for true recognition, Elesin cannot resist pursuing the byway he has opened, and the solution he finds is perfectly balanced. The apodictic expression of need gains its force from the reworking of the metaphysical imagery of the ritual itself ('I needed you as the abyss across which my body must be drawn'), although, as we saw earlier, that simile *might* suggest a slight distancing or coming apart. The word 'perhaps' is crucial. It both draws attention to the fiction of modesty that separates what is to come from his previous invocations of blame, just as it opens up into a new justification, a renewed attempt not to acknowledge failure.

The final two sentences are the most complex, and a fitting end to such a balanced and complex confession. It is here that the word 'confess' is actually used, along with the almost conspiratorial vocative, highlighting the privacy of the moment, and, implicitly, the privileged truth of what is to follow. In the event, he reminds us once more of the partial blame that the white man must take (notice the care he takes in using those two strong words 'abomination' and 'violently'), and then offers a *false* individual motive, that of longing to remain. Yet this risk and danger is constitutive of the ritual itself, for without the unique challenges of will, the implicit acknowledgement of the danger that earth's lure *must* present, the scale is lost – for something which requires little will is accessible to all, and no great challenge. I have said that this is a false pairing, and this is confirmed in the following sentence, in which Elesin states that the longing would not have mattered, *had indeed already been overcome*, until, he repeats, the white man arrived.

This extraordinary instance of narrative temptation and self-indulgence and guilt masking as confession before the safety of a silent 'addressee', gains relief in the subsequent exchange with Iyaloja. Only here, the addressee will not remain silent before his narrative explanations or his attempts to apportion blame, to attain an understanding which reaches for fictive illusions rather than the full and heavy silence of acknowledgement, as in the following exchange:

ELESIN: Enough Iyaloja, enough.
IYALOJA: We called you leader and oh, how you led us on. What we have no intention of eating should not be held to the nose.

ELESIN: Enough, enough. My shame is heavy enough.
IYALOJA: Wait. I came with a burden.
ELESIN: You have more than discharged it.
IYALOJA: I wish I could pity you.
ELESIN: I need neither your pity nor the pity of the world. I need understanding. Even I need to understand. You were present at my defeat. You were part of the beginnings. You brought about the renewal of my tie to earth, you helped in the binding of the cord. (68-9)

Elesin seeks to impose his own terms, which is another way of controlling confession, or closing one's ears to the voice of consequence. His attempt to resolve the sense of Iyaloja's burden through wordplay ('You have more than discharged it'), utterly failing to anticipate its terrible literal import ('burden' being the corpse of his own son), is Soyinka's critique of such an attitude, and is all the more terrible as it is an echo of Elesin Oba's earlier question – 'Shall I step burdened into the unknown?' – which has, in turn, become the fate of the entire community.

Iyaloja, who knows the literal weight of the burden, reacts to Elesin's misunderstanding without pity – a moment of great pathos, for there can be no greater condemnation of Elesin's failure. And it is also the occasion of Elesin's second misunderstanding, as he proceeds to take 'pity' in its weakest form, something akin to 'feeling sorry for', rather than the depth of feeling which is held in the Latinate etymology, that of compassion or understanding of suffering; pity, that is, as the deepest expression of understanding available to humans, a movement of the mind and moral imagination. Instead, he opposes pity and understanding in terms that we must not miss: for the understanding that he craves from others is merely antidote to the isolations in which shame encloses us – remember Elesin's first words after his arrest in the previous act: 'Leave me alone! Is it not enough that you have covered me in shame!' (60). Following his previous confession, then, a sort of trial-run before a mute public, he casts out his narrative net once more, aligning within this narrative commentary the characters whose hands are dirty. The anaphora of 'you', directed at Iyaloja, builds up through an intensification of verbs: you were present, you were part of, you brought about, you helped in, that final verb also carrying that deeper shade of 'collaboration'. And observe that coherent confluence of metaphors earlier deployed: ties and cords and bindings here explicitly associated to earth.

It is astonishing just how this second retrospective diagnostic narrative differs in confidence from the first, how it makes of his own failure a general model, of his particular case a universal one:

> ELESIN: What were warnings beside the moist contact of living earth between my fingers? What were warnings beside the renewal of famished embers lodged eternally in the heart of man? But even that, even if it overwhelmed one with a thousand-fold temptations to linger a little while, a man could overcome it. (69)

This pull is well held by the usage of the impersonal abstraction 'man/one', rather than the former 'my', and it is consolidated immediately afterwards by the apodictic general law as to the workings of relief:

> ELESIN: It is when the alien hand pollutes the source of will, when a stranger force of violence shatters the mind's calm resolution, this is when a man is made to commit the awful treachery of relief, commit in his thought the unspeakable blasphemy of seeing the hand of the gods in this alien rupture of his world. (69)

This seems to me far less clear-cut than what a superficial reading might suppose to be a confession, and certainly it is important to avoid the lures of considering this astonishing piece of writing as if it more properly belonged to the isolating beauty of an anthology piece. Firstly, the originary or causal link between failure and the white man persists, although here, that yearning of earth-bound limbs, and the sense that he would soon overcome such longing, has disappeared, or rather been transmuted into the 'calm resolution' of the mind. If I have spoken too boldly of a causal link – such logical connectors are deliberately denied us, and instead we are left with the awkward and indistinct repetition of 'It is when... this is when' – the passivity of 'man' being 'made' to commit treachery is important. So here, the confession is reworked: the white man or alien or stranger force of violence, comes in upon calm resolution, forcing it to commit blasphemy. What comes after ('I know it was this thought that killed me...') is contingent upon this *primus motus,* this first movement, derives therefrom, and the new-found assurance of this retrospective diagnosis – recall that earlier 'perhaps', the effaced nuance – cannot be separated from the narrative commentary as solution.

There is, however, a key departure. Before, Iyaloja responds, recalls her warnings, but it is this very response, albeit biting and angered and dismayed, which legitimates, through participation, Elesin's move into narrative. I find this an utterly plausible expression of the problem: to what extent should we try to understand? to what extent does the imaginative understanding of crime or infraction attenuate responsibility, or even render us complicit? to what extent does refusal to understand betoken a refusal of moral responsibility? The word 'understanding', however, carries a stain (recall Elesin's 'I need understanding' [69]), and Iyaloja will not make the same mistake again:

> IYALOJA: Explain it how you will, I hope it brings you peace of mind. The bush-rat fled his rightful cause, reached the market and set up a lamentation. 'Please save me!' – are these fitting words to hear from an ancestral mask? 'There's a wild beast at my

heels' is not becoming language from a hunter. (69)

This is a refusal to invite narrative, a refusal to engage. And it is crucial that following her deliberate intimation of the individualistic therapeutic objectives of Elesin's stories, Iyaloja expresses her rebuke in terms of rhetoric ('fitting words'), in terms of the language proper to a given context. There can be no casuistical or verbal resolution of an all-or-nothing situation; there can be no further 'credit' for Elesin, where the 'houseposts of trust' (15) have suffered total collapse, and such is the difference between his early request during the ritual (quoted in the chapter epigraph), and standing this side of death. Iyaloja's silent stance before he who was once called Elesin Oba is an instance of the old maxim: there is only what works for society and what does not.

Earlier, I argued in the direction of two false moments of anagnorisis. The first, in Simon Pilkings, as ignorance announces, according to convention, a passing into knowledge, only to continue serenely to the last; and in Jane, as ignorance reaches the sort of negative recognition of her own limits, though resolutely held in this colonial context. In truth, Aristotle reserved anagnorisis for the major peripeteia of the protagonist – and that undoubtedly comes with Elesin Oba. Only, again, Elesin too enacts a moment of recognition which does not induce and bespeak the full burden of knowledge before what has happened: however terrible it is for him to be confronted with total failure before his son, it does not trigger a passage from ignorance to full knowledge but rather, as we have seen, the self-justifications and equivocations of casuistical rhetoric. Anagnorisis comes not as Elesin Oba looks upon his living son, but only as he looks upon him *'rolled up in the mat, his head and feet showing at either end'* (75). This is the sense of that silence whose awfulness will be a measure of the success of the dramatic production. It is the silence of a full knowledge that no words can attenuate or dissipate or evade; a knowledge that leads to suicide.[317]

There is an alternate structural thread of the play, first suggested in Elesin's instruction to his new wife as she emerges from the bridal chamber:

> ELESIN: Our marriage is not yet wholly fulfilled. When earth and passage wed, the consummation is complete only when there are grains of earth on the eyelids of passage. Stay by me till then. (40)

Joseph's lines, something of a classic in modern African literature –

> JOSEPH: Madam, this is what I am trying to say: I am not sure. It sounds like the death of a great chief and then, it sounds like the wedding of a great chief. It really mix me up (30) –

remain perfectly consistent with the formal possibilities of this consummation. And yet in the closing actions of the play, the young wife '*takes up a little earth, walks calmly into the cell and closes Elesin's eyes. She then pours some earth over each eyelid and comes out again.*' (76) Consummation is completion and fulfilment, and it is powerful that this should be the closing action of the play, the fulfilment which we might have sought as audience members offered to us as a reminder of what could have been, in its shadowed enactment of consummation, its purely formal presentation. Those byways of the word 'earth' we continue to hear, in the staging of a coherent conclusion, well-prepared, when the meaning or completion of fulfilment is no longer available; a final, all-too literal appearance of earth, to seal the passing of the empowering word, and end with words' equivocations once and for all.

---

[317] It is tempting to think of the silence at the climax of *Things Fall Apart*, as the five court messengers come to curtail the village meeting. See Achebe, *Things Fall Apart*, 148: 'In that brief moment the world seemed to stand still, waiting. There was utter silence. The men of Umuofia were merged into the mute backcloth of trees and giant creepers, waiting.'

Conclusion

The English poet John Keats once reflected upon Shakespeare's talent as a writer in the following words:

> [...] at once it struck me, what quality went to form a Man of Achievement especially in Literature – which Shakespeare possessed so enormously – I mean *Negative Capability*, that is when man is capable of being in uncertainties, Mysteries, doubts, without any irritable reaching after fact – reason. Coleridge, for instance, would let go by a fine isolated verisimilitude caught from the Penetralium of mystery, from being incapable of remaining content with half knowledge. This pursued through Volumes would perhaps take us no further than this, that with a great poet the sense of Beauty overcomes every other consideration, or rather obliterates all consideration.[318]

There is much in Keats' critical reflection to admire: how it is content to acknowledge the claims of fact, without conceding that fact should dictate to literature; its clear insight that the truth of literature is not one which is susceptible to exhaustive conceptions of truth – how, indeed, the truth of literature shows up the folly of the impulse to a completeness of understanding (Coleridge's 'being incapable of remaining content with half knowledge'); and how the expression of this truth in what he calls a 'Man of Achievement', comes in the quality of 'negative capability', the writer's ability to move in

---

[318] John Keats, *The Complete Poetical Works and Letters of John Keats* (Cambridge: Houghton, Mifflin and Co., 1899), 277.

uncertainty and doubt and mystery, without yielding to the claims of particular truths. Keats was writing on William Shakespeare, but his words seem to me astonishingly pertinent to the example of Wole Soyinka.

I take scepticism to be constitutive of the literary condition. It is not, in my sense, a closeted theoretical questioning of the grounding of the possibilities of knowledge; conversely, it does not aspire to a condition of ataraxia or equanimous sophrosyne, as if the point of life were to detach oneself from decisions or choice or responsibility, to avoid receiving life's complications; nor does it leave us without a sense of good and bad, deprived of a moral compass before a sudden multiplying of possibilities, adrift in ambiguity. Scepticism in literature, rather, is a quality of the poetic intelligence by which a writer inhabits uncertainty and doubt and mystery, giving the fullest of range and expression to competing claims. In the ideal reader, or audience, it hones and deepens our moral imagination. This it achieves through language.

I began this study by talking of 'language', by which I meant something as apparently simple as Soyinka's words, the poetry of his language. Poetry is the terrain of negative capability, and the language of Soyinka's major works unyieldingly lays bare our irritable attempts to reach after fact. Arguably, this is less clear in the early apprentice-work of *The Lion and the Jewel* and *The Trials of Brother Jero,* two relatively simple exercises in the rhetoric of persuasion. In *The Lion and the Jewel,* the triumph of the practised language of a libidinous old reactionary, Baroka, ensures that all Lakunle's heading skyward in words' 'untrammelled climb', to borrow a phrase from Seamus Heaney,[319] brings the young man no closer to the prize, though we forgive him, and he recovers quickly; it is Baroka who shows us the dangers of learning to like a

---

[319] Heaney, *Finders Keepers,* 266.

thought as one dances alone among the shadows, like a jubilant Sadiku, for thoughts are not transparent upon life; and Baroka again who enables us to see that even in disarming seduction there might be a lesson in life and language, a double-issue.

Yet literary language is not merely a matter of showing persuasion in action. Soyinka's more suggestive plays enact, as they progress, a movement from one world of language convention to another, and an essential part of these plays' intention is that we experience that passing in and through language; that is, that we hear words becoming and become strange, against the grain of new worlds. In *Jero's Metamorphosis*, the inconsequential and comic language of trickery and astuteness thickens through its closeness to military 'justice', into a suggestion of violence which cannot be fully contained by comedy. Which is to say Soyinka responds to the advent and prolonging of military rule in Nigeria by investing and turning genre from within. This gains grip through the audience's generic expectations (we know Brother Jero from before), against which a new language emerges.

In *The Road*, generic expectations are again stretched through history beyond their stock-expression – this time in the form of the Nigerian dramatic type of the teacher turned by reading. Just as with the later *Jero's Metamorphosis*, it is the stretching of genre, how Professor is at once familiar and utterly unknown, which allows for the impact and effect of language, the strange coherence of what Professor is saying; how his words, however idiosyncratic, also possess their own coherence within his linguistic and social milieu. To the extent to which we *understand* his language, we too are mad. In turn, where the simple *idea* of 'madness' in *The Road* is incapable of speaking to the ways in which his words might penetrate and inhabit us, in *Madmen and Specialists*, too, any *ideas* we might have regarding anarchy or nihilism mean little without seeing how we *come* to anarchy or nihilism in language, how we might be led there by not attending to our words, by not holding them to basic principle. Again, it is important that we are witness to the passage, that we hear the words of the old women as strong, just as we sense that strength is fading or retiring, or becoming lost to us; and, at the same time, we understand Soyinka's dramatic critique of how thinking thinking thinking, the drift and unlatching of words from reality, is not without its terrible consequences.

It is unsurprising that a sceptical temper such as Soyinka's should be led to interrogating, through literature, a posture of objectivity, of standing beyond the compromises and uncertainties and doubts of experience. Eman, the strongest of the community, the strongest of us all, achieves a certain moral transcendence in his sacrifice, but it is nonetheless a self-sacrifice whose causes, and violent expression, are sufficiently indistinct to be perplexing. In *A Dance of the Forests* and *The Bacchae of Euripides,* the hypothesis of an Archimedean point of view which gathers all difference into a coherent perspective, a vantage point which guarantees justice, is subjected to severe sceptical interrogation, though the dramatic scale is greater than that which we saw in *The Strong Breed.* Leonardo da Vinci once remarked that the sun has never seen shadow ('Il sole non vide mai nessuna ombra'), and there is a sense in which Soyinka, in his onlooking and divinely-stained characters (Forest Head and Tiresias), is always careful to show how absolute clarity of vision strangely cohabits with blindness, an inability to see shadow, or shade, or nuance; an inability, that is, to perceive and *feel* what it is to be human, the deeper understanding. This curious cohabitation either expresses itself in a curiously a-poetic language, a language proper to emptiness, as with Forest Head, as if experience constantly anticipated and never lived has never subjected his *language* to the enriching stresses of experience; or it is a cohabitation only curtailed by stepping into the *wordless* music of communion, Tiresias shedding the curse of emptiness to know ecstasy.

We should not dismiss, too quickly, the importance of the wordlessness of music (by invoking, say, a 'progressive' viewpoint which criticizes Soyinka for not offering a 'political' expression of revolution), for the dramaturgical gambit of *The Bacchae of Euripides* is predicated, deliberately and quite precisely, on the extent to which we are prepared, *momentarily*, to subdue our impulse to reach after fact, to resist the obliteration of consideration, to paraphrase Keats, in a wider communion – the lesson, finally, of Senghor. It seems to me that to take the play seriously, is to take this intention seriously.

Some might object that I have, over the course of this study, neglected talk of Ogun. This is, in part, due to certain reservations as to the concrete usage which a symbol can assume in the hard-headed business of analysing *words*. It is also, however, a way of safeguarding a certain interpretative independence from the exciting history of Soyinka criticism, a criticism which has, perhaps by now, saturated the symbol to such an extent that it requires extraordinary analytical skill and patience for theory to clarify, rather than to occlude or elide.[320] A sharp focus on words, on language, might hold us to the meanings of, for example, a single chapter in *The Man Died*, more than any talk of the Will or self-assertion is ever able to (Keats' pursuit through volumes). For there, *language* is responding directly to milieu: to literal poverty, to the attendant breakdown of Soyinka-prisoner's basic assumptions – as to existence, as to his own limitations, as to the remit of his Will; is, indeed itself, subject to breakdown. But it is also

---

[320] Biodun Jeyifo's *Wole Soyinka: Politics, Poetics, and Postcolonialism* is a memorable example of just such an analytical achievement, with regards to Ogun in Soyinka's oeuvre.

capable of reformulating and rebuilding and remaking itself. Literature alone can show this before us as a process which we can apprehend.

There can be a no more deserving question of our attention than the words and rhetorical tools we draw on to express a loss of being more complete than physical death; our utter stripping down, our reduction to nothing (and this no doubt explains the rather grandiloquent history of critical writing on tragedy). In *Death and the King's Horseman*, the ritual journey well enacts the constitutive tensions of a certain thread in Yoruba oral poetry: the fear of loss and drift and perambulation in life, as in language. The failure of that ritual, and its consequences greater than physical death, receive expression in an *order* of language, rather than in description. That is to say, the passage into a loss more terrible than the simple curtailment of existence, receives its fullest expression in an order of language which belongs to existentialism, to casuistry, to the retrograde justifications of an isolated self. And this gains pathos precisely against the language of the mutual constitutions in word and being, of the ritual which is already fading from our minds.

I have tried throughout not to subject the reader to accidental chronological distinctions, instead holding open the many possibilities of Soyinka's language, as they respond to 'first idea' and general artistic intention, with and against each other, in a spirit of mutual enrichment. I have resisted completeness of conclusion, not for the sake of political correctness, but because I do not know how, fully, to account for the specific sort of understanding which we can come through to literature, and nothing else; I do not know whether I can render the sense of 'knowledge' which I feel renewed, and undermined, on every contact with the works I have here studied. The little I know is that I am richer for having been confronted, and defeated, by such problems; and for having experienced them, as much as is possible, with those characters on the stage, and the words in which they live, and move.

Bibliography

Primary Sources I: Cited Works Of Wole Soyinka

Plays

Wole Soyinka: Collected Plays 1: A Dance of the Forests (1-78), *The Strong Breed* (113-146), *The Road* (147-232), *The Bacchae of Euripides* (233-307) (London: Oxford University Press, 1973).

Wole Soyinka: Collected Plays 2: The Lion and the Jewel (1-58), *The Trials of Brother Jero* (143-172), *Jero's Metamorphosis* (173-214), *Madmen and Specialists* (215-276) (London: Oxford University Press, 1974).

Death and the King's Horseman (London: Methuen, 1975).

The Invention and The Detainee: The Invention (Pretoria: University of South Africa, 2005 [1959]),17-61.

Poetry

Idanre & Other Poems (London: Methuen & Co. Ltd., 1967).

A Shuttle in the Crypt (London: Rex Collings, 1972).

The Novel

The Interpreters (London: Collins, Fontana Books, 1965).

Biography and Autobiography

The Man Died. Prison Notes of Wole Soyinka (Middlesex: Penguin Books, 1975 [1972]).

Ìsarà: A Voyage Around Essay (London: Methuen, 1989).

Aké: The Years of Childhood (London: Methuen, 2001 [1981]).

Essay Collections

Myth, Literature and the African World (Cambridge: Cambridge University Press, 1976).

Art, Dialogue and Outrage: Essays on Literature and Culture (Ibadan: New Horn, 1988).
Art, Dialogue and Outrage: Essays on Literature and Culture (London: Methuen, 1993).
The Burden of Memory, The Muse of Forgiveness (Oxford; New York: Oxford University Press, 1999).

Uncollected Essays

"And After the Narcissist?" *African Forum*, Vol.1, No.4 (Spring, 1966), 56-64.
"EXILE: Thresholds of Loss and Identity," *Anglophonia/ Caliban 7*, ed. Christiane Fioupou (Toulouse: Presses Universitaires du Mirail, 2000), 61-70.
"The Tolerant Gods," in *Orisa Devotion as World Religion: The Globalization of Yorùbá Religious Culture*, eds. Jacob Olupona and Terry Rey (Wisconsin: The University of Wisconsin Press, 2008), 31-50.

Primary Sources II: Literary And Philosophical Works Cited

ACHEBE, Chinua, *Things Fall Apart* (London: Heinemann, 1958).
_____, *Arrow of God* (London: Heinemann, 1964).
_____, *Beware, Soul Brother: poems* (London: Heinemann, 1972).
ARMAH, Ayi Kwei, *Two Thousand Seasons* (London: Heinemann Educational, 1979).
BARRIE, J.M., *Peter Pan or The Boy Who Would Not Grow Up* (London: Hodder and Stoughton, 1928).
BECKETT, Samuel, *Happy Days* (London: Faber and Faber, 1961).
BORGES, Jorge Luis, *Ficciones* (Buenos Aires: Debolsillo, 2012 [1941]).
CARROLL, Lewis, *Alice's Adventures in Wonderland & Through the Looking-Glass*, ed. Peter Heath (London: Academy editions, 1974).

CERVANTES, Miguel de, *El Ingenioso Hidalgo Don Quijote de la Mancha*, http://quijote.bne.es/libro.html.
CHINWEIZU, *Energy Crisis and Other Poems* (New York; London; Lagos: Nok Publishers, 1978).
DESCARTES, René, (*Œuvres et Lettres* (Paris: Gallimard, 1953).
EURIPIDES, *The Bacchae*, in *Euripides V*, eds. David Gene and Richard Lattimore (Chicago; London: Chicago University Press, 1959), 154-228.
HENSHAW, James Ene, *This Is Our Chance* (London: University of London Press, 1957).
ISOLA, Akinwunmi, *Iku Olokun-Esin* (Ibadan: Fountain Publications, 1989).
KANE, Cheikh Hamidou, *L'Aventure Ambigüe* (Paris: Julliard, 1961).
KEATS, John, *The Complete Poetical Works and Letters of John Keats* (Cambridge: Houghton, Mifflin and Co., 1899).
LADIPO, Duro, *Oba Waja* in *Three Yoruba Plays: Oba Koso, Oba Waja and Oba Moro by Duro Ladipo*, trans. Ulli Beier (Ibadan: Mbari Publications, 1964), 74-89.
MEMMI, Albert, *Portrait du colonisé. Portrait du colonisateur* (Paris: Gallimard, 1957).
MILTON, John, *Paradise Lost*, ed. Alastair Fowler (London; New York: Longman, 1968).
ORWELL, George, *Shooting an Elephant and Other Essays* (London: Secker and Warburg, 1950).
RILKE, Rainer Maria, *The Notebooks of Malte Laurids Brigge*, trans. William Needham, ebook.
SEKYI, Kobina, *The Blinkards* (Ibadan; Nairobi; Lusaka: Heinemann Educational Books, 1974 [1915]).
SEMBÈNE, Ousmane, *Les Bouts de Bois de Dieu* (Paris: Presses pocket, 1971).
SENGHOR, Léopold Sédar, *Chants d'ombres*, suivis de *Hosties noires* (Paris: Seuil, 1956).

SHAKESPEARE, William, *The Riverside Shakespeare*, ed. G. Blakemore Evans (Boston; Atlanta; London: Houghton Mifflin Co., 1974).

STEVENS, Wallace, *The Palm at the End of the Mind: Selected Poems and a Play*, ed. Holly Stevens (New York: Vintage Books, 1972).

THURBER, James, *My Life and Hard Times* (Paris: Hachette, 1955).

WORDSWORTH, William, "The Tables Turned," in *Lyrical Ballads and Other Poems, 1797-1800*, ed. James Butler and Karen Green (Ithaca; London: Cornell University Press, 1993), 108-9.

YEATS, W.B., *The Collected Poems of W.B. Yeats*, ed. Richard J. Finneran (New York: Simon and Schuster Inc., 1996).

The Authorized King James Version of The Bible. Introduction and notes by Robert Carroll and Stephen Prickett (Oxford: Oxford University Press, 1998). Print.

Secondary Sources I: Essays, Articles and Critical Works Cited

ABIODUN, Rowland, "Who Was the First to Speak? Insights from Ifá Orature and Sculptural Repertoire," in *Orisa Devotion as World Religion: The Globalization of Yorùbá Religious Culture*, eds. Jacob Olupona and Terry Rey (Wisconsin: The University of Wisconsin Press, 2008), 51-69.

ACHEBE, Chinua, *Hopes and Impediments: Selected Essays 1965-1987* (New York: Anchor Books, 1988).

———, *Home and Exile* (Oxford; New York: Oxford University Press, 2000).

———, *The Education of a British-Protectorate Child* (London: Penguin, 2009).

ADORNO, T.W., "The Essay as Form," trans. Bob Hullot-Kentor and Frederic Will, *New German Critique* 32 (Spring-Summer, 1984), 151-171.

AGETUA, John, ed., *When the Man Died: View, Reviews and Interviews on Wole Soyinka's Controversial Book* (Benin City: Bendel Newspapers Corporation, 1975).

ANDERSON, Benedict, *Imagined Communities: Reflections on the Origin and Spread of Nationalism* (London; New York: Verso, 1993).

ARENDT, Hannah, "The Imperialist Character (On Kipling)," in *Reflections on Literature and Culture*, ed. and trans. Susannah Young-ah Gottlieb (Stanford, California: Stanford University Press, 2007), 167-171.

ARISTOTLE, *Poetics*, ed. and trans. Stephen Halliwell (Chicago: University of Chicago Press, 1998).

ARROWSMITH, William, Introduction to *The Bacchae* by Euripides, in *Euripides V*, eds. David Gene and Richard Lattimore (Chicago; London: Chicago University Press, 1959), 141-153.

ASHTON, John, *Understanding the Fourth Gospel* (Oxford: Oxford University Press, 2007 [1993]).

BAKHTIN, M.M., *The Dialogic Imagination: Four Essays*, trans. Caryl Emerson and Michael Holquist (Austin: University of Texas Press, 1981).

BARBER, Karin, "How Man Makes God in West Africa: Yoruba Attitudes Towards the Orisa," in *Africa*, Vol. 51, No.3 (1981), 724-44.

_____, *I Could Speak Until Tomorrow: Oriki, Women, and the Past in a Yoruba Town* (Edinburgh: Edinburgh University Press, 1991).

_____, *The Anthropology of Texts, Persons and Publics: Oral and written culture in Africa and beyond* (Cambridge: Cambridge University Press, 2007).

BARBER, Karin, John Collins and Alain Ricard, "Three West African Popular Theatre Forms: A Social History" in *West African Popular Theatre*, eds. Karin Barber, John Collins and Alain Ricard (Bloomington and Indianapolis: Indiana University Press; Oxford: James Currey, 1997), 1-55.

BARBER, Karin and P.F. de Moraes Farias, eds., *Self-Assertion and Brokerage: Early Cultural Nationalism in West Africa* (Birmingham: African Studies Series 2, 1990).
BASCOM, William, *Ifa Divination: Communication Between Gods and Men in West Africa* (Bloomington and London: Indiana University Press, 1965).
BEIER, Ulli, *"Esu-Elegbara*: Ambivalence in Yoruba Philosophy," in The *Hunter Thinks the Monkey Is Not Wise... The Monkey Is Wise, But He Has His Own Logic. A Selection of Essays*, ed. Wole Ogundele (Bayreuth: Bayreuth African Studies Series 59, 2001).
BLOOM, Harold, *The Anxiety of Influence: A Theory of Poetry* (New York; Oxford: Oxford University Press, 1997 [1975]).
BONNEFOY, Yves, *Shakespeare and the French Poet*, trans John Naughton (Chicago; London: University of Chicago Press, 2004).
BROCKBANK, Philip, "Blood and Wine: Tragic Ritual from Aeschylus to Soyinka" [1983], in *Perspectives on Wole Soyinka: Freedom and Complexity*, ed. Biodun Jeyifo (Jackson: University Press of Mississippi, 2001), 77-90.
CAMUS, Albert, *Le Mythe de Sisyphe: essai sur l'absurde* (Paris: Gallimard, 1942).
CANNADINE, David, "Splendor out of Court: Royal Spectacle and Pageantry in Modern Britain, c. 1820-1977," in *Rites of Power: Symbolism, Ritual, and Politics Since the Middle Ages*, ed. Sean Wilentz (Philadelphia: University of Pennsylvania Press, 1985), 206-243.
_____, *Ornamentalism: How the British Saw Their Empire* (London: Penguin Books, 2001).
CAVELL, Stanley, *Disowning Knowledge in Seven Plays of Shakespeare* (Cambridge: Cambridge University Press, 2003).
CHINWEIZU, "Prodigals, Come Home!" *Okike: An African Journal of New Writing*, No.4 (1973), 1-12.

———, Introduction to *Voices From Twentieth-Century Africa* (London; Boston: Faber and Faber, 1988), xvii-xl.

CHINWEIZU, Onwuchekwa Jemie and Ihechukwu Madubuike, *Toward the Decolonization of African Literature: African Fiction and Poetry and Their Critics* (London; Boston; Melbourne; Henley: KPI, 1985 [1980]).

COHN, Dorrit, *Transparent Minds: Narrative Modes for Presenting Consciousness in Fiction* (Princeton, New Jersey: Princeton University Press, 1978).

CROW, Brian, 'Soyinka and the Romantic Tradition' in *Before Our Very Eyes: Tribute to Wole Soyinka*, ed. Dapo Adelugba (Ibadan: Spectrum Books, 1987), 147-169.

DE QUINCEY, Thomas, *Miscellaneous Essays* (Boston: Ticknor, Reed, and Fields, 1851).

DIAGNE, Souleymane Bachir, *Léopold Sédar Senghor: l'art africain comme philosophie* (Paris: Riveneuve éditions, 2007).

DREWAL, Henry, "Introduction: Yoruba Art and Life as Journeys," in *The Yoruba Artist: New Theoretical Perspectives on African Arts*, eds. Rowland Abiodun, Henry Drewal and John Pemberton III (Washington D.C.; London: Smithsonian Institution Press, 1994), 193-200.

EAGLETON, Terry, *Sweet Violence: The Idea of the Tragic* (Oxford: Blackwell Publishing, 2003).

ECHERUO, Michael J.C., *Victorian Lagos: Aspects of Nineteenth Century Lagos Life* (London; Basingstoke: Macmillan, 1977).

———, "Aha m efula: A Matter of Identity".
http://ahiajoku.igbonet.com/1979/

ELIAS, Norbert, *La société de cour*, trans. Pierre Kamnitzer (Paris: Calmann-Lévy, 1974).

EMPSON, William, *Seven Types of Ambiguity* (Middlesex: Penguin, 1930).

———, '"Hamlet" When New,' *The Sewanee Review*, Vol.61, No.1 (Winter, 1953), 15-42.

ESSLIN, Martin, *The Theatre of the Absurd* (London: Eyre and Spottiswoode, 1962).
FIOUPOU, Christiane, Avant-propos to *la Route* by Wole Soyinka, trans. Christiane Fioupou and Samuel Millogo (Paris: Hatier, 1988), 3-12.
―――, *La Route: réalité et représentation dans l'oeuvre de Wole Soyinka* (Amsterdam; Atlanta: Rodopi, 1994).
―――, "Salut à toi Saint Atunda... Grand iconoclaste dès la genèse: récits de création, traditions yoruba et réappropriations littéraires," paper delivered for the conference 'Avatar des commencements: récits de genèse,' Université de Toulouse-Le Mirail, December 4, 2012.
FRYE, Northrop, *The Great Code: The Bible and Literature* (London; Melbourne; Henley: Ark Paperbacks, 1982).
GIBBON, Edward, *The History of the Decline and Fall of the Roman Empire*, Vol.4, 1996 Project Gutenberg Edition ebook.
GIBBS, James, ed., *Critical Perspectives on Wole Soyinka* (London; Ibadan; Nairobi: Heinemann, 1980).
―――, "The Masks Hatched Out," in *Theatre Research International*, Vol.7, No.3 (Autumn 1982), 180-206.
―――, "Neglected Masterpiece: Responses to a UK Production of a Major Wole Soyinka Play," *West Africa* (1-7 April, 1991).
GINZBURG, Carlo, *Occhiacci di legno: Nove riflessioni sulla distanza* (Milan: Feltrinelli, 1998).
GOMBRICH, E.H., *Art and Illusion: A Study in the Psychology of Pictorial Representation* (London: Phaidon, 1960).
HARRIS, Wilson, "The Complexity of Freedom," in *Perspectives on Wole Soyinka*, ed. Biodun Jeyifo (Jackson: University Press of Mississippi, 2001), 51-61.
HAYS, Richard B., "The Canonical Matrix of the Gospels," in *The Cambridge Companion to the Gospels*, ed. Stephen C. Barton (Cambridge: Cambridge University Press, 2006), 53-75.

HAZARD, Paul, *La Crise de la conscience européenne* (Paris: Gallimard, 1968).
HEANEY, Seamus, *Finders Keepers: Selected Prose 1971-2001* (London: Faber and Faber, 2002).
HOBSBAWM, E.J. and Terence Ranger, eds., *The Invention of Tradition* (Cambridge: Cambridge University Press, 1983).
IMBO, Samuel O., "Okot p'Bitek's Critique of Western Scholarship on African Religion," in *A Companion to African Philosophy*, ed. Kwasi Wiredu (Oxford: Blackwell Publishing, 2004), 364-373.
IRELE, Abiola, "Tradition and the Yoruba Writer," in *Critical Perspectives on Wole Soyinka*, ed. James Gibbs (London: Heinemann, 1980),45-68.
_____, *The African Experience in Literature and Ideology* (London; Exeter, N.H.: Heinemann, 1981).
_____, "In Praise of Alienation," in *The Surreptitious Speech: Présence Africaine and the Politics of Otherness 1947-1987*, ed. V.Y. Mudimbe (Chicago: University of Chicago Press, 1989), 201-225.
_____, *The African Imagination: Literature in Africa and the Black Diaspora* (New York: Oxford University Press, 2001).
_____, Foreword to *The Invention* and *The Detainee* by Wole Soyinka (Pretoria: University of South Africa, 2005), ix-xi.
_____, *Négritude et condition africaine* (Paris: Editions Karthala, 2008).
IRELE, F. Abiola and Simon Gikandi, Preface to *The Cambridge History of African and Caribbean Literature*, eds. Abiola Irele and Simon Gikandi (Cambridge: Cambridge University Press, 2004), xi-xx.
IZEVBAYE, Dan, "Language and Meaning in Soyinka's *The Road*," in *Critical Perspectives on Wole Soyinka*, ed. James Gibbs (London: Heinemann, 1980),
_____, "Elesin's Homecoming: The Translation of The King's Horseman," in *Research in African Literatures*, Vol.

28, No.3 (1997),154-170.

_____, "West African Literature in English," in *The Cambridge History of African and Caribbean Literature*, eds. Abiola Irele and Simon Gikandi (Cambridge: Cambridge University Press, 2004), 90-103.

JAKOBSON, Roman, "Linguistics and Poetics," in *Style and Language*, ed. T. Sebeok (Cambridge, Massachusetts: M.I.T. Press, 1960), 350-377.

_____, "Two Aspects of Language and Two Types of Aphasic Disturbances," in *Selected Writings II: Word and Language* (The Hague; Paris: Mouton, 1971), 239-259.

JEYIFO, Biodun, *The Yoruba Popular Travelling Theatre of Nigeria* (Lagos: A Nigeria Magazine Publication, 1984).

_____, *The Truthful Lie: Essays in a Sociology of African Drama* (London: New Beacon Books Ltd., 1985).

_____, ed., *Perspectives on Wole Soyinka: Freedom and Complexity* (Jackson: University Press of Mississippi, 2001).

_____, *Wole Soyinka: Politics, Poetics and Postcolonialism* (Cambridge: Cambridge University Press, 2004).

_____, " 'Oguntoyinbo': Wole Soyinka and "Igilango Geesi",' *Philosophia Africana*, Vol.11, No.1 (March 2008), 21-36.

JONES, Eldred Durosimi, *Othello's Countrymen. The African in English Renaissance Drama* (London: Oxford University Press, 1965).

_____, *The Elizabethan Image of Africa* (Charlottesville: University Press of Virginia, 1971).

_____, *The Writing of Wole Soyinka* (London: James Currey, 1988 [1973]).

KATRAK, Ketu H., *Wole Soyinka and Modern Tragedy: A Study of Dramatic Theory and Practice* (New York; Westport; Connecticut; London: Greenwood Press, 1986).

KERMODE, Frank, Introduction to *The Tempest* by William Shakespeare (London; New York: Methuen, 1954).

_____, *The Genesis of Secrecy: On the Interpretation of*

Narrative (Cambridge, Massachusetts: Harvard University Press, 1979).
_____, *The Sense of an Ending: Studies in the Theory of Fiction* (Oxford:Oxford University Press, 2000 [1966]).
KERMODE, Frank, *Shakespeare's Language* (New York: Farrar, Straus, Giroux, 2000).
KIRK-GREENE, Anthony, *On Crown Service: A History of HM Colonial and Overseas Civil Services 1837-1937* (London; New York: I.B. Tauris Publishers, 1999).
_____, *Symbol of Authority* (London; New York: I.B. Tauris, 2006).
KOYRÉ, Alexandre, *Du Monde clos à l'univers infini*, trans. Raissa Tarr (Paris: Gallimard, 1973).
LANHAM, Richard, *A Handlist of Rhetorical Terms* (Berkeley; Los Angeles; London: University of California Press, 1991).
LEJEUNE, Philippe, *On Autobiography*, trans. Katherine Leary (Minneapolis: University of Minnesota Press, 1989).
LEVI, Primo, *I sommersi e i salvati* (Torino: Einaudi, 2007).
MANNHEIM, Karl, *Ideology and Utopia: An Introduction to the Sociology of Knowledge*, trans. Louis Wirth and Edward Shils (San Diego; New York; London: HBJ, 1985).
MARX, Karl, *Political Writings, Vol. 3: The First International and After*, ed. David Fernbach (New York: Random House/Vintage Books and Monthly Review Press; London and Harmondsworth: Penguin Books and New Left Review, 1974).
MASTRONARDE, Donald, *Contact and Discontinuity: Some Conventions of Speech and Action on the Greek Tragic Stage* (Los Angeles; London: University of California Press, 1979).
MENKITI, Ifeanyi, "On the Normative Conception of a Person," in *A Companion to African Philosophy*, ed. Kwasi Wiredu (Oxford: Blackwell Publishing, 2004), 324-331.
MORETTI, Franco, *Signs Taken for Wonders: On the Sociology*

of Literary Forms (London; New York: Verso, 2005 [1983]).
MOTSA, Zodwa, Introduction to *The Invention* and *The Detainee* by Wole Soyinka (Pretoria: University of South Africa, 2005), 1-16.
MSISKA, Mpalive-Hangson, *Postcolonial Identity in Wole Soyinka* (Amsterdam; New York: Rodopi, 2007).
NINO, Carlos Santiago, *Radical Evil On Trial* (New Haven; London: Yale University Press, 1996).
NUTTALL, A.D., *The Alternative Trinity: Gnostic Heresy in Marlowe, Milton, and Blake* (Oxford: Clarendon Press, 1998).
_____, *Shakespeare* the *Thinker* (New Haven; London: Yale University Press, 2007).
OBIECHINA, Emmanuel, *An African Popular Literature: A Study of Onitsha Market Pamphlets* (London: Cambridge University Press, 1973).
OBILADE, Tony, "The Stylistic Function of Pidgin English in African Literature: Achebe and Soyinka," in *Research on Wole Soyinka*, eds. James Gibbs and Bernth Lindfors (Trenton, New Jersey: Africa World Press, 1993), 13-24.
OGUNBA, Oyin, *The Movement of Transition: A Study of the Plays of Wole Soyinka* (Ibadan: Ibadan University Press, 1975).
OKPEWHO, Isidore, "Soyinka, Euripides, and the Anxiety of Empires," in *African Drama and Performance*, eds. John Conteh-Morgan and Tejumola Olaniyan (Bloomington: Indiana University Press, 2001), 55-77.
OLANIYAN, Tejumola, *Arrest the Music! Fela and his Rebel Art and Politics* (Bloomington and Indianapolis: Indiana University Press, 2004).
OLUPONA, Jacob K., *City of 201 Gods: Ile-Ife in Time, Space, and the Imagination* (Berkeley, Los Angeles; London: University of California Press, 2011).
OSOFISAN, Femi, "Tiger on Stage: Wole Soyinka and Nigerian Theatre," in *Theatre in Africa*, eds. Oyin Ogunba and Abiola Irele (Ibadan: Ibadan University Press, 1978), 151-174.

OSOFISAN, Femi, *The Nostalgic Drum: Essays on Literature, Drama and Culture* (Trenton, New Jersey: Africa World Press, 2001).

OSOFISAN, Femi, Intervention in "Ninth Dialogue: The Word in Disguise,' in *The Power of the Word/ La Puissance du Verbe*, ed. T. J. Cribb (Amsterdam; New York: Rodopi, 2006), 177-178.

OSUNDARE, Niyi, "Yorùbá Thought, English Words: a Poet's Journey Through the Tunnel of Two Tongues," in *Kiss and Quarrel: Yorùbà/English, Strategies of Mediation*, ed. Stewart Brown (Birmingham: African Studies Series 5, 2000), 15-31.

——, "Stubborn Thread in the Loom of Being: The Writer as Memory of the World," slightly modified version of the S.A. Yoder Memorial Lecture presented to the Convocation of Goshen College, Indiana, October 21, 1998, in *Thread in the Loom: Essays on African Literature and Culture* (Trenton, New Jersey: Africa World Press, Inc., 2002), 13-20.

PEEL, J.D.Y., *Aladura: A Religious Movement Among the Yoruba* (London: Oxford University Press, 1968).

——, *Religious Encounter and the Making of the Yoruba* (Bloomington and Indianapolis: Indiana University Press, 2000).

PRICKETT, Stephen, "The Bible in Literature and Art," in *The Cambridge Companion to Biblical Interpretation*, ed. John Barton (Cambridge: Cambridge University Press, 1998), 160-178.

QUAYSON, Ato, *Aesthetic Nervousness: Disability and the Crisis of Representation* (New York: Columbia University Press, 2007).

SEDLAK, Werner, "Prison Memoirs by African Writers (Ngugi, Pheto, Soyinka): The Cultural Unity and Complexity of Resistance" in *Fusion of Cultures?* eds. Peter O. Stummer and Christopher Balme (Amsterdam: Rodopi, 1996), 183-192.

SERRES, Michel, *Le Système de Leibniz et ses modèles mathématiques* (Paris: Presses Universitaires de France, 1968).
SHKLAR, Judith N., *The Faces of Injustice* (New Haven: Yale University Press, 1990).
SHKLOVSKY, Viktor, *Theory of Prose*, trans. Benjamin Sher (Illinois: Dalkey Archive Press, 1990 [1925]).
STAROBINSKI, Jean, *L' Œil vivant II. La relation critique* (Paris: Gallimard, 1970).
———, *Montaigne en mouvement* (Paris: Gallimard, 1982).
STEINER, George, *The Death of Tragedy* (London: Faber and Faber, 1961).
———, *After Babel: Aspects of Language and Translation* (London; New York; Toronto: Oxford University Press, 1975).
SUVIN, Darko, "The Mirror and the Dynamo: On Brecht's Aesthetic Point of View," *TDR*, Vol.12, No.1 (Autumn, 1967), 56-67.
———, *To Brecht and Beyond: Soundings in Modern Dramaturgy* (Sussex: The Harvester Press, 1984).
———, *In Leviathan's Belly: Essays for a Counter-Revolutionary Time* (Rockville, Maryland: Wildside Press LLC, 2012).
THOMPSON, E.P., *Whigs and Hunters: The Origin of the Black Act* (Harmondsworth: Peregrine Books, 1977).
TOWA, Marcien, *L'idée d'une philosophie négro-africaine* (Yaoundé: Éditions Clé, 1979).
WHEELER, Michael, *St. John and the Victorians* (Cambridge: Cambridge University Press, 2012).
WILENTZ, Sean, ed., *Rites of Power: Symbolism, Ritual and Politics since the Middle Ages* (Philadelphia: University of Pennsylvania Press, 1999).
WILLBERN, David, "Shakespeare's Nothing" in *Representing Shakespeare: New Psychoanalytic Essays*, eds. Murray M. Schwartz and Coppelia Kahn (Baltimore and London: The John Hopkins University Press, 1980), 244-263.

WILLIAMS, Bernard, *Descartes: The Project of Pure Enquiry* (Sussex: The Harvester Press, 1978).

WIREDU, Kwasi, "Amo's Critique of Descartes' Philosophy of Mind," in *A Companion to African Philosophy*, ed. Kwasi Wiredu (Oxford: Blackwell Publishing, 2004), 200-206.

—————, Introduction to *Decolonizing African Religions: A Short History of African Religions in Western Scholarship* by Okot p'Bitek (New York: Diaspora Africa Press, 2011), xi-xxxvi.

WOOD, James, "God Talk: The Book of Common Prayer at Three Hundred and Fifty," *The New Yorker*, October 22, 2012. http://www.newyorker.com/arts/critics/atlarge/2012/10/22/121022crat_atlarge_wood?currentPage=all

YAI, Olabiyi Babalola, "Issues in Oral Poetry: Criticism, Teaching and Translation," in *Discourses and its Disguises: The Interpretation of African Oral Texts*, eds. Karin Barber and P.F. de Moraes Farias (Birmingham: Centre of West African Studies, African Studies Series 1, 1989), 59-69.

—————, "In Praise of Metonymy: The Concepts of "Tradition" and "Creativity" in the Transmission of Yoruba Artistry over Time and Space," in *The Yoruba Artist: New Theoretical Perspectives on African Arts*, eds. Rowland Abiodun, Henry Drewal and John Pemberton III (Washington D.C.; London: Smithsonian Institution Press, 1994), 107-118.

—————, "The Path is Open: The Herskovits Legacy in African Oral Narrative Analysis and Beyond," PAS Working Papers, No.5 (1999), pp.36.

—————, "Tradition and the Yoruba Artist," *African Arts*, Vol. 32, No.1, Part 2 (Spring 1999), 32-5+93.

—————, "Seuils pour repenser la traduction des poésies orales africaines," in *Anglophonia/Caliban* 7, ed. Christiane Fioupou (Toulouse: Presses Universitaires du Mirail, 2000), 225-237.

YAI, Olabiyi Babalola, "Ninth Dialogue: The Word in Disguise," in *The Power of the Word/La Puissance du Verbe*, ed. T.J. Cribb (Amsterdam; New York: Rodopi, 2006), 163-180.

Secondary Sources II: Select Bibliography

ABIMBOLA, Wande, *Sixteen Great Poems of Ifá* (Niamey: UNESCO, Organization of African Unity Centre for Linguistic and Historical Studies by Oral Tradition, 1972).

ABIODUN, Rowland, Henry John Drewal and John Pemberton III, *Yoruba Art and Aesthetics in Nigeria* (Zurich: The Center for African Art and the Rietberg Museum, 1991).

ABRAHAM, W.E., *The Mind of Africa* (Chicago; London: The University of Chicago Press, 1962).

ADOTEVI, Stanislas, *Négritude et négrologues* (Paris: Union Générale d'Éditions, 1972).

APPIAH, K.A., *In My Father's House: Africa in the Philosophy of Culture* (New York: Oxford University Press, 1992).

AUERBACH, Eric, *Mimesis: The Representation of Reality in Western Literature*, trans. Willard R. Trask (Princeton, New Jersey: Princeton University Press, 1953).

AUSTIN, J.L., *How To Do Things With Words* (Cambridge, M.A.: Harvard University Press, 1962).

BELLO, Bankole, *Wole Soyinka, Citizen-poet*, 5 Continents — La Sept — Fr. 3 — BB Films & Video, 1990.

BLUMENBERG, Hans, *La leggibilità del mondo*, trans. Remo Bodei (Bologna: Societa editrice, 1984).

BRECHT, Bertolt, *Brecht on Theatre: The Development of an Aesthetic. (A Selection from Brecht's Notes and Theoretical Writing.)*, ed. and trans. John Willet (London: Methuen & Co., 1964).

CHINWEIZU, *The West and the Rest of Us: White Predators, Black Slavers and the African Elite* (New York: Random House, 1975).

CURREY, James, *Africa Writes Back: The African Writers Series and the Launch of African Literature* (Oxford: James Currey, 2008).
DREWAL, Margaret Thompson, *Yoruba Ritual: Performers, Play, Agency* (Bloomington and Indianapolis: Indiana University Press, 1992).
DUNTON, Chris, *Nigerian Drama in English Since 1970* (London; New York: Hans Zell Publishers, 1992).
ECHERUO, Michael J.C., *Joyce Cary and the Novel of Africa* (London: Longman, 1973).
_____, *Joyce Cary and the Dimensions of Order* (London: Macmillan Press, 1979).
ERLICH, Victor, *Russian Formalism: History – Doctrine* (New Haven; London: Yale University Press, 1981 [1965]).
FALOLA, Toyin and Matt D. Childs, eds., *The Yoruba Diaspora in the Atlantic World* (Bloomington and Indianapolis: Indiana University Press, 2004).
FIOUPOU, Christiane, "Variations on Wole Soyinka's *Death and the King's Horseman*," in *New Theatre in Francophone and Anglophone Africa*, ed. Anne Fuchs (Amsterdam; Atlanta: Editions Rodopi, 1999), 229-240.
_____, "African Literature and Theory: The Cart Before The Horse?" in *Commonwealth: Essays and Studies*, Vol.24, No.2 (Spring 2002), 5-16.
FUENTES, Carlos, *Cervantes o la crítica de la lectura* (Alcalá de Henares: Centro de Estudios Cervantes, 1994 [1972]).
GABEL, John B., Charles B. Wheeler and Anthony D. York, *The Bible as Literature: An Introduction* (New York; Oxford: Oxford University Press, 1996).
GATES, Henry Louis Jr., ed., *'Race', Writing, and Difference* (London: The University of Chicago Press, 1985).
_____, *The Signifying Monkey: A Theory of African-American Literary Criticism* (New York; Oxford: Oxford University Press, 1988).

GILROY, Paul, *The Black Atlantic: Modernity and Double Consciousness* (Cambridge, M.A.: Harvard University Press, 1993).
GOODY, Jack, *The Domestication of the Savage Mind* (Cambridge; London; New York; Melbourne: Cambridge University Press, 1977).
_____, *The Expansive Movement: The Rise of Social Anthropology in Britain and Africa (1918-1970)* (Cambridge: Cambridge University Press, 1995).
GÖTRICK, Kacke, "Soyinka and *Death and the King's Horseman* or How Does Our Knowledge – or Lack of Knowledge – of Yoruba Culture Affect Our Interpretation," in *African Literature Association Bulletin*, Vol.16, No.1 (Winter 1990), 1-9.
HALLIWELL, Stephen, *Aristotle's Poetics* (Chapel Hill: The University of North Carolina Press, 1986).
_____, *The Aesthetics of Mimesis: Ancient Texts and Modern Problems* (Princeton; Oxford: Princeton University Press, 2002).
IDOWU, E. Bolaji, *Olódùmarè: God in Yoruba Belief* (Ikeja: Longman, 1962).
IRELE, Abiola, *The Negritude Moment: Explorations in Francophone African and Caribbean Literature and Thought* (Trenton; New Jersey; London: Africa World Press, 2011).
JAUSS, H.R., *Pour une esthétique de la réception*, trans. Claude Maillard (Paris: Gallimard, 1978).
KESTELOOT, Lilyan, *Les écrivains noirs de langue française: naissance d'une littérature* (Bruxelles: Université Libre de Bruxelles, 1963).
KIRK-GREENE, Anthony, ed., *Glimpses of Empire:* A Corona Anthology (London; New York: I.B. Tauris Publishers, 2001).
LARSEN, Stephan, *A Writer and His Gods: A Study of the Importance of Myths and Religious Ideas to the Writings of*

Wole Soyinka (Stockholm: University of Stockholm Department of the History of Literature, 1983).
LERNER, Laurence, *The Uses of Nostalgia: Studies in Pastoral Poetry* (London: Chatto and Windus, 1972).
LÖWITH, Karl, trans. M.-C. Challiol-Gillet, S. Hurstel and J. -F. Kervégan, *Histoire et salut: Les présupposés théologiques de la philosophie de l'histoire* (Paris: Gallimard, 2002).
MBEMBE, Achille, *Essai sur l'imagination politique dans l'Afrique contemporaine* (Paris: Karthala, 1999).
MBITI, John S. *African Religions and Philosophy* (Oxford: Heinemann, 1989 [1969]).
MUDIMBE, V.Y., *The Invention of Africa: Gnosis, Philosophy, and the Order of Knowledge* (Oxford: James Currey, 1989).
NGUGI wa Thiong'o, *Decolonizing the Mind: the Politics of Language in African Literature* (London: James Currey, 1986).
NOOTER, Mary H., ed., *Secrecy: African Art that Conceals and Reveals* (New York: The Museum for African Art; Munich: Prestel, 1993).
NORTON, David, *A Textual History of the King James Bible* (Cambridge: Cambridge University Press, 2004).
NUTTALL, A.D., *A New Mimesis: Shakespeare and the Representation of Reality* (London; New York: Methuen, 1983).
NWOGA, Donatus and Chukwuma Azuonye, eds., *The Hero in Igbo Life and Literature* (Enugu: Fourth Dimension Publishers, 2002).
OFEIMUN, Odia, "Africa's Many Mansions," *West Africa* (20-26 July, 1992), 1231-2.
OGUNBIYI, Yemi, ed., *Drama and Theatre in Nigeria: a Critical Source Book* (Lagos: Nigeria Magazine, 1981).
_____, *Perspectives on Nigerian Literature 1700 to the Present*, Vol.2 (Lagos: Guardian Books Nigeria Limited, 1988).
OLORUNYOMI, Sola, *Afrobeat! Fela and the Imagined*

Continent (Ibadan: IFRA, 2005 [2003]).
OMOTOSO, Kole, *Achebe or Soyinka? A Study in Contrasts* (London; Melbourne; Munich; New Jersey: Hans Zell Publishers, 1996).
PERRIS, Simon, "Our Saviour Dionysos: Humanism and Theology in Gilbert Murray's *Bakkhai*," *Translation and Literature* 21.1 (2012), 21-42.
PRICKETT, Stephen, *Words and* The Word: *Language, Poetics and Biblical Interpretation* (Cambridge: Cambridge University Press, 1986).
QUAYSON, Ato, *Strategic Transformations in Nigerian Writing* (Oxford: James Currey; Bloomington and Indianapolis: Indiana University Press, 1997).
RAJI-OYELADE, Aderemi and Oyeniyi Okunoye, eds., *The Postcolonial Lamp: Essays in Honour of Dan Izevbaye* (Ibadan: Bookcraft, 2008).
RICARD, Alain, *Théâtre et nationalisme* (Paris: Présence Africaine, 1972).
———, *Wole Soyinka ou l'ambition democratique* (Paris: Les nouvelles editions africaines, 1989).
RISÉRIO, Antonio, "De Oriquis," *Revista Afro-Ásia*, No.15 (1992), 36-55.
SAID, Edward, *Culture and Imperialism* (London: Vintage Books, 1994).
SENGHOR, Léopold Sédar, *Liberté I: Négritude et humanisme* (Paris: Seuil, 1964).
SLOCHOWER, Harry, *Mythopoesis: Mythic Patterns in the Literary Classics* (Detroit: Wayne State University Press, 1970).
TODOROV, Tzvetan, ed. and trans., *Théorie de la littérature: Textes des formalistes russes* (Paris: Seuil, 2001 [1965]).
WALDRON, Jeremy, *The Law (Theory & Practice in British Politics)* (London; New York: Routledge, 1990).
WALI, Obi, "The Dead-end of African Literature," *Transition,*

No.11 (September 1963), 13-18.
WATT, Ian, *The Rise of the Novel* (London: Chatto and Windus, 1957).
WELLEK, René, *A History of Modern Criticism: 1750-1950. Volume 5 English Criticism, 1900-1950* (New Haven; London: Yale University Press, 1986).
WILLIAMS, Raymond, *Modern Tragedy* (California: Stanford University Press, 1966).
WILSON KNIGHT, George, *The Wheel of Fire: Interpretations of Shakespearian Tragedy* (London; New York: Routledge Classics, 1930).
WIREDU, Kwasi, *Philosophy and an African Culture* (Cambridge: Cambridge University Press, 1980).
WRIGHT, Derek, *Wole Soyinka Revisited* (New York: Twayne Publishers, 1993).
YAI, Olabiyi, ed., *African Studies Quarterly*, Vol. 2, No.4 (1998).

Index of Names

Abiodun, Rowland, 304
Achebe, Chinua, 8, 9, 10, 11, 12, 34, 63, 64, 71, 112, 178, 210, 212, 239, 245-249, 252, 291, 311, 315, 316, 322, 329
Adedeji, Joel, 267
Adorno, Theodor W., 28
Aeschylus, 3, 4, 143
Agetua, John, 213
Amo, Anton Wilhelm, 238
Anderson, Benedict, 262, 263, 265, 281, 282, 285, 286
Arendt, Hannah, 198, 262, 263, 265
Aristophanes, 55, 65
Aristotle, 272, 273, 328
Armah, Ayi Kwei, 289, 290
Arne, Thomas, 282
Arrowsmith, William, 181, 186, 192
Ashton, John, 81
Auden, W.H., 17

b/
Badejo, Peter, 321
Bakhtin, Mikhail, 56, 57, 96
Barber, Karin, 27, 52, 211, 258, 259, 294, 298, 302
Barrie, J.M., 263
Bascom, William, 71
Beckett, Samuel, 116, 117, 121, 122, 126
Beier, Ulli, 39, 277
Benda, Julien, 110
Béti, Mongo, 26
Bloom, Harold, 295
Bonnefoy, Yves, 70, 72

Borges, Jorge Luis, 109, 110, 232
Brecht, Bertolt, 159, 185
Brockbank, Philip, 4, 143, 191, 255
Brown, Stewart, 17
Bunyan, John, 24
Burns, Robert, 27

c/
Camus, Albert, 116
Cannadine, David, 280, 281
Carroll, Lewis, 248
Cavell, Stanley, 5, 320
Cervantes, Miguel de, 70, 109
Charron, Pierre, 236
Chinweizu, 61
Ciroma, Adamu, 213
Cohn, Dorrit, 76, 219
Cole, Herbert, 301
Coleridge, Samuel Taylor, 330
Conrad, Joseph, 156
Cranmer, Thomas, 116, 117
Crow, Brian, 152, 186

d/
da Vinci, Leonardo, 333
de Quincey, Thomas, 247, 248
Descartes, René, 235, 236, 237, 238, 240, 245, 246, 250, 251
Diagne, Souleymane Bachir, 250
Dickens, Charles, 140, 266
Drewal, Henry, 312

e/
Eagleton, Terry, 211
Echeruo, Michael, 10, 295

Elias, Norbert, 283
Eliot, T.S., 5
Empiricus, Sextus, 236
Empson, William, 74, 75, 206
Enahoro, Peter, 213
Esslin, Martin, 122
Euripides, 3, 180, 181, 182, 185, 186, 188, 191, 192, 193, 194, 196, 203, 301

f/
Fagg, William, 208
Fagunwa, Daniel O., 2
Fenimore Cooper, James, 318
Fioupou, Christiane, 79, 84, 85, 103, 105, 160, 254, 298
Franklin, Benjamin, 252
Frye, Northrup, 84
Fugard, Athol, 156

g/
Gates Jr., Henry Louis, 264
Gibbon, Edward, 22
Gibbs, James, 142, 155, 263, 264
Gikandi, Simon, 17
Ginzburg, Carlo, 167
Gombrich, Eric, 255

h/
Harris, Wilson, 156, 157, 158
Hays, Richard B., 84
Hazard, Paul, 251
Heaney, Seamus, 16, 17, 18, 331
Hegel, Georg Wilhelm Friedrich, 114
Henshaw, James Ene, 27
Hobsbawm, E.J., 279, 280

i/
Irele, Abiola, 2, 17, 52, 155, 156, 160, 198, 213, 245, 257, 299, 305, 311, 319, 320

Isola, Akinwunmi, 296
Izevbaye, Dan, 2, 73, 74, 80, 96, 106, 296

j/
Jakobson, Roman, 297, 302
James, William, 109
Jemie, Onwuchekwa, 61
Jeyifo, Biodun, 1, 29, 96, 97, 98, 103, 107, 162, 260, 277, 294, 316, 334
Joffe, Adolfe, 229
Johnson, Samuel, 6, 84
Jones, Eldred, 3, 113

k/
Kafka, Franz, 76
Kane, Cheikh Hamidou, 239, 244, 245, 289, 290
Katrak, Ketu, 102, 105, 160
Keats, John, 330, 331, 334
Kenner, Hugh, 121
Kermode, Frank, 3, 4, 5, 6, 7, 8, 9, 12, 162, 231, 297
Kierkegaard, Søren, 220
Kirk-Greene, Anthony, 268, 279
Koyré, Alexandre, 240
Kyd, Thomas, 75

l/
La Mothe le Vayer, François de, 236
Ladipo, Duro, 276, 277
Lanham, Richard, 297
Lejeune, Philippe, 214
Levi, Primo, 229
Lindop, Grevel, 264

m/
Madubuike, Ihechukwu, 61
Mahood, Molly, 17
Mangakis, George, 216
Mannheim, Karl, 259, 260
Marlowe, Christopher, 17, 19

Marx, Karl, 252, 253
Mastronarde, Donald, 193, 194, 301, 302
Memmi, Albert, 264, 265, 266, 283
Menkiti, Ifeanyi, 299
Milton, John, 253, 254, 255
Montaigne, Michel de, 200, 236
Moore, Henry, 156
Moretti, Franco, 98, 99, 100
Motsa, Zodwa, 155
Msiska, Mpalive-Hangson, 19
Muldoon, Paul, 16

n/
Nabokov, Vladimir, 282
Ni Dhomhnaill, Nuala, 16
Nino, Carlos Santiago, 198
Nuttall, A.D., 24, 66, 114, 135, 201

o/
O'Brien, Conor Cruise, 213
Obiechina, Emmanuel, 31
Obilade, Tony, 49
Ogunba, Oyin, 53, 110, 111, 160, 161
Ogunbiyi, Yemi, 206
Okpewho, Isidore, 180
Okri, Ben, 233
Olaniyan, Tejumola, 299
Olupona, Jacob, 256
Omotoso, Kole, 213
Orwell, George, 284, 285
Osofisan, Femi, 4, 5, 52, 70
Osundare, Niyi, 17, 23, 24
Ovid, 18
Owen, Wilfred, 129

p/
p'Bitek, Okot, 80, 81, 238
Pascal, Blaise, 240, 241, 242, 245, 246
Peel, J.D.Y., 51, 52, 58, 59, 60, 61, 62, 63, 66, 67, 83
Picasso, Pablo, 156

Prickett, Stephen, 254
Puttenham, George, 266

q/
Quayson, Ato, 117
Quintilian, 266, 297

r/
Radin, Paul, 214
Ranger, Terence, 279, 280
Rilke, Rainer Maria, 245
Russell, Bertrand, 109

s/
Schmidt, Michael, 264
Sedlak, Werner, 221
Sekyi, Kobina, 27
Sembene, Ousmane, 270
Senghor, Léopold Sédar, 14, 142, 197, 198, 201, 202, 203, 204, 205, 208, 249, 250
Serres, Michel, 241
Shakespeare, William, 3, 4, 5, 7, 31, 70, 75, 117, 134, 135, 162, 185, 255, 295, 315, 316, 330, 331
Shklar, Judith, 140, 141
Shklovsky, Viktor, 14, 15, 78, 93, 158
Sowemimo, Sobo, 213
Sowemimo, Segun, 215, 217
Spinoza, Baruch, 5
Starobinski, Jean, 200, 201, 218
Steiner, George, 19, 20, 21, 251, 252, 253
Stevens, Wallace, 122, 123, 125, 126, 231
Suvin, Darko, 7, 15, 117, 121, 159, 251

t/
Tennyson, Alfred, 192, 266
Thompson, E.P., 260, 261
Thurber, James, 6, 79
Towa, Marcien, 250

Trotsky, Leon, 15, 229
Tutuola, Amos, 2, 87

w/
Weber, Max, 60
Wheeler, Michael, 83
White, James, 51
Willbern, David, 134, 135
Williams, Bernard, 236, 237
Wiredu, Kwasi, 212, 237, 238, 239, 251
Wood, James, 117
Wordsworth, William, 138

y/
Yai, Olabiyi, 6, 7, 72, 198, 257, 258, 298, 302, 303
Yeats, William Butler, 8, 9, 11, 12, 178, 249

www.ingramcontent.com/pod-product-compliance
Lightning Source LLC
Chambersburg PA
CBHW050527300426
44113CB00012B/1979